Contents

Foreword

Fred P. Piercy

This book is a timely gift to our field. McDowell, Knudson-Martin, and Bermudez offer us both the theory and practical guidelines we need to support equity in the face of sociocultural factors at play in all relationships. They explain socioculturally attuned family therapy as a set of transtheoretical considerations that they apply to family therapies to support third order change. That is, they provide a way to understand and address sociocultural factors that promote and maintain unearned privilege and misuses of power.

The authors explain that it is not possible for a therapist to be neutral in the face of power imbalances. Tolerance and acceptance are not enough. We must address the dynamic interplay between societal systems that privilege some over others. Uneven influence and opportunities can be, as the authors explain "based on social class, gender, race, ethnicity, languages, sexual orientation, age, nation of origin, abilities, and (even) looks." The authors show family therapists how they can integrate sociocultural attunement within a wide range of family therapy theories.

As a long-time author and editor, as I read this book, I reflected on the qualities that I value in professional writing. For example, does the author answer the "so what?" question. Why is a work important? What does it add to the field? This book's potential impact is easy to see. There is no more important issue in our field than how to provide culturally attuned therapy that appreciates the strengths of one's culture and family, identifies inequities, addresses inequities, and applies our family therapies in a manner that addresses these inequities.

As an editor, I also look for interventions that are theoretically grounded and brought to life through clinical dialogue and practical exercises. McDowell, Knudson-Martin, and Bermudez do this in every chapter. They introduce each major model of family therapy, discuss its history and application, identify the enduring concepts of each model, then show how sociocultural attunement might be applied to each particular theory. I particularly liked their last chapter, that identified the steps in their approach that can be applied to any existing family therapy.

As for accessibility and tone, other editorial values of mine, McDowell, Knudson-Martin, and Bermudez have made difficult concepts clear, engaging, and eminently transferrable to practice. Also, in this era of political and societal bullying, the authors' approach doesn't shame or bully. They work with clients in a sensitive and kind manner that invites understanding and collaboration.

Perhaps the most important value in contemporary family therapy is cultural sensitivity. Indeed, the authors support greater cultural understanding, equity, and critical social conscientiousness. Their work is both impressive and important. I can see it transforming the way we practice family therapy, regardless of model. It is good that we are talking about social justice in our field. The authors operationalize this concept for family therapists. They provide an accessible, useful, affirming socioculturally attuned family therapy that examines

Socioculturally Attuned Family Therapy

Guidelines for Equitable Theory and Practice

Teresa McDowell, Carmen Knudson-Martin, and J. Maria Bermudez

Routledge
Taylor & Francis Group

NEW YORK AND LONDON

First edition published 2018
by Routledge
711 Third Avenue, New York, NY 10017

and by Routledge
2 Park Square, Milton Park, Abingdon, Oxon, OX14 4RN

Routledge is an imprint of the Taylor & Francis Group, an informa business

Library of Congress Cataloging-in-Publication Data
Names: McDowell, Teresa, author. | Knudson-Martin, Carmen, author. | Bermudez, J. Maria, author.
Title: Socioculturally attuned family therapy : guidelines for equitable theory and practice / Teresa McDowell, Carmen Knudson-Martin, and J. Maria Bermudez.
Description: New York, NY : Routledge, 2017. | Includes bibliographical references and index.
Identifiers: LCCN 2017032515 | ISBN 9781138678200 (hardcover : alk. paper) | ISBN 9781138678217 (pbk. : alk. paper) | ISBN 9781315559094 (e-book)
Subjects: | MESH: Family Therapy | Culturally Competent Care | Sociological Factors
Classification: LCC RC488.53 | NLM WM 430.5.F2 | DDC 616.89/156—dc23
LC record available at https://lccn.loc.gov/2017032515

ISBN: 978-1-138-67820-0 (hbk)
ISBN: 978-1-138-67821-7 (pbk)
ISBN: 978-1-315-55909-4 (ebk)

Typeset in Bembo
by Swales & Willis Ltd, Exeter, Devon, UK

Socioculturally Attuned Family Therapy

Socioculturally Attuned Family Therapy addresses the need for socially responsible couple, marriage, and family therapy that infuses diversity, equity, and inclusion throughout theory and clinical practice. The text begins with a discussion of societal systems, diversity, and socially just practice. The authors then integrate principles of societal context, power, and equity into the core concepts of ten major family therapy models, paying close attention to the "how to's" of change processes through a highly diverse range of case examples. The text concludes with descriptions of integrative, equity based family therapy guidelines that clinicians can apply to their practice.

Teresa McDowell, EdD, is a professor of marriage, couple, and family therapy and chair of the Department of Counseling Psychology at Lewis & Clark Graduate School of Education and Counseling in Portland, Oregon. She is a licensed marriage and family therapist, AAMFT clinical fellow, and approved supervisor. Her work includes a focus on applying critical social theory to family therapy practice.

Carmen Knudson-Martin, PhD, LMFT, is a professor and director of the marriage, couple, and family therapy program at Lewis & Clark Graduate School of Education and Counseling. She is a past president of the American Association for Marital and Family Therapy—California Division, and recipient of the 2017 Distinguished Contribution to Family Therapy and Practice award from the American Family Therapy Academy. She is a founder of socioemotional relationship therapy.

J. Maria Bermudez, PhD, is an associate professor in the marriage and family therapy program in the Department of Human Development and Family Science at the University of Georgia. She is an AAMFT clinical fellow, approved supervisor, and licensed marriage and family therapist. Her work is anchored in feminist-informed and culturally responsive approaches to therapy, research, and supervision.

Toward a more equitable future,
we lovingly dedicate this book to the next generation:
to our students, our children, and our grandchildren

sociocultural structures, supports relational equity, and thus social justice. McDowell, Knudson-Martin, and Bermudez' book will not only transform our practices and our clients, but ourselves as well.

Fred Piercy, PhD, recently retired from the family therapy doctoral program at Virginia Tech, Blacksburg, VA. From 2012 through 2017, he was the editor of the *Journal of Marital and Family Therapy*.

Preface

Introducing Ourselves

As socioculturally attuned family therapists, we want readers to know who we are, our social locations, our intentions, our values, and some of our individual and collective herstory in the field of family therapy. We have a lot in common with each other. We are all family therapy educators, supervisors, and clinicians with various types of professional experiences. All three of us are highly relational beings, dedicated to putting relationships first, including our relationships with each other. We are hard workers who have shared our energy and creativity over the course of writing this text, struggling to make sense of how, as family therapists, we can all expand our work to support more just relationships. We have deeply valued the differences between us, which allows each of us to see with more than our own eyes. Next, we each share a few thoughts about our journeys thus far in the field of family therapy.

Teresa

I became a family therapist in the 1980s. I remember walking around amazed, gaping at patterns I was seeing everywhere. I was hooked! Wrestle as I might, I couldn't pull myself away from a field that was teeming with energy, pushing to find new ways of creating change. I fell in love with counterintuitive thinking; with the MRI model, structural and strategic family therapy, and the work of Milton Erickson. As the field developed, I embraced solution focused and narrative practices. Being active, intuitive, and imaginative—taking risks using experiential techniques—became central to my practice. I balanced the burden of trying to do therapy right with an entrepreneurial drive to think creatively. I reminded myself often in the early years that they called it practice for a reason . . . I was just practicing.

Along the way I became deeply disconcerted about social inequity and began looking outside family therapy for answers. A doctorate in liberation based adult education helped me rethink family therapy and set the stage for challenging my own Eurocentric thinking, unexamined whiteness, heterosexual and cisgender privilege, and middle-class legacy. During the first half of my career I looked to family therapy to help me understand the world. During the second half I searched in and out of family therapy to find ways to understand and challenge unjust social and familial arrangements.

When I find an idea in my travels (usually in the land of critical social theories), I drag it home to family therapy and find somewhere to put it—somewhere it might make a difference. Of course others have been doing the same, creating momentum for socially just family therapy. Carmen, Maria, and I tasked ourselves with systematically inventorying and mapping relationships between many of these collective ideas, relying on our years as family therapists to develop guidelines for just practice across models. Working with Carmen and Maria has been a gift. Beyond their friendship, scholarly acumen, and clinical expertise, they have helped me find a place to belong—a home where I can remain unsettled—in constant motion between the center and the borderlands of family therapy.

Carmen

Before I came to this field, I taught family life education in high schools. I found myself fascinated by students who struggled, not by their "problem behavior," but by their stories of hurt, pain, and unfairness. Seeing students labeled as troublemakers while misdeeds of "good" students (as I had been) escaped notice heightened my curiosity about the systemic dynamics that create and maintain these inequities.

Then I moved to Iran. As a young woman of Scandinavian heritage raised on a farm in North Dakota, I experienced being on the outside and had to learn how to negotiate a social system organized so differently than I was used to. How did I buy groceries? How did I get from one place to another? Who could I trust? When the Tehran-American School hired me to teach family life education and psychology, I had to consider human behavior and relationships from perspectives different than my own. Later, living in Senegal and then teaching at international schools in Jordan and Costa Rica, I learned to see my North American world from the outside and to take apart and examine my taken-for-granted expectations. I experienced the privileges accorded English speakers and U.S. citizenship.

In 1983 I began to study family therapy as part of a PhD in sociology. This was pure luck! Since then I have focused on how the larger societal context operates in the moment-by-moment of therapy. New collaborators in each place I worked (Montana, Georgia, Southern California, and Oregon) stretched my thinking and a diverse range of students and clients gave me windows into their worlds. As a white, monogamous, cisgender, heterosexual, temporarily able-bodied wife, mother, and grandmother, I am continually humbled by the limits of my understanding and the ease with which I am usually able to walk through this world. Yet as a therapist, I regularly witness the effects of societal inequalities. To me, promoting equitable relationships is both an ethical and clinical issue. Grappling with the intricacies of this work with Teresa and Maria has been exceedingly challenging and enriching. Our understandings will always be a work in progress.

Maria

I have been a practicing couple and family therapist for over 24 years. I consider myself a "purist" in family therapy. I graduated from two COAMFTE (Commission on Accreditation for Marriage and Family Therapy Education) graduate programs and have taught in two COAMFTE graduate programs, and my studies have been strongly rooted in academic departments of human development and family studies. What initially drew me to the field of family therapy was the focus on families in therapy. Simple enough. But what fascinated me was the way in which family therapists think. I enjoy examining the multiple contexts of people's lives and seeing complex processes as they unfold. I greatly value all the family therapy theories and models, but being from Honduras, I was especially drawn to ideas that reflected my collectivistic and collaborative values, such as with postmodern and social constructionist approaches to family therapy.

Nonetheless, I didn't fully immerse myself in diversity studies until I started teaching an undergraduate course called Gender Roles across the Lifespan. I taught it every semester for five years. It was life-changing and learning from my colleagues in women's studies was empowering. Learning critical theories helped me examine how structural, systemic, and relational dynamics shape our identities, social location, and lived experiences. Learning from feminist scholars profoundly altered the way I integrated family studies and family therapy models and theories into the different aspects of my work. It was a paradigm shift that expanded my worldview and pushed me to deepen my understanding of diversity, social justice, and equity—professionally and personally.

I remember first being aware of disparities at a young age. During my childhood and adolescence, my mother and I traveled to Honduras to see my father and my family there. We went four times; at age 4, 11, 15, and 19. It was impactful for me. Not only was it strange for me that everyone fussed over my fair skin and light blue eyes (awareness of my white privilege), I was extremely unsettled by seeing young children in the street, begging for money, selling gum and candy, and staring into the windows of the restaurants where we ate (awareness of my class privilege). It was confusing to me and no one explained to me what was happening. I wasn't exposed to this in the U.S. Although my family in Honduras and the U.S. was mostly "working" middle-class, as I got older, I developed a sincere and deep gratitude and appreciation for our privilege. We had a house, consistent electricity, food, clean water, washing machines, a reliable postal system, good public education, new clothes and shoes, and a peaceful way of life. We did not come here fleeing persecution or escaping violence or financial distress. Instead, my mother, who learned to speak English in school and worked in an office as an accountant, brought us to the U.S. for a "better way of life." My father, who was well-regarded for his work as an auto mechanic, did not want to immigrate, but conceded because of the opportunities that were not possible for us there. Although I could not name what I knew, early in my life I learned about the effects of immigration, transnational families, colorism, language fluency, colonization, and mixed documentation status.

What I later learned through my studies is that this "better way of life" is not accessible to everyone in the same way; not in the U.S. or anywhere. The structural barriers and the trajectories of cumulative advantage and disadvantage lay the groundwork for the ways in which the "American dream" can be accessed and lived. The course of my life was altered with immigration, as it is for so many of us, almost all of us in the U.S. Although I was the only one of my siblings to obtain a college degree, I would not have been in the position to influence others in the way I do today if my mother had not been able to change the course of our lives. As a consequence, I am greatly humbled and honored to co-author this book with such outstanding scholars in the field of family therapy. It is my hope that our theorizing and critical lens will help the readers of this text critically evaluate and attune, with a sense of urgency, to the factors that shape our lives and our ways of working. It is time for another paradigm shift!

In Conclusion

Stepping out of what is familiar and trying something new takes a special mix of courage, excitement, and humility. As authors putting forth the new ideas in this text, we have been immersed in that mix. We pass our work on to you now with the hope that you will have the courage to both use and challenge our ideas, that you will bear the humility of not always doing social justice based family therapy "right," and that you will join in our excitement about the future of family therapy.

Acknowledgments

Maria

It is such an honor to co-author my first book with two scholars that I greatly admire. I want to first thank Drs. Teresa McDowell and Carmen Knudson-Martin for giving me the amazing opportunity to embark on this journey with them. It has truly been a privilege. Our process was richly generative, collaborative, and inspiring. I am hopeful that our body of work will be generative to others as well and that it will serve to move our field forward in important and necessary ways.

The richness of my journey could not have been possible without walking alongside the remarkable people that have paved the way for me. I would first like to thank my family, who laid such an important foundation for my life; especially my mother, Judith Silva Perez, who was my first feminist mentor. She taught me what it meant to be a strong, independent, courageous woman, mother, and professional. She would say, "If you are going to do something, do it right." I can still hear her say, "Hágalo bien y con amor!" And to my father, Rene Enrique Perez, who passed away during my adolescence; he was a gentle and kind man and I have such sweet memories of him. I would also like to thank my siblings and their spouses for their constant love and support of me; Zoila and Mario, Eddy and Toni, Ruy and Sandra, Manuel and Amalia, Gerardo and Rosana, and Renee and Marcelo, as well as my nieces and nephews, and their spouses and children. Let's keep dancing and celebrating life together. And to my family of choice, my lifelong best friends in Texas, I am so grateful for each one of you!

I would also like to thank and acknowledge other important giants in my life—my feminist mentors/professors/colleagues/friends who strengthened me with their critical consciousness, highest standards of excellence, and undying passion for marriage and family therapy and family science; Drs. Lorna Hecker, Joe Wetchler, Anne Prouty, Katherine Allen, Saliha Bava, Karen Wampler, Gwen Sorell, Elizabeth Sharp, Nancy Robinson, Tom Stone Carlson, Christi McGeorge, and Yajaira Curiel. I find myself repeating your words and phrases with my students and our conversations consistently echo in my mind. I hope that I will be able to influence my students the way you have influenced me. And to my community of scholars from the University of Georgia, especially Drs. Jay Mancini, Jerry Gale, Desiree Seponski, Morgan Stinson, Bertranna Muruthi, and soon to be doctors, Andrea Farnham, Ashley Walsdorf, Valerie Maxey, and Josh Boe—I appreciate how you help me acknowledge what I know, while simultaneously keeping me in an unsettled "not-knowing" stance. You continuously move my thinking forward. I would also like to thank and acknowledge my clients and research participants, who are a constant source of challenge and inspiration for me. Without them, I would not be able to theorize, learn, and grow in the ways I do.

I would also like to thank my partner and best friend, Romulo (Ronnie) Rama for giving me "for better and better" and sharing his life with me. And I am also grateful to Meg and Nicolas, Eric and Leah, and Mandy, for welcoming me into their lives. I am looking forward to our future together!

And last, I would like to thank my incredible daughters, Lucia, Aida, and Giana, to whom I dedicate this book. They are my world and I am so thankful for them each and every day. I love you and I hope you all continue confidently on your paths toward becoming strong, resilient women who are passionate, caring, critical thinkers. Remember to always err on the side of kindness, compassion, and connection!

Carmen

Working with Teresa and Maria on this book is the most significant professional challenge I have undertaken. We love this field and hold deep respect for all the family therapists and social scientists who advanced systems/relational thinking and practice before us. Along our different journeys each of us was also transformed by critical, feminist, and social construction-ist scholars and activists. As the three of us discussed this book and what it might accomplish, we spoke of our legacies as family therapists—the courage of our founders to question and transform the assumptions, practices, and ethics of mainstream mental health treatment; the wisdom of Bateson and other systemic thinkers who helped us see individual consciousness and behavior as part of a much larger whole; and the strength of the many female family thera-pists who said, "Enough!" At the same time, we challenged ourselves to trust our own voices and experience. We set for ourselves a delicate balance between getting concepts "right" and telling the family therapy story through our own lens. Working collaboratively with Maria and Teresa on every chapter produced something new that none of us could have done alone. I like to imagine that this is how our field has always evolved—challenging each other to try to solve a puzzle, clarify a systemic lens, or develop a new practice.

This is not my first collaboration. When I started my doctoral program at the University of Southern California under the direction of Carlfred Broderick, Tom and Marcia Lasswell, Connie Ahrons, and others, I felt like I had come "home." Housed in a sociology department, a common mantra was "the fallacy of individual reductionism." We learned that one could not explain behavior on the basis of individual action or choice alone. Shortly after beginning my first family therapy assistant professor and program director position at Montana State, I went to a Groves Conference and met Anne Mahoney. Though a full professor of sociology who had taught at Denver University for 17 years, Anne engaged with me as a peer. We researched and wrote together for 20 years. Anne was always willing to look for the holes in our thinking. Through her example, she taught me to write clearly and simply. She modeled working relationally, and I have tried to follow her lead as I engaged with younger colleagues, putting relationship before product. She remains a trusted friend and mentor.

When I moved to Loma Linda University in 2000 to lead a new family therapy doctoral program, I found Douglas Huenergardt. Doug and I discovered that, though living many states apart, we had each had Irv Borstein as a clinical supervisor. Doug had also been part of a clinical group with Marianne Walters, one of the founders of the women's movement in family therapy. Doug and I began to do co-therapy and invited students to watch. In 2008 we decided to formalize the process in an action research project focused on how to address gender, power, and culture in couple therapy. Together with a team of over 20 doctoral students across almost 10 years, we developed socio-emotional relationship therapy (SERT). Since moving to Lewis & Clark College a few years ago, Doug and I no longer work together directly, but I channel him almost every day. Working with Doug and the Loma Linda doc-toral students was an amazing gift that continues to evolve as our former students continue to develop the SERT approach and share it with their students. Ketsia Lafontant and Les Bishop helped us develop training vignettes. Melissa Wells and Sarah Samman helped me edit a volume on our SERT research with contributors Jessica ChenFeng, Julie Estrella, Mona Fishbane, Naveen Jonathan, Young Joo Kang, Lana Kim, Veronica Kuhn, Mia Pandit, Jason Richards, Kirstee Williams, and Elisabeth Esmiol Wilson. Many of us continue to work together to advance the SERT approach. Thank you all, especially Lana, Elisabeth, and Lindsey, with whom I have current projects.

I may be the first person in my family to go to college, but I learned how to work hard and contribute to the larger good from my parents Phoebe and Nels Knudson. They would be proud to see this book, but not surprised. My husband John Knudson-Martin joined his name with mine many years ago. We are a good team. Thank you, John, for understanding the life of a scholar-practitioner and for your steadfast support. My children Chris and Kyara and their partners Melanie and Jerome give me purpose and perspective. Grandsons Ethan and Kai are the light of my world. Above all, I could not have written this book or had any guidance to offer if it had not been for the many clients who put their faith in our process together and allowed me into the hidden corners of their lives. Thank you for your inspiration and willingness to seek new possibilities. Your stories inform every page.

Teresa

By the time I was in my twenties I had given up my professional dreams. Before I knew it I was married, living in a cabin, and caring for two children, without electricity or running water. Fast forward a few years (finally had enough of going back to nature!) and I got a phone call. Mom was in treatment at the Meadows in Wickenburg, Arizona. I was expected to attend something called family week. I went to several family weeks as different members went through treatment. The Meadows saved our family and their staff changed the course of my life. I thank them for their wisdom and dedication to families like mine. I thank my family for being loving and courageous enough to heal.

Eventually I applied to Pacific Lutheran University (PLU). I was thrilled when they let me in . . . and terrified. I don't know where my life would have gone if my professor, mentor, and eventual colleague and friend, Charlie York, hadn't opened that door and shown me the way. Years later Cheryl Storm became my supervision mentor, colleague, and dear friend. Charlie and Cheryl gave me the opportunity to supervise and teach at PLU. Their mentorship, faith in my potential, practical guidance, and professional example set the stage for the rest of my career. I want to deeply acknowledge their importance to my professional journey.

I worked as a rural family therapist in Aberdeen, Washington, for over a decade. Being the only family therapist in two counties allowed me to work with all kinds of families. I also had the opportunity to serve as a consultant and trainer for local social service agencies and businesses. I was privileged to walk alongside agency staff who were on the front lines of some of the most challenging work in the community. I loved being a rural practitioner and hold sacred the hours I spent with families in Aberdeen. I am honored to have been invited into the intimate moments of their lives. I am grateful for all they taught me.

When my sons left home I found a full-time position running the family therapy clinic at Northern Illinois University (NIU). It was at NIU that I met She-Ruei Fang. She was to become one of my closest colleagues and friends. I am so grateful to She-Ruei for helping guide me toward work in diversity and social equity. Scholar activist, Phyllis Cunningham, was a major professor in my doctoral program at NIU. I thank her almost every day for holding me accountable for using my privilege to make social change.

After graduating from NIU, I took a position as the director of the master's and doctoral programs at the University of Connecticut (UCONN). It was at UCONN that I was afforded the opportunity to engage in international work. I began lasting relationships with colleagues in Egypt, Uganda, and India. I discovered a kindred spirit in Hanan Hosney from Menoufia University in Egypt. Being an ongoing part of Paschal Kabura's work at the Bishop Magambo Counselor Training Center in Ft. Portal, Uganda, has been life-changing. Likewise, collaborating with Bros. Mathew Panathanath and George Padikara at Montfort College in Bangalore, India, has deeply enriched my professional journey.

I came to Lewis & Clark because the graduate school places value on faculty social awareness, critical research, liberation based teaching, and practice that promotes social equity. I want to thank my colleagues at Lewis & Clark for giving me the space and support to grow in my understanding of the relationship between critical social theory and family therapy. I also want to thank Pilar Hernández-Wolfe, Rhea Almeida, and Andraé Brown for their inspirational work and collaboration.

I want to make sure to acknowledge family, which is at the heart of it all. Years pass and the family you grew up in is no longer; parents go on their way as grandchildren are born. The sweetness of relationships is marked with moments of bitter pain and loss. My grandchildren are what keeps me solidly in the present. When I am with them the rest of the world melts away. From youngest to oldest I would like to acknowledge the deep and positive impact they have on my life. Rooney, Ewan, Nina, Adina, William, Elizabeth, and Lindsey–I love you. My sons Quentin and Flynn, and stepson Rob, are men I am deeply proud of as they take their place in the world—each in his own way. Their partners, Lauren, Alice, and Janelle, are my dearest daughters. I also want to acknowledge John, who has stood by me for the last 45 years through every twist and turn of family life. I am truly blessed to be surrounded by a large, loving family.

Finally, hats off and pens down! I want to acknowledge the unrivaled synergy of our team. I emerged from the haze of co-authoring this work with a meaningful and forever bond with my sister scholars, Carmen and Maria.

From All of Us

We applaud the work of our colleague, Fred Piercy, who has been a leader in diversity and social equity in family therapy. He has dedicated his life to our field and we hold him in the highest regard. Thank you, Fred, for writing the Foreword for this text. We thank Josh Boe for his tireless work researching, editing, formatting, and in many other ways contributing to this text. We also thank Juleen McGonigal for careful expert review of every single word!

1 Why Sociocultural Attunement and Equity Matter

It would be difficult to find a family therapist today who does not believe culture and societal context are important. Sometimes the effects are obvious; a woman seeks therapy for depression and we quickly realize she is embedded in a relationship that strips her of dignity and voice. This woman's plight can be linked to a broader society in which women are systematically disempowered. A gay couple living in a conservative rural community turn the effects of their oppression inward, heightening conflict between them. White members of a biracial family fail to understand the full impact of racism on those they love, creating tension between them. Other times the effects are less obvious; a white, upper-middle-class, heterosexual couple argue over one of their spending habits, or a teenage boy in a seemingly stable middle-class family acts out in the community.

When we see links across individual, relational, community, and societal systems, we often don't know how to intervene in helpful ways. We question how we should use our awareness of social dynamics, including the impact of social location (e.g., race, social class, sexual orientation, nation of origin, abilities, gender, religion/spirituality, region) and societal systems (e.g., capitalism, patriarchy, democracy, social welfare institutions, educational institutions) to help families. We wonder how to fluidly move between assessing the impact of societal systems and making specific socioculturally attuned clinical interventions. Here we address what we find most challenging, which is how to do this while adhering to, or being informed by, family therapy models.

In *Socioculturally Attuned Family Therapy: Guidelines for Equitable Theory and Practice* we address the need for socially responsible family therapy that infuses diversity, equity, and inclusion throughout theory and clinical practice. This includes attention to societal systems that shape our daily lives at intimate, local, national, and global levels. A variety of family therapy theories and models are routinely taught in advanced educational programs and practiced by clinicians worldwide. We join those who struggle to teach these models while helping students and supervisees integrate social awareness into actual practice. As practitioners ourselves, we share difficulties professionals face in realizing truly just practice without abandoning their theoretical foundations. The primary question that guides our work is: How do we continue to use the models we so value in family therapy in ways that integrate the impact of culture, societal context, and power as essential considerations in therapeutic change?

⤙⤚

Sociocultural attunement refers not only to awareness of societal systems, culture, and power, but to a willingness to pay close attention and be responsive to the experience of others.

⤙⤚

Family Therapy and Societal Context: A Brief Historical Overview

The field of family therapy challenged the dominant system of its time, i.e., the medical model. Psychotherapists were trained to understand and treat dysfunction. The family was considered primary in creating and maintaining psychopathology. Early family therapists were rebels using new systemic perspectives and involving family members in therapy. As a consequence, clinical models emerged that were separate and unique from those in psychology and social work.

As the field developed, so did ideas about cultural and societal context (Hair, Fine, & Ryan, 1996). Auerswald (1968, 1972) was one of the first to develop an ecosystemic approach to families, integrating community systems into practice. It was during their years working with Auerswald at the Wiltwyck School that Minuchin and colleagues turned their focus toward families living on low incomes, developing the framework for structural family therapy. Early on, this group (Minuchin, Montalvo, Guerney, Rosman, & Schumer, 1967) recognized the impact of poverty, discrimination, and oppression on family well-being. Although not always practiced with the broader context in mind, structural family therapy's origins in structural functionalism encouraged us to conceptualize the family as a social institution in systemic interaction with other social institutions. This includes an understanding of the potential impact of extra-familial forces and stressors on family roles and power dynamics. Aponte (1976, 1990) built on these ideas, developing an ecostructural approach to working with families in the context of their communities. Others, including Wynne (1967) and Keeney (1979), argued for an ecosystemic epistemology that links open systems at multiple levels including individual, family, community, societal, and environmental (Hair et al., 1996).

Imber-Black (1992) described families as part of multiple embedded systems within society. Over time, cultural and societal context became foundational to understanding and treating families (Falicov, 2014; Ho, Rasheed, & Rasheed, 2004; McGoldrick, Giordano, & Garcia-Preto, 2005). The feminist movement (e.g., Hare-Mustin, 1978; Luepnitz, 1988; McGoldrick, Anderson, & Walsh, 1989; Walters, Carter, Papp, & Silverstein, 1988) shattered the view of families as apolitical, reciprocal systems by connecting intimate interaction to power dynamics in the broader society.

The argument that family therapists are in a position to create positive social change and should intentionally promote social equity is also not new (Raskin, 2010). For example, in 1988 Goodrich, Rampage, Ellman, and Halstead wrote:

> Whether intended or not, [family therapy's] impact on individual families . . . leads to an impact on our collective social life . . . . This influence serves either to support or to change prevailing structures of belief and action regarding family life. Those of us who want this influence to be in the direction of changing prevailing structures must work to reform fundamental aspects of our professional field.
>
> (p. 180)

Several approaches routinely conceptualize and intervene across multiple systems in ways that support social and relational equity. Critical conversations were introduced in family therapy by Eliana Korin in 1994. Korin (1994) argued that critical conversations based on the work of Paulo Freire could be used to create emancipatory change in family therapy. According to Freire (1970/2000), critical consciousness, or conscientização, can be raised through dialogue and reflection, which in turn leads to informed action. Martín-Baró , Aron, and Corne (1994, p. 40) also built on this tradition, arguing that "people must take hold of their fate, take the reins of their lives, a move that demands overcoming false consciousness and achieving a critical understanding of themselves as well as of their world and where they stand in it."

The cultural context model (CCM) (Almeida, Dolan-Del Vecchio, & Parker, 2007) relies heavily on raising social awareness, believing clients can better solve problems once they understand how societal systems affect their relationships. Narrative family therapy (White & Epston, 1990) and just therapy (Waldegrave & Tamasese, 1994) share roots in social constructivism. Societal context is highly relevant in these approaches as dominant social discourses shape not only how we think about ourselves, but how we interact with and think about others—the meaning we assign to all experience through language. Feminist family therapy (Prouty Lyness & Lyness, 2007) and SERT (Knudson-Martin & Huenergardt, 2010) are examples of approaches that routinely pay attention to how culture and societal systems create and maintain relational power imbalances that in turn create individual and relational symptoms. Similar to these models, our work centers relational equity as necessary for success in therapy.

The Impact of Inequity on Mental Health and Relational Well-Being

According to the U.S. Center for Disease Control and Prevention (2013), determinates of health include social class, sexual orientation, race, gender, age, and abilities. Oppression and discrimination affect individuals and families by creating and exacerbating mental health and emotional problems, straining relationships, and limiting strategies for coping with stress. For example, racism affects the likelihood of imprisonment and consequent negative effects of being incarcerated. Discrimination increases the risk of developing substance addictions and problem gambling. People of color in the U.S. suffer higher rates of illness and die younger than whites (Jones, 2000). The National Institute of Mental Health (2014) reported that women in the U.S. are 60%–70% more likely to experience anxiety or depression. LGBTQ (lesbian, gay, bisexual, transgender, queer/questioning) youth are at significant risk, being far more likely to attempt suicide and/or experience homelessness (Garofalo, Wolf, Wissow, Woods, & Goodman, 1999; Kruks, 1991). Researchers have identified connections between lower socioeconomic class and higher rates of mental health problems (McCulloch, 2001). How children develop and the opportunities available as they enter adulthood are deeply impacted by social class (Lareau, 2011). This includes the influence parents have in intervening on their children's behalf, resources for learning and educational opportunities, and exposure to the "rules of the game" in various social contexts. These trajectories often lead to a lifetime of cumulative advantage or disadvantage (Merton, 1968).

The list goes on. The bottom line is that those with adequate income to live in safe neighborhoods, meet educational needs, and enjoy food security—those whose social locations place them at the center free from discrimination—aren't under the same type of stress as those who are at constant risk. Social status impacts our ability to influence others, the choices available to us, the resources we have to enjoy life and overcome problems, and the way others treat us on a daily basis.

Changes in Practice Standards

Increased awareness has resulted in greater commitment to diversity and social equity in accreditation standards across helping fields, calling all of us into action. In this text we explore how we might answer this call; how we might take action. The complete picture of changing standards is beyond the scope of this chapter; however, it is clear from just a few examples from marriage and family therapy, professional counseling, social work, and psychology that competent practice includes attention to diversity and social equity. According to the Commission for Accreditation of Marriage and Family Therapy Education (COAMFTE), programs must:

> demonstrate their commitment throughout the program to diversity and inclusion. This includes providing a multiculturally-informed and globally-minded education that addresses a range of diversity; a safe, respectful, inclusive learning climate; student experiences

with diverse, marginalized, and/or underserved communities; and a commitment to the ethical and social responsibility . . . to diverse, marginalized, and/or underserved communities.

(COAMFTE, 2014, Version 12, Standard II, para. 1)

Likewise, the Commission for Accreditation of Counseling and Related Educational Programs (CACREP) requires a focus on social and cultural diversity that includes:

theories and models of multicultural counseling, cultural identity development and social justice and advocacy, multicultural counseling competencies, the impact of heritage, attitudes, beliefs, understandings, and acculturative experiences on an individual's views of others, the effects of power and privilege for counselors and clients . . . strategies for identifying and eliminating barriers, prejudices, and processes of intentional and unintentional oppression and discrimination.

(CACREP, 2016, Section 2, para. 4)

These expectations have been, and continue to be, a hallmark of the field of social work. According to the Council on Social Work Education Commission on Accreditation (CSWE COA), social workers must:

understand how diversity and difference characterize and shape the human experience and are critical to the formation of identity. The dimensions of diversity are understood as the intersectionality of multiple factors including but not limited to age, class, color, culture, disability and ability, ethnicity, gender, gender identity and expression, immigration status, marital status, political ideology, race, religion/spirituality, sex, sexual orientation, and tribal sovereign status. Social workers understand that, as a consequence of difference, a person's life experiences may include oppression, poverty, marginalization, and alienation as well as privilege, power, and acclaim. Social workers also understand the forms and mechanisms of oppression and discrimination and recognize the extent to which a culture's structures and values, including social, economic, political, and cultural exclusions, may oppress, marginalize, alienate, or create privilege and power.

(CSWE, 2015, Competency 2.1.4, para. 4)

APA guidelines for multicultural education, research, practice, and organizational change for psychologists include the following statement (APA, 2002):

All individuals exist in social, political, historical, and economic contexts, and psychologists are increasingly called upon to understand the influence of these contexts on individuals' behavior. The Guidelines on Multicultural Education, Training, Research, Practice, and Organizational Change for Psychologists reflect the continuing evolution of the study of psychology, changes in society-at-large, and emerging data about the different needs for particular individuals and groups historically marginalized or disenfranchised within and by psychology based on their ethnic/racial heritage and social group identity or membership. These Guidelines . . . reflect knowledge and skills needed for the profession in the midst of dramatic historic sociopolitical changes in U.S. society, as well as needs from new constituencies, markets, and clients.

(p. 1)

The growing expectation that family therapists will pay attention to societal systems, culture, and power is clear. What remains obscure, however, is how to do so while continuing to use models and practices foundational to our field. In other words, how can family therapists integrate awareness of societal systems, culture, and power across models into their everyday work with individuals, couples, and families?

Definition of Sociocultural Attunement

What we are calling *socioculturally attuned family therapy* is a set of transtheoretical considerations that can be integrated into existing family therapy models. We use the term *sociocultural* to describe interconnections of societal systems, culture, and power. This includes not only shared meanings that define culture, but dynamic interplay between societal systems that privilege some over others, resulting in uneven influence and opportunities based on social class, gender, race, ethnicity, language, sexual orientation, age, nation of origin, abilities, and looks. Patterns that occur at individual, relational, and societal levels are recursive and continuous vs. discrete and unilateral. Families impact community and society and vice versa.

For example, consider a middle-class family that is eager to ensure their children excel in school, stand out in athletics and music, and demonstrate qualities of prosocial leadership. These efforts are aimed at maintaining or improving the social class of the next generation. This in turn reinforces the values, ideology, and cultural practices of those with the greatest influence in societal institutions to set these norms, e.g., those who are in positions to grant college scholarships and offer employment. In other words, the interconnection between societal systems, culture, and power supports hegemony, i.e., dominant cultural group control over major societal systems. Left uninterrupted, the routine practices, rules, and values of societal systems (e.g., education, government, professional associations, commerce) continue to benefit those with the greatest social influence.

We use the term *attunement* to imply not only heightened consciousness, social awareness, and intellectual understanding, but a willingness to pay close attention to the experience of others and be responsive (e.g., D'Aniello, Nguyen, & Piercy, 2016). The worldview of those in non-dominant groups is often marginalized, creating what Fricker (2007) termed epistemic injustice. This includes those in centered, dominant groups routinely devaluing or dismissing the testimony of those in marginalized groups (Tatum, 1997). It also includes difficulties members of marginalized groups may have in assigning credibility to their own experience due to fewer shared resources for identifying and legitimizing collective meaning. Attunement infers being at one with others, bearing witness to their testimony, and helping them make meaning of their social experience. Sociocultural attunement, therefore, requires foundational knowledge of culture, societal systems, and power dynamics as well as the willingness and ability to tune in and effectively respond.

Sociocultural Attunement and Common Factors

Common change factors have received a great deal of attention in the helping fields, including family therapy (Sprenkle, Davis, & Lebow, 2009). Debates have ensued regarding the relative importance or unimportance of models, including the argument that common factors work through or enhance models (Sexton, Ridley, & Kleiner, 2004). Although the same factors are not uniformly defined across theorists, they are frequently categorized as client and extratherapeutic factors, therapist factors and therapeutic alliance, hope and expectancy for change, and use of models and techniques. D'Aniello et al. (2016) encouraged family therapists to enhance common factors through cultural sensitivity and attunement. In the following sections we discuss how common factors are positively impacted by sociocultural attunement.

Client and Extratherapeutic Factors

Social location (i.e., intersection of identities such as race, gender, sexual orientation, and social class within specific local, social, and global contexts) determines many of the social and economic resources clients have to help solve problems. Socioculturally attuned family therapists pay close attention to the impact of identity within societal structures as well as standpoints that shape clients' experiences. Consider a white, middle-class, heterosexual couple in the U.S. who are in their mid-sixties. They enter therapy when the wife announces her intention to divorce. The husband begins the conversation by expressing his utter dismay at his wife's dissatisfaction for what he has experienced as a good marriage. From his perspective, they have had their share of problems raising kids, making financial ends meet, and getting along, but nothing he wouldn't expect. They have both worked and he has always respected his wife's right to make decisions on her own. From the wife's perspective, she has spent a lifetime accommodating a difficult man who seems to remain unaware of her experience regardless of the number of times she tries to tell him he is controlling and dismissive. She reports a lifetime of mediating relationships between her husband and children, endless efforts to keep the peace in the family, and a desire to be on her own during the final stages of life. How could these perspectives be so different when the couple identify as the same race, age, social class, and sexual orientation? Understanding the complexity of gendered power dynamics and being aware of changing gender roles in the U.S. are foundational to understanding this couple's differing perspectives and experiences. This includes awareness of the extratherapeutic factors that have affected their journey together (e.g., gender oppression, women's rights movement, male privilege, religious heritage).

Therapist Characteristics and Therapeutic Relationship

Cultural awareness is core to therapeutic alliance. Family therapists are expected to know themselves; to identify and work on their cultural and personal biases in order to prepare for working with all families. Sociocultural attunement takes this expectation a step further. Socioculturally attuned family therapists must be able to take a multi-ocular view, simultaneously attending to the (1) complexities of societal structures and clients' social locations within those structures, (2) significance of standpoint and worldview in individuals and relationships between individuals, (3) nature of presenting problems as embedded within local, national, and global contexts, and (4) impact of societal systems on power dynamics in all relationships. Attending to sociocultural context is primary to accurately empathizing with each member of the family and the family as a whole, which in turn enhances therapeutic alliance.

Within-system alliance, that is the alliance and bond between family members as well as their agreement on therapeutic goals and tasks, is also predictive of successful therapeutic outcome. Anderson and Johnson (2010) researched the relationship between therapist-client alliance, couple alliance with each other, and levels of distress in early stages of heterosexual couples' therapy. They found when therapists formed stronger alliances with more powerful partners (in this case men), less powerful partners (in this case women) became more distressed. The opposite did not hold true. Men did not become distressed over therapists forming initially stronger alliances with their female partners. The authors suggested this outcome challenges the belief that when therapists are not able to join with all family members equally, they should form an alliance with the most powerful and/or distant family member. This practice, which is intended to keep families in therapy, seems to be counterindicated as it reinforces unjust social arrangements. It makes sense that those in less powerful positions would become concerned and disheartened, perceiving therapists as maintaining the status quo and/or contributing to relational inequity. In short, therapeutic alliance is impacted by power dynamics in societal context. Socioculturally attuned family therapists must be able to assess the nuances of power in relationships (Knudson-Martin, 2013), connect intimate relationships to larger social forces, and navigate their roles in ways that support relational equity. This includes improving within-system alliances by encouraging attunement of more powerful members to the experiences, feelings, and needs of less powerful family members (Knudson-Martin, 2013).

Socioculturally attuned family therapists integrate multiple knowledges, including disciplinary, interdisciplinary, and non-disciplinary knowledge. Disciplinary knowledge draws from family therapy theory, models, and techniques. Interdisciplinary knowledge includes sociology, economics, political science, and other areas of study that inform how we conceptualize families in societal context. Non-disciplinary knowledge honors indigenous knowledges, lived individual and family experiences, children's knowledge, non-Western knowledge, and the multiplicity of lifeworlds. Non-disciplinary knowledge is key to practicing from a decolonizing stance that embraces multi-directional pluriversal practice. Consider a European American family that entered therapy when the oldest daughter, 19, experienced some anxiety about going away to college. During the initial interview, the therapist learned that although the family had a large house, all three children, ages 7–19, piled into their parents' room to sleep on weekends. The therapist, working from a Bowenian perspective, immediately wondered if the family was emotionally fused (anxiety leaving home + co-sleeping during adolescence = fusion) and began following that line of questioning. Only the father considered the family's sleeping arrangements a problem. The rest of the family reported that they have fun on those nights and enjoy the sense of being together. The therapist was struggling between disciplinary, interdisciplinary, and non-disciplinary knowledge. The model she was using has the potential to support the most powerful member of the family—in this case the father—who wants consistent, uninterrupted access to his wife. If the therapist had not examined her own cultural bias, she may have assumed the father was right. Without careful examination, the therapist might have fallen into a dominant discourse about women not being able to separate from their children. This would serve to further a pattern of male dominance and Western, androcentric perspectives that value independence and autonomy. The therapist might have justified this decision by describing the family as European American, generalizing cultural values and practices to all families of similar descent. The therapist's alliance would have been strained with the mother, who would feel even more distressed. The therapist would have also failed to improve the alliance between the mother and the father by inadvertently supporting the inequity that maintains relational problems. The lived experience and preferred ways of being of most of the family, i.e., the children's and mother's knowledge (non-disciplinary knowledge), did not fit broader cultural/societal expectations (interdisciplinary knowledge), including the father's perspective, which is mirrored by Euro and androcentric assumptions of a particular family therapy model (disciplinary knowledge).

Expectancy for Change

Families come to therapy seeking relief from emotional and/or relational problems. They set the agenda for change along with the therapist. Clients also enter therapy at the will of others, including child welfare institutions and the justice system. At times, societal institutions expect family therapists to serve as social control agents by influencing families to change in what is considered prosocial ways. Care must be taken not to recreate unjust social arrangements. Socioculturally attuned family therapists ask questions such as "Who is expecting change and why? What is my role in facilitating change?" And "How is my role contributing to maintaining the status quo of inequity and/or promoting social equity?"

Understanding the complexities of societal systems, culture, and power allows socioculturally attuned family therapists to identify opportunities for change. That is they recognize and support resistance that draws from and leads to resilience, which in turn inspires authentic hope. Consider a heterosexual couple who entered therapy when Miguel became depressed. Miguel identified as Mexican American and Sally identified as European American. They met each other when working to support the rights of migrant workers in the Southwest U.S. They shared political and social ideology. Miguel was the only Latino engineer at a manufacturing firm where he routinely experienced racism from colleagues. He felt isolated in a white neighborhood and community, remaining there at Sally's request. Sally described herself as anti-racist, offering her activism as proof. The therapist noticed, however, that Sally rarely acknowledged Miguel's experiences of oppression and marginalization. Unraveling this dynamic, including the differences in their racial experiences and daily stressors, led to increased hope for change. The husband's depression lifted as the couple began routinely attending to acts of daily racism, considering together how to resist racism, and entertaining the idea of moving to a more supportive context.

Application of Models

Sociocultural attunement improves the ability to use existing models in ways that support social equity. Models enhance change by offering clients and therapists a coherent framework from which to understand and find relief from problems. They serve as road maps that can inspire hope and confidence in the therapeutic process. The primary purpose of this text is to offer conceptual clarity and practical guidelines for socioculturally attuned practice across family therapy models, enhancing their role in the change process.

What Follows

The focus of this text is on bridging theory to practice; maintaining the integrity of established models while integrating contemporary understanding of diversity and social justice. In this first chapter, we argued for the importance of paying attention to how societal context and power dynamics affect mental health and relational well-being. Chapter 2 includes definitions of societal systems, diversity, and socially just practice, offering transtheoretical guidelines for practice. We highlight the relevance of third order change (McDowell, 2015) in socially transformative practice. Therapists encourage third order change by inviting families to inspect systems of systems, raising awareness and questioning the impact of societal context on presenting problems in an effort to promote relational equity. We argue that third order change occurs when families are able to recognize the impact of societal systems on their relationships, envision relationally equitable alternatives, and take liberatory action.

In Chapter 3, we explore self-of-the-therapist and ethical considerations for practicing socioculturally attuned family therapy. In the chapters that follow (Chapters 4–13), we integrate principles of societal context, power, and equity into the core concepts of major family therapy models, paying close attention to the "how-tos" of change processes. Each of these chapters includes numerous amalgamous, deidentified case illustrations. The final chapter (Chapter 14) provides readers with a more detailed description of transtheoretical guidelines for socioculturally attuned practice.

Chapters on family therapy models offer variety in how concepts are explained and examples are offered, however each follows a similar format. We first introduce the model, offering examples of its application and historical highlights. We do not attempt to offer a thorough overview of how to practice each therapeutic approach, but identify what we consider the most enduring concepts of each model. We then integrate principles of sociocultural attunement relying on theories of societal systems and power that are particularly applicable to the family therapy model at hand. We offer guidelines for practicing the model from a socioculturally attuned perspective and apply these guidelines to a case illustration.

Limitations

There are limits associated with any perspective or practice framework. What we advocate for is no exception. Many of the limits will follow in critiques of our work. We are aware, however, of a number of limiting decisions. The first is what we chose to include. We offer an overview of what we consider enduring concepts from each of 10 family therapy models. We did not attempt to include all models of family therapy. We have been deeply engaged in identifying enduring concepts across models in a field to which we have devoted most of our working lives. We are aware, however, that others may choose different concepts as primary in each of the models we present, or at least define these concepts differently. The second limit involves the decision to offer an overarching framework of each model rather than an exhaustive overview. This decision relies on readers accessing fuller historical and in-depth practice knowledge of each model from other sources. Third, we chose not to offer extensive details of the work so many of our colleagues are engaged in that integrates social justice into family therapy practice. That would be a volume in itself. We deeply appreciate their work and have used it to inform ours for many years. Finally, this is a first attempt at defining socioculturally attuned family therapy and considering its application across existing models. We expect our work to be critiqued and that others will build on our ideas. Our hope is to further the ongoing conversation about how to bridge the gap between the growing emphasis on social awareness as primary in professional preparation and guidelines for practices that promote just relationships.

References

Almeida, R., Dolan-Del Vecchio, K., & Parker, L. (2007). *Transforming family therapy: Just families in a just society.* Boston, MA: Allyn & Bacon.

American Psychological Association. (2002). *Guidelines on multicultural education, training, research, practice, and organizational change for psychologists.* Retrieved from http://www.apa.org/pi/oema/resources/policy/multicultural-guideline.pdf

Anderson, S. R., & Johnson, L. N. (2010). A Dyadic analysis of the between-and within-system alliances on distress. *Family Process, 49*(2), 220–235.

Aponte, H. J. (1976). The family-school interview: An ecostructural approach. *Family Process, 15*(3), 303–311.

Aponte, H. J. (1990). Too many bosses: An eco-structural intervention with a family and its community. *Journal of Strategic and Systemic Therapies, 9*(3), 49–63.

Auerswald, E. H. (1968). Interdisciplinary versus ecological approach. *Family Process, 7*(2), 299–303.

Auerswald, E. H. (1972). Families, change, and the ecological perspective. *Family Process, 10*(3), 263–280.

Center for Disease Prevention and Control. (2013). *Health disparities and inequalities report.* Retrieved from http://www.cdc.gov/mmwr/pdf/other/su6203.pdf

Commission for Accreditation of Counseling and Related Educational Programs. (2016). *2016 CACREP standards.* Retrieved from http://www.cacrep.org/for-programs/2016-cacrep-standards/

Commission on Accreditation for Marriage and Family Therapy Education. (2014). *Accreditation standards: graduate and post-graduate marriage and family therapy training programs.* Retrieved from http://www.coamfte.org/iMIS15/COAMFTE/Accreditation/Accreditation_Standards_Version_12.aspx

Council on Social Work Education. (2015). *Core competencies and practice behaviors.* Retrieved from https://www.ecu.edu/cs-hhp/socw/customcf/docs/field/CSWE_Core_Competencies.pdf

Council on Social Work Education Commission on Accreditation (2015). *2015 Educational policy and accreditation standards.* Retrieved from http://www.cswe.org/Accreditation/Standards-and-Policies/2015-EPAS

D'Aniello, C., Nguyen, H., & Piercy, F. (2016). Cultural sensitivity as an MFT common factor. *American Journal of Family Therapy, 44*, 234–244.

Falicov, C. (2014). *Latino families in therapy* (2nd ed.). New York, NY: Guilford Press.

Freire, P. (2000). *Pedagogy of the oppressed.* New York, NY: Bloomsbury. (Original work published in 1970).

Fricker, M. (2007). *Epistemic injustice: Power and the ethics of knowing.* New York, NY: Oxford University Press.

Garofalo, R., Wolf, R. C., Wissow, L. S., Woods, E. R., & Goodman, E. (1999). Sexual orientation and risk of suicide attempts among a representative sample of youth. *Archives of Pediatrics & Adolescent Medicine, 153*(5), 487–493.

Goodrich, T., Rampage, C., Ellman, B., & Halstead, K. (1988). *Feminist family therapy: A casebook.* New York, NY: W. W. Norton.

Hair, H., Fine, M., & Ryan, B. (1996). Expanding the context of family therapy. *The American Journal of Family Therapy, 24*(4), 291–304.

Hare-Mustin, R. T. (1978). A feminist approach to family therapy. *Family Process, 17*(2), 181–194.

Ho, M. K., Rasheed, J. M., & Rasheed, M. N. (2004). *Family therapy with ethnic minorities* (2nd ed.). Thousand Oaks, CA: SAGE.

Imber-Black, E. (1992). *Families and larger systems: A family therapist's guide through the labyrinth.* New York, NY: Guilford Press.

Jones, C. P. (2000). Levels of racism: A theoretic framework and a gardener's tale. *American Journal of Public Health, 90*(8), 1212–1215.

Keeney, B. P. (1979). Ecosystemic epistemology: An alternative paradigm for diagnosis. *Family Process, 18*(2), 117–129.

Knudson-Martin, C. (2013). Why power matters: Creating a foundation of mutual support in couple relationships. *Family Process, 52*(1), 5–18.

Knudson-Martin, C., & Huenergardt, D. (2010). A socio-emotional approach to couple therapy: Linking social context and couple interaction. *Family Process, 49*(3), 369–384.

Korin, E. (1994). Social inequalities and therapeutic relationships: Applying Freire's ideas to clinical practice. In R. V. Almeida (Ed.), *Expansions of feminist family theory through diversity* (pp. 75–98). New York, NY: Haworth Press.

Kruks, G. (1991). Gay and lesbian homeless/street youth: Special issues and concerns. *Journal of Adolescent Health, 12*(7), 515–518.

Lareau, A. (2011). *Unequal childhoods: Class, race and family life with an update a decade later* (2nd ed.). Oakland: University of California Press.

Luepnitz, D. A. (1988). *The family interpreted: feminist theory in clinical practice.* New York, NY: Basic Books.

Martín-Baró, I., Aron, A., & Corne, S. (1994). *Writings for a liberation psychology.* Cambridge, MA: Harvard University Press.

McCulloch, A. (2001). Social environments and health: Cross sectional national survey. *BMJ, 323*(7306), 208–209.

McDowell, T. (2015). *Applying critical social theories to family therapy practice.* New York, NY: Springer.

McGoldrick, M., Anderson, C., & Walsh, F. (Eds.). (1989). *Women in families: A framework for family therapy.* New York, NY: W. W. Norton.

McGoldrick, M., Giordano, J., & Garcia-Preto, N. (2005). *Ethnicity and family therapy* (3rd ed.). New York, NY: Guilford Press.

Merton, R. K. (1968). The Matthew effect in science: The reward and communication system of science. *Science, 159*(3810), 56–63.

Minuchin, S., Montalvo, B., Guerney, B., Rosman, B., & Schumer, F. (1967). *Families of the slums: An exploration of their structure and treatment.* New York, NY: Basic Books.

National Institute of Mental Health. (2014). *Women and depression: Discovering hope.* Retrieved from http://www.nimh.nih.gov/health/publications/women-and-depression-discovering-hope/index.shtml

Prouty Lyness, A., & Lyness, K. (2007). Feminist issues in couple therapy. *Journal of Couple & Relationship Therapy, 6*(1/2), 181–195.

Raskin, J. (2010). Constructing and deconstructing social justice counseling. In J. Raskin, S. Bridges, & R. Neimeyer (Eds.), *Studies in meaning 4: Constructivist perspectives on theory, practice and social justice* (pp. 247–276). New York, NY: Pace University Press.

Sexton, T., Ridley, C., & Kleiner, A. (2004). Beyond common factors: Multilevel-process models of therapeutic change in marriage and family therapy. *Journal of Marital and Family Therapy 30*(2), 131–149.

Sprenkle, D. H., Davis, S. D., & Lebow, J. L. (2009). *Common factors in couple and family therapy: The overlooked foundation for effective practice.* New York, NY: Guilford Press.

Tatum, B. D. (1997). *"Why are all the black kids sitting together in the high school cafeteria?" and other conversations about race.* New York, NY: Basic Books.

Waldegrave, C., & Tamasese, K. (1994). Some central ideas in the "Just Therapy" approach. *Family Journal, 2*(2), 94–103.

Walters, M., Carter, B., Papp, P., & Silverstein, O. (1988). *The invisible web: Gender patterns in family relationships*. New York, NY: Guilford Press.

White, M., & Epston, D. (1990). *Narrative means to therapeutic ends*. New York, NY: W. W. Norton.

Wynne, L. (1967). Discussion of the "individual and the larger contexts." *Family Process, 6*, 148–154.

2 Guiding Principles for Socioculturally Attuned Family Therapy

Socioculturally Attuned Family Therapy is a transtheoretical framework that builds on existing family therapy models in ways that expand our abilities to understand the impact of societal systems and power on presenting problems and to tailor interventions accordingly. Following, we describe and relate principles of socioculturally attuned family therapy, emphasizing the concept of third order change (McDowell, 2015). This includes how dimensions of power and societal context can be integrated into family therapy models to guide practices that support just relationships (see Figure 2.1.).

Societal Context

Ecosystems include both living and nonliving organisms in particular places at particular times. A family in rural Uganda awakens in a modest thatch roofed hut to the sound of their farm animals—pigs, chickens, and goats—waiting to be fed. Their morning water must be boiled to drink the local tea. The air is clear and the sun is reliably bright. Their beautiful tropical setting is rampant with malaria-bearing mosquitos. The economy suffers from a history of colonization, civil war, and global capitalism. Oil has been found beneath the ground, which signals social change as companies from China and the West begin circling. The family's ecosystem includes the entire context in which they are embedded, from the smallest insect to the largest land mass.

Societal context refers to the organization of human activity that emerges within and is dependent on all other aspects of ecosystems. A European American family wakes up in a small apartment in a large city in the U.S. They hear familiar street noises and the sounds of neighbors arguing. The refrigerator holds nothing suitable for school lunches so children are gathering coins from between couch cushions as the family cat looks on. A parent hurries the children, scolding the oldest for not making sure lunches were ready, while grabbing an umbrella to walk the children safely to school against their objections. Clean water runs out of the tap, but the air is polluted. Buildings along the way are being remodeled as

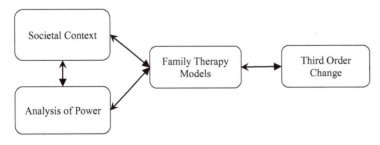

Figure 2.1 Conceptual framework for socioculturally attuned family therapy.

the neighborhood becomes gentrified, soon to be too expensive for the family to remain. Several miles away an African American family rushes to grab ready-to-eat breakfast bars as a father warns his only child to be in the car in 10 minutes or he will face having to walk to school. James, 15 years old, throws his iPad into a backpack that contains shorts and a t-shirt for afterschool sports. He is worried that the Nike shoes he picked out for basketball might be too bright and will draw the wrong kind of attention from his teammates. James' mother is calling out spelling words they studied together the night before. They look forward to dinner out that evening. These families' morning activities and interactions have already been deeply shaped by differing incomes within their urban ecosystem.

When we use the term "societal context" we are referring to shared meanings that define culture, inform identities, and situate experience, as well as the dynamic interconnection of social systems that shape constraints and opportunities within specific spatial settings. The family in Uganda is headed by a 15-year-old girl, Dembe. Her maternal grandmother is alive but living on a separate family plot. She has two younger brothers and a younger sister. She is one of more than half of the families in her village that are child-headed, most of whom lost their parents to AIDS. She and her 13-year-old brother, Jimiyu, are HIV positive but are receiving recently available antiretroviral (ARV) treatment. Dembe must stay on the family land to protect the family belongings from those who might steal them when they are away at school. Jimiyu has been challenging Dembe, siding with their late father's family who argue that the land and children should go back to the paternal clan as is customary when no adults are living. Dembe knows this will leave her and her siblings with nothing and refuses their interference, relying on Ugandan laws that protect the young family's right to their parents' property. Jimiyu has been yearning for items from the West, now increasingly advertised on the internet and television. He recently accepted a pair of Nike shoes from a local NGO. Dembe is angry, fearing peers and extended family will be jealous and no longer help if they believe an NGO is supporting the family. Jimiyu is refusing his sister's and maternal grandmother's authority as women and elders.

Every moment of Jimiyu and Dembe's life is affected by the complex nature of sociopolitical and ecological contexts, including traditional gender roles affected by colonization, tribal and clan customs, Western NGOs, Ugandan government and laws, access to physical space and ownership of property, world economy, international power dynamics that influence availability of ARV treatment, and so on. Societal systems are not simply benign organizational patterns that create a sense of wholeness. They are theaters where struggles for power, influence, and material advantage are acted out.

Social Structures

Social structures include socioeconomic stratification, social institutions, and other large systems. They shape the meaning we make of our lives and relationships, the organization of our daily (even most intimate) interactions, the material realities in which we are situated, and the location and expression of our emotional, spiritual, and existential experiences. Social institutions include (among others) family and kinship, community, religion, social welfare and health care, education, economy, mass media, and government/politics. Social structures impose constraints and opportunities over possible individual, group, and institutional actions. For example, the U.S. legal structure includes laws for governing actions and systems for controlling law-breaking behavior, as well as avenues to protect civil rights and seek compensation for wrongdoing.

Social structures largely determine the material realities of our lives, which in turn deeply affect our well-being. The U.S. family mentioned earlier is also female-headed. Melinda is 35; her oldest daughter, Maya, is 15, followed by a 9-year-old daughter and a 6-year-old son. Melinda fled from her physically abusive husband and spent 6 months in a family shelter before finding a job and apartment. Her daily schedule includes working the night shift as an aid in a nursing home before coming home to help her children get to school. As a white woman, Melinda makes approximately 80% of what a white male counterpart would make with a similar educational background (yet considerably more than a woman of color). Systems of male dominance and patriarchy that promote and maintain violence against women that have deeply affected her family continue to be prevalent worldwide. The increasing focus on capitalism and the individual in the U.S. has driven a trend toward warehousing the elderly, creating a need for professional caretakers. This provides Melinda with work, but work that is not highly valued in an ageist society that prioritizes productivity. Melinda must rely on her oldest daughter to help run the family. When she enters family therapy because one of her children is failing in school, the therapist pathologizes Melinda for Maya's role as a "parentified child."

Our relationships are shaped by context, but contexts are not neutral.

All societies are plagued with social structures and institutions that promote and maintain unearned privilege, power imbalances, and misuses of power. Our interconnected identities— race, social class, age, sexual orientation, gender, nation of origin, language, migration status, looks, abilities, and other identity markers—shape our opportunities and constraints. People who hold greater social power typically have the strongest influence over the creation of social institutions, including their governing values, norms, and rules. For example, in the U.S., most universities and knowledge produced through universities privilege Western, Euro-centered cultural frameworks. Social welfare institutions likewise set expectations for family interaction and parenting based on dominant middle-class, Euro-centered cultural assumptions. As family therapists, we are in a unique position to analyze, navigate, and intervene in these systems.

Culture

Culture refers to beliefs, values, and traditions, ways of being and doing, collective meaning-making, shared knowledge and attitudes, and conceptual frameworks for understanding the universe including spirituality and religion. Culture is fluid and continually shifts as we collectively adapt to changing circumstances. Both Melinda and Dembe value their families and put the needs of others first. This is a cultural expectation for women in most societies. While it plays out differently in each cultural context, as women they are both struggling with patriarchy and both are deeply affected by global capitalism. Dembe holds cultural values of filial piety and respect for elders. This contributes to her conflict as elders in her father's clan to whom she might have turned no longer have her best interests in mind. Cultural traditions that once helped children in her situation now work against her as the dearth of resources leaves most of the country in need. When there were few children left without parents (there was no word for orphan in Dembe's native language prior to civil war and the AIDS pandemic) and clans had enough to share within tribal structures, children would have been protected when their holdings were turned over to elders along with their care. In the U.S., Melinda personally cares for elders within a context that has created a growing demand for paid professional caretakers, but within a cultural context that devalues the elderly. Maya and Dembe are both 15-year-old girls who love and support their younger siblings. They both spend time each day making sure their siblings are fed, sleep well, and follow family rules. What their dedication means and how it is valued or supported, is vastly different across the cultural contexts of the U.S. and Uganda.

Maya and James live in the same city in one of the most prosperous countries in the world, yet their lives are quite different. James, also 15, gets annoyed with the constant attention of his parents, but knows he can rely on them for meeting the majority of his needs. He feels pressured to do well in school as both parents are highly educated and expect him to maintain the family's social class advantage. Lately his grades have been dropping as he spends increasing amounts of time in the privacy of his own room late at night gaming on the internet. When they enter therapy, the therapist fails to understand the nuances of internet addiction. She prioritizes Euro-centered cultural values of privacy and autonomy, subtly discouraging James' parents from insisting they have access to his room or that he is not allowed to access the internet.

Let's now compare their lives with the life of Aziza, also 15 but living in a village in rural Egypt that has been supported across many generations through rug weaving. Aziza has been training in a local rug-making business since she was 7 years old, teaching her nimble fingers to work quickly across carpet threads. She and her family are considered blessed because of her natural abilities, which have been enhanced by long hours of work. Those who become master weavers must train from a very young age. Without these apprentices, the village as a whole would suffer. A 17-year-old boy, Ammon, has just been appointed the new supervisor; a position for which Aziza had secretly been hoping and working. Ammon and Aziza's relationship is about to change as the power dynamic between them becomes further unbalanced. Ammon is not as deft a weaver but as a male he must be able to support a wife before he can marry. This led to the decision to promote him over Aziza. He must pay for an apartment and provide for all the daily needs of a family. Aziza's income will be her own when she marries, to spend on her children and extended family as she chooses. The market for handmade rugs is changing, however, as more and more goods are created by machines and available at cheaper prices. A Western therapist might encourage Aziza's parents to advocate for her rights and/or dissuade parents in the village from allowing their children to train at young ages, viewing this practice as neglectful or abusive child labor. As apparent in these examples, family therapists must struggle with tensions inherent in all societies and cultures (e.g., between continuity and change, conflicting values and beliefs, prioritizing individual or collective well-being.)

It is generally agreed that culture is largely a social construction, a shared system of meaning-making and agreed upon knowledge. What is often less clear, however, are the dynamics of power relative to what we refer to as shared knowledge and meaning. In the example of Aziza and Ammon, issues of child labor and male privilege are center stage to many of us in the Western world. Our social construction of childhood in Western societies includes a focus on learning and play, responsibility for self but not for others. The social arrangement in rural Egypt just described, however, makes sense in context. Those with wealth purchase the rugs that have for centuries been proudly made by a community that depends on their production and sale. Children are chosen because of their early aptitudes; much like young athletes around the world who also spend their days in physical training (an activity that is generally lauded in most of the world). Islamic law attempts to balance power and gender by requiring a man to financially care for his wife/wives. Many young men in rural Egypt have no prospects and are losing hope of marriage. Women are expected to have their own holdings to protect them and help them provide for themselves and their families if needed. These traditional relationships are unique in some ways, yet share many gender inequities with the rest of the world as women are also expected to work the "second shift," are promoted at a slower rate, often make less than men, and are vulnerable to male dominance.

The term "shared" in relation to culture conjures a sense of equal participation and influence that can disguise the impact of power differentials in the creation of what is considered true and right. Our attitudes and beliefs, the meaning we make of our roles in society, and social discourses privilege those with the most power to shape collective discourse or rhetoric (Hair, Fine, & Ryan, 1996). As can be seen throughout examples in this chapter, these constructions result in real material consequences, including the uneven distribution of goods, leisure time, access to adequate housing, social influence, and prestige.

According to Bourdieu (1986), those whose cultural practices are closest to dominant groups have the greatest advantage in society. This includes language, interactional styles, speech patterns, attitudes, and beliefs that can be instrumental in upward class mobility. Bourdieu used the term *cultural capital* to refer to the advantage of being able to navigate and mirror the culture of those in the center who have the greatest access to influence and economic advantage. In the U.S. the most valued and centered cultural capital is that of white, middle- and upper-class, heterosexual, able-bodied, young to middle-aged men. Those most closely affiliated with this group secure lateral advantage and vertical advantage is secured via their legacies. Walk into most banks in the U.S. and notice who is sitting at the managerial desks. Most often these positions are filled by white men, followed by white women and men of color. They typically share the dress, language, and mannerisms of the white corporate world. Those already established in the system maintain cultural capital by hiring others who are culturally like them, adhering in turn to organizational culture. Cultural capital promotes social capital and social networks that reproduce in-group advantage. In our example, the social capital necessary to move up in corporate structures provides entrance into social networks. The bank managers mentioned earlier are hand-picked by those with power in the corporation's social network. This capital is the most valued currency in societal systems and social institutions, reifying the privilege of some and marginalizing others. This same dynamic is at play in most therapeutic settings.

Consider, for example, differences that are likely to occur in therapy for high- and low-status clients. High-status clients are likely to have greater choice in where they go for services. They have greater access to a different therapist should they dislike their provider or feel uncomfortable in a particular context. In contrast, it is likely that stressors which exacerbate problems in the first place (e.g., inadequate transportation, lack of flexibility in work hours, economic stressors) contribute to difficulties families with low status might have in even attending therapy. This in turn may be interpreted as low motivation for change by therapists in agencies that have strict "no show" policies. The currency of cultural and social capital also impacts the work of therapy. Think for a moment about how you might think and feel as you are getting ready to see a Supreme Court judge in couples therapy versus a single mother who has been court mandated for parenting skills.

The processes just mentioned are similar to colonial processes in which the culture and knowledge of colonizers is centered and imposed as superior. Colonization often relies on the meta-narrative that military strength, technological advancement, and scientific knowledge are evidence of a natural, linear progression of societies. Colonization is internalized as those being colonized are compelled to adopt colonizer language, dress, social practices, values, and beliefs. Let's refer back to our example of the child-headed family in Uganda. Dembe and her siblings are Christians and benefit from the help of their church. They speak English and dress in Western clothes provided by church members in the U.S. Jimiyu is being inducted into the world market through media exposure to goods he has come to expect and view as superior but cannot afford. He is beginning to internalize Western values that privilege self over the collective, creating conflict between what he wants and what Dembe expects from him as a brother.

Colonization happens within societies as well. As therapists, we are often faced with externalized and internalized superiority and/or oppression (e.g., racism, sexism, classism, homophobia, ableism, ageism, nationalism) in ourselves and in those with whom we work. Left unchecked, our own practices as family therapists can be oppressive and colonizing.

For example, consider a family entering therapy because their 3-year-old is having trouble sleeping in her own room. The therapist may inadvertently promote Euro-centered cultural values of independence and individuality if she simply assumes this is a problem that will result in long-term dependence or is a sign something is going wrong in the child's development. Wherever the child ends up sleeping, it is important that the therapist is able to help the parents think through their assumptions and how their concerns may be being influenced by dominant values with which they themselves may or may not agree.

Spatial Setting

Physical space, which includes all nonliving and living organisms and beings, is essential to understanding worldview and culture. Bourdieu (1986) argued that it is within what he called *habitus*, i.e., physical and social space, that we develop shared values, beliefs, and ways of thinking and doing. Let's revisit our example from rural Egypt. In this habitus there are limited opportunities for employment. There is almost no movement to and from other villages. The community is far from the fertile valley of the Nile. Nearly all members of the community are Muslim, responding to the call for prayer that rings out into the streets five times a day. Family and social systems are well established within a widely held religious and monocultural milieu. For most of us who live in highly diverse social contexts, this type of cultural uniformity is almost unimaginable. However, even in the most diverse societies we tend to share space with those who are similar to us culturally and who have similar social capital. In effect, space is organized via social, including power, arrangements which in turn are shaped by space. According to Soja (2010):

> Viewed from above, every place on earth is blanketed with thick layers of macrospatial organization arising not just from administrative convenience but also from the imposition of political power, cultural domination, and social control over individuals, groups, and the places they inhabit.
>
> (p. 540)

The emotional and relational impact of where families live, the safety and comfort of homes and neighborhoods, and the level of control and privacy they have over their immediate environment are rarely considered in family therapy. This is in spite of consistent evidence that living in adverse conditions due to poverty negatively impacts mental and physical health (Hudson, 2012). Inadequate physical space limits meeting basic human needs including the need for privacy and personal space, social interactions, and safety (Fitzpatrick & LaGory, 2000). By considering the need for privacy, personal space, desired social interaction, and safety within homes, neighborhoods, and communities, therapists can account for what is often invisible in the therapy room. For example, think about helping a parent use consequences rather than anger to curb negative child behavior. Place this family in a home with bedrooms for each child and a fenced back yard. Now place this same family in a small apartment where the parent sleeps on the couch and children cannot go outside alone.

Mobility is also often overlooked as part of the matrix of privilege and oppression (Jensen, 2011). The freedom and means to move from one place to another, including movement required for social mobility, is unevenly distributed. Those with the greatest privilege enjoy the best environmental space, safest and most comfortable living places, greatest mobility, and least surveillance by others. Consider again our example of one of the families living in a large U.S. city. Melinda and her children are safe from domestic violence that once existed within their home, but they live in an apartment slated for demolition in which they can hear and be heard by their neighbors. Melinda is unsure of her children's safety when they walk to school. Those moving in and gentrifying the neighborhood are exercising their class and economic privilege to transform the space for the upwardly mobile. Melinda and her family will be forced to search for new housing which is likely to be less desirable. Melinda does not have the means to start fresh in a new community. Her move will have to be carefully calculated to maintain access to her job and meet her children's needs while again saving for first and last month's rent. A therapist who underestimates this situation and is working to help Melinda become empowered or raise her self-esteem may be baffled by Melinda's caution when relating to her employer or considering a move.

On the other hand, James lives in a relatively safe community but must deal with the very real impact of racism when he leaves his home. He may be viewed as dangerous in spite of never having committed a crime or even losing his temper. His parents instruct him on what to do if he is profiled by the police and how to handle racism on a daily basis. Part of their anxiety about his lowered grades is from living in a societal context that requires James as a young black man to outperform his white counterparts. A therapist working with James who fails to recognize the dangers of racism may interpret James' parents' reluctance as resistance to therapy and/or as an attempt to keep him from eventually leaving home.

Power

++ →+

Power is a set of social processes by which individual and collective interests are determined.

++ →+

Social context and relational equity are not add-ons but central to the development and maintenance of symptoms. At the beginning of the chapter we referred to a married, heterosexual woman entering therapy for depression. Locating the depression inside of her as an individual would likely limit treatment to helping her think differently, encouraging her to increase her physical activity and/or begin taking anti-depressants, and offering a venue for her to express her feelings and concerns. Now imagine we include these potentially useful interventions but in the context of relationships. We help the couple develop an equal, mutually attuned relationship in which they both feel heard and connected. They eventually share equal influence with each other as they negotiate getting their needs met within the relationship, as well as the social awareness to traverse a societal context which routinely privileges one over the other.

Power dynamics are central to understanding emotional and relational well-being. There is ample evidence that equality in adult relationships promotes individual and relational well-being, and analysis of nuanced power dynamics between couples has become increasingly sophisticated (Knudson-Martin, 2013). According to Knudson-Martin (2013, p. 6) "the ability of couples to withstand stress, respond to change, and enhance each partner's health and well-being depends on their having a relatively equal power balance." She further contended that, "clinical change is hard to sustain unless therapists assess for and attend to the power processes underlying . . . relational dynamics." This calls for therapists to be able to assess and interrupt power imbalances rather than maintaining the illusion that one can be neutral in the face of relational inequity.

Early Thoughts about Power in Family Therapy

Originally, family therapists tended to view power as a pragmatic issue relevant to symptom formation and maintenance within family systems. Early communications theorists (Jackson & Jackson, 1968) identified couple relationships as complementary or symmetrical. Although these terms are now used somewhat differently, at that time complementary relationships were perceived as not equal. One partner was viewed as in charge and leading and the other was seen as following; one dominant and the other submissive. This may play out in a number of ways. Consider ideal Christian marriages in which a male partner is required to serve his family, listen carefully to the concerns and input of his wife, and be guided by a higher power to make final decisions that benefit the collective over himself. Consider in contrast abusive relationships in which one partner holds dominion over the other via emotional, physical, and/or sexual violence.

Symmetrical relationships were defined as equal, but originally defined as in danger of creating competition and escalating conflict. Think about couples that fight over everything without compromise. Both demand to be heard and accommodated, refusing to be influenced by the other. Consider a couple who argued continuously about most things, including whether the plants in the yard should be watered in the morning before it got hot or in the evening after it cooled down. One would start watering, the other would turn off the hoses—both with certainty of their right to do so. Eventually one of them simply cut the plants to the ground. As is true in most power dynamics, the one who was willing to go the furthest won the battle, but at uncalculated cost to the relationship. It is interesting that the idea of complementary and symmetrical relationships emerged during a time in U.S. society in which most families were dominated by males.

Returning to an historical perspective, Minuchin (1974) considered vertical and horizontal power in family systems through a focus on hierarchy and boundaries. From this point of view it is important and necessary for parents to have enough power to teach and protect children. Consider parents who are so preoccupied with the struggle for power and influence in their own relationship that they cannot agree on how to parent their children. As the children grow, each aligns with one of the parents, disrupting the sibling relationships and leaving the field wide open for children to act out. Or, a parent who is determined to control children may use excessive anger and punishment that in turn results in the children resisting oppression through withdrawing, arguing back, constantly attempting to accommodate, or running away. Madanes (1981) considered relational power imbalances as central to understanding and treating symptoms, the symptom itself being part of the power equation.

In the families just described, a runaway child might be seen as a metaphor for a power imbalance in the couple relationship that leaves one of the parents wanting but not feeling able to permanently leave the relationship. Relational power dynamics were not often placed in societal context. Hierarchical incongruences and power imbalances were not routinely linked to systems of privilege and oppression. There was little, if any, mention of male privilege or patriarchy being supported by the broader society and providing the backdrop for couple power dynamics until the feminist critique.

Critical and Postmodern Conceptualizations of Power

More recently critical social theory (e.g., critical race theory, feminist neo-Marxism, critical geography, and critical sociology) has been applied to broaden the understanding of and contextualize relational power in family therapy (McDowell, 2015). Critical social theorists tend to view power as relational and bi-directional. Those with greater available resources are in positions to impose their objectives or will on others. For example a parent often has greater physical presence that can be imposed, as well as social power and financial resources needed by a child. The child can bring refusal to cooperate and emotional withdrawal to bear on the relationship, but a parent can deny the child movement within and beyond the home, withhold food and other wants or needs, and threaten or use physical and emotional pain to exert influence. Ultimately the child has the power of social institutions that protect children, but only if parents exert power that causes harm beyond what is allowed by law.

Descriptions of power mentioned earlier fall within a modern, structural functional paradigm. Postmodern approaches to family therapy attend to power in a different way, primarily based on the work of Michel Foucault (1972). What in the modern era was considered universal and natural came under further attack with the postmodern critique in which knowledge and power are seen as inseparable, i.e., what is considered knowledge depends on societal power relations. Power is not held, but enacted. According to this view, we don't possess power; power is constructive and generative as well as constraining. Power is not simply coercive, but a productive organizing force in society. All members of a family come to the table when called, sit and wait for the blessing to be said, pass food to others, begin eating using prescribed manners, and engage in lively conversation. Everyone knows what to do in this common social practice. If all family members don't come to the table, someone is designated to go and get them. Power is generated via the interactional choreography. In effect, we exist in a network or web of power that shapes who we are, what we do, and the nature of our relationships. What we believe to be real, true, and right governs our views, causing us to in effect police each other and ourselves.

Critical Postmodern Conceptualizations of Power

It can be difficult to reconcile postmodern, modern, and critical analyses of power to effectively use them in family therapy practice. Viewing power from a critical postmodern perspective allows us to (1) acknowledge the impact of multi-directional power and pervasiveness of dominant discourses in our daily lives, while (2) considering the real material consequences of uneven distribution of power. McDowell (2015) offered the following description that integrates modern, postmodern, and critical understandings of power:

> Power is pervasive and unevenly distributed; systematic and idiosyncratic. Imagine power as everywhere shaping our collective and individual decisions about how to interact with each other across diverse contexts. We basically know what to expect within our cultural groups and familiar settings. We maintain social practices by policing each other and ourselves. Now imagine that power also pools up or thickens in some places; that some of us have more resources and greater influence to bring to bear in shaping singular and collective interactions. Collectively, those with greater resources and influence shape cultural practices and ideologies in ways that benefit their own group and maintain greater access to resources. Now imagine all of this in motion with those being threatened reacting to potential and actualized power by yielding, withdrawing, navigating and/or pushing back . . . . In other words, imagine a complex web of influence that is systematically designed to maintain power and access to resources of some over others but is also filled with idiosyncratic, highly nuanced power dynamics in local specific contexts. It is this type of complexity we deal with daily in the practice of family therapy.
>
> (pp. 6–7)

Power dynamics reverberate across all levels of societal systems and social structures, including our most intimate family relationships. Our face-to-face interactions are impacted by our access to power and resources on societal levels. Another family gathers for dinner; however, when children come to the table they sit quietly out of the view of their father who often performs power through scowling or demanding silence. The mother attempts to mediate the effects of the father's exertion of power by predicting his needs, sending non-verbal cues to children if they complain about the food, and keeping dinner moving swiftly. This family performs a common social practice of having dinner together while reflecting broad organizing principles of their society in which women must be more attuned to the needs and desires of men as men take on more authoritative roles; male privilege and dominance in the family mirroring males being centered and dominant in government, business, religious, and other social institutions.

Decisions about Using Power and Influence

We are all deeply influenced by broad social power dynamics, yet as individuals within relationships we still have choices about how to enact and/or garner influence with each other. We consider a plethora of immediate and long-term consequences of our actions. We may attempt to limit another's power over us by reducing their potential to overpower. At times we accommodate others to avoid harm or access power by proxy. We decide purposefully or inadvertently how to exert influence—what methods to use and how far to press. We evaluate the costs of persuading or demanding that others bend to our will, calculating the nature and history of the relationship and how others are likely to respond. For example, one of the partners in a same sex couple demands the other come out to family and friends as their relationship moves toward the possibility of marriage. Has the situation become unbearable, warranting the risk of losing the relationship if there is a refusal to live openly married? Is the demand unreasonable, creating unwarranted risk or emotional stress for the partner who wants to move more slowly? We also consider our own values and ideal selves as well as how we want others to see us. Was it difficult for the partner to make such a demand, as doing so goes against an easygoing, caring view of self?

Power and Resistance

Wherever there is oppression there is also resistance to oppression. Presenting problems can sometimes be identified as resistance to oppressive relationships. This can be imagined throughout the previous examples: children run away or constantly fight with parents; a partner refuses to listen when feeling pushed by the other's demands; a family accommodates a domineering power figure but only in that figure's presence; a withdrawal into the safety and power of depression. Routine responses to being overpowered can become automatic, creating problems in future relationships. Resistance can, however, also create resilience and promote relational equality. For example, family members who learned to constantly accommodate an oppressive parent fine-tune their abilities to read moods, context, and nuanced power dynamics. The child who fights back develops the ability to speak out and weather conflict.

◂—➤

When we miss power dynamics, we not only overlook the opportunity to build on resistance and resilience but risk inadvertently contributing to the problem.

◂—➤

Less powerful persons can be pathologized and/or made to carry the greater burden for change when well-meaning therapists center their attention on simply removing symptoms of oppression. For example, it is not uncommon for a partner who is in a one-down position to feel dismissed by a more powerful and (therefore) less attuned partner. This may lead the one-down partner to commonsense solutions such as repeating arguments and escalating anger in attempts to influence the relationship. When the couple arrives in therapy, the therapist is faced with one partner who seems unreasonable and out of control and one who presents as cool and collected, even patiently enduring unreasonable wrath. In these situations, we may inadvertently reinforce relational inequity by resting our attention on calming the partner who resorts to screaming and nagging, seeing this partner's actions as the greater problem. If one of the partners is diagnosed, it is likely to be the one who is (actually attempting to be) out of control. When we miss power dynamics we also run the risk of missing what cannot be said in families. Although this is often highly nuanced, the most ready example occurs where there is intimate partner violence. Hopefully all family therapists now screen for violence, spending at least some time with each partner to offer opportunity for disclosure. Just as being overpowered can lead to angry outburst, physical and emotional symptoms, and withdrawal, it can also lead to silence.

First, Second, and Third Order Change

↤→

What is commonly understood as true or common sense often reflects the views, and maintains the privilege, of those with the greatest influence over its definition.

↤→

We often refer to first order solutions as "common sense," knowing their impact will be limited and make no real lasting difference in the way relationships are organized. For example, new parents who are arguing over who gets up at night with the baby might be coached to alternate, one taking odd days and the other taking even days. This might be helpful, but it rings of common sense, first order change that fails to address the dynamics that prevented the couple from agreeing on this kind of obvious arrangement in the first place. Family therapists routinely target second order change, i.e., qualitative, discontinuous change that alters a system's rules, structure, and/or order (Watzlawick, Weakland, & Fisch, 1974).

Second order change is said to have occurred when system rules and shared meaning change along with interactions. Compared to second order change, we often consider first order change as cursory because it does not alter the structure or rules of a system, maintaining meaning frameworks or schemas. Second order change might involve addressing power dynamics that have been exacerbated and made more urgent by the couple becoming parents. Looking a little closer at the concept of common sense reveals the ubiquitous nature of the relationship between power and knowledge, i.e., the dynamic between dominant cultural worldviews or discourse and what we consider to be the natural order of things (Gramsci, 1971).

When purposefully considered and carefully sequenced, first and second order change are both essential to the practice of family therapy. Second order shifts are followed by a series of first order changes within the new meaning-making schema and system rules. When new alternatives are created, everyday patterns of interaction shift as a result, which in turn support second order change. The new parents exemplified earlier might engage in second order change as they increase their attunement toward each other's needs and began to share more equal influence. First order change such as alternating nights might then be a practical extension of this more foundational level change. First order change can also be important when a family is in crisis and needs stability. First order change is only a problem in therapy when it takes precedence or is present without attention to second order dynamics.

↤→

Third order change is a shift in relationship to sociocultural systems that expands possibilities and enables transformation of one's life.

↤→

Even though third order change is a new concept in family therapy (McDowell, 2015), it is not necessarily a new practice in family therapy. When therapists integrate sociocultural awareness into their approaches and open space for socially transformative change, they are engaging in third order change (e.g., CCM, SERT, just therapy). When therapists engage in third order change they help families connect their lived experience to broader systems of systems, raising awareness and questioning the impact of cultural norms, values, and societal power structures on relational dynamics and presenting problems. The new parents previously mentioned might now reflect on gender roles and gender equity, systems of patriarchy across families and social institutions, the impact of living in a capitalist society relative to social class and work demands, and so on.

Consider as another example, an intergenerational pattern of sons in conflict with their fathers. At a second order change level, a father might be encouraged to remember what it was like when he was a boy trying to please his father, feeling that no matter what he did he could not live up to his father's expectations. This might soften his approach and increase his emotional attunement to his own son. If the therapist were to engage the family in dialogue or socioeducation about the bind in which fathers and sons often find themselves in patriarchal societies, e.g., sons being invited into patriarchy by their fathers who also insist on maintaining power over them, the family might be able to see how they participate in a widespread system that informs conflict within the family. These types of revelations promote third order change that can be liberating, releasing families from imposed societal structures.

Bateson (1972, p. 298) referred to four levels of learning in *Steps to an Ecology of Mind*, the first two of which correlate with what has become commonly understood as first and second order change. The following excerpt reflects a parallel between Bateson's levels of learning and first and second order change, as well as what has been introduced elsewhere as third order change (Bartunek & Moch, 1987; McDowell, 2015):

> Learning I is change in specificity of response by correction of errors of choice within a set of alternatives. Learning II is change in the process of Learning I, e.g., a corrective change in the set of alternatives from which choice is made, or it is a change in how the sequence of experience is punctuated. Learning III is change in the process of Learning II, e.g., a corrective change in the system of sets of alternatives from which choice is made.
>
> (Bateson, 1972, p. 298)

According to Bateson, first level learning or first order change occurs when change is made but relationship dynamics and schemas remain the same (Bartunek & Moch, 1987). Possibilities for difference are limited to what is available within what he referred to as a set of alternatives; in other words what can be imagined within a schema. Second level learning or second order change is change in the schema itself and resulting change in sets of alternatives. It focuses on the process level of relationships, creating new schemas (Bartunek & Moch, 1987). This allows relationships to be punctuated differently and members of a system to choose from different sets of alternatives.

Third order change or third level learning involves major shifts in how we see the world (Ecker & Hulley, 1996), through a focus on meta-processes and meta-narratives. Third order change—what Bateson referred to as level 3 learning—necessitates a meta-perspective in which we consider sets of alternatives, leading to being able to choose not only between sets of alternatives but between schemas (Bartunek & Moch, 1987). When therapists target third order change they are active and intentional, working in a space in which taken-for-granted assumptions are inspected, taken apart, and disrupted to reveal multiple perspectives and possibilities. This critical meta-perspective is in itself a paradigm shift; a shift in how we think and how we know what we know.

From Principles to Practice

Socioculturally attuned therapists sensitively apprehend and resonate with clients' social contexts (D'Aniello, Nguyen, & Piercy, 2016; Pandit, Kang, ChenFeng, Knudson-Martin, & Huenergardt, 2014). Therapists must be vigilant in our understanding and consideration of the impact of intersecting social, historical, economic, religious, political, and cultural systems each time we intervene in a local "here and now" context. We must keep multiple systems levels in mind while considering the interaction between these systems, societal power processes, and specific family dynamics. In other words, therapists engage by continually connecting the dots between broad social levels and intimate and family relationships. As family therapists we are familiar with adopting a multi-ocular lens when considering specific relational patterns within multiple systems dynamics.

Socioculturally attuned family therapists continuously make the connection between power dynamics at larger social levels and problems at the most intimate relational levels. The concept of isomorphism is familiar to family therapists and can be used to understand the ways in which family systems reflect the organization of larger social systems in which they are embedded. Sociologists refer to isomorphism as mimetic, normative, or coercive (DiMaggio & Powell, 1983). Families are affected by all three of these processes, i.e., they often mimic the organization, structure, and rules of larger social systems (e.g., patriarchy); follow social norms and values that govern institutions across societies (e.g., valuing hard work); and/or experience pressure from outside systems to conform to particular ways of being (e.g., parenting in socially sanctioned ways). From postmodern perspectives, families are thought to reflect and make meaning of their experiences through dominant social discourses. In turn, these discourses affect every aspect of life, including how we feel and what we do.

Finally, therapists working from a socioculturally attuned perspective need to be diligent not to inadvertently reproduce the status quo of societal context and power relations in the therapy process. Not noticing or intervening in relational inequity, failing to address sexism and racism, and practicing from white middle-class perspectives are just a few of the many ways we contribute to unjust systems. Third space (Soja, 2010) can be created by engaging in critical dialogue and reflection (Freire, 1970/2000), imagining and supporting just relationships, and collaborating with families to create strategies for action that support third order change.

Practicing socioculturally attuned family therapy requires us to infuse the practice of family therapy models with an understanding of how societal context and power dynamics contribute to mental health and relational problems. The transtheoretical goal of socioculturally attuned practice that supports equity can be integrated into interventions within all family therapy models. The following guidelines help to disrupt inequalities in social relationships that are largely invisible, taken-for-granted, or assumed natural and open options for relational systems that equitably support the health and well-being of all. They include:

↤→

Attune:	*Understand, resonating with, and responding to experience within societal contexts.*
Name:	*Identify what is unjust or has been overlooked—amplify silenced voices.*
Value:	*Acknowledge the worth of that which has been minimized or devalued.*
Intervene:	*Support relational equity—disrupt oppressive power dynamics.*
Envision:	*Provide space to imagine just relational alternatives.*
Transform:	*Collaborate to make what is imagined real—third order change.*

↤→

In this text we demonstrate how family therapists can apply these general guidelines to promote ethical and equitable practice using a variety of models. We offer a number of ways of looking at the world from critical, culturally sensitive, and socially just traditions. We welcome readers to challenge and rethink our ideas, to expand on what follows by integrating unique perspectives and practices that further efforts toward equity based practice. Our hope is that collectively we can imagine more possibilities for practice and expand the vision of practicing family therapy in ways that actively support equitable relationships.

References

Bartunek, J., & Moch, M. (1987). First-order, second-order, and third-order change and organizational development interventions: A cognitive approach. *The Journal of Applied Behavioral Science, 23*(4), 483–500.

Bateson, G. (1972). *Steps to an ecology of mind.* London, UK: Jason Aronson.

Bourdieu, P. (1986). The forms of capital. In J. G. Richardson (Ed.), *Handbook of theory and research for the sociology of education* (pp. 241–258). New York, NY: Greenwood Press.

D'Aniello, C., Nguyen, H., & Piercy, F. (2016). Cultural sensitivity as an MFT common factor. *American Journal of Family Therapy, 44,* 234–244.

DiMaggio, P. J., & Powell, W. W. (1983). The iron-cage revisited: Institutional isomorphism and collective rationality in organizational fields. *American Sociological Review, 48*(2), 147–160.

Ecker, B., & Hulley, L. (1996). *Depth oriented brief therapy: How to be brief when you were trained deep and vice versa.* San Francisco, CA: Jossey Bass.

Fitzpatrick, K., & LaGory, M. (2000). *Unhealthy places: The ecology of risk in the urban landscape.* New York, NY: Routledge.

Foucault, M. (1972). *The archeology of knowledge.* London, UK: Routledge.

Freire, P. (2000). *Pedagogy of the oppressed.* New York, NY: Bloomsbury. (Original work published in 1970).

Gramsci, A. (1971). *Selections from the prison notebooks of Antonio Gramsci.* New York, NY: International.

Hair, H., Fine, M., & Ryan, B. (1996). Expanding the context of family therapy. *The American Journal of Family Therapy, 24*(4), 291–304.

Hudson, C. (2012). Disparities in the geography of mental health: Implications for social work. *Social Work, 57*(2), 107–119.

Jackson, W. J., & Jackson, D. D. (1968). *The mirages of marriage.* New York, NY: W. W. Norton.

Jensen, A. (2011). Mobility, space and power: On the multiplicities of seeing mobility. *Mobilities, 6*(2), 255–271.

Knudson-Martin, C. (2013). Why power matters: Creating a foundation of mutual support in couple relationships. *Family Process, 52*(1), 5–18.

Madanes, C. (1981). *Strategic family therapy.* San Francisco, CA: Jossey Bass.

McDowell, T. (2015). *Applying critical social theory to family therapy practice.* New York, NY: Springer.

Minuchin, S. (1974). *Families and family therapy.* Cambridge, MA: Harvard University Press.

Pandit, M., Kang, Y. J., ChenFeng, J., Knudson-Martin, C., & Huenergardt, D. (2014). Practicing socio-cultural attunement: A study of couple therapists. *Journal of Contemporary Family Therapy, 36,* 518–528.

Soja, E. (2010). *Seeking spatial justice.* Minneapolis: University of Minnesota Press.

Watzlawick, P., Weakland, J., & Fisch, R. (1974). *Principles of problem formation and problem resolution.* New York, NY: W. W. Norton.

3 Self-of-the-Therapist and Ethical Considerations in Socioculturally Attuned Family Therapy

Sociocultural attunement is essential to ethical and effective family therapy practice. Our cultural lens deeply impacts how we view the world, including how we think about clients and approach presenting problems (Baker, 1999). This includes the ability to respect another's values without attempting to change them or feeling the need to give up one's own (Hardy & McGoldrick, 2008). It also requires the courage to break social norms, such as talking about race, class, and gender, and to disrupt power systems to which we have been socialized to conform. Ethical practice requires therapists to have an advanced awareness of themselves within complex societal contexts in order to ethically and effectively practice socioculturally attuned family therapy.

At the very minimum, ethical positioning is a stance in which one is clear about the need to engage with clients in ways that are consistent with ethical guidelines and principles. There are nine standards in the American Association for Marriage and Family Therapy (AAMFT) Code of Ethics. It is noteworthy that the very first standard, 1.1, is non-discrimination. It reads as follows: "Marriage and family therapists provide professional assistance to persons without discrimination on the basis of race, age, ethnicity, socioeconomic status, disability, gender, health status, religion, national origin, sexual orientation, gender identity or relationship status" (AAMFT, 2015, para. 1). In spite of its primary position in the code of ethics, many students and licensed family therapists intentionally or unintentionally position themselves in ways that are not aligned with this standard. Rejecting this standard may be overt, involving a conscious choice due to conflicting personal codes of morality, values, religious beliefs, cultural norms, or biases (Caldwell, 2013; Priest & Wickel, 2011). For example, the statement "I don't believe I can work with same-sex couples because I cannot in good conscience support their union or marriage or help them work toward their clinical goals" is a stance that knowingly contradicts our non-discrimination standard. Failing to align with this standard may also be relatively unintentional. In these cases, family therapists are not likely to realize they are engaging in discrimination. Examples include working harder with a client with high status than with a client with low status, failing to acknowledge one's own racial, class, gender, or sexual orientation privileges, using Eurocentric models without considering cultural fit, and expecting women to take on the majority of emotional work in couples therapy.

This chapter engages readers in the ethics of equity based practice and the role of self-of-the-therapist in socioculturally attuned family therapy. We review the myth of neutrality in the practice of family therapy, consider the importance of developing the contextual self-of-the-therapist, and explore the role of power in clinical practice. We discuss dialectical tensions, offering examples of common struggles in equity based clinical practice. Our hope is that highlighting these contextual issues and ethical tensions will help all of us to become more socioculturally attuned, regardless of the models to which we adhere.

Myth of Neutrality

Early on, therapists were expected to be objective and neutral to avoid contaminating or negatively affecting clients' clinical processes with their own biases and assumptions (Slife, Smith, & Burchfield, 2003; Tjeltveit, 1986). Boszormenyi-Nagy and Spark (1973) challenged this idea when they argued instead for multi-directed partiality in which the therapist advocates for all family members, including those not present (Boszormenyi-Nagy & Krasner, 1986). Therapists are neither neutral umpires nor ones who stand above the conflict; rather, they take the side of each family member, being empathic and fair toward everyone while positioning their work to promote just relationships. Each person is important and deserves to be understood and valued. For Boszormenyi-Nagy and Spark (1973), the therapist must argue the case from each family member's perspective, purposely avoiding an attitude of benevolent neutrality. They asserted that multi-directional partiality is vital in gaining and restoring mutual trust within the family and for maintaining credibility as a therapist.

Feminist family therapists likewise challenged the myth of neutrality, pointing to ethical concerns surrounding the assumption that therapists can be objective. Early on, Betty Carter (1985, p. 78) argued that, "You cannot not act out of your age, gender, sibling position, experience, belief system, and wisdom, or lack of it. Your only choice is whether to do this consciously or unconsciously." Bograd (1984) and Goldner (1985) challenged family therapists to rethink foundational notions of circularity, neutrality, and complementarity, arguing that these concepts do not address issues of power and control inherent in family life and therapeutic processes. These theorists helped family therapists understand that neutrality is in fact far from neutral. A new wave of postmodern family therapists continued the argument against the myth of neutrality, asserting that therapists operate from a value position (Melito, 2003). Our stances, biases, values, beliefs, and perspectives guide who we are and what we do. In addition, therapists have power to influence clients in significant and lasting ways.

Issues of power and control continue to be areas of concern as they are blatantly evident in most frameworks (e.g., the medical model, clinical theories and models, research methods). It is imperative that we develop deep understandings of how societal systems, power structures, clinical frameworks, and therapeutic stances can maintain the status quo of privileging some at the expense of others. Family therapists must engage in ongoing, thoughtful, contextual self-reflexivity in order to take an intentional stance that supports just relationships in equity based practice.

Contextual Self-of-the-Therapist

Contextual self-of-the-therapist encourages accountability for one's own social location in relationship to power and privilege (or lack thereof) and for uncovering and correcting our own biases that contribute to social inequity. It also refers to acknowledging the potential impact on therapeutic practice of one's own family of origin, current relationships, and experiences across societal systems. Cultural awareness and being able and willing to attune to those in cultures different from our own is essential (D'Aniello, Nguyen, & Piercy, 2016).

Therapist Social Location

↤↦

Ethical positioning is not possible without self-reflexivity, critical social awareness, and the ability to support relational justice.

↤↦

Self-reflectivity and critical social awareness are especially important for those in structurally ascribed positions of power, including family therapists. Arguably, those who have the most social capital and ability to influence are most responsible for facilitating necessary and important changes that lend themselves to equitable and just practices (Almeida, Dolan-Del Vecchio, & Parker 2008; Hernández & McDowell, 2010). Socioculturally attuned family therapists need to develop contextual consciousness in addressing issues of gender, societal power, and culture in clinical practice. This includes attending to one's own experience of racial privilege and oppression (McDowell et al., 2005) as well as the impact of one's own cultural background (Ellenwood & Snyders, 2006; Hardy & Laszloffy, 1995; Hardy & McGoldrick, 2008).

It is vital for family therapists to reflect on their heterosexist biases, and heterosexual and cisgender therapists to examine their privilege (Adams & Benson, 2005; McGeorge & Stone Carlson, 2011; Nealy, 2008). Additionally, we must develop awareness of how internalized oppression, such as internalized sexism and racism, operate within us to perpetuate patriarchal structures, white privilege, and androcentric norms (Sharp, Bermudez, Watson, & Fitzpatrick, 2007).

Power that is inherent in the very nature of being an expert (i.e., role power as a therapist) does not necessarily ameliorate power based on social location. Therapists with less privileged social positions may need to use their power to gain credibility and influence when clients are unconsciously discrediting them or needing more leadership. For example, therapists who are young and/or persons of color may not be afforded the privilege of lowering their professional position of power when their structural and systemic levels of power threaten their stance as therapists. It is at times necessary for people in less powerful social or structural positions (e.g., women, persons of color, or those with a particular disability or difference) to embrace and elevate their power in order to help clients achieve their goals. This is done carefully, with humility and confidence that therapists know how to use their power as leverage to help them be effective, credible, and compassionate.

Therapists must be able to maintain their positions as experts while addressing interactions in ways that encourage a client's accountability and change. Let's consider racism directed at a therapist of color as an example. McDowell et al., (2003) described their participation in a group working on racial awareness and taking anti-racist stances in therapy. Following is an excerpt from their paper (pp. 189–190).

Client: I always thought when you called someone Mexican that it was derogatory.

Cecilia: Why do you think that?

Client: I guess it's just the way people use it. I've always tried to use Hispanic because I thought it was much more proper.

Cecilia: When you use the word Mexican, what do you think of? . . . . You are not going to offend me.

Client: It's like there are different classes. When I think of Mexican I think of people in a lot of trouble, people who don't speak English, more straight from Mexico. When I think of Hispanic it could be anybody else.

Cecilia: So Mexican conjures up bad things for you.

Client: They are a different class of people.

Cecilia: So for you when you think of Mexican, the terms that come up for you are not as good as White.

Client: Yeah, mm hmm.

Cecilia: So now that you know I am Mexican, (Cecilia used this term purposefully to challenge the client's view of Mexicans) what does that mean to you?

Client: No matter what race anyone is, it doesn't bother me. I'm not racist; the only thing that bothers me is when someone can't speak English. I think they are ignorant. I can't help it.

Cecilia:	But I am still wondering, does the fact that you know I am Mexican, does that affect how you think of me?
Client:	I don't think of you as Mexican. I think of you as Latina.
Cecilia:	What if I would have called myself Mexican instead of Latina, would you have thought differently of me?
Client:	No, I would have thought of you as Hispanic. The only people that fit my negative view of Mexicans are people I don't know. Everyone I have ever gotten to know doesn't fit the stereotype.
Cecilia:	Once you meet someone that doesn't match the stereotypes . . . . What do you do?
Client:	Every Hispanic person I have ever met doesn't fit the stereotype.
Cecilia:	This is very interesting. What is it like for you for us to be talking about race like this?
Client:	I like it, I guess I'm not racist, but maybe I have a lot of misconceptions. I don't want that. My parents were very prejudiced.
Cecilia:	So is it okay if we talk about this again as it comes up?
Client:	Yes, I would like to get into the topic of race. Like I have always wanted to date cross racially but don't know how I would deal with my family.
Cecilia:	Okay. We are learning together here. You are helping me understand also. We can work together on this.
Client:	I'd like to talk to my family about it.
Cecilia:	Yeah, race is a difficult thing to talk about. It seems important that we find a way for you to talk to your family about this.

The authors (McDowell et al., 2003) discussed Cecilia's ability to regulate her own emotions while her client expressed overt racism toward her. They pointed out that the therapist was able to maintain an inquirer stance, slow the process down to allow space for the client to explore thoughts about race/ethnicity, and connect the client's (lack of) racial awareness to therapeutic goals. The therapist in this scenario had the knowledge, fluency, and self-awareness to challenge what was happening in the moment while leading a conversation that allowed the client to openly express and begin inspecting his racism.

Self-Disclosure in Context

Socioculturally attuned family therapists recognize these complexities and navigate self-disclosure in ways that allow them to use their identities to encourage equitable relationships in families. In the earlier example, Cecilia decided to disclose her Mexican heritage to help her client recognize racism and its effects. The decision to disclose was carefully timed to both maintain and leverage the positive relationship between the client and therapist.

Issues around therapist self-disclosure are complex (Roberts, 2005). There are some aspects of our identities that are (correctly or not) assumed by clients and other aspects that we have control over sharing. For example, we often "announce" our sex/gender through dress, mannerisms, and general appearance. Those with cisgender privilege and those who identify as transgender experience choices around sex and/or gender disclosure quite differently. Abilities, sexual orientation, race, and actual age may be visible or invisible. Some therapists of color, like Cecilia in the previous example, can "pass" as white if they choose to do so. Religious therapists can "pass" as secular.

We have choice over how much and what we share about our life experiences. This is the topic most associated with training in self-disclosure. We are used to asking ourselves questions like "Am I sharing this to help the client? How will it be helpful? How will it impact our therapeutic relationship?" and "How does self-disclosure fit into the model I am using?" But what about differences that put the therapist in a one-down position relative to the broader societal context? How are these decisions made when the therapist has a choice about whether or not to disclose an experience or social identity? What about when a gay or lesbian therapist is working with a homophobic client? Or a family in which a teen is coming out to parents who are fundamentalists? When does the therapist disclose sexual orientation to show solidarity and ally with a client or some members of a family?

Cultural Democracy

Socioculturally attuned family therapists must go beyond the concept of culture as difference to embrace cultural democracy (Košutić & McDowell, 2008), which demands equal valuing of all cultures and resists dominance of one culture over another. This concept is closely linked to the practice of decolonization in which therapists resist the privileging of ideology, practices, and membership of a dominant culture over colonized peoples (e.g., European American male ideology, cultural practices and identity in the U.S.). Paulo Freire's (1970/2000) critical pedagogy, which included raising critical consciousness to encourage self-determination and liberation, is an example of decolonizing practice. Freire engaged learners in dialogue and reflection to raise awareness of the impact of societal forces on their thinking and actions. Critical social awareness allows us to consider alternatives to the status quo rather than seeing social arrangements as natural and unchangeable. Freire argued that dialogue and reflection should lead to action that challenges the status quo of inequitable social relationships.

Garcia, Košutić, and McDowell (2015) added to Freire's liberatory framework by integrating emotion into the process of critical dialogue, reflection, and action. They argued that emotion is an integral part of self-reflection and the process we go through as we become more socially aware. Emotion itself is influenced by power and social position (Wetherell, 2012). Our perspectives, thought process, emotions, and worldview are intertwined. In other words, emotions are socially constructed rather than natural, internal, or exclusively related to thoughts; emotion is in effect a bridge from our internal experience to the outside world. For example, those with significant social privilege are likely to experience fewer negative emotions in relationship to social location until their privilege is exposed and they must grapple with the discomfort of holding unearned advantage and/or losing advantages.

It can be difficult to attune to emotions of those in social positions that differ from our own. In fact we often assume that what we feel or imagine ourselves feeling in another's situation is normal without considering culture, relational power, or societal context. Exploring sociocultural context, including our own positionality, perspectives, and emotions relative to societal contexts, is vital to our ability to assess and analyze power dynamics on both broad social and intimate relational levels, and as much as is possible, take in and resonate with another's sociocultural experience.

Power in Practice

Power dynamics are ubiquitous. We are often blinded by our own positions of power and the mechanisms that support our privilege. This occurs by simply failing to inspect and acknowledge the ways in which our epistemological frameworks marginalize the lifeworlds and experiences of others (Fricker, 2007). We also engage in subtle cultural wars in daily practice as we press colleagues and clients to accept our practice models and perspectives of mental and relational health. That said, we often hear beginning family therapists say they want to "flatten the hierarchy in order to empower clients." They appear nervous about taking a stance, perhaps assuming that influencing clients is by its very nature unethical. We join others who have postulated that attempts to reject the power we hold as therapists can inadvertently support the status quo of social inequity. This raises a variety of practical and ethical concerns, including the fact that our ways of knowing and positions of power have real material consequences (McDowell, 2015) regardless of our ability to identify how we and our clients are affected by them.

The decision to be directive versus collaborative is a false dichotomy. Larner (1995) examined issues of power and interventions in family therapy from the perspective of Derrida's philosophy in which power is presented as both real and socially constructed. He challenged therapists to consider the wider social context in which a "not-knowing" or "non-intervening" conversation takes place. Socioculturally attuned family therapists need to be aware that power, knowledge, and influence are always intertwined in the experience of therapy and in clients' expectations of change. It is necessary to continuously gauge one's position of power without assuming one can or should flatten the hierarchy inherent in the client–therapist relationship.

↤ →↦

Awareness of power is a critical first step in engaging in ethical practice, regardless of theoretical orientation.

↤ →↦

We must also attend to power outside the therapy room, relative to our communities and practice settings. Not all therapists and supervisors, however, are in a position to challenge systems in which families are embedded or in which therapy takes place. Supervisors from the dominant culture may be surprised to learn that supervisees are not willing to challenge people in a system that exacerbates their vulnerability. For people of color, women, those with disabilities, immigrants, etc. this vulnerability may always be present, regardless of the years of experience, educational degrees, or positions of power (Hernández, Taylor, & McDowell, 2009). Challenging powerful people within a system has to be done carefully, always gauging and balancing risk and reward. It is vital that we work together, sharing our power to collectively interrupt and transform harmful power dynamics.

Tensions in Socioculturally Attuned Practice

There are a number of tensions we experience as we come to define ourselves as socioculturally attuned family therapists. At times these tensions seem like irreconcilable differences. At other times it seems perfectly compatible to take a both/and position. We encourage readers to not see these tensions as dichotomous, but as continuums or at times competing values and goals. Although there are many tensions in ethical equity based work, we have chosen to emphasize the importance of recognizing the ways in which societal systems constrain personal agency, helping clients grapple with decisions about resistance to oppression, and honoring clients' perspectives and/or being culturally sensitive while challenging oppression. We do not attempt to offer universal solutions; rather, we hope the following will help readers consider the complexities and prepare to make decisions involved in equity based therapy.

Recognizing Societal Constraints on Personal Agency

Equity based therapists are often in a position of reconciling tensions between encouraging clients' personal empowerment and helping them negotiate societal constraints that limit their agency. Many of us fall into the trap of thinking everyone can choose a different way of thinking, being, and living. This is a privileged perspective that leads us to assume we all have (enough) choice. We often assume clients can achieve anything they put their minds to if they change their thoughts and perspectives, or assume responsibility for their situation and actions. This rings of the myth of meritocracy, which is a common belief that we can "pull ourselves up by our bootstraps" in order to overcome adversity, be successful, or achieve our goals. We can fail to acknowledge that all of us, to varying degrees, have social and structural constraints that block our agency. For example, worldwide, women and girls are still prevented from having equal access to education, safety, control, voice, leadership, and equal pay. LGBTQ people live with the daily oppression of heteronormativity and homophobia. People of color continue to experience the oppressive effects of colorism/racism, white privilege, and internalized racism. Those who live on low income are often geographically limited without equal freedom of movement or access to food or employment opportunities (McDowell, 2015).

++ →→

Therapists help families identify strengths and tap into resilience, yet when the session is over, many return to oppressive contexts.

++ →→

It is difficult and disconcerting to acknowledge the complexity of social position, inequity, and socioeconomic status. People reared in a privileged or even moderate income bracket are often oblivious to the struggles of those living on severely low income. Economic security buffers many of us against the real material consequences of limited or scarce resources (McDowell, 2015). For example, in a natural disaster, state of emergency, or crisis situation, wealthy individuals and families have greater access to resources that help buffer the crisis. The real life consequences of inequitable access is tangible and affects how we embody space, pursue or access resources, and both perceive and realistically gauge our choices. Furthermore, mechanisms of marginalization and oppression have a cumulative effect, placing those in the most disadvantaged positions at higher risk which in turn creates greater disadvantage across the lifespan (Merton, 1973, 1988). Therapists can help clients resist internalizing oppressions while navigating the effects and maximizing agency within constraining contexts. Therapists can also be allies for change by supporting clients' efforts to transform social arrangements within their spheres of influence e.g., individual, family, community, broader society.

Case Example

Marty, a white middle-class lesbian family therapist, landed her first job out of graduate school providing in-home therapy to primarily people of color living on low income. She exuded positivity and consistently demonstrated the ability to deeply care about all of those with whom she worked. She had firsthand experience of marginalization, oppression, and microaggressions that stemmed from homophobia. She was nervous but excited to get to work, to help her clients change their lives. She engaged clients in hopeful conversations drawing on a strength based therapeutic approach. Within a few months, Marty found herself feeling increasingly less competent, even dreading the work she had once been so excited about. After a particularly frustrating family session, she finally blurted out "I just don't see what I am doing wrong! Why my clients aren't getting better!" Marty's supervisor asked her to explain what she meant by "getting better" as Marty's clients typically reported that therapy was going well. During the supervisory conversation, Marty was surprised to realize she held the assumption that anyone can change their social status if they overcome psychological and relational problems. She held unquestionable good will and an unwavering belief that clients have the strengths they need to overcome problems. What she hadn't realized is that the assumption she held about her work—that as a therapist she could help clients overcome poverty by encouraging individual and relational change—was not only naive but inadvertently blamed clients for their own oppression. With time and experience, Marty would begin to recognize her role in supporting clients being able to both navigate and transform unjust systems within their families and community.

Working with Complexities and Potential Costs of Resistance

Another common tension is related to assessing the extent to which clients respond to subjugation by resisting, coping, or a combination of both. For example, some people respond to intimate partner violence by enduring for a while, for a long time, or indefinitely. Another option is to fight back using covert or overt resistance. In many cultures, such as those in Latin America, women are valued for emulating the Virgin Mary by being submissive, virtuous, and enduring hardship or suffering with acceptance and grace (Falicov, 1992). Even when faced with maltreatment and subjugation, girls and women in strongly patriarchal and misogynous cultures are taught to endure, "aguantarse" as stated in Spanish, as a badge of honor (Falicov, 1992; McGoldrick, Giordano, & Garcia-Preto, 2005). These cultural values can create tension in equity based work that values both culture and liberation. Solutions may need to be complex, including covert resistance if clients cannot leave a violent or oppressive system. Decisions to resist and about the forms of resistance to use must balance what is healthy, necessary, and useful with very real and tangible potential consequences.

There are many forms of resistance to abusive or subjugating power. Strategies include education about societal systems and power dynamics (Freire, 1970/2000), disloyalty or disobedience to oppressive systems, identity movements, coalition building to take collective action, engaging in revolution, and refusing to accept dichotomous thinking and choices (Heldke & O'Connor, 2004). Other types of resistance include yielding when the cost of overtly challenging is too high, withdrawing when situations are unbearable, and understanding how to navigate dynamics of power and oppression. Directly challenging oppressive and dominant systems can be risky. Potential costs include not being believed and/or being labeled as a problem. These must be weighed against the likelihood of positive change. Those with the greatest privilege take the least risk in speaking out directly to promote change in family, community, and societal systems. They are most likely to be believed and be able to influence change with the most modest personal consequences. Conversely, those most marginalized take the greatest risk, being less likely to be believed and potentially paying the greatest personal cost (McDowell, 2004). Another way to resist is to recognize and challenge how unexamined thoughts and emotions inadvertently maintain oppressive structures (Medina, 2013). Refusing to explore our own perspectives, or those of others, may be a fear based reaction, particularly for members of dominant groups (Goodman, 2011).

Case Example

Consider Kecia and Deidra, a female African American couple in a small Southern town who kept the intimate nature of their relationship a secret from their families and church. If their therapist believed that openness is a mark of emotional differentiation and that the couple suffered from having to maintain their closeted position, she may have engaged the couple in discussions about "coming out" without recognizing the important role the black church played in their lives and how important maintaining the story that they are "just friends and roommates" may have been in their ability to access other important forms of support and resilience.

Honoring Perspectives, Being Culturally Sensitive, and Challenging Oppression

‹‹—››

Socioculturally attuned therapists honor clients' cultural values and personal perspectives while simultaneously challenging oppression.

‹‹—››

Clients' beliefs and preferred directions for therapy may seem in opposition to what is just. How do therapists honor client beliefs, values, and goals when we believe they may inadvertently support a client's own subjugation or the oppression of another? This goes hand in hand with considering unintended consequences of raising critical consciousness, including disruption to family relationships as worldviews change. The goal of being culturally sensitive can obscure the decision between what is acceptable and what is unjust—what should be supported as part of someone's culture and what should be challenged even if culturally supported.

It is often difficult to discern when to be confident in our knowing, when to be transparent, when to be cautious, or when to make a direct statement that challenges or affirms a stance. Receiving feedback from therapists can be important and helpful to clients (Sundit, 2011). This includes professional knowledge that helps families to see their situation from outside themselves. Professional knowledge, however, has the potential to be liberating and/ or oppressive. An example of this is the Harry Benjamin International Gender Dysphoria Association, now known as World Professional Association for Transgender Health, which was first created in 1979 to establish the standard of care for transgender people seeking hormone replacement therapy. The strict guidelines were meant to help ensure that the health and well-being of clients was held in the highest regard, even though the professional guidelines may have not been aligned with the client's goals or timeline. These guidelines have proven to be liberating in some ways, including legitimizing hormone replacement therapy as a medical need. They also continue to be oppressive as clinicians and agencies often require an undue number of sessions and a process of intrusive questioning before being willing to support medical treatment.

Equity based therapists view understanding of societal context and power dynamics as part of their professional knowledge which, like other professional knowledge, has the potential to help solve presenting problems and improve clients' lives. Honoring clients' choices seems reasonable enough, but it is not always easy when a therapist believes choices are harmful to clients or others in their lives. Can we truly respect clients' choices if we believe they are unjust? In the end, there are times when therapists must take a both/and stance, instead of an either/or stance. We can honor a family's way of knowing and doing, respect their choices and decisions, and question institutional and structural practices that negatively affect the family, while still honoring the practices of the profession. We can help clients explore the nuances and implications of cultural practices, knowing that taken-for-granted cultural assumptions are not always just. Cultures are not monolithic and oppression is routinely met with resistance in all societies.

Case Example

Thomas, an Asian heterosexual, middle-class, male therapist entered therapy with a family that immigrated to the Southern U.S. from China. Thomas noticed during his initial meeting with Tina, a 45-year-old daughter, and her 81-year-old mother, Maylee, that Maylee was often sharp tongued and critical of Tina. Tina described being married, working in a demanding job, and caring for two teenage children in addition to caring for her aging mother. Thomas recognized the importance of intergenerational family life and shared Tina's value of caring for elders, the situation resonating with his having grown up with his own grandmother in his parents' home. As he listened to Tina, he reflected on what it must have been like for his mother, who was the primary caregiver to his paternal grandfather. Thomas noticed that Tina was reluctant to stand up to verbal abuse from her aging parent and found himself at a loss for how to help. Thomas got caught between the shared value of caring for and respecting elderly members of the family and the need to help his clients confront an unjust and abusive parent-child relationship. Thomas needed to be able to help Tina name this conflict and work with her to explore her options.

Using Power to Balance Power

Family therapists are in the unique and challenging position of facing competing dominant discourses and societally supported power dynamics that differently affect clients in the same family, often privileging some over others. Practicing from an equity based perspective requires therapists to be both countering and collaborative, moving flexibly between the two in order to analyze power dynamics, connect and collaborate with all family members, and position themselves to be able to disrupt oppressive relationship dynamics.

⤝⤞

Socioculturally attuned therapists value all voices in the family, not allowing any voice to overpower that of others.

⤝⤞

Therapists must be able to challenge power to create opportunities for equitable relationships to develop. Consider adult children who are trying to impose or dictate what they think their parents must do in their final years. If an aging parent is able to make choices, their voice must be heard. The therapist must intervene when the loudest voice is not that of the one who is most negatively affected by decisions being made. The therapist is confronted with their own power. What does this mean for the therapist? Should a therapist use their position as an expert of the therapeutic process to challenge power imbalances in families? A study of how equity based family therapists address this issue showed that they regularly balance interventions that actively counter injustice with maintaining a collaborative relationship (D'Arrigo-Patrick, Hoff, Knudson-Martin, & Tuttle, 2017). These therapists tended to deal with their power by asking questions rather than telling and being open and transparent as they used inquiry to help clients make connections about social issues that impact their lives.

Case Example

Kimberly, a white, young, heterosexual female therapist-in-training began working with a heterosexual, middle-class, white couple. The wife, Amy, had persuaded her husband, Kurt, to enter therapy after a particularly volatile argument. Although they both reported that their relationship had never been violent, they agreed that the level of rage and conflict was not what either wanted or expected in their marriage. During the first session, Kimberly was careful to talk to both Amy and Kurt in order to ensure they both felt heard. She noticed, however, that Amy often repeated her complaints to Kurt, who routinely dismissed them. When Kimberly attempted to interrupt and redirect, Kurt dismissed her as well. Kimberly firmly adhered to her interpretation of a collaborative stance in therapy, not wanting to impose her agenda on clients. This stance left her deadlocked, unable to find a way to challenge the power dynamic that fueled the couple's conflict. Without a way to facilitate the therapeutic process and use her influence as an expert to challenge Kurt's more powerful position, Kimberly was unable to intervene to support Amy or help the couple develop a more just relationship.

Conclusion

Equity based family therapists are faced with difficult ethical decisions and tensions relative to our role in the change process. It is not possible for therapists to take a truly neutral stance. We must make decisions about how to use our power to promote health and well-being for all family members. This includes interrupting power dynamics that privilege some over others. At times this means challenging the common cultural practices that are oppressive.

It also requires us to find hidden strengths in all cultures that may have been minimized or marginalized. To engage in ethical socioculturally attuned family therapy, we must rigorously examine our cultural assumptions, values, beliefs, and attitudes (Bermudez, 1997; Hardy & Laszloffy, 1995). We must find ways to develop accountability systems that identify when we are actively or passively oppressive in our practices. This includes moment-by-moment awareness and self-reflexivity in the process of therapy as we implement our clinical models. In the following chapters we offer practice guidelines that help address these tensions.

References

Adams, A., & Benson, K. (2005). Considerations for gay and lesbian families. *Family Therapy Magazine, 4*(6), 20–23.

Almeida, R. V., Dolan-Del Vecchio, K., & Parker L. (2008). *Transformative family therapy: Just families in a just society*. Boston, MA: Pearson Education.

American Association for Marriage and Family Therapy. (2015). *User's guide to the AAMFT code of ethics*. Washington, DC: The American Association for Marriage and Family Therapy.

Baker, K. A. (1999). The importance of cultural sensitivity and therapist self-awareness when working with mandatory clients. *Family Process, 38*(1), 55–67.

Bermudez, J. M. (1997). Experiential tasks and therapist bias awareness. *Contemporary Family Therapy, 19*(2), 253–267.

Bograd, M. (1984). Family systems approaches to wife battering: A feminist critique. *American Journal of Orthopsychiatry, 54*(4), 558–568.

Boszormenyi-Nagy, I., & Krasner, B. (1986). *Between give and take*. New York, NY: Brunner/Mazel.

Boszormenyi-Nagy, I., & Spark, G. M. (1973). *Invisible loyalties: Reciprocity in intergenerational family therapy*. Oxford, UK: Harper & Row.

Caldwell, B. E. (2013, September/October). Conscience clauses: When do the therapist's moral values outweigh a client's request for help? *Family Therapy Magazine, 12*(5), 20–27.

Carter, B. (1985). Ms. intervention's guide to "correct" feminist family therapy. *Family Therapy Networker, 9*, 78–79.

D'Aniello, C., Nguyen, H., & Piercy, F. (2016). Cultural sensitivity as an MFT common factor. *American Journal of Family Therapy, 44*, 234–244.

D'Arrigo-Patrick, J., Hoff, C., Knudson-Martin, C., & Tuttle, A. (2017). Navigating critical theory and postmodernism: Social justice and therapist power in family therapy. *Family Process, 56*, 574–588.

Ellenwood, A. E., & Snyders, R. (2006). Inside-out approaches to teaching multicultural techniques: Guidelines for family therapy trainers. *Journal of Family Psychotherapy, 17*(1), 67–81.

Falicov, C. J. (1992). Love and gender in the Latino marriage. *American Family Therapy Newsletter, 48*, 30–36.

Freire, P. (2000). *Pedagogy of the oppressed*. New York, NY: Bloomsbury. (Original work published in 1970).

Fricker, M. (2007). *Epistemic injustice: Power and the ethics of knowing*. New York, NY: Oxford University Press.

Garcia, M., Košutić, I., & McDowell, T. (2015). Peace on Earth/war at home: The role of emotion regulation in social justice work. *Journal of Feminist Family Therapy, 27*(1), 1–20.

Goldner, V. (1985). Feminism and family therapy. *Family Process, 24*(1), 31–47.

Goodman, D. J. (2011). *Promoting diversity and social justice: Educating people from privileged groups*. New York, NY: Routledge.

Hardy, K., & Laszloffy, T. A. (1995). The cultural genogram: Key to training culturally competent family therapists. *Journal of Marital Family Therapy, 21*(3), 227–237.

Hardy, K., & McGoldrick, M. (2008). Re-visioning training. In M. McGoldrick & K. Hardy (Eds.), *Re-visioning family therapy* (2nd ed.) (pp. 442–460). New York, NY: Guildford Press.

Heldke, L., & O'Connor, P. (2004). *Oppression, privilege, & resistance: Theoretical perspectives on racism, sexism, and heterosexism*. New York, NY: McGraw-Hill.

Hernández, P., & McDowell, T. (2010). Intersectionality, power, and relational safety in context: Key concepts in clinical supervision. *Training and Education in Professional Psychology, 4*(1), 29–35.

Hernández, P., Taylor, B., & McDowell, T. (2009). Listening to ethnic minority AAMFT approved supervisors: Reflections on their experiences as supervisees. *Journal of Systemic Therapies, 28*(1), 88–100.

Košutić, I., & McDowell, T. (2008). Diversity and social justice issues in family therapy literature: A decade review. *Journal of Feminist Family Therapy, 20*(2), 142–165.

Larner, G. (1995). The real as illusion: Deconstructing power in family therapy. *Journal of Family Therapy, 17*(2), 191–217.

McDowell, T. (2004). Exploring the racial experiences of graduate trainees: A critical race theory perspective. *The American Journal of Family* Therapy, *32*(4), 305–324.

McDowell, T. (2015). *Applying critical social theories to family therapy practice.* New York, NY: AFTA SpringerBriefs in Family Therapy.

McDowell, T., Dashiell, W., Holland, C., Ingoglia, L., Serizawa, T., & Stevens, C. (2005). Raising multiracial awareness in family therapy through critical conversations. *Journal of Marital and Family Therapy, 31*(4), 399–411.

McDowell, T., Fang, S., Gomez Young, C., Brownlee, K., Khanna, A., & Sherman, B. (2003). Making space for racial dialogue: Our experience in a marriage and family therapy training program. *Journal of Marital and Family Therapy, 29*(2), 179–194.

McGeorge, C., & Stone Carlson, T. (2011). Deconstructing heterosexism: Becoming an LGB affirmative heterosexual couple and family therapist. *Journal of Marital and Family Therapy, 37*(1), 14–26.

McGoldrick, M., Giordano, J., & Garcia-Preto, N. (Eds.). (2005). *Ethnicity and family therapy* (3rd ed.). New York, NY: Guilford Press.

Medina, J. (2013). *The epistemology of resistance: Gender and racial oppression, epistemic injustice, and resistant imaginations.* New York, NY: Oxford University Press.

Melito, R. (2003). Values in the role of the family therapist: Self determination and justice. *Journal of Marital and Family Therapy, 29*(1), 3–11.

Merton, R. K. (1973). The Matthew effect in science. In N. Storer (Ed.), *The sociology of science* (pp. 439–459). Chicago, IL: University of Chicago Press.

Merton, R. K. (1988). The Matthew effect in science, II: Cumulative advantage and the symbolism of intellectual property. *ISIS, 79*(4), 606–623.

Nealy, E. C. (2008). Working with LGBT families. In M. McGoldrick & K. V. Hardy (Eds.), *Re-visioning family therapy: Race, culture, and gender in clinical practice* (2nd ed.) (pp. 289–299). New York, NY: Guilford Press.

Priest, J. B., & Wickel, K. (2011). Religious therapists and clients in same-sex relationships: Lessons from the court case of Bruff v. North Mississippi Health Service, Inc. *The American Journal of Family Therapy, 39*(2), 139–148.

Roberts, J. (2005). Transparency and self-disclosure in family therapy: Dangers and possibilities. *Family Process, 44*(1), 45–63.

Sharp, E. A., Bermudez, J. M., Watson, W., & Fitzpatrick, J. (2007). Reflections from the trenches: Our development as feminist teachers. *Journal of Family Issues, 28*(4), 529–548.

Slife, B., Smith, A., & Burchfield, C. (2003). Psychotherapists as crypto-missionaries: An exemplar on the crossroads of history, theory, and philosophy. In D. Hill & M. Krall (Eds.), *About psychology: At the crossroads of history, theory, and philosophy* (pp. 55–72): Albany: State University of New York Press.

Sundit, R. (2011). Collaboration: Family and therapist perspectives of helpful therapy. *Journal of Marital and Family Therapy, 37*(2), 236–249.

Tjeltveit, A. C. (1986). The ethics of value conversion in psychotherapy: Appropriate and inappropriate therapist influence on client values. *Clinical Psychology Review, 6*(6), 515–537.

Wetherell, M. (2012). *Affect and emotion: A new social science understanding.* Los Angeles, CA: SAGE.

4 Socioculturally Attuned Structural Family Therapy

The development of structural family therapy by Salvador Minuchin and colleagues (Minuchin, Montvalo, Guerney, Rosman, & Schumer, 1967, 1974) gave the field a way to map the organization of families and concisely describe their dynamics. This approach enabled practitioners to think about families as a unit and make sense of complex interactions. In structural family therapy, families are understood as open systems that respond and adjust to the outside world. Presenting problems reflect and maintain family structures. Structural family therapy focuses on interactional patterns and the relative power of family members to influence these patterns. Structural family therapists recognize the inherent strength of families to positively adapt to changing circumstances. Therapeutic goals include restructuring interactions in ways that support the development of the family system and well-being of all members.

↠↞

Socioculturally attuned structural family therapy invites families to consider third order change in how they organize their lives in relationship to broader societal contexts.

↠↞

In socioculturally attuned structural family therapy, families are encouraged to **attune** to how societal systems and power dynamics impact all members; to **name** and **value** the experience of each family member within subsystems, family hierarchy, and the broader society. Therapists **intervene** in structures that support and condone privilege of some at the expense of others. Families are encouraged to **envision** alternatives in order to more consciously choose how they organize their relationships. Through this process, families **transform** their relationships to share power equitably with each other, working together to face societal injustices.

In this chapter we highlight enduring concepts in structural family therapy and demonstrate a link between family and societal structures. We illustrate how therapists can integrate principles of sociocultural attunement in assessing family problems and offer practice guidelines that can lead to third order change.

Primary Enduring Structural Family Therapy Concepts

Following are six concepts core to practicing structural family therapy. The first three focus on how families are organized, including repetitive patterns of interaction, family and individual development, and family structure and hierarchy. The other three focus on interventions, including the importance of joining, challenging assumptions, and restructuring.

Patterns of Interaction

One of the earliest discoveries of Minuchin et al. (1967, 1974) was that families engage in repetitive patterns. Patterns are essential to daily functioning and living predictable lives. When patterns become rigid, however, they constrict the range of possible behaviors. Problems occur when families get caught in patterns of interaction that they find unsatisfactory yet difficult to alter. Patterns interlock and repeat across situations. Even the most routine interactional patterns can reflect and reinforce broader problematic relational dynamics. Think about a simple morning routine, e.g., getting up, managing breakfast, getting ready for school, and going to work. Consider John, Emanuel, and their 16-year-old son, Max. John came from a white, upper-middle class family. Emanuel's Mexican American family was working class. Max was adopted and is multiracial. John and Emmanuel share a business in which John takes the lead and serves as the "face" of the business while Emanuel manages the finances and personnel. John also attempts to take the lead at home, resulting in the couple arguing over tasks and struggling to negotiate differences. Now let's go back to the simple routine of getting up and getting ready for the day. Emanuel is the first one awake. He makes coffee and prepares breakfast for Max and John. When John gets up he is anxious to get to work and calls out to Max to wake up. Max delays his response until John opens his door and yells "Get up now!" Max slowly gets ready for school and avoids eye contact with John when he sits down to eat. No one talks until John leaves for work. Once alone, Emanuel and Max enjoy a relaxed and playful conversation as Emanuel takes Max to school. Similar patterns of interaction occur across situations, leading the family to define Emanuel and Max's relationship as "close" and Max as "rebellious."

These repetitive, observable patterns of interaction are the basic unit of analysis for describing family structure. Through observing repeated sequences of behavior among multiple family members, structural family therapists hypothesize about how a family is organized; who is in charge, who is aligned with whom, and the nature of individual, subsystem, and family boundaries. Exploring family members' thoughts and feelings that both inform and result from patterns of behavior provides information about family rules and roles as well as the impact of family structure on the well-being of each individual.

Family Development

Structural family therapists assume families evolve through stages of development. Each stage creates new demands and opportunities. The family must continuously accommodate changing needs of its members as each grows and ages. The family must also accommodate changes in circumstances (e.g., economic shifts, illnesses, political climates, moves) through time (Minuchin & Nichols, 1993). A well-functioning family promotes and supports the development of all family members and can adapt to necessary changes. Family relationships, or structures, that limit the growth and development of children or adults are considered problematic.

Structural family therapists do not take it upon themselves to determine ideal family structures per se; however, the link between how a family is organized and the development of its members guides decision-making relative to restructuring. Consider a family in which there were two white, heterosexual parents—Jim and Lacey. They had three adolescents. The oldest was a 17-year-old girl, Laura. The second was a 15-year-old boy, Jimmy, and the third was a 13-year-old boy, Tim. Lacey worked as an administrative assistant to put Jim through medical school before staying home to care for their three children. She went back to work managing Jim's practice when all three kids began middle school. Once both parents worked full time, they relied heavily on Laura to cook meals and watch after Jimmy and Tim. Jim and

Lacey bought Laura a car with the stipulation that she pick up her younger brothers and get them to sports events after school. The couple entered therapy when Lacey discovered Jim had an affair with a woman who worked at the hospital.

It was important to the family for Lacey to spend her time raising the children. She appreciated an upper-middle-class lifestyle and the status associated with being married to a physician. She was devastated by the affair, feeling vulnerable and angry. Jim threw off her concern with a promise that the affair meant nothing and would not happen again. This family structure privileged the developmental needs of the males, expecting females to play supportive roles. Jim's career was primary and although the couple worked together toward his success, it was he who had been able to fulfill his developmental potential and was in a more powerful role. Lacey's development had been routinely compromised in favor of the development of all others in the family. Jim's affair highlighted the unfairness of the relationship, leaving Lacey increasingly disillusioned and resentful of the inequity between them. During therapy it became clear that Laura was being ushered into a similar inequitable arrangement as a young woman. In her role as a sister, she was expected to place the needs of her brothers before her own, mirroring her mother's role as a wife who is expected to sacrifice her adult development for the sake of her husband's.

Family Structure and Hierarchy

The use of structure as a metaphor for describing this observable organization reflects Minuchin's early training as a physician who understood the human body as a system with an internal structure (Minuchin & Nichols, 1993). The observable interactional patterns in families that are referenced as a family's structure include who is close with whom (alliances), who sides with each other (coalitions), who is grouped together based on role, common interests, age (subsystems), who has access to whom and what type of access (boundaries), and who has more or less influence over others (hierarchy).

Family maps are often used to describe, communicate, and track the way a family is organized. The map typically starts with drawing circles or using names, initials, or roles (e.g., mom) to indicate how close family members are to each other and their relative influence or power. For example, in the case just described, Jim and Lacey were both in a parental or executive subsystem and a spousal subsystem, however they were not equal in power in either of these. A therapist might start the map addressing the structure of the spousal subsystem when Jim was having the affair and once the affair was over (see Figure 4.1).

Both maps acknowledge that Jim had more power in the relationship. The map on the left shows an open boundary between Jim and the woman at work with whom he had an affair. The map on the right of Figure 4.1 shows a solid line of disconnection once the affair ended. The individual boundary between Jim and Lacey shows more distance between them when Jim was having the affair. Now the therapist might add the rest of the family (see Figure 4.2).

The map in Figure 4.2 describes the family in the following way. Jim had more power than his wife and co-parent. The solid line beneath the subsystem demonstrates that Jim

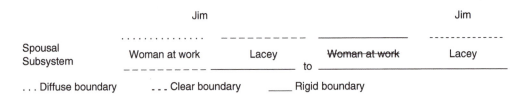

Figure 4.1 Boundaries within spousal subsystem when an affair is present.

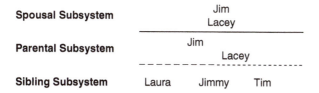

Spousal Subsystem	Jim Lacey		
Parental Subsystem	Jim Lacey		
Sibling Subsystem	Laura	Jimmy	Tim

Figure 4.2 Entire family map including subsystems and how power influences subsystems.

and Lacey kept their adult relationship as partners private and didn't share their relationship problems with their children. As parents they each had different boundaries with the children. Lacey was more accessible to them than Jim, who maintained more distance. At this point, what we know about the family leaves some questions regarding the power dynamics among siblings. At first glance it would seem that Laura, as the oldest child and the one who is responsible for helping her parents with the younger two kids, would be above her brothers in the hierarchy. The therapist would need to investigate further, however, to determine if her brothers listen to her, if her parents back her up, if she is in more of a supportive than authoritative role, and so on.

The therapist might have noticed that mom and Laura had a close connection as the two females in the family. This might be considered an alliance between mom and Laura. Upon further investigation we might discover that Lacey and Laura frequently complained to each other about Jim's authority and undermined him when they thought he was being unreasonable. This would be described as a coalition between them against dad.

Joining

Structural family therapists recognize the necessity of joining with all family members to be able to both challenge and invite them to entertain alternatives. The family will only follow a therapist's directives if members feel connected and cared for. Joining is an ongoing process throughout therapy, a relational commitment from start to finish. According to Minuchin, "Joining has nothing to do with pretending to be what you are not. It means tuning in to people and responding to the way they move you" (Minuchin & Nichols, 1993, p. 42). Joining requires that the therapist treat each family as unique. According to Minuchin, Reiter, and Borda (2014), joining is "a mindset constructed out of respect, empathy, curiosity and commitment to healing" (p. 4). This can be difficult at times.

Think about working with a family in which a parent is emotionally and verbally abusive to a teenage child. It may be quite easy for many of us to identify and join with the child, but more difficult to genuinely join with the parent. The therapist must find a way to be equally respectful, empathetic, curious and committed to the well-being of all family members in order to help them restructure the system. Structural family therapists join with families by using the family's language and reflecting the family's relational style. They glean information about the family by becoming part of the system without getting caught in the system. Let's consider a family therapist getting caught in the system with Jim and Lacey's family described earlier.

Jim: It is tough working every day to support this family. Between office hours, hospital rotations and being on call I put in 70 hours a week! I don't think they really appreciate how hard I work to get everything this family needs and wants!

Lacey:	Of course we do. This is not about how hard you work! How hard any of us work.
Jim:	How hard any of us work? I'm the one out there busting my back . . .
Therapist:	Clearly you work hard, Jim, but I think what Lacey is saying . . .
Jim (interrupts therapist):	You know, Lacey, for once I would just like to see you . . .
	Therapist falls silent as she begins thinking how unfair Jim is being . . .

It is likely in this scenario that although the therapist was trying to connect with all family members and ensure everyone felt understood, she got caught in the pattern of Jim dominating conversations and setting the terms by which discussions occur. The therapist was drawn into what was likely to be Lacey's experience of being overridden by Jim. In this way, the therapeutic system became isomorphic or parallel to the family system.

Challenging Assumptions

When families enter therapy they typically "know" what the problem is and often have an idea of what (and who) needs to change. They have tried a number of solutions based on their definition and understanding of the problem. These attempted solutions have not worked or the family would most likely not be seeking help. Most clients expect help to come in the form of alternative solutions, not in alternative definitions of the problem. Minuchin et al. (2014) asserted that the family's certainty in their definition of the problem works against change. It is up to the therapist to engage the family in co-constructing new ways of viewing the problem that will lead to different types of solutions. A mantra in structural family therapy is "make sure you are solving the right problem." Too often therapists accept the family's definition of the problem and get caught in attempting commonsense and/or linear solutions. Next is an excerpt from a session with John, Emanuel, and Max in which the therapist gets caught in content, inadvertently increasing the certainty family members have of the problem.

John:	The problem is that Max is having trouble growing up and taking responsibility.
Emanuel:	He is a teenager! Your problem is you want everyone to be just like you!
John:	I thought we agreed to focus on Max.
Max:	(sighs and rolls his eyes)
Therapist:	Lots of families worry about teenagers learning to take responsibility and it is normal for teens to rebel a little. In fact it is healthy!

Although the therapist in this interaction attempted to normalize and smooth over the conflict, she was paying more attention to content (e.g., a teenager taking responsibility) than process (e.g., parents not acting as a team).

Family therapists need to introduce alternatives in how families think about problems. When problems are viewed differently, families are often able to see new possibilities and solutions. As mentioned previously, certainty of the problem and resulting sets of solutions are often the crux of how families get stuck. Although early structural family therapists were more likely to determine a new framework and use their expert stance to get the family to accept a different reality (i.e., reframe), many contemporary therapists (Minuchin et al., 2014) see this process as one of co-construction. Let's continue with John, Emanuel, and Max to see how the therapist might have invited a new understanding of the problem.

Emanuel:	Yes, we understand that teenagers often rebel but Max is a good kid. John just expects too much.
John:	(rolls his eyes and looks away)
Max:	This is stupid!
Therapist:	As fathers you expect different things from your son?
John:	I expect Max to act his age and take responsibility.
Emanuel:	He does. Max is doing great in school.
Therapist:	Max, it seems like your dads have different ways of looking at things. What is it like for you when they argue about you?
Max:	What do you think? I hate it!
Therapist:	John and Emmanuel how are you at being a team in other parts of your lives besides parenting? Your business? Your relationship?

Here the therapist moved the focus from Max to the parents working together. The therapist was trying out a new way to view the problem, inviting the family to see things differently. This effectively moved Max out of the role of being the problem. As long as there is a person designated by the family as "the problem" it is difficult to move out of linear, individual, commonsense solutions in favor of relational, contextual change. In the example offered earlier, the therapist might have got caught in the view that Max was the problem because he was being rebellious, or that John was the problem because he was controlling, or that Emanuel was the problem because he failed to back up his co-parent. Accepting Max as the identified problem would have invited the therapist to get stuck where the family was stuck.

Challenging assumptions includes exploring family rules and expectations relative to family roles. The nature of assumptions is that they guide thinking, feeling, and interacting, often without being overtly discussed or intentionally considered. They operate without inspection, limiting alternatives. In the previous example, John and Emanuel are operating from ideas they each have about how to be a parent, who, if anyone, should be in the lead, what teenagers need from parents, what Max's intentions are, and so on. The therapist would guide enactments in which these assumptions could be identified, made overt, and intentionally altered or agreed upon. Following is an example of how a therapist might have challenged assumptions when working with Jim and Lacey in a couple session.

Therapist:	Jim and Lacey, would you tell each other what you hoped your relationship would be like? You know when you first decided to marry? Lacey can you start? Jim, while Lacey is talking will you please do your best to really listen. Then you will have a turn and it will be Lacey's turn to listen.
Lacey:	I guess I thought we were going to be in this together. You know, me and you the whole way.
Jim:	We are! We work together, live together . . . we're together 24/7! What more do you want?
Therapist:	I want to make sure each of you understands what the other expects without interrupting each other. You have different ideas about what it means to be together through life. Lacey, can you say more about what you meant when you said "I thought we were going to be in this together?"

The therapist would continue to explore assumptions each holds about gender and power, paid versus family work, time together in contrast to making decisions together, the meaning of intimacy, and so on. The therapist would also explore family roles: What does each expect of a father, mother, husband, wife? Where were these ideas about roles formed? In what ways are expectations around family roles helpful or not helpful to the family as a whole; to each individual?

Restructuring

Enactments are a cornerstone intervention in structural family therapy. A significant part of each session includes directing family members to talk directly to each other while the therapist pays attention to and helps shape interaction. Talking directly to each other in therapy offers families a new experience of purposefully rather than spontaneously interacting (Minuchin et al., 2014). The therapist can notice how they interact, watching for patterns that are problematic as well as those that work well. Enactments allow therapists to help families modify their interactions, set clear boundaries, better understand each other, and connect with each other emotionally. At first, the therapist is likely to want to observe even when communication escalates, is derailed by other family members, and/or reaches a stalemate. This provides important firsthand information about family dynamics. The therapist often comments on the interaction to help families take a meta-perspective of their relationships, i.e., learn to "talk about how they talk."

Therapists do more than observe and learn about family patterns through enactments. They interrupt, pause for interpretation, ask for emotional expression, and coach communication. They help distant family members come closer emotionally, help establish clear boundaries, and encourage members of subsystems to work together in part by using enactments. Butler and Gardner (2007) suggested five stages of enactments depending on the family's ability to successfully talk directly with each other. When conflict is high and direct communication seems to do more harm than good, they suggest asking family members to talk through the therapist. The therapist becomes less of a "go between," interrupts less often, and coaches interactions less when family members are able to communicate directly and the communication leads to solving problems. Following is an example of an enactment using the earlier example of John, Emanuel, and Max, a little later in therapy.

Therapist:	John and Emanuel, I am going to ask the two of you to talk directly about your vision of parenting together. What kind of team are you hoping to be? John, will you turn your chair to face Emanuel and Emanuel, will you start the conversation?
Emanuel:	John, I want us to work together to be more understanding of Max.
John:	I think we are understanding. Maybe too understanding.
Max:	This is hopeless!
Therapist:	For now, Max, I am going to ask you to let your dads talk. It can be tempting to interrupt them to help, but let's see how they do.
Max:	I wasn't trying to help. It just drives me crazy when they do this.
Therapist:	(turns away from Max and back to parents) Ok John, can you tell Emanuel what being a team looks like to you?
John:	I think we should set rules and back each other up.
Emanuel:	Yes, but you are setting the rules and then expecting me to follow them just like Max.
Therapist:	So are you both saying that you want to set rules together and back each other up, but you want to really agree? Is that right?
Emanuel:	(looking at therapist) Yes, but it can't all be on John's terms.
Therapist:	Emanuel, can you look directly at John and say that to him rather than to me?
Emanuel:	(looking at John) It can't all be on your terms.
Therapist:	Emanuel, you also said earlier that you wanted the two of you to be more understanding of Max. Can you tell John directly what you mean?

The therapist in this scenario was unbalancing the system by offering Emanuel support in making his perspective heard by John. This temporarily disrupted the power dynamic in which John has more voice in the family. The therapist also unbalanced the system by ensuring the couple interaction is not detoured through Max. Unbalancing is an important concept in structural family therapy. It is assumed that the therapist has the necessary influence or power in the therapeutic system to direct interactions and can "lend" power to family members. Interrupting typical dynamics that stabilize conflict, such as detouring, is also a way to unbalance the system, opening possibilities for alternative interactions and solutions. Another typical unbalancing technique is to raise intensity. Therapists can raise intensity in a number of ways, including pressing the family to continue interactions at the point in which they typically stop and slowing down interactions to explore and express deep emotions.

Structural family therapists consider boundaries across all interventions. In the previous example, the therapist worked on helping the family set a clear boundary between the parental and child subsystems by not allowing Max to interrupt his parents or help them out of their conflict. The therapist would not always have Max in the room, respecting the separation between spousal/parental and child/sibling subsystems. In this conversation, Max being there gave the therapist the opportunity to block him from becoming part of the parental subsystem. It is likely that more conversations about fathering and about the couple's relationship would need to occur without Max present. Max, as a teenager, would also likely need to meet with the therapist alone from time to time to discuss his experience and prepare for how to talk to his parents about his needs.

Integrating Principles of Sociocultural Attunement

In this section we explore connections between societal systems and family systems, between societal rules and structures and family rules and structures. This includes attention to how interactional patterns and power dynamics are reproduced across levels and settings in complex social systems.

Societal Context and Structure

↞→

Socioculturally attuned structural family therapy expands the structural analysis of families to a structural analysis of families within society.

↞→

Socioculturally attuned structural family therapy assumes that organizational patterns affect and are affected by all levels of interlocking systems, including families, communities, and societies, as well as by social locations that intersect these systems (e.g., gender, race, social class, sexual orientation). On a societal level the metaphor of structure refers to systems of systems at a macrolevel. Repeated patterns of interaction among groups within and across social contexts serve to create and maintain social stratification, patterned group relationships, and institutional organization. These systems are hierarchical. Access to influence and resources differ according to one's individual and group position in society.

The work of French philosopher and sociologist Pierre Bourdieu offers a bridge between our understanding of family structure and societal structure, family rules in relationship to social rules, and the material world in relationship to the social world. The question "how can behaviour be regulated without being the product of obedience to rules?" (p. 65) particularly intrigued Bourdieu (1986). In other words, he questioned how personal agency and social structures (including predictable interactions) might be reconciled. Above all, Bourdieu viewed reality as relational, making many of his ideas helpful in linking family systems and social theory. Bourdieu's concepts of habitus, field, capital, and symbolic violence are particularly applicable to practicing socioculturally attuned structural family therapy.

Enduring Patterns Across Contexts

Bourdieu (1986) argued that it is within social space, or habitus, that we learn, internalize, and embody shared ways of thinking and doing, values, and beliefs. Habitus is a concept that expands our thinking beyond dichotomies to consider relationships between dualistic concepts; internal/external, objective/subjective, agency/structure, and personal/social. For example, a family may be concerned that a child is too shy. They attribute the behavior to an intrinsic quality of the child (internal). A family therapist is likely to look at the behaviors the family identifies as shyness, watching for patterns of communication and interaction that help make sense of these behaviors (external). At the same time a family therapist may attribute the problem of identifying the child as shy (internal to the individual) to family dynamics alone (internal to the family) rather than considering how social dynamics including gender, class, sexual orientation, race, and specific contexts influence behavior and patterns of interaction (external to the individual and family). In effect, family therapists must hold what is commonly described as internal and external in the same space, being most interested in the relationship between these conceptual frameworks.

Habitus refers to a combination of history and disposition within time and space that shapes our thinking and guides our behavior in relationships. In effect, societal norms and expectations as expressed through social class, culture, and family contexts, together with our unique qualities, create dispositions. Dispositions are lasting but also changeable over time and transferable across settings (Bourdieu, 1986). This includes how we tend to think, feel, and act in various situations or relational fields. Take humor, for example, which is assigned to some people as an individual characteristic. They tend to make people laugh across many (but not all) settings. Humor is developed in habitus. Most "funny people" know how to read contexts well enough to predict what those around them might find amusing. In effect humor is a relational dynamic at the crossroads of habitus and disposition within relational fields.

According to Maton (2014):

> Habitus links the social and the individual because the experiences of one's life course may be unique in their particular *contents* but are shared in terms of the *structure* with others of the same social class, gender, ethnicity, sexuality, occupation, nationality, region and so forth.
>
> (p. 52)

In other words, although individuals and families are unique, they are also inseparable from the contexts in which they exist. Habitus, or enduring patterned ways of being and doing, include family upbringing, past choices, social class, education, cultural norms, spatial setting, and much more; the sum of what makes us "who we are." This is both structured and structuring. In other words, our social context, history, and social location structure our thinking, attitudes, beliefs, emotions, and actions. At the same time our patterned participation in society furthers the very structures that influence us. In fact, social structures become embodied through identity based constructions such as gender, race, social class, ethnicity, and sexual orientation.

Let's consider Jim and Lacey from the earlier example as a case in point. Lacey embodies her social identity as a heterosexual, white, upper-middle-class female in many ways, including the way she thinks about her body and performs her social role. Her relationship to self and others is deeply influenced by her perception of a broader social gaze. She "watches her weight," gets her hair cut at an expensive salon, shops for clothes that enhance her "figure," participates in make-up consultations, and carries a name brand purse. Jim does the same. He "keeps in shape" by participating in individual athletics, dresses in business casual sportswear when not at work, keeps his hair trimmed and face clean shaven, and wears designer eyeglasses. Jim is reassured through his affair at work that he is still vital and attractive. The same affair leaves Lacey believing she has "lost her looks" (and the privilege her looks have afforded her). Both Jim and Lacey inadvertently maintain their white privilege by adhering to the belief and teaching their children that race doesn't matter. Their attempts to conform to social expectations inadvertently contribute to social inequity by serving to maintain the status quo.

Group Relational Systems

Relational systems develop as groups differentiate from each other, developing semi-autonomous spheres of action that over time become increasingly specialized. Power relations within and among what Bourdieu called "fields" serve to structure and shape patterns of interaction. Bourdieu (1977) used the term "doxa" to refer to the "rules of the game" within a field. These rules are typically not spoken or overt, but assumed as if natural and inevitable. The rules limit the actions of agents within the field while benefiting those who know how the game is played. The positions we take in these fields, or relational systems, serve to maintain or disrupt power relationships; to keep the rules and power dynamics the same or change them. Agents in these fields use their positions, or power, to establish and enforce the rules which advantage them/their group. Take for example the highly contested ban on bilingual education in the U.S. state of California. Native English speakers have the advantage in the field of education and professional positions over those for whom Spanish was their dominant language in childhood. This advantage is secured from preschool forward. Bilingual education threatens this advantage creating a more equal playing field; a change in the rules that would redistribute power.

Power and Capital

+←→+

Family hierarchy and boundaries are directly impacted by power dynamics in society.

+←→+

From a structural perspective, power can be seen as connected to capital. According to Bourdieu (1986), economic, social, cultural, and symbolic capital all play a role in determining our degree of social influence and access to resources (Garcia & McDowell, 2010). Economic capital refers to money as well as capital that can be used to secure money without relying on one's own labor (e.g., investment capital). Social capital refers to social networks; relationships that provide opportunities to share resources and/or secure resources (e.g., insider knowledge of a job, reference letters for court or school). Symbolic capital is earned and unearned prestige (e.g., the title of "doctor," a high status family name). These are all closely linked to cultural capital which refers to that which can be used to gain upward mobility (e.g., language and speech patterns, looks, relational styles). Cultural capital is an important concept relative to power and equity as those whose cultural practices are centered and dominant tend to have an advantage.

In the U.S. the cultural practices, speech patterns, values, and attitudes of white, upper-class heterosexuals are typically centered and dominant. Being conventionally good looking, male, able-bodied, young, U.S. born, and masculine tends to further increase social advantage. In other words, those with the most influence and greatest resources tend to reproduce their group's advantage by privileging their own cultural practices. This creates lateral advantage for those most closely resembling and affiliated with dominant groups and vertical advantage through inheritance. This social dynamic affects family dynamics. Consider a white family in which parents have transitioned from lower-class childhoods to the middle-class by working hard, taking out student loans, adopting middle-class language and relational styles, and making sure they made connections that would provide them with as much advantage as possible. Now that they are stable in the middle-class, they expect their children to enjoy and benefit from their work to secure economic and social resources. Let's imagine now that their teenager is spending her time with lower-class friends, not doing homework, and abusing substances. This is likely to be a problem for the family for many reasons, among them her squandering of the family's social and cultural capital.

Bourdieu's (1986) term *symbolic violence* refers to when social rules or practices (including family rules and practices) that support the superiority of one group (or family member) over another are misunderstood as inevitable. The superiority of one group over another is viewed as the natural order of things rather than socially constructed. This view is widely accepted and internalized by members of both groups. Bourdieu (1986) offered many examples of this, including social class and gender relations. Relative to social class, those in the upper classes are often seen by all classes as smarter, more diligent, and superior to those in lower classes. This creates the illusion that social class largely depends on the character and effort of individuals. Now let's consider this dynamic relative to gender in family structure, using Lacey and Jim as a case in point. The idea that Jim's career should come first and that his needs and comfort are more important reflects pervasive symbolic violence in most societies in which men are routinely privileged.

Symbolic violence occurs when constructions of male superiority are internalized by both males and females; when heterosexual relationships are seen as "normal" and homophobia is internalized; when industrialized societies are seen as "advanced"; when those who don't identify as male or female are seen as "other" (cisgenderism); when whiteness is centered (racism); and so on. This is not to say that resistance to these constructions doesn't exist or that those who are oppressed routinely don't realize inequity is not the natural order of things. In fact, family members who are marginalized or oppressed are often acutely aware of their experience even when uncertain of the broader social dynamics that inform family power dynamics. Continuing with our example of Jim and Lacey's family, Laura is likely to feel conflicted—being pleased that her parents bought her a car while feeling slighted by her brothers' after school needs being prioritized over her own. The therapist would make covert rules overt, in this case bringing to light and challenging symbolic violence. This process would allow Laura and her family to identify the dynamics in which they are caught, make sense of their experience, and have more choice about what to do.

Third Order Change

Socioculturally attuned structural family therapists target third order change by engaging families in ways that raise awareness and question the impact of societal context on presenting problems. For example, a therapist might ask couples to speak directly to each other about what they learned about gender/race/social class/sexual orientation when growing up. This would include messages from parents, extended family, peers, and the media. As clients are coached to talk directly to each other about these influences, the therapist asks probing questions and offers opportunities for reflection that increase collective social awareness in the therapeutic system.

＊←→＊

The therapist is active and intentional, creating space where assumptions can be inspected—taken apart and disrupted—to reveal multiple perspectives and possibilities.

＊←→＊

This critical meta-perspective is in itself a paradigm shift; a shift in how we think and how we know what we know.

Practice Guidelines

There are a number of important steps for practicing socioculturally attuned structural family therapy including (1) expanding the family map, exploring the interplay between habitus and field to connect family to societal structures, (2) identifying societal influences on family power dynamics, rules, and roles through exploring the impact of capital on families, (3) encouraging families to explore and commit to equity based relationships that resist the impact of symbolic violence, and (4) helping families restructure to support developmentally appropriate relational equity.

1. Connecting Family and Societal Structures

Socioculturally attuned structural family therapists are familiar with the impact of worldview, family history, intergenerational dynamics, and social context on family functioning and the importance of attending to these in therapy. When they join with clients, they are exploring, attending to, and in some ways entering, a family's habitus. They are aware of the need to continually join throughout the process of therapy to ensure a deep understanding of each family's world. Socioculturally attuned structural family therapists map families within societal context, recognizing that family members go in and out of various social fields, which further influences their relationships with each other.

In our example of Jim and Lacey, Jim functioned daily in a medical field in which doctors are highly privileged and assigned significant relational power over patients and other staff. This, in combination with his male privilege, affected the course of his affair with the nurse in his workplace. Belonging to the medical field provided economic, social, symbolic, and cultural capital that placed Jim at an advantage in his relationship with Lacey, and also afforded him greater opportunity to have an affair without suffering significant relational consequences. A socioculturally attuned structural family therapist would include these fields in the family map and understanding of family habitus. She would invite family members to explore how their individual positions in these social contexts affect their relationships, including the rules they live by as a family.

2. Identifying Societal Influences on Family Power Dynamics

Socioculturally attuned structural family therapists look beyond the overt and covert rules of the family to understand their relationship to "rules" of various fields families inhabit. Consider our example of John and Emanuel, who were raised in very different fields or contexts. Emanuel understood the intricacies of relational dynamics within lower-class, Mexican American communities. He knew the rules. When John entered this field, he was somewhat lost about what to do—how to be. Likewise, John grew up in upper-class fields that supported white privilege and dominance of white upper-class values, attitudes, and behaviors. When Emanuel entered John's world, he also didn't know all of the rules. This created complex and problematic dynamics for the couple. Their therapist would need to explore not only broad societal themes related to social class, race, and ethnicity, but also work with the couple to help them identify the "rules of the game" in each field they enter. This would ensure they can work together to navigate very different social situations in ways that they both feel supported as a couple. Rules within fields tend to support existing societal structures (e.g., taboos against talking about race support white privilege; believing those who have more are worth more supports existing class systems). Therapy is a place where these rules can be broken by making them overt, discussing their impact, and establishing greater agency over their influence.

3. Exploring and Committing to Equity Based Relationships

By connecting family to societal structures and identifying societal influences on family power dynamics, socioculturally attuned structural family therapists are poised to explore the impact and cost of relational inequality on individual and family well-being. Family members become increasingly aware of how societal dynamics affect their most intimate relationships as therapists initiate conversations that raise social awareness and expose power dynamics. These conversations include exploring the relational costs of power imbalances. Back to Jim and Lacey. Jim enjoyed disproportionate power which allowed him to be more influential in setting the emotional climate in the home, meet more of his individual needs, and enjoy being accommodated by the rest of the family. When the costs of this power were carefully explored, it became clear to all (including Jim) that the children were closer to their mother and often resented their father. Jim had lost the respect of his wife and children, and the females in the family were routinely disempowered. This was very likely not what Jim and Lacey hoped for and may be in contrast to their stated values of raising strong children, supporting equal opportunity for their daughter, and Jim's desire to be close and revered by the family.

4. Restructure to Support Developmentally Appropriate Relational Equity

Socioculturally attuned structural family therapists share the assumption that families should be structured in ways that support optimal development for all members. Oppressive relationships and societal structures block equal opportunity for health and well-being, including individual and relational development. Influence and accountability must be balanced. For example, as children gain autonomy and influence, they are expected to become increasingly accountable for their actions and to consider the impact of their decisions on others. Parents may be in charge of most decisions but are expected to make decisions that benefit their children and consider the needs of the group. When one adult overpowers another, when the needs of one become routinely privileged over another, it is likely to create an imbalance that creates and maintains presenting problems. Addressing these imbalances and encouraging structural equity is central, rather than auxiliary, to treatment.

Case Illustration

Let's continue with our example of Emanuel, John, and Max. Emanuel was born in the U.S. from parents who had migrated from Mexico without documentation. His early life was spent in the state of Arizona. When Emanuel was 4 years old his father was stopped for a traffic citation and deported when it was discovered that he did not have proper documents. From the time Emanuel was 4 until he was 12, his father was deported to Mexico and returned to Arizona four times. The family finally made the decision that Emanuel and his mother would go to the state of New Mexico to live with his mother's sister. Emanuel's older siblings stayed behind as U.S. citizens with jobs in Arizona. Emanuel rarely saw his father after that time.

John grew up in the state of Texas. His family owned a large, successful business. His father inherited the business from John's grandfather and succession of the business to John as the son and only child was carefully planned and executed. Emanuel and John met in college in New Mexico. After college they moved back to Texas so John could run his family business. John and Emanuel passed as friends and roommates while living in Texas among John's family and the conservative business community. After John's father died, John liquidated the family business to start something new with Emanuel. This was an opportunity for the couple to move to Massachusetts to secure legal marital status and begin the process of Emanuel legally adopting Max.

Max was born in Texas. His biological father was white and in the military and his mother was the young daughter of John's Latina family housekeeper. John's family's influence cleared the way for him to privately adopt Max as an infant. The adoption was arranged before Max was born and the expenses of the delivery were covered by John's parents, who saw this as an opportunity for their son to have a child and for them to have a grandchild. John, Emanuel, and Max lived on John's parents' estate in a guesthouse and both worked in the family business for the duration of their stay in Texas.

The couple made the decision to be openly out as a married gay couple when they moved to Massachusetts. The business was put in both of their names and they bought a home together. They were able to openly father together and developed a supportive community of friends and colleagues. Things went smoothly with John taking the lead in the business and Emanuel taking the lead parenting until Max became a teenager.

Connecting Family and Societal Structures

The therapist working with John and Emanuel's family asked questions that raised social awareness in the therapeutic system. As the therapist analyzed the connections between societal and family dynamics, the family developed critical social awareness of the systems in which they were embedded. These conversations provided information that informed the process of mapping the family in societal context, which in turn provided direction for restructuring interventions. Following is an example of therapeutic dialogue between the therapist, Lisa, and the couple, John and Emanuel, that served to raise critical consciousness while assessing family in societal structure.

Lisa identified as a white, middle-class, bisexual, gender queer family therapist who had lived in Boston since childhood. Lisa had personal experience with homophobia, sexism, and cisgenderism. Lisa's self-of-the-therapist work included critically examining how their interconnected identities provided privilege in some ways (white, middle-class, and living in a progressive city) and marginalization or oppression in others (bisexual, gender fluid). Understanding how societal systems and power dynamics impact their own life helped prepare Lisa to engage in critical consciousness with John, Emanuel, and Max.

Lisa:	So John, you mentioned that when you and Emanuel first moved to the family property in Texas the two of you lived as friends. Can you talk more about that decision . . . how the decision was made?
John:	My family is really conservative. By the time I met Emanuel, my parents knew I was gay, but I promised not to tell anyone in our hometown because of the family business.
Lisa:	Who was most concerned about someone finding out and what were they worried might happen if others knew?
John:	Mostly my dad. He had worked really hard to build the business. I think he assumed we would lose business if the community knew I was gay.
Lisa:	What was that like for you and how did you approach Emanuel about your father's wishes?
John:	I didn't like it, but my dad always called the shots. I told Emanuel it was something we just had to do if we eventually wanted the family business.
Lisa:	Emanuel, can you tell John directly what it was like for you to be told to stay closeted in John's world? To have John and his father make this decision for you?

Emanuel: I felt so uncomfortable with your family anyway, John. They knew I didn't come from money. I'm not white. Plus my being around seemed to just remind everyone that you are gay. I agreed because I love you, but I never felt like I fit. I still don't.

John: Well you fit as far as I am concerned. I wish you just wouldn't worry about my family. We left Texas, started a new life, sold the family business . . .

Lisa: So it sounds like the two of you are trying to talk about your differences in social class and race, how racism and classism have affected your relationship.

Emanuel: It is hard for us to talk about, but it has a big effect on us.

John: Really? I think we have done pretty well to overcome those kinds of prejudices.

Lisa: You have overcome a lot just to be a couple. At the same time it makes sense to me that you, Emanuel, would notice the effects more. John, I know I am usually most unaware of the impact of my own privileges. This is much bigger than the two of you, but can we start by giving you some time, Emanuel, to really talk to you, John, about your experience?

This line of questioning eventually led John and Emanuel to better **attune** to each other and see how their relationship was affected by broader societal structures. Increased social awareness prepared them to depersonalize differences and begin to work together to support each other and their son within an unjust society.

Identifying Societal Influences on Family Power Dynamics

By talking openly about racism, classism, patriarchy, and homophobia, Emanuel and John were better able to understand dynamics in their own family. John tended to take the lead in major decisions, to be more demanding of Max, and to dismiss Emanuel's experience. Many therapists would connect this pattern to an intergenerational dynamic and socialization of males, but a socioculturally attuned structural family therapist would also identify this pattern as inheritance of white, male, upper-class privilege. The process of raising critical consciousness through dialogue and reflection would guide action toward liberatory change (Freire, 1970/2000; Korin, 1994). Following, Lisa **names** the inequities stemming from families of origin and John and Emanuel's social locations in the broader society.

Lisa: John, you mentioned that your dad made all the big decisions in your family. He even made the decision for you and Emanuel to live closeted in Texas. How do you make sense of this?

John: He was just the head of the household. I think men back then ran everything.

Lisa: Do you remember what that was like for you and your mom?

John: I hated it. He was always on me. I think my mom just checked out.

Lisa: Always on you?

John: He expected a lot. He put me in charge of running a whole section of the business when I was 15! If I complained he would tell me to "be a man." I thought he was going to have a heart attack when I told him I was gay!

Lisa: So being gay was not being a man?

John: I guess not.

Lisa: Working hard, not complaining, excelling at your job . . . what else does being a man mean? Being in charge of your family?

John: Yeah. He was just trying to help me grow up and be successful.

Lisa: Passing the baton? So you could be successful and in charge of your own family?

John: When you put it that way . . .

Lisa:	How about you, Emanuel? What did your family pass down to you about being a man? Being in a family?
Emanuel:	For us, family was everything. I learned you do what you have to for the family. My dad had to keep his head down . . . keep a low profile when he was in the States. My mom was strong and independent when he was gone but did whatever he said when he was around. It was confusing. I guess I sort of resented him.
Lisa:	So even though your fathers both learned men should be in charge of the family, they had real differences in their power and privilege in the world. How do the differences in what you learned and the differences in race and social class impact the power dynamic in your relationship with each other? What messages do these dynamics send to Max?

A socioculturally attuned structural family map might look something like the one in Figure 4.3:

Exploring and Committing to Equity Based Relationships

Lisa **valued** all voices in the family as they helped the couple identify their egalitarian **values.** Emanuel and John described their ideal relationship as one in which they equally shared the responsibilities of running their business and parenting their son. They were committed to a fair and just relationship. At first, they saw the issues in their family being about personalities. Max was drawn to Emanuel because he was more patient and "laid back." John was a driven

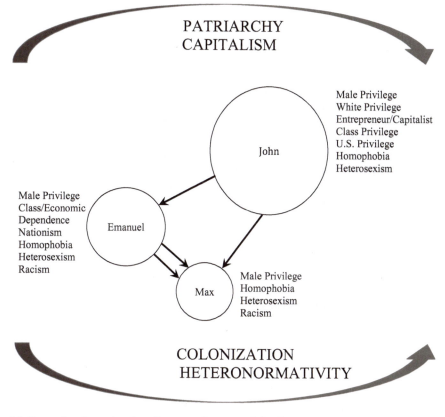

Figure 4.3 Example of a socioculturally attuned structural family map.

perfectionist who liked to be in control. Over time, what they viewed as internal dispositions were exposed as existing between the internal and external—between individuals and relationships, relationships and societal context. As Max grew up he expected to enter adulthood in a family that prided itself on being democratic. This mirrored not only the values of the democratic society in which they lived, but the value John and Emanuel both placed on having a fair and egalitarian marriage. Emanuel and John wanted Max to become increasingly autonomous yet accountable to others. Their own fathers were in more powerful positions in the family and lacked the emotional and relational attunement they wanted in their intimate relationship as well as in their parenting. They also wanted Max to be socially aware and know how to challenge racism, sexism, classism, and homophobia. All three family members readily engaged in visioning changes in their relationships that promoted equity and closeness. This family had a multitude of strengths and experience facing and overcoming oppression that could be jointly mobilized.

Restructure to Support Developmentally Appropriate Relational Equity

John and Emanuel were committed to dismantling the effects of patriarchy in their relationship. This included rethinking how to help Max "become a man." One of the ways Lisa **intervened** was by helping John find ways to connect with Max that did not rely on giving him advice or demanding performance. For example, Lisa asked John and Max to spend a session together in which they were guided in talking directly to each other and coached to communicate in ways that increased understanding between them. This included expression of feelings. John was also asked to spend time with Max between sessions. John had to learn to deal with anxiety surrounding letting go of control and to trust Emanuel as a co-parent and business partner. Lisa engaged John and Emanuel in discussions about power dynamics, social class, gender, and race to raise their social awareness and help them **envision** change. Lisa also worked directly with the couple to encourage them in direct communication, making certain Emanuel's voice was heard in the therapy process. John learned to listen more carefully and attune to his partner's needs and feelings. John also learned to seek out Emanuel's input on decisions after realizing that although he thought the relationship was equal, he often made unilateral decisions. Emanuel became more outspoken, disagreeing with John directly when needed rather than seeking the comfort of Max when he felt misunderstood by John. Lisa assigned homework in which John and Emanuel were to regularly meet to discuss the business. Over time this helped them **transform** from a patriarchal business model (typically supported in capitalist economies) to a more collaborative, team-driven model. They also began routinely checking with each other about parenting decisions. They both enjoyed individual relationships with Max that did not undermine Max's relationship with their co-parent. Lisa openly talked about race with the couple and helped them talk with Max to better prepare him to resist racism. Their increasing awareness prompted an interest in Max to engage in community activism. Overall, the family became increasingly feminist and collaborative, valuing relationships over tasks; mutual involvement over control.

Summary: Third Order Change

Max, Emanuel, and John engaged in first, second, and third order change throughout the process of being in family therapy. In this case, first order change included things like asking Emanuel and John to spend one night a week on a "no-problems date." The therapist did not expect this type of commonsense solution to change the relationship dynamics per se, but saw it as a step toward second order change in which the couple redefined their relationship as one that was closer and more equal. Second order change included Emanuel and John becoming more equal as parents and business partners and Max developing more balanced relationships with both of his parents. Third order change included an active decision by Emanuel and John to resist patriarchy in their relationships with their fathers and each other. This included challenging gender stereotypes that pressure men to be competitive versus co-operative, to be autonomous versus collaborative, and stoic rather than vulnerable. In the end, they were able to structure their family in a more egalitarian and loving way. This included becoming more aware and committed to dismantling multiple dynamics of oppression, including racism, sexism, heterosexism, and classism within their family and beyond. The family became fluent in discourses of liberation by taking a meta-view of their relationships in societal context. This expansion of relational options was liberating while holding each member accountable for unearned privilege and misuse of power in intimate relationships.

References

Bourdieu, P. (1977). *Outline of a theory of practice* (R. Nice, Trans.). Cambridge, MA: Cambridge University Press. (Original work published 1972.)

Bourdieu, P. (1986). The forms of capital. In J. G. Richardson (Ed.), *Handbook of theory and research for the sociology of education* (pp. 241–258). New York, NY: Greenwood Press.

Bourdieu, P. (1990). *In other words: Essays towards a reflexive sociology* (M. Adamson, Trans.). Stanford, CA: Stanford University Press. (Original work published 1987).

Butler, M., & Gardner, B. (2007). Adapting enactments to couple reactivity: Five developmental stages. *Journal of Marital and Family Therapy, 29*(3), 311–327.

Freire, P. (2000). *Pedagogy of the oppressed.* New York, NY: Bloomsbury. (Original work published in 1970.)

Garcia, M., & McDowell, T. (2010). Mapping social capital: A critical contextual approach for working with low-status families. *Journal of Marital Family Therapy, 36*(1), 96–107.

Korin, E. C. (1994). Social inequalities and therapeutic relationships: Applying Freire's ideas to clinical practice. *Journal of Feminist Family Therapy, 5*(3/4), 75-98.

Maton, K. (2014). *Habitus.* In M. J. Grenfell (Ed.), *Pierre Bourdieu: Key concepts* (2nd ed.) (pp. 48–65). New York, NY: Routledge.

Minuchin, S. (1974). *Families and family therapy.* Cambridge, MA: Harvard University Press.

Minuchin, S., Montalvo, B., Guerney, B., Rosman, B., & Schumer, F. (1967). *Families of the slums: An exploration of their structure and treatment.* New York, NY: Basic Books.

Minuchin, S., & Nichols, M. P. (1993). *Family healing: Tales of hope and renewal from family therapy.* New York, NY: Free Press.

Minuchin, S., Reiter, M., & Borda, C. (2014). *The craft of family therapy: Challenging certainties.* New York, NY: Routledge.

5 Socioculturally Attuned Brief and Strategic Family Therapies

Brief and strategic family therapists introduced the idea that change can happen quickly and that small changes can lead to more substantial desired change. Families are often viewed as trying to solve problems in ways that make sense but don't work, requiring therapists to think counterintuitively to intervene in family dynamics. Therapists using these approaches focus on the here and now, helping families change interactional patterns that maintain the very problems they often wish to eliminate.

A number of important approaches to working with families fall under the broad heading of brief family therapy. These include the work of leading figures at the Mental Research Institute (e.g., Watzlawick, Beavin Bavelas, Jackson, 1967), the Milan group (e.g., Palazzoli Selvini, Boscolo, Cecchin, & Prata, 1980), and strategic family therapists (e.g., Haley, 1973; Madanes, 1984). As with many family therapy models developed in the second half of the 20th century, brief models were based on Bateson's concept of families as systems. The focus was on the family unit and tailoring interventions to specifically meet the needs of each family. Relatively little attention was paid to the broader social context. These approaches were originally influenced by Milton Erickson's counterintuitive approach to change (de Shazer, 1982; Haley, 1973) and have endured many rounds of influential thought including social constructionism. New approaches have emerged from these frameworks over time including post-Milan (Brown, 2010) and brief strategic family therapy (Szapocznik & Williams, 2000). Strategic family therapists target specific interactional patterns in ways that simultaneously eliminate the presenting problem and change family dynamics.

++→

Socioculturally attuned strategic family therapists promote third order change by factoring broad societal dynamics into hypotheses and interventions.

++→

Socioculturally attuned strategic family therapists attune and help family members **attune** to each other's views—from views of the problem to views of the world. Therapists **name** societal power dynamics expressed as symptoms or metaphors of the problem. They **value** the voices of those not fully heard or in one-down positions and **intervene** in incongruent hierarchies by making the covert overt. Families are encouraged to **envision** and try on possibilities that lead to **transformation** in which relationships are no longer limited by what is socially ascribed. In this chapter we describe enduring concepts and practices related to brief and strategic family therapy. We illustrate how therapists can integrate principles of sociocultural attunement and offer practice guidelines. We then share a case illustration to demonstrate how integrating societal systems and attention to power can lead to third order change.

Primary Enduring Brief and Strategic Family Therapy Concepts

There are a number of tenets common across brief models, including a focus on the here and now, the assumption that change doesn't require insight and can happen quickly, and the idea that small change can lead to bigger change (Nardone & Watzlawick, 2005). Brief and strategic family therapists highlighted that we can't not communicate (Watzlawick et al., 1967). Even silence is a form of communication and communication may have more than one referent. Symptoms are sometimes viewed as metaphoric communication with interactional cycles around one problem representing patterns around another, less approachable problem (Madanes, 1984). For example a family may complain of an adolescent repeatedly running away when in fact the shared concern is that one of the parents wants to leave the marriage. Strategic family therapists consider how families are organized using the metaphor of family hierarchy, but focus on power dynamics in ways that differ from structural family therapists.

In strategic therapy, problems are viewed as metaphors and/or resulting from incongruent hierarchies, or imbalances of power (Madanes, 1981). Those who carry the symptom are often resisting power dynamics that family members are unable to address. Interventions share the expectation that therapists will be active and carefully target directives to disrupt problematic relational patterns (Nardone & Watzlawick, 2005). Therapeutic teams are sometimes used to form hypotheses, observe live sessions, and carefully design interventions for therapists to deliver during and/or at the end of sessions.

In this section, we offer enduring core concepts in the practice of brief and strategic family therapies, including circularity and circular questioning, viewing problems as attempted solutions, thinking counterintuitively, and assessing power imbalances. We describe what makes an intervention strategic, and emphasize the expectation that therapists be active agents of change.

Circularity

Patterns of interaction and thinking non-linearly remain hallmarks of the practice of family therapy. Brief and strategic family therapists used the term "circular causality" to refer to the idea that it is not necessary to discover where a problem started in order to find a solution. Each part of a pattern, or each action, is also a reaction, affecting and being affected by all surrounding actions (Watzlawick et al., 1967). Patterns can therefore be interrupted anywhere to create change. Later in this chapter we will advocate for integrating analysis of power into circular thinking, arguing that therapists must be careful not to assume that family members have equal influence over the formation or resolution of problems or that families are solely responsible for symptoms.

Circular questioning provides a means of feedback while continually opening new possible explanations and views of the problem (Palazzoli Selvini et al., 1980). The therapist asks questions to check out hypotheses about what is creating and maintaining problems. At the same time, family members are asked to share how they view relationships between other family members, as well as what they think others might think, say, or feel. This adds new information to their understanding of each other and the problems they face. The family not only hears about each member's views and experience, but about what each assumes are the views and experiences of others. All questions reflect assumptions and answers confirm or deny hypotheses.

For example, if I ask a family member, "When would your brother say this problem started?" I am sharing my assumption that there was a time when the problem did not exist and inferring that knowing the circumstances and timing of the problem's origin will help solve it. By asking one family member to assume the position of another, the therapist is adding information to the system (i.e., what one brother thinks the other thinks) while forming a hypothesis about why the problem is occurring. When the family member answers "He would say it started soon after our mother died," the therapist begins to build a hypothesis that the problem is associated with the death of the mother. She then asks, "Who was closest to your mother?" hypothesizing that the problem is connected to loss of a close relationship. When the client answers "None of us. In fact we never felt we could live up to her expectations," the new information leads the therapist to rethink her hypothesis. It also leads the family and therapist to shift how they are making meaning of the situation together.

Hypothesizing is seen as suppositional, providing direction and making sense of problems relationally. Rather than seeking truth, therapists use hypotheses to guide treatment. Family members are invited to meta-communicate, which in turn contributes to new ways of thinking and doing. Let's consider the example of the Bernadines, a white, middle-class couple (Lily and Tom), who entered problem gambling treatment with their adult daughter, Mavis.

Therapist:	So Lily, I am wondering who you think is most concerned about Mavis's gambling?
Lily:	Well I think Mavis is.
Mavis:	Really?!
Therapist:	If I were to ask you that same question, Mavis, what would you say? Who do you think is most concerned about the gambling?
Mavis:	Mom is—definitely! She's the one who calls me worrying all the time. She gets Dad all worked up about it too.
Therapist:	So how would you describe their relationship? Mom and Dad's?
Mavis:	I don't know . . . I guess happy. Dad seems happy with their relationship. I'm not sure Mom is. Maybe she wants him to be around more—pay more attention to what is going on.
Therapist:	And how do you think your mom would describe her relationship with your dad?
Mavis:	She would probably say they love each other, that all couples have to deal with differences, you know . . . the usual. She might say he is a grump no matter what she tries to do to make him happy (laughs and smiles at dad).
Therapist.	If your brother Mark were here, what would he say about your parents' relationship?
Mavis:	He would take Mom's side. I think he would say Dad is kind of in his own world. Besides, Mark thinks I am a total loser!
Therapist:	So your brother would say Mom is most concerned about the gambling and that Dad is not as involved with things? How about your dad, who would he say is most concerned about the gambling?
Mavis:	Well you can ask him, but he will say Mom is.
Therapist:	Dad?
Tom:	I suppose Mavis is right. It really bothers her mom.
Therapist:	If Mom were bothered less by the gambling would it still be a problem?
Tom:	Well of course. It's not like I don't care! Lily is just the most tuned in to it.
Therapist:	So Mom, maybe they are saying you carry most of the worry? Is that how you see it?
Lily:	I suppose so.

In this brief exchange, the therapist was able to help the family identify a number of patterns, including how the family might be organized around the problem. Lily receives new information, i.e., that her husband and daughter believe she is most concerned about the problem. The family is offered a new idea, i.e., mom is carrying most of the burden of the problem.

Problems as Attempted Solutions

According to Watzlawick, Weakland, and Fisch (1974), there are three primary ways attempted solutions become, or contribute to, problems. The first is when families underestimate the need to take action. For example, a wife may complain that she does not have equal influence in relation to her husband, who in turn uses his power in the relationship to dismiss her concerns. This pattern continues until the wife leaves the relationship. The husband may then realize the need to respond, but responds too late.

The second type of attempted solution is when families overestimate action needed to solve a problem. For example, a newly blended heterosexual couple comes into therapy because a stepfather is concerned that his adolescent stepson is not doing as he is told. When the therapist investigates, she discovers that the son is doing well in school, observes curfews, does the majority of his chores, and is generally respectful to his parents. The stepfather is focused on the son's failure to pick up his room and to complete chores on demand, such as folding the laundry when asked. The stepfather's focus on minor non-compliance is inadvertently creating a problem as the mother feels the need to defend her son and the son is withdrawing from both parents. This overreaction to a minor issue adds to the tension in emerging stepparent-child relationships and exacerbates the power imbalance between the couple by highlighting the mother's lack of influence over the stepfather's unrealistic expectations.

The third type of attempted solution is when families repeat commonsense solutions even when they exacerbate problems. Let's go back to the example of the Bernadines. Mavis (age 28) was having difficulty living on her own without the financial help of her parents. She worked at a minimum wage job and spent most of her free time in diners playing on electronic gambling machines. Tom and Lily worried about their daughter being evicted from her apartment, not having food, or being able to pay her phone bill. They were dedicated, as most parents are, to helping their daughter be successful and happy. They refused to give Mavis money to gamble, but when she needed money for rent or food they felt compelled to help. They took over her phone bill to make sure they could always reach her and she could call on them when she needed support. Providing financial support to encourage their daughter to be on her own is a commonsense solution that is effective in some situations. In this case, parents were being held hostage by the gambling. They knew their daughter lost the money she needed but didn't want her to face difficult consequences. Lily and Tom trying to help their daughter succeed and Mavis relying on financial support (which inadvertently supported gambling) became a pattern of attempted solutions that made the problem worse.

Counterintuitive Thinking

Brief and strategic therapies were influenced by Milton Erickson's counterintuitive approach (de Shazer, 1982; Haley, 1973). Viewing problems from a counterintuitive lens can lead to creative solutions. In fact, how the family is thinking about and defining the problem is part of the problem or at least keeps them stuck and unable to discover a solution. In de Shazer's words (1982) "the therapist's worldview must help him [sic] see beyond the client's worldview. The therapist must see the client's problem from a different angle" (p. 21). In essence, the therapist reframes how the problem is understood, helping clients see it differently to lead to different sets of solutions. According to Nardone and Watzlawick (2005), non-ordinary logic is key to unlocking the self-maintaining logic of most problems. They argued that "The strategic approach to therapy, linked directly to the contemporary philosophy of constructivism knowledge . . . is based on the assertion of the impossibility . . . of offering an absolutely true and definitive explanation of reality" (p. 38). It is precisely these many possible realities that opens space for counterintuitive thinking.

Rather than being concerned over the cause of a problem, brief and strategic family therapists are interested in uncovering and disrupting what is maintaining the problem. The therapist must help families view problems differently in order to inspire greater options for change. Take for example a couple who entered therapy because a wife, who had the majority of power in the relationship, was unhappy about a husband who consistently acquiesced to her wishes. During the first session the wife told the therapist they had come in so the therapist could get the husband to stand up to her. This couple was stuck in a self-defeating logic loop. The only way the husband was able to stand up to the wife was by refusing her demand that he do so. If the therapist accepted the client's position on the problem they would worsen the problem by ineffectively trying to get the husband to be more assertive.

Therapists may find differences in family members' views to be part of the problem (de Shazer, 1982). For example, one partner may insist that sharing emotion is primary while the other views emotion as counterproductive. Joining with one view over the other typically leaves the therapist stuck as part of the system attempting to use the same logic. A therapist would need to shift into a new level or type of solution. This might involve suggesting that it is not that one approach is better than the other, but the judgmental attitude each partner takes of the other that is problematic (Atkinson, 2005). This requires therapists to think beyond their own worldview about how problems should be solved. There are many ways of looking at what is true. A strategic therapist is most concerned with what works and what inspires hope for change (Haley, 1976). Haley was convinced that therapists need to help families construct problems that could be solved rather than ones that were by some objective measure, true.

Incongruent Hierarchies

Like structural family therapists, strategic family therapists consider power dynamics and family hierarchy as central to presenting problems. They differ in their view of power, however, being primarily concerned with imbalances of power and incongruent hierarchies. According to Madanes (1981),

> when one is dealing with a family . . . there is inevitably an issue of hierarchy because the participants are not all equal. They have status differences based on such issues as age, control of funds, and community-vested authority and responsibility.
>
> (p. 5)

Madanes argued that all couples deal with issues of power and control as they typically divide areas of responsibility. She noted that family members have the potential to overpower each other, along with the potential to nurture and care for each other. Incongruent hierarchies occur when family members' influence does not match expectations for their roles. Consider a child who worries over and takes care of a parent with a drinking problem. Not only is the parent unable to consistently fulfill the role of caretaker and protector, but the child is placed in a position of taking charge of the parent. Unequal relationships between parents are sometimes balanced by one or more children siding with a one-down parent, but may also be balanced through symptomatic behavior (Madanes, 1981).

Take for example a heterosexual couple in which the husband has more power to influence major decisions and sets the mood in everyday interactions. The wife accommodates him for the most part, but from time to time goes on spending sprees. She apologizes profusely when bills come in, but can't seem to stop. The husband is rendered helpless over his wife's spending, which he is unable to control. In this way, the symptom of overspending might be seen as serving to balance power in an unequal relationship. This perspective of power does not clearly differentiate overt power from acts of resistance to power. When therapists view the most symptomatic person in the family as the most powerful, they often overlook the symptom as a form of resistance to the non-negotiable power of another family member.

Therapist as Agent of Change

Strategic interventions have become almost synonymous with the use of paradox, which has largely fallen out of favor. Nardone and Watzlawick (2005) argued that there is no ethical dilemma when delivering non-transparent interventions because therapy is not a zero sum game—the therapist has the best interest of the client in mind and the therapist and clients win or lose together. There have also always been clear guidelines, including the imperative that interventions should never cause harm (Haley, 1980). Paradoxical interventions must be win/win, i.e., helpful whether or not the family follows the directive.

What makes an intervention strategic is not that it is paradoxical or delivered in non-transparent ways, but the fact that it is specifically tailored to target and interrupt a problematic interactional pattern. The therapist's responsibility is to be active and direct the family, supplying interventions that create change within unique family and societal contexts. According to Haley (1980, p. 10) a useful theory "should guide a therapist to action rather than to reflection. It should suggest what to do." In fact Haley placed the responsibility to create change squarely on the shoulders of the therapist. This mandate has changed over time to a greater reliance on collaboration between therapists and clients; however, the importance of therapists being active and accountable for intervening in problematic dynamics has endured.

Descriptions of the wide variety of strategic interventions are beyond the scope of this work and have been described in depth elsewhere. These include the Milan group's use of invariant prescription, paradox, and counterparadox, therapy teams, and family rituals (Boscolo, Cecchin, Hoffman, & Penn, 1987; Selvini-Palazzoli & Viaro, 1988); Haley's (1984) ordeal therapy and reframing techniques; and prescribing the symptom, pretending, seeing symptoms as metaphors and replacing their function (Madanes, 1981). The following examples are intended to give the reader the flavor of typical strategic interventions.

Interventions range from direct and transparent to indirect with relatively hidden agendas. The obvious logic of some strategic interventions is apparent to the therapist and the family, or at least the adults in the family. Take for example a common pattern between siblings and a parent. Joe (age 7) and Walter (age 5) fluctuate between playing well together and arguing. When the arguing gets loud and they start calling each other names, their custodial grandmother, Mary, enters the room to tell them to stop. If they don't stop, Mary raises her voice and sends them to their rooms. Mary is tired of the fighting and wants a new solution. The therapist asks Joe and Walter what they most enjoy and learns they especially love going with their grandmother to the store where they are allowed to spend a dollar each on anything they like. Mary agrees with the therapist to offer the dollar to each of them in a new way. Each week she will exchange 2 dollars for 40 nickels. Mary is directed to place 20 nickels in each of two jars. Whenever she hears Joe call Walter a name, she simply goes to Joe's jar, takes out a nickel and places it in Walter's jar. She does likewise when she hears Walter call Joe a name. If either child protests they lose another nickel. This intervention interrupts the pattern of Mary intervening in sibling arguments while maintaining her rule as a parent that there will be no name calling. Both children have control over keeping their money and when they choose to spend it on name calling it benefits the sibling whom they intend to insult.

The therapist might offer a family an explanation without fully disclosing the reasoning behind an intervention. This doesn't necessarily mean the reason given isn't true, but the truth of the explanation is less relevant than the change in pattern. For example, a family enters therapy because their 4-year-old is throwing fits several times a day. When she does this, parents get upset with her and try to get her to stop, which seems to escalate the behavior. The therapist (after exploring all other potential causes for sudden disruptive behavior) discovers that the child did not throw tantrums until recently and shows concern that the child may have missed the important developmental stage in which young children learn they can't control everything around them, i.e., the terrible twos. The therapist reassures the family that it is better for a 4-year-old to go through the terrible twos now than as a teen and encourages them to make sure their daughter has at least one tantrum a day to get through this developmental stage as quickly as possible.

The therapist and family carefully lay out exactly what is to happen when the child has a tantrum and how to insist on a tantrum if she hasn't had one all day. They rehearse prompting a tantrum during the session. When they have to resort to prompting a tantrum they are asked to sit together and have a cup of hot cocoa once it is all over. Prescribing the symptom creates change in how the symptom is viewed and each family member's action/reaction. Once you have voluntarily done something that felt out of control you are more likely to take a meta-view that makes repeating the same behavior in the same old way nearly impossible.

Haley (1984) proposed therapists help families abandon problems by creating ordeals that made problems too troublesome to maintain. For example, a family entered therapy after seeing a physician and learning there was no medical cause for their 13-year-old's headaches, which had kept him out of school for several weeks. It was imperative that he return to school as soon as possible, but the family was uncertain about what to do as the headaches persisted. The therapist explored developmental issues, problems at school, family dynamics, and so on, only to find that the boy's headaches seemed to center around some mild anxiety which avoiding school exacerbated. The longer he was out, the more anxious he became about returning. In this case, the therapist elicited the help of parents and grandparents who were eager to see the problem resolved. Each of the adults agreed to be on call to spend one or two days a week in the school nurse's office. The school agreed that a parent or grandparent could sit with the student when he wasn't feeling well. This way he would at least be at school, but never without someone to nurture him when he wasn't feeling well. The boy returned to school, but not to the nurse's office, relinquishing his headaches to avoid the social embarrassment of having a parent or grandparent with him at school.

Integrating Principles of Sociocultural Attunement

Sociocultural attunement requires expanding practice beyond family systems to consider the relationship between families and society. The idea of circularity, or that interactions occur in repetitive patterns, remains useful in challenging linear cause and effect thinking; however, the relative power family members have to create and maintain patterns must be taken into account. Likewise, it is important to understand parallel societal processes that promote imbalances of power and their effects on incongruent hierarchies and presenting problems. Socioculturally attuned brief and strategic therapists are called on to not only think counter-intuitively but to think in ways that counter hegemony.

⤝→

From a socioculturally attuned perspective, symptoms are carefully considered to determine if and how they may serve as acts of resistance to unjust systems.

⤝→

Societal Context

One of the strengths of brief and strategic therapies has been a focus on families as relatively unique; each to be carefully considered in order to tailor treatment accordingly. Socioculturally attuned brief and strategic therapists are tasked with understanding how family interactions and the meaning of problems are impacted by culture and societal dynamics. Conceptualizing circularity and problem formation on a societal level can help therapists develop contextually informed strategic hypotheses.

Circularity in Context

Circular causality has been heavily criticized as promoting an assumption that problems are self-perpetuating and that all family members have equal opportunity to create change. Feminist family therapists challenged the assumption that family members have equal influence and that problems reside solely within families rather than reflecting power dynamics in the broader society (James & McIntyre, 1983). According to Goodrich, Rampage, Ellman, and Halstead (1988),

> Circularity is another systemic construct that operates in women's disfavor. The idea that people are involved in recursive patterns of behavior, reactively instigated and mutually reinforced results either in making everyone equally responsible for everything or no one accountable for anything.
>
> (p. 17)

Haley (1980) actually voiced a related concern when he argued that "Systems theory, as it was applied to families, tended to describe participants as equals . . . a primary problem . . . is the way systems theory takes away individual responsibility" (p. 15).

Perhaps the metaphor of patterns as circular is itself a problem as it elicits a sense of equality and equidistance, like sitting at a round table at standard intervals. There is no one at the head of the table and everyone has the same amount of space. You can see and hear everyone equally. Although the practice of continuing to track interactions until they loop back or "circle around" to the starting point remains helpful, in reality, patterns of interactions are more likely uneven, unequal, and asymmetrical; actions more or less voluntary, with participants having various levels of influence and choice across situations. Interactions are influenced by societal dynamics which afford some greater power and influence in families than others. Likewise, choices are often narrowed by social constraints, cultural norms, and power dynamics which limit actions and reactions.

Consider an Egyptian Muslim family in which an adult son, Mohamed, is unable to earn enough money to marry due to the country's long-term economic depression. He begins to stray from family and religious values in favor of hanging out and drinking alcohol with a group of peers who are in the same situation. He and his father, Achmed, engage in verbal conflict when he arrives home. His mother, Magda, attempts to intervene but is quickly dismissed by both males. The conflict escalates until Mohamed angrily leaves the house. Magda and Achmed then argue about how the situation was handled until Magda withdraws. Call to prayer calms and centers both Achmed and Magda who then come together in a loving embrace. Culturally, Mohamed is expected to be a capable provider before he marries. Global economic disparities leave him caught between childhood and adulthood. He acts out in an adult way (e.g., drinking with friends) that leaves him paradoxically stuck in childhood (e.g., being scolded by his father). As a female, Magda enjoys economic rights and protection under Egyptian law, which interprets the Qur'an as guaranteeing those rights (Al-Mannai, 2010), yet like most women in the world, she has less power to influence men in a patriarchal society. Their religious beliefs and common cultural experience of being called to prayer five times a day serve as a source of resilience that helps them maintain connection in spite of conflict. This circular pattern is shaped by economic, religious, and cultural constraints and opportunities.

Problem Formation at a Societal Level

We must understand how societal dynamics contribute to problem formation and how some social problems are exacerbated by attempted solutions on a societal level. Consider financial aid from high resource countries to low resource countries. This makes good common sense to most of us. This aid ensures a positive political alliance and often enhances military strength that supports multiple governmental agendas. The countries receiving aid are hopefully in better positions to defend themselves through military force, build infrastructures, encourage trade, and lessen poverty. The dynamics of national lending and debt, however, create new problems. Those in power to disburse funds can do so in ways that benefit themselves, maintain their power, and/or support reforms that eventually fail. Low resource countries can become increasingly indebted to powerful international lenders. This reinforces existing international imbalances of power (Soederberg, 2013). These commonsense solutions can have unintended effects at local levels. In this case, poverty, and the many emotional, relational, and health problems associated with poverty, may become increasingly difficult for families to overcome as governments must pay back their loans even when it means depriving families of basic needs such as health care and education.

It is not uncommon for societies to under respond or over respond in ways that contribute to large scale formation of social problems. For example, many societies significantly under respond to intimate partner violence, poverty, racism, homophobia, and other social problems. Failure to adequately respond leaves vulnerable family members and families most marginalized in society without protection and/or equal access to resources. The effect on families is widespread, contributing to many of the problems family therapists are only too aware of (e.g., medical problems, depression, anxiety, interpersonal conflict).

Families are also influenced by cultural and societal contexts in their attempts to solve problems. Consider parents over responding to children earning poor grades. Poor academic performance may result in fear, anger, and family conflict. These reactions are informed in part by economic systems that rely on education as a means of securing middle- and/or professional-class status. At some level, a second grader's poor academic performance threatens the family's and child's long-term economic security.

Power

Strategic therapists carefully analyze power imbalances; however, symptom removal remains the primary goal (Madanes, 1981), rather than necessarily promoting relational equity. This may lead therapists to intervene in ways that mirror power dynamics and fail to help families consider more equitable and just alternatives. For example, many years ago Teresa saw a family in which a teenage daughter and her mother got into chronic arguments. The father sometimes took the side of his wife and sometimes took the side of his daughter, typically being the one to make any necessary final decisions. As a then strategic therapist, Teresa asked the family to reenact the arguments in session and assigned the father the task between sessions of flipping a coin each time mother and daughter fought in order to decide whose side he would take. This intervention eliminated the pattern of mother and daughter fighting and father stepping in, but failed to address the societal dynamic of male dominance that maintained the father's one-up position in the family.

Post-Milan practice (Brown, 2010) emerged in response to the critique of the Milan group's lack of attention to power (e.g., Goldner, 1985, 1993; Hoffman, 1985) and the introduction of social constructivism. Therapists began to be thought of as engaging with families to mutually understand problems within societal context. Hypothesizing broadened to include social influences and analysis of power dynamics.

Societal Impact on Power Imbalances

In the example offered earlier, it didn't occur to Teresa that the symptom or pattern in which the family was stuck reflected an incongruent hierarchy on a societal level. Patriarchy promotes the assumption that sex and gender are conflated, dichotomous, and natural. Men and masculinity are more greatly valued and assume a one-up position in relationship to women and femininity, even in societies such as the U.S. that tout democracy and equality. At a societal level men are more often the decision makers as was true in this family. By asking the husband/father to make an arbitrary decision about supporting either his wife or teenage daughter, Teresa was reinforcing the problem even while eliminating the symptom. She was also ignoring what may have been a form of resistance to male dominance by the mother and daughter.

Culture and Power

Family therapists often view culture as a matter of difference. Cultural competence is vital to ethical, effective practice and therapists support cultural democracy by viewing all cultures as equally legitimate. There is a tendency, however, even among culturally competent therapists, to overlook the centering and dominance of some cultures over others, which potentially offers those in the majority culture greater social influence and access to resources (see Chapters 2 and 4; Bourdieu, 1986).

Culture affects how we attempt to solve problems, and what we consider intuitive or logical is often unexamined dominant cultural logic. For example, European Americans in the U.S. tend to value independence and individuality. When a family enters treatment with a 3-year-old who is having trouble sleeping on her own it can be easy to follow the family's commonsense logic of the importance of toddlers sleeping separately from parents. Commonsense solutions (e.g., night light, door ajar, reward system) attempt to resolve what has been culturally framed as a problem. Family therapists might believe they are thinking "outside the box" when hypothesizing that the child's refusal to sleep alone is a function of family interactions (perhaps a problem in the couple's relationship) while failing to examine the expectation that healthy toddlers sleep alone privileges European American cultural dominance. The therapist in this situation would not necessarily discourage the parents from their goal, but could help parents put their decision in cultural perspective.

Symptoms as Forms of Everyday Resistance

Everyday resistance is often overlooked as a response to oppressive power dynamics in families and societies. According to Afuape (2011),

> aspects of everyday resistance include the ways people always resist oppression; the ways we all struggle with contradictory positions and ways of responding to oppression that can coexist; the back and forward movement toward liberation that is forever shifting and changing; the place of our relationships and social circumstances in supporting or constraining movements in our preferred direction; and the possibility of being both oppressor and oppressed.
>
> (p. 72)

⊷⇥

What we identify as problems might also be sites of everyday resistance, better understood as symptoms of power imbalances in society.

⊷⇥

For example, demonstrating depression may be both a genuine physical and emotional struggle and a way to resist an oppressive marriage or job. Strategic therapists notice this dynamic and hypothesize symptoms as exerting a type of power that can balance incongruent hierarchies.

Practicing from a socioculturally attuned framework extends this idea beyond the family to link oppression to broader societal contexts. Women who are displaying depression as a form of resistance to a male partner's dominance are also resisting a much broader force of male dominance which maintains this power dynamic in intimate relationships. A client showing depression or panic attacks in response to a workplace may also be resisting much larger issues (e.g., class privilege, racism, sexism) that promote and maintain unjust working conditions.

Resistance in the form of symptoms is also frequently overlooked as a site of resilience (McDowell, 2015). Consider a set of twins in a family in which a socially powerful parent is verbally and emotionally abusive. One twin argues back continuously and is labeled as a problem because she disrupts the family on a daily basis. The other withdraws, eventually relying on drug use to resist oppression. The first twin's behavior contributes to her resilience by helping her learn not to give up and to stand up even when under attack. The second twin resists by engaging in drug abuse which is temporarily empowering within drug using contexts, but disempowering in the larger society (Stanton & Todd, 1982).

Third Order Change

Third order change occurs when there are shifts in how families see the world, allowing them to consider more possibilities for how to understand and negotiate their relationships. Socioculturally attuned brief and strategic therapists co-construct hypotheses with clients that include awareness of the impact of societal context on presenting problems. Raising social awareness helps families to realize the impact of these broad social arrangements on their most intimate relationships and more directly and knowingly participate in dismantling incongruent hierarchies and relational patterns. This deeply impacts family rules and collective meaning making.

←→

Third order change occurs in socioculturally attuned strategic family therapy when families unlock incongruent societal hierarchies in favor of adopting equity based relational systems.

←→

Practice Guidelines

Practicing socioculturally attuned brief and strategic family therapy requires thinking beyond the family, broadening the circle of interactions and hypotheses to include power dynamics in societal context. Symptoms are viewed through a lens that considers their value as forms of resistance and symptom free resistance is supported. Rather than being neutral observers who intervene to remove symptoms, therapists take a number of steps including broadening the circle, thinking counterintuitively to counter hegemony, including societal power imbalances in hypotheses, affirming symptom free resistance, and intervening to support just relationships.

1. Broadening the Circle

Socioculturally attuned brief and strategic family therapists expand their view to **attune** to the interconnection of individual thoughts and behaviors, patterns of interaction, cultural lifeways, and societal dynamics. Consider the Bernadines mentioned previously, who presented with a gambling problem. Treatment for problem gambling is likely to include attention to biological (e.g., chemical changes in the brain, neuro-pathways), psychological (e.g., magical thinking, fantasies of the future), behavioral (e.g., gambling rituals), affective (e.g., emotional triggers), relational (e.g., attachment styles, family patterns around gambling behavior), contextual (e.g., financial issues, allure of gambling contexts), cultural/social (e.g., meaning of money, economic system, definition of success), and existential (e.g., illusion of control, beliefs around chance) considerations (McDowell & Berman, 2016). These areas are not discrete or dichotomous but deeply intertwined. For example, it is not possible to understand the meaning of money, the thought process around gambling, the family's reaction to problem gambling, or the allure of gambling contexts without understanding the society's economic system and cultural definition of luck and success. Even the dopamine released in the brain when taking a gambling risk is influenced by the economic system and cultural value of wealth.

Circular questioning with the Bernadines from a post-Milan framework that includes the larger context might continue as follows:

Therapist:	So I am thinking about why so often in families moms seem to carry most of the worry. Tom, what do you think most people would say if I asked them why women seem to worry a lot about everyone else?
Tom:	I think most people would say that's just what mothers do.
Therapist:	And what do you think they would say about fathers?
Tom:	Well I think most people would say fathers care a lot about their families too but just show it in different ways . . . working . . . doing things for the family.
Therapist:	Mavis, if I were to ask your brother Mark the same questions, what would he most likely say?
Mavis:	Well Mark just stays out of things.
Therapist:	Yes, of course I notice he didn't come today (everyone laughs). But if you were to venture a guess, what might he say if he were here?
Mavis:	I think Mark and I both go to Mom when we need things because she is more likely to understand, so maybe she just knows us better and so worries more.
Therapist:	Mavis what do you think your friends would say about the role of women being caretakers in the family?
Mavis:	Most of my friends are not so interested in doing that. They want partners who will be more equal and to be able to do more of what they want to do.
Therapist:	And your mom's friends? What might they say?
Mavis:	I don't think they like it, but maybe they would say they are stuck being the ones who hold the family together. Most of them do a lot of making sure everyone else is OK . . . especially their husbands (laughs).

By broadening questions to include social discourse, the therapist was able to **name** and pursue gender and power dynamics within and beyond the family.

2. Think Counterintuitively to Counter Hegemony

According to Brown (2010), circular thinking must include therapists' awareness of their own beliefs and values as well as the impact of dominant social discourses on families and presenting problems. Being able to take a meta-view of dominant social discourses and the dynamics of broad societal systems allows therapists to develop the critical consciousness necessary to think counter hegemonically as well as counter intuitively. We use the term hegemony to refer to mechanisms that maintain the status quo of unequal power distribution in society through social, political, economic, and ideological control. This includes, but goes beyond, the concept of dominant discourses to include laws, corporate and educational practices, social services, and so on. The therapist's critical awareness contributes significantly to how problems are framed and consciousness raising takes on a more central role in creating third order change. The therapist **values** sources of resilience and silenced voices of resistance. This is exemplified in the case illustration at the end of this chapter when the family and therapist work together to raise critical consciousness in order to develop a hypothesis that is socioculturally attuned.

3. Include Societal Power Imbalances in Hypothesis

Socioculturally attuned brief and strategic therapy expands hypotheses to include societal power dynamics. Children typically have less power and responsibility than their parents. Power imbalances, however, are not part of the natural order of adult relationships. Viewing power imbalances as existing solely within the boundaries of families tends to pathologize individual relationships and limits how we are able to **intervene.** Consider a European American family in which there is an aging parent living with an adult child and two adolescent grandchildren. The rest of the family talks only to each other and frequently overlooks the grandparent when making plans. The grandparent is expected to go along with whatever decisions are made. This family is deeply influenced by a youth-oriented culture which devalues those who are no longer financially producing. If the grandparent is female and less than fully able-bodied, the power imbalance worsens as the family is likely to unintentionally act out the ageism, sexism, and ableism of dominant U.S. society. The family enters treatment because the grandparent is having angry outbursts. If the therapist non-reflexively shares the worldview that older adults are worth less than younger adults and children, he is likely to view the grandparent's outbursts as a symptom of adjusting to old age rather than societal dynamics impacting the family.

4. Affirm Symptom-Free Resistance

Resistance is a healthy response to oppression. Strategies for resistance may be quite varied, including withdrawing physically or emotionally, standing up and speaking out, yielding in order to get through oppressive situations, and trying to understand in order to navigate power dynamics (McDowell 2004). Socioculturally attuned family therapists are in a position to help clients **envision** how to strategize against oppression in ways that don't cause them further harm.

Consider a firefighter who was the only female in her rural station. Her co-workers referred to her as an opportunity hire and excluded her from chances to perform. She was in a relationship with a man who shared the traditional gender role expectations of her family of origin and most of her community. She was referred to therapy by a physician after exhaustive tests could not determine a physical cause for her inability to swallow food. The therapist gathered information about all of the client's relationships before hypothesizing that the symptom was a metaphor of the client's resistance to being overpowered. The client and therapist began exploring dynamics in the client's life that she was "not willing to swallow." Identifying the oppression and attempts to resist oppression was a powerful consciousness raising intervention. The client joined a group for women in male dominated workplaces that the therapist started after seeing many women in the community dealing with similar dynamics. Over time, the therapist, women in the group, and the client developed alternative approaches to resisting oppressive situations.

5. Support Just Relationships

According to Knudson-Martin (2013), it is not possible for a therapist to be neutral in the face of power imbalances. If a therapist fails to address relational inequity, he unwittingly contributes to it by default. On the other hand, if the therapist encourages shared power, he may be criticized for promoting his own agenda. This would seem to be an impossible ethical bind if it were not for the fact that power imbalances often create and maintain the very symptoms the therapist and family are trying to eliminate (McDowell, 2015). From this perspective, the therapist is obligated to address what is harming the family. As noted earlier, therapy is not a zero sum game (Nardone & Watzlawick, 2005). Shifting the power from the oppressor to the oppressed is not a successful outcome as it maintains a power-over system that will continue to be problematic.

←→

Transformative action requires socioculturally attuned therapists to be aware of the impact of societal systems on all family members, including those who are acting in oppressive ways.

←→

Case Illustration

Tiana (age 16) come to family therapy with her brother, Jamar (age 10), and parents, Brandon (age 40) and Kisha (age 42). The family lives in a relatively safe middle-class neighborhood. All family members identify as black, heterosexual, and able-bodied. Brandon and Kisha met 20 years prior while in college. Brandon grew up in a working-class family in which most of the men were in the building trades. Kisha's parents were upper-middle-class and held important positions in the government. Tiana and Jamar are both doing well in a private, Roman Catholic school. The family entered treatment with Ladonna, who works for Catholic Community Services. Ladonna identifies as a black, heterosexual woman. She grew up living in poverty, however, her professional career now provides a stable middle-class income. The family explains to Ladonna that they are experiencing growing conflict.

During their initial visit, Jamar responds to Ladonna's question about why the family came to therapy by resentfully stating, "My *sister* yells all the time." Brandon glances at Jamar with a slight grin. Kisha interrupts with "There is too much fighting between everyone," glancing at Jamar with a disapproving brow. The family describes a repetitive pattern of conflict. They offer a typical example in which Brandon makes a demand of Tiana (e.g., go close the door, fold this laundry). Tiana ignores her father, Brandon repeats the demand in an angry tone, Jamar offers to do the chore ("I'll do it dad!"), Brandon tells him to stay out of it and pursues Tiana, repeating his demand in an angry, physically threatening tone and posture. Kisha intervenes asking him to calm down, while Tiana screams at her father as she withdraws to her room. Kisha tells Brandon "You can't just boss her around! She is almost 17!" Brandon withdraws in anger until Jamar comes and sits on his lap.

Broadening the Circle

The pattern of interaction described here seems relatively straightforward. At first glance it appears to be a simple case of a teenager acting out and parents needing to agree on how to parent together as a team. Part of the problem, however, is that parents disagree on how strict to be with their daughter and Kisha disapproves of Brandon's approach. Brandon is not easily influenced by Kisha and in spite of her cautions, continues what Kisha considers overly aggressive parenting of their daughter. When Ladonna explores other areas of the parent's relationship she discovers this is a pattern. Brandon is far more likely to influence Kisha than Kisha is to influence Brandon. Kisha frequently attempts to persuade Brandon to see her perspective, but is left feeling that she is the one who must accommodate him.

Ladonna broadens the circle by exploring race, gender, and social class dynamics in society and how these dynamics impact this particular family. Expectations that Kisha will accommodate Brandon based on gender overshadow her coming from a higher social class background and are, in part, a response to the lack of respect Kisha knows Brandon experiences as a black man in the broader society. For example, despite his competence, Brandon was not promoted as quickly from superintendent to project manager as his male counterparts in his white dominated construction firm. Internally he is always on guard, careful not to upset others, knowing that men like him are often viewed as dangerous. At home he feels more entitled to relax his guard and expect obedience. Kisha wishes Brandon would treat Tiana less harshly, yet knowing he is so often denigrated outside the home, she tends to protect his status in the family (see Cowdery et al., 2009). Ladonna also explored differences in societal expectations, issues of safety, and avenues for success for Tiana and Jamar as young black women and men in the current U.S. context.

Thinking Counterintuitively to Counter Hegemony

When family members' actions didn't attain the desired result, they repeated them anyway because they made sense. When Brandon made a demand of Tiana and she didn't comply, he continued with more of the same, repeating his demands more forcefully. Kisha repeatedly attempted to get Brandon to understand, using the same arguments each time she was frustrated with how he was approaching their daughter. And so on, with each member of the family repeating the same type of commonsense response even though nothing changed. Thinking counterintuitively includes considering what message this problem pattern may be communicating and how the problem may be balancing an incongruent hierarchy.

＊←→

Thinking in ways that counter hegemony includes considering how family communication may reflect imbalances of power on a societal level.

＊←→

When Ladonna asks Brandon more about his concern over his daughter not doing as he asks, he explains "I only ask her to do a few simple things!"

Ladonna:	So you don't ask much of your daughter.
Brandon:	No. Plus, what I tell her to do isn't difficult. Just keep the house up, help her mom with the dishes . . .
Ladonna:	Really basic stuff.
Brandon:	Yes, what I tell her to do is easy.

Ladonna recognizes Brandon's response as one that perpetuates female dependency and underachievement. She is especially concerned because she is keenly aware of the myth of the black matriarch that can dismiss the ways black women lack power (Hill, 2005). She goes on to challenge this societally informed belief.

Ladonna:	Actually, that concerns me a little.
Brandon:	What, that it's easy!
Ladonna:	Well yes. Mom, what do you think Tiana is capable of doing?
Kisha:	She is a pretty competent young woman. She gets good grades, is on the student council at school, helps me teach preschool on Sundays at our church. He's right. What we expect of her at home isn't much.

Ladonna:	Tiana, is your mom right?
Tiana:	I guess so. I just don't like being bossed around all the time!
Ladonna:	I am wondering why your parents don't expect more of you. (Tiana rolls her eyes) No, I don't mean more time or more tasks, but things that are harder to do . . . more fitting to your abilities. You are almost 17 right? Next year is your last year in high school . . . then what?
Tiana:	I am going to college.
Ladonna:	So Mom and Dad, what are you hoping she will learn from you in the next year before she goes to college?
Brandon:	To be responsible so she can take care of herself.
Kisha:	Well that, yes. And to be confident. She is a good person. I want her to hold onto herself and her values when she gets out on her own.

Ladonna continues to explore expectations for Tiana to be grown up; to take care of herself, make good decisions, and "stand up for what she believes in." Tiana agrees this is what she wants for herself and for her brother when her brother grows up. Brandon was stuck in a commonsense, self-perpetuating cycle of asking less and less of his daughter in more and more demanding ways. He inadvertently undervalued his daughter's abilities and dismissed his wife's concerns and advice. He also used anger and aggression as a means to get what he wanted. Ladonna was thinking counterintuitively when suggesting the parents ask their daughter to do more difficult tasks rather than doing less. If Ladonna had simply encouraged Brandon to treat his daughter in a more developmentally appropriate way, (e.g., give her tasks for the week that she completes as she has time) she would be joining her mom's voice and either be dismissed as another female in the therapeutic system or be demonstrating that she had more influence over Brandon's decision than did Kisha.

Ladonna was also setting the stage to counter patriarchy. Expecting too little of a 16-year-old daughter reflects low expectations for young adult females. Tiana was obviously capable of more adult contributions to the family. Ladonna engaged the family in discussions about what they wanted their daughter to be able to do as a black female in society. Brandon agreed that he wanted his daughter to have the same rights and say in her life as men. This opened the door to talking about the couple's gendered relationships in which Brandon had more say than anyone else in the family and how this pattern inside the family might be exacerbated by racism that takes a toll on the whole family. Ladonna led the family in a discussion about how that came about, the cost to the family relationships, and what they envisioned instead.

Including Societal Power Dynamics in Hypothesis

The socioculturally attuned therapist working with this family began by asking questions that helped the family work with her to hypothesize how what was going on within the family reflected broader societal dynamics. The family was caught in an incongruent hierarchy found more generally in society and played out across many specific contexts in their lives. For example, Kisha and Brandon worked for the same company and had the same educational background. Both experienced being routinely marginalized by white peers, building customers, and company owners as the only two black employees. The company was also highly organized around gender. The office employed only women and only men worked in the field. Although both Kisha and Brandon held highly skilled leadership positions in the company, the women in the office were frequently diminished and dismissed by male employees who (unlike Brandon) put off requests to complete paperwork, referred to getting "nag mail" from the office, and circulated sexist jokes.

Ladonna and the family worked together to develop a hypothesis that included a gendered power imbalance shaped by broader societal racial dynamics that left dad making unilateral decisions and exerting power. This dynamic cost Brandon some of his connection with his wife and oldest daughter. His use of aggression came at a particularly high price as family members sometimes accommodated out of fear. Jamar joined his dad's side, which also cost him closeness with his mother and sister and perpetuated the privilege sons sometimes have in African American households due to their lack of advantage in the larger society (Hill, 2005). Tiana needed to learn to stand up for herself in a context in which males continue to have greater privilege and expect women to accommodate them. Kisha and Brandon needed to learn, and demonstrate for their children, how to share equal influence in a world that marginalized each of them in somewhat different ways.

Affirming Symptom-Free Resistance

The therapist in this situation affirmed the parents' desire to make certain their daughter was prepared for adulthood. This included among other things being able to take responsibility and complete difficult tasks independently. Ladonna, Kisha, and Brandon needed to guide Tiana in how to resist gender and racial oppression, including how to "stand up for what she believes in" as a young black woman. She also affirmed Brandon's desire to be connected, Kisha's right to have equal say in what happens in the family, and the need for Jamar to not have to take sides. Kisha, Brandon, and Tiana agreed on chores that were more challenging, would help prepare her for adulthood, and that she could fit into her busy schedule. This included helping her father change the oil in their cars, doing the weekly grocery shopping for the family, and giving her brother a ride at least three times a week.

Ladonna and the parents agreed to help Tiana practice asserting herself in effective and respectful ways. Brandon agreed to make arbitrary demands of Tiana from time to time without the use of a loud voice or physically aggressive posture. Tiana agreed to respectfully decline or offer a time when she would be able to accommodate the request. Kisha was then to review Tiana's efforts, coaching her as needed. Anyone in the family who noticed Brandon sharing power by thinking about others first, asking instead of demanding, or negotiating respectfully, was to warmly approach him and give him a kiss on the cheek. This strategic intervention prescribed the symptom but in ways that supported a shift toward greater connection and equality in the family.

Supporting Just Relationships

This family presented with a relatively simple problem, but one that reflected a much broader social and family dynamic. The symptom was a form of resistance to male dominance in the home and community context. It was vital that Tiana find ways to resist demands that undervalued her potential contribution, required accommodation, and were enforced through physical displays of aggression. Kisha could not support her co-parent because she agreed with her daughter, who in some ways spoke for them both. Tiana was preparing to launch from the family and had less to lose by being the one to stand up than did Kisha. Jamar was left deciding which team he should join and made the move to be on the more powerful one. This left him at risk for learning only accommodation as a response to male dominance. By supporting just relationships, the therapist was able to help the family remove the symptom, but not without first recognizing the symptom as a form of resistance.

Summary: Third Order Change

The family in the previous illustration engaged in first, second, and third order change. Changing the types of chores Tiana was asked to do was a form of first order change. This intervention alone would not lead to second order or process level change which is qualitative and discontinuous, altering the system's rules, structure, and/or order (Watzlawick et al., 1974). Changing the meaning of Tiana's refusal to comply with doing chores on demand from a form of rebellion to a necessary skill for adulthood led the way for second order change. Second order change included Kisha having more equal say in parenting and Tiana being supported by both parents in more developmentally appropriate ways. Third order change occurred in this family when there were major shifts in how they saw the world (Ecker & Hulley, 1996). The family was able to consider more possibilities for how to organize their relationships when they were able to take a meta-view of gender, race, and power in society. This helped them realize the impact of these broad social arrangements on their most intimate relationships and to make more conscious choices about how they wanted to live. The therapist invited the family into third order change by working with them to develop a hypothesis that included awareness of the impact of societal context on the family's presenting problem. This, in turn, led to *further* second order change as they altered family rules about the meaning and impact of gender in relationship to influence and competence.

References

Afuape, T. (2011). *Power, resistance and liberation in therapy with survivors of trauma: To have our hearts broken*. New York, NY: Routledge.

Al-Mannai, S. (2010). The misinterpretation of women's status in the Muslim world. *Digest of Middle East Studies, 19*(1), 82–91.

Atkinson, B. (2005). *Emotional intelligence in couples therapy: Advances from neurobiology and the science of intimate relationships*. New York, NY: W. W. Norton.

Boscolo, L., Cecchin, G., Hoffman, L., & Penn, P. (1987). *Milan systemic family therapy: Theoretical and practical aspects*. New York, NY: Harper & Row.

Bourdieu, P. (1986). The forms of capital. In J. G. Richardson (Ed.), *Handbook of theory and research for the sociology of education* (pp. 241–258). New York, NY: Greenwood Press.

Brown, J. (2010). The Milan principles of hypothesising, circularity and neutrality in dialogical family therapy: Extinction, evolution, eviction . . . or emergence. *The Australian and New Zealand Journal of Family Therapy, 31*(3), 248–265.

Cowdery, R., Scarborough, N., Knudson-Martin, C., Lewis, M., Shesadri, G., & Mahoney, A. (2009). Gendered power in cultural contexts part II: Middle class African American heterosexual couples with young children. *Family Process, 48*(1), 25–39.

De Shazer, S. (1982). *Patterns of brief family therapy*. New York, NY: Guilford Press.

Ecker, B., & Hulley, L. (1996). *Depth-oriented brief therapy: How to be brief when you were trained to be deep and vice versa*. San Francisco, CA: Jossey-Bass.

Goldner, V. (1985). Feminism and family therapy. *Family Process, 24*(1), 31–47.

Goldner, V. (1993). Power and hierarchy: Let's talk about it! *Family Process, 32*(2), 157–162.

Goodrich, T., Rampage, C., Ellman, B., & Halstead, K. (1988). *Feminist family therapy: A casebook*. Ontario, Canada: Penguin Books.

Haley, J. (1973). *Uncommon therapy: The psychiatric techniques of Milton H. Erickson, M.D.* New York, NY: Norton.

Haley, J. (1976). *Problem-solving therapy: New strategies for effective family therapy*. San Francisco, CA: Jossey-Bass.

Haley, J. (1980). *Leaving home: The therapy of disturbed young people*. New York, NY: McGraw-Hill.

Haley, J. (1984). *Ordeal therapy: Unusual ways to change behavior*. San Francisco, CA: Jossey-Bass.

Hill, S. A. (2005). *Black intimacies: A gender perspective on families and relationships*. Walnut Creek, CA: AltaMira Press.

Hoffman, L. (1985). Beyond power and control: Toward a "second order" family systems therapy. *Family Systems Medicine, 3*(4), 381–396.

James, K., & McIntyre, D. (1983). The reproduction of families: The social role of family therapy? *Journal of Marital and Family Therapy, 9*, 119–129.

Knudson-Martin, C. (2013). Why power matters: Creating a foundation of mutual support in couple relationships. *Family Process, 52*(1), 5–18.

Madanes, C. (1981). *Strategic family therapy.* San Francisco, CA: Jossey-Bass.

Madanes, C. (1984). *Behind the one-way mirror: Advances in the practice of strategic therapy.* New York, NY: Jossey-Bass.

McDowell, T. (2004). Exploring the racial experiences of graduate trainees: A critical race theory perspective. *The American Journal of Family Therapy, 32*(4), 305–324.

McDowell, T. (2015). *Applying critical social theory to the practice of family therapy.* New York, NY: Springer.

McDowell, T., & Berman, E. (2016). *Best of both worlds: Integrating relational models into problem gambling treatment.* National Council on Problem Gambling conference, Tarrytown, NY, U.S.

Nardone, G., & Watzlawick, P. (2005). *Brief strategic therapy: Philosophy, techniques, and research.* Lanham, MD: Jason Aronson.

Palazzoli Selvini, M., Boscolo, L., Cecchin, G., & Prata, G. (1980). Hypothesizing—circularity—neutrality: Three guidelines for the conductor of the session. *Family Process, 19*(1), 3–12.

Selvini-Palazzoli, M., & Viaro, M. (1988). The anorectic process in the family: A six-stage model as a guide for individual therapy. *Family Process, 27*(2), 129–148.

Soederberg, S. (2013). The politics of debt and development in the new millennium: An introduction. *Third World Quarterly, 34*(4), 535–546.

Stanton, M. D., & Todd, T. C. (Eds.). (1982). *The family therapy of drug abuse and addiction.* New York, NY: Guilford Press.

Szapocznik, J., & Williams, R. (2000). Brief strategic family therapy: Twenty-five years of interplay between theory, research and practice in adolescent behavior problems and drug abuse. *Clinical Child and Family Psychology Review, 3*(2), 117–134.

Watzlawick, P., Beavin Bavelas, J., & Jackson, D. (1967). *Pragmatics of human communication: A study of interactional patterns, pathologies, and paradoxes.* New York, NY: W. W. Norton.

Watzlawick, P., Weakland, J., & Fisch, R. (1974). *Change: principles of problem formation and problem resolution.* New York, NY: W. W. Norton.

6 Socioculturally Attuned Experiential Family Therapy

Joel, age 16, slouches in a chair in the therapy room with arms folded scowling at the floor. Joel's mother is animated as she explains her concerns about her son. Joel's father looks away, obviously frustrated with both his son and wife. Their therapist searches for ways to help the family express their thoughts and feelings to each other, with her own anxiety triggered by the family's fear that they cannot withstand hearing each other's true feelings. An experiential therapist in this situation moves toward the unexpressed emotion that the family seems to be avoiding, helping family members explore their inner worlds and express themselves to each other. Her goal is to make room for growth by encouraging family members to listen and have empathy for each other—to attune to each other. Discovering and sharing authentic experience shifts the way the family thinks, feels, and relates to each other. As a result they become more connected, genuine, authentic, and flexible as they demonstrate the ability to tolerate individual desires, fears, anxieties, hopes, and dreams.

Experiential therapy emerged from existential humanism during the 1950s and 1960s and was developed primarily by Virginia Satir (1964/1967) and Carl Whitaker (Napier & Whitaker, 1978). Satir focused on communication and positive human potential while Whitaker concentrated on the symbolic nature of family interaction. They were both charismatic, relying on their ability to be fully present to guide families into new and genuine experiences. Whitaker was well known for sharing stories from his own life and making playful, even absurd, interventions that symbolized what was going on in the family and/ or created temporary chaos to help the family reorganize without symptoms. The impact of Satir's use of self—her warmth, intuition, and authenticity—was sometimes referred to as magic (Banmen & Maki-Banmen, 2014). Many doubted the ability to reproduce experiential therapy as a model because it seemed to rely so heavily on self-of-the-therapist rather than theory and technique. Whitaker and Satir inspired generations of therapists to be hopeful and positive about human potential, to trust growth as an inevitable outcome of honest self-exploration and emotional expression, to rely on the transformative power of therapeutic experiences, and to use self-of-the-therapist in genuine and authentic ways.

Third order change in experiential family therapy involves the family going beyond understanding each other within an intimate relational framework to awareness of the impact of societal forces on their experience and the experience of those around them.

⤆⤇

Third order change in socioculturally attuned experiential family therapy requires identifying, putting into words, sharing, and hearing felt experiences of marginalization, oppression, and privilege.

⤆⤇

Attuning to and **naming** sociocultural experience is core to socioculturally attuned experiential family therapy. As family members **value** each other's experience and how societal systems preload their relationships, they become more willing and able to **envision** alternatives. Therapists participate in this process, **intervening** in inequitable relationships along the way and helping families take **transformative** action to liberate themselves from unwanted sociorelational contracts (e.g., male dominance and patriarchy, higher wage earners having greater voice, heteronormative family dynamics).

⊷⇥

Attuning to ways in which some are supported and draw power from the societal context at the expense of others paves the way to envision and create more equitable relationships.

⊷⇥

In this chapter we describe some enduring family therapy concepts and practices related to experiential family therapy, including communication, identifying and sharing emotions, use of experiential interventions, and therapist's use of self. We then illustrate how therapists can integrate principles of sociocultural attunement into experiential approaches to broaden awareness of self and others in societal context. We argue that it is not possible to fully understand ourselves —how we think, feel, and act—without realizing the impact of culture, societal systems, and power dynamics on our everyday lives. To this end, we offer a set of guidelines for considering human potential within societal context and explore the role of power dynamics in emotion and emotional expression. We then share a case illustration to demonstrate an application of socioculturally attuned experiential family therapy that integrates societal systems and attention to power in ways that can lead to first, second, and third order change.

Primary Enduring Experiential Family Therapy Concepts

The focus in experiential therapies is on each individual within a family system. Having multiple members of a family, including more than one generation, participate in therapy offers the therapist greater leverage for change and provides the family with greater continuity. The family is seen as blocking or supporting individual desires that drive self-actualization, which in turn weakens or strengthens the family as a whole. The approach focuses on the present, expecting change to occur through therapeutic experiences in the here and now. We have identified four enduring family therapy concepts associated with experiential therapies: communication, sharing emotions, experiential interventions, and therapists' use of self.

Communication

Experiential therapists help family members get in touch with themselves and communicate with each other in ways that are genuine and congruent. According to Satir (1967, p. 63), communication "includes all those symbols and clues used by persons in giving and receiving meaning." This includes verbal and nonverbal expression. It is not uncommon for people to communicate more than one message at the same time, prompting confusion in the message receiver. Accountability for communication is key. Experiential therapists interrupt attempts to send messages without taking responsibility for meaning. For example, one may say "I said I am not angry!" in a tone that clearly sends the message that they are in fact mad. The receiver is likely to believe the way the message is sent over its content, but has no way to verify meaning. They are thereby stuck, unable to resolve conflict and difference.

Communication traps like this one derail authentic connection. Take John, who won't tell his partner, Emily, what he wants, but becomes surly when Emily chooses a restaurant with a long line or goes to bed early on a night John feels amorous. When Emily questions John, he denies that he is unhappy yet remains quiet, withdrawn, and sullen. In a situation like this, an experiential therapist would encourage Emily and John to identify and accept their individual desires, hopes, anxieties, and frustrations, helping them put their thoughts and feelings into words. The therapist might ask the couple to demonstrate or communicate about their relationship through an experiential exercise. For example, she might ask them to sit back-to-back and talk to each other so their facial expressions can't be used to relay unclaimed messages. Or she might use a story from her own life, perhaps telling them about trying to understand what her pre-verbal toddler needs and how upset he gets when she guesses incorrectly.

Experiential therapy promotes democratic ideals of all family members deserving their own yearnings, choices, feelings, and needs, which they have the right and responsibility to clearly communicate. Little attention has been paid to the relationship between power dynamics and communication. These approaches tend to expect communication and understanding to lead to agreement and the meeting of all family members' needs equally.

Sharing Emotions

Experiential therapists help people identify their emotions and then communicate them effectively. Consider Lars, a 70-year-old Norwegian American Vietnam veteran, who is being cared for by his adult daughter, Vina. They come to therapy because Vina is "at her wits' end" with her father being cross and demanding. She agreed that he could move into her home and wants to be a good and caring daughter. She reports, however, that no matter what she does, Lars "refuses to be happy." During the therapeutic conversation, the therapist, Greta, notices a moment when Lars becomes quiet and puts his head in his hands.

Greta: Lars, what are you experiencing right now?

Lars: I am just listening. (looks up)

Greta: I noticed for a moment you looked down and put your head in your hands. What are you feeling as your daughter talks about you being difficult to please?

Lars: I don't know. Nothing.

Vina: That's the trouble dad! You don't care what I have to say.

Greta: Vina, how do you feel when your father turns away from you like that?

Vina: Angry! Hurt! Pissed off!

Greta: Lars, let's take a moment . . . I am going to ask you to help me here.

Lars: OK.

Greta: (stands up, walks over to Lars and sits next to him) Will you put your head in your hands and look down like you did a moment ago?

Lars: (follows the therapist's instructions and sits quietly)

Greta: (lowers her tone and moves in close to Lars) What are you feeling in your body right now? In your back, legs, stomach, heart, arms . . .

Lars: My chest is tight. (pause) Maybe I am having trouble swallowing.

Greta: So you're tight in your chest and throat. How about your head and hands?

Lars: I just want to disappear.

Greta: Your throat and chest get tight and you want to hide . . . disappear. What feeling might that be? Hurt, anger, embarrassment, shame, disappointment, fear . . . .?

Lars: (with heads still in hands) Maybe shame.

Greta: So shame . . . anything else? (allows a pause)

Lars: Disappointment in myself.

Greta: (in low and caring tone) That sounds really difficult Lars—those feelings of being ashamed and disappointed in yourself.

Greta accepted that Lars had trouble accessing and naming his emotions. Vina was quickly able to identify emotions but not able to effectively share them in part because her father refused to listen and acknowledge hearing her. Feelings need to be both expressed and validated. Vina's frustration came from having to guess what her father thought and felt. She assumed he did not care when he reported not feeling anything. By slowing down the interaction, warmly supporting Lars while challenging him to identify and express himself, Greta was able to create a new experience. This moment of understanding would need to be followed and expanded over time for there to be the type of change needed for Lars and Vina to support each other in being fully themselves.

Greta did not address the context or power differences between Lars and Vina. Vina had a lifetime of being the daughter of a demanding and difficult father. She was a female and expected to be a caregiver who accommodated her father's wishes. Lars was a Vietnam veteran with untreated trauma and shame, which he held tightly inside. As a white heterosexual male, he expected others to simply deal with his moods. He had never stopped to really think about his daughter's experience of him or the sacrifices she made to assume his care. Lars was a second generation Norwegian American who was raised to keep his emotions intact and unexpressed. Military training and being socialized as a male in his generation furthered that mandate.

Satir (Banmen & Maki-Banmen, 2014) made the point that it is not just our feelings that are important but how we feel about our feelings. She argued that we are often disappointed in ourselves or ashamed of our feelings. We try to dismiss, change, or hide how we feel from others rather than fully exploring and expressing ourselves. This prevents our growth and leads to convoluted communication. Let's go back to the example of John and Emily. John struggles with telling Emily what he wants and also with how he feels when his needs aren't met. This is due, in part, to John wanting to please Emily. He rejects his own needs to be the kind of person who puts his partner's needs first. When this leads to his feeling irritated, frustrated, or disappointed, John is displeased with his own emotion and attempts to deny how he really feels to himself and others. Emily then presses him to share his thoughts and feelings, eventually becoming frustrated herself. Now John is even more unhappy as his efforts to be selfless and please Emily have had the opposite result.

Experiential family therapy highlights emotion without ignoring cognition. In fact thinking, acting, and feeling are interconnected determinants of our experience. According to Connell, Mitten, and Bumberry (1999), "The goal of symbolic-experiential therapy is to provide an experience that flips the family's way of thinking. It must contaminate their way of perceiving reality and project them into a different way of interpreting and embracing life" (p. 2). Experiential therapists differ in their emphasis on helping clients connect their present emotions and experiences with the past. For example, Whitaker did not think clients needed to understand the current or historical cause of a problem to solve it, but Satir encouraged clients to become increasingly aware of themselves and to explore the lasting impact of childhood family of origin experiences.

Experiential Interventions

Experiential interventions are part of the process of therapy that unfolds as families talk about their situations, relationships, and experiences. The therapist takes the lead in structuring and guiding the therapeutic system toward growth that will resolve symptoms rather than setting specific goals with the family at the beginning of the encounter. The therapist does not encourage clients to set their sights on specific outcomes at the beginning of the therapy process as is common in many other models.

The therapist assumes positive outcomes will occur as a result of the therapeutic process; that given the right conditions, humans grow into their full, symptom-free potential.

Experiential family therapists take an active role in ensuring conditions for growth are met through identifying and sharing feelings and experiences. According to Napier and Whitaker (1978) the therapist must win "the battle for structure" (p. 10) while ensuring the family takes the initiative for change. The therapist must be able to facilitate what happens in therapy, but it is the family's motivation that drives change. In other words, the therapist must be in charge of the process and engage fully as part of the therapeutic system without knowing the outcome of interventions.

Experiential therapists guide families through experiences that prompt awareness of self in relationship to others. Many forms of expression are available, including, but not limited to, movement, dance, drawing, and sculpting. Demonstrating, rather than simply discussing, family dynamics provides avenues for understanding through embodied experience and felt memory. Sculpting is one of the most common experiential techniques (Papp, Scheinkman, & Malpas, 2013). The therapist asks a family member to place others and themselves in the room in relationship to each other. The therapist helps the sculptor decide who is in the middle and who is outside; who is turned inward and who is turned away; who is up on a stool and who is lying on the floor, and so on. She also helps the sculptor determine if someone should have a fist up, or a hand out, or a head down. No interpretations are solicited. Once all are in place the therapist moves from one to another inviting felt experience of being in the position each has been placed.

Sculpting provides a way to begin addressing power, emotional distance, protection, closeness, and other relational dynamics. Each person is encouraged to share individual experience and feelings that result from family dynamics. All are held in place, listening to others' experiences from the positions they hold in the family. Family members don't always see the dynamics in the same way and more than one sculpt can be completed to explore other perspectives. For example, consider a family in which the father often became loud, stood up and moved toward his wife and children when he wanted his way. The therapist asked the family to engage in a sculpt of these situations, slowly and carefully exploring each family member's experience and emotions during these moments. When the sculpt was completed, the father sank into his chair in shock stating "I had no idea I was frightening them!" Even though he consistently relied on creating fear in those around him to get them to do what he wanted, it became clear through sculpting that he did not fully understand what their experience was like or the relational cost of his use of power.

Therapist's Use of Self

According to Roberts (2005) experiential therapy relies heavily on self-disclosure "as a way to mold shifting boundaries, help subjectivity to emerge, and add affect" (p. 51). This requires therapists to be diligent in dealing with their own self-awareness; their own emotional and relational health. Therapists must guide the therapeutic process while being open to experiencing therapeutic encounters. This includes being able to tolerate intense emotions in self and others. Consider entering a room with parents whose teenager has recently committed suicide. Most of us are filled with a sense of dread around the emotions we will encounter. Experiential work requires us to move in close to even the most painful experiences and honor the humanity of all involved. This is possible in part by viewing emotions as natural, helpful, and potentially healing. As Connell et al. (1999, p. 28) argued "pain is not the enemy." Attempting to help others simply feel better short circuits the growth process.

Experiential therapists are authentic, using themselves in a variety of ways. They might share a feeling they are having while in the room with a family making a statement like "I am feeling some anger and I don't know where it is coming from. Is anyone feeling angry?" In this situation the therapist points to what is already in the room, using her own experience and taking the kind of chance she expects clients to take. Experiential therapists might use images that come to them while sitting with clients to suggest the symbolic nature of family interactions. For example, a therapist might say "I keep getting this picture popping in my head. I don't know if this makes sense or helps us at all, but I am envisioning the two of you in combat gear, dusty and tired, arm in arm coming out of a combat zone."

Likewise, they might use hunches to interpret things like family drawings. Consider a family in which a 9-year-old boy is described by parents as being depressed, even suicidal. The therapist asks the boy and his 7-year-old brother to draw a picture of the family that included each family member doing something while she talks with the mother and father. When drawings are complete, The therapist notices the 9-year-old's drawing includes himself pointing at a rat in the corner while the rest of the family looks away. This prompts the therapist to turn to the family and ask "Who else feels depressed?" The mother looks at the father, who responds "I do." Once the 9-year-old gets everyone to look at the rat he is free to feel better, leaving the therapist in charge of helping his dad.

Integrating Principles of Socioculturally Attuned Experiential Family Therapy

Experiential therapy relies on humanist assumptions that given a supportive context, free of barriers to positive growth, individuals and families can actualize their full potential. Social equity is paramount, therefore, to individual, family, and group development across all contexts as it assures the widest access to that which promotes health and well-being (e.g., respect, inclusion, opportunity, affirmation of worldview, physical and psychological safety, access to education and health care, right to love whomever you choose, financial security).

Societal Context

++ →→

Awareness of the impact of societal context on perspectives, feelings, and desires helps individuals and families take initiative to remove and/or better navigate barriers to growth.

++ →→

Regardless of what is accomplished in therapy, many clients still face racism, sexism, nationism, homophobia, heterosexism, ableism, and poverty. These oppressive and marginalizing forces deeply affect physical, psychological, emotional, and relational health. Awareness of the impact of societal systems can, however, help us see which barriers are movable. This includes internalized "isms," the negative effects of socially supported relational power imbalances, and adherence to societal norms and expectations that are contrary to our well-being.

Experience and Broader Societal Context

Socioculturally attuned experiential family therapists recognize the importance of social awareness in the use of contextual self-of-the-therapist. Let's go back to our example in which the therapist, Greta, worked with Lars and Vina. Greta described herself as a second generation German American. Greta grew up in a German enclave in Ohio, U.S. As is true for most of us, Greta worked extensively on understanding her own family background. For Greta this included exploring the impact of her German American heritage. She explored her ability to identify, express, and elicit emotions. This included overcoming her initial discomfort in asking others to openly express feelings. Now let's imagine that Greta wants to become more socioculturally attuned so she engages in additional work on her contextual self-of-the-therapist. This includes learning about the history of the civil rights movement in the U.S., exploring the impact of power dynamics on gender roles, understanding historical and contemporary identity movements, learning about the politics of war over the past century, and analyzing how societal systems such as patriarchy, social class, democracy, and colonization affect intimate family life.

As Greta becomes better able to understand herself in social context, she will be able to help others, like Lars and Vina, explore how context shapes their feelings and experiences in relationship to each other. She would recognize how Lars having a lifetime of white male privilege dovetailed into his stoic masculine Norwegian attitudes and wartime experience. Greta would contrast this with Vina's challenge of being a respectful and caring daughter while maintaining her expectation of gender equality in all of her relationships, including her relationship with her father. Greta's personal and social awareness would allow her to help Vina and Lars navigate the landscape of being a father and daughter in a specific societal and historical context.

Socioculturally attuned experiential family therapists can also use self-disclosure to raise social awareness and support just relationships. For example, a socioculturally attuned family therapist might, at the right moment, share with a family her experience of watching her own father work so hard yet never enjoy the relationship connections he desired, or her own struggle as a woman to balance being a mother with working. Another example would be a therapist disclosing how difficult it was to watch her brother come out as gay to parents who were confused and afraid of his sexual orientation. This type of disclosure helps normalize experience and open conversations about social and contextual influences on families.

Experience in Community Context

Although experiential interventions often attend to relational space within the family, the family's physical context and community are frequently overlooked as impacting experience. The context of community includes both space and place. Space can be thought of as the ecosystem, including all that is living and nonliving in a physical environment. Place refers to how we experience space. It is within a place that we meet our basic human needs for personal space, privacy, social interaction, and safety (Fitzpatrick & LaGory, 2000; McDowell, 2015). The spaces we inhabit, our sense of place, and our ability to secure our basic needs are highly dependent on societal dynamics of privilege, power, and oppression. For example, communities with low status often go without neighborhood maintenance, suffer more than their share of pollution, and have limited access to basic needs such as fresh food, public transportation, and safety.

Socioculturally attuned experiential family therapists consider where families live, work, get medical care, shop, receive education, recreate, and so on relative to spatial justice. They recognize and address the consequences of dynamics of power and privilege on physical resources and community geography. McDowell (2015) proposed *family cartography* as a method for exploring the experience of families within particular space and place. According to McDowell (2015) this is a way to "capture family life within the spaces family members inhabit in order to better understand the relationship between power, privacy, personal space, social interactions, safety, and the problems presented in therapy" (pp. 61–62). Family cartographies are maps that do not need to be drawn to scale or use a predetermined legend. Rather, the therapist facilitates drawing a picture of the family's community, including neighborhoods, relevant parks and place of worship, shopping and educational resources, sources of pollution, noise, danger/risk, and so on. Anything relevant to the family's daily lives can be included using symbols the family chooses. McDowell suggested a number of questions that might be used to develop a family cartography of any period in a client's past or the present (see Figure 6.1).

Sample Questions on How to Create a Family Cartograph
1   Describe the setting—physical environment, climate, town, and neighborhood in which you live/lived/grew up. (Map the territory.)
2   What kinds of social interactions are/were available to you in this setting? Where are/were you and your family able to go and not go in this setting? How safe do/did you feel? What level of privacy and personal space does/did this setting provide?
3   Describe the power dynamics in this setting. Include race, class, gender, sexual orientation, abilities, nation of origin, language, and any other signifiers that are relevant. (Add these to the map using symbols.)
4   How do/did these power dynamics affect you and your family? In what ways do/did you and/or your family members participate in the oppression or marginalization of others? How are/were you and your family oppressed or marginalized?
5   Describe the home in which you live/lived. (Add to map as an excerpt.) What kinds of social interactions are/were available to you in and around your home? In what areas of the home did you spend the most time and why? Where are/were you able to go and not go in your home and why? How safe do/did you feel in various spaces in your home? What level of privacy and personal space does/did this setting provide?
6   Who is/was in your family? Who has/had the most power? How is/was the power enacted? (Draw a map excerpt to show family.) How do these power dynamics reflect the broader power dynamics in your community?
7   What spaces on your map reflect sites of oppression? Describe the relationships in these sites. (Add oppression symbols to the map.)
8   Where are sites of resistance? Describe the relationships in these sites. (Add resistance symbols to the map.) How do/did you and/or your family resist oppression? Where, what, and how do/did you learn to resist oppression?
9   What types of resiliency do/did you develop as a result of this geography? (Add resilience symbols to the map.)
10 What else would you like to add to the map?

Figure 6.1 Creating a family cartograph. From *Applying Critical Social Theories to Family Therapy Practice* (p. 63), by T. McDowell, (2015), New York, NY: Springer. Adapted with permission.

Once the community map is complete, the therapist can ask the family to draw their home within the community. This can include all rooms and outdoor space, how each room felt, who had the most influence or impact on the emotional "weather" in the home, and so on. This provides a physical reference for remembering and sharing experience and emotion. The exercise helps the therapist understand the experience of clients within a physical context while raising social awareness and relational insight among family members.

Cultural Attunement and Cultural Democracy

Socioculturally attuned experiential family therapists extend the humanistic value of each person having worth and deserving voice by striving for cultural democracy. The ideal of cultural democracy goes beyond acknowledging that many cultures exist within most societies to supporting the right each group has to its values, beliefs, and practices without marginalization or oppression by more dominant cultures (Košutić & McDowell, 2008). The concept of democracy (even cultural democracy) reflects Western thought by extending the focus on rights of individuals to rights of groups. Democracy within a collectivist framework focuses on individuals cooperating in order to best meet the needs of all. The value of doing what is best for the group does not ignore individual needs; rather, it assumes all individuals will share the likelihood of having needs met through the group or family.

+←→+

Practicing socioculturally attuned family therapy requires auditing what we assume is "good therapy" from a cultural perspective.

+←→+

At a meta-level, therapists must view each culture as equally valid and work within cultural frameworks to support the growth and well-being of all family members. This includes recognizing the tremendous diversity within cultural groups and families, along with challenging culturally supported power differentials. The practice of socioculturally attuned experiential family therapy includes asking questions such as: How do we understand the cultural context of emotion? How do we find ways for clients to express emotion to us and each other in culturally supported ways? What might it look like to be vulnerable within various cultures and groups? Sharing thoughts and emotions directly with family members is not prized or adaptive in all cultures. For example, in many Asian cultures expressing one's own needs is counter to collectivist values that place the well-being of the group before that of the individual (Quek & Knudson-Martin, 2006). Sharing one's feelings and needs may be viewed as placing a burden on others. According to ChenFeng, Kim, Knudson-Martin, and Wu (2017), Asian American couples often carry "intangible loss" from generations of migration, loss of homeland, and marginalization in the host country. Each carries this burden on their own in "quiet fortitude" without leaning on others, not believing "that they should or could expect or ask for intimate emotional attention" (p. 5). Duty and loyalty to the family may be implicitly expected, while focus on oneself may be viewed as selfish. A socioculturally attuned experiential therapist would need to work within this cultural framework to slowly acknowledge losses and "scaffold their movement towards vulnerability so that it did not leave the couple feeling raw and unsafe" (ChenFeng et al., 2017, p. 562). These authors suggested that "when quiet fortitude is valued, decisions are often centered around logic, reasoning, and tangible outcomes rather than emotional consequences" (p. 562).

Consider Neeb, the aging father in a Hmong family who moved to the U.S. after the Vietnam war. Neeb had, like many Hmongs, left his village in the hills of North Vietnam to fight alongside the U.S. When the war was over, Neeb, his wife, Me, and their daughter, Kiab, took refuge in a midwestern U.S. city. Their daughter, Luv, was born in the U.S. Luv now cares for her aging father, Neeb, just as Vina cares for her father, Lars. Neeb is not overtly demanding of Luv. He carries the burden of his past trauma in quiet fortitude. He is grateful that his children are thriving. Luv's sister, Kiab, tells their father how good he looks, how well he must be eating, to compliment Luv. Luv and Kiab are deeply grateful to their father and protect him from any additional burden after all he has lost and suffered. Kiab knows it is difficult for her sister to be the primary support for their father, but rather than stating this directly, she invites Neeb to spend more time with her family, explaining how this would be good for her children. A therapist working with this family would need to share the deep respect for the father and the way the family quietly shares their burdens. Greta, who has just walked out of a session with Lars and Vina, is now talking with Neeb, Luv, and Kiab for the first time. Neeb has been reluctant to leave his home for more than short errands. Greta is helping them renegotiate care for Neeb so Luv can meet her goal of completing a college degree.

Greta: Neeb, I see your daughters take very good care of you.
Neeb: I am blessed to have such wonderful children.
Kiab: We love him very much.
Luv: We are grateful to have a good father that would do anything for his family.
Greta: Yes, I can see that. Luv you live with your father, or he lives with you?

Luv: Yes, we live together. My mother is gone so it is just us in the house now.
Greta: And you are in school? College?
Luv: Yes I am getting a degree in advertising.
Greta: Neeb, now both of your children will have college degrees! Kiab, where do you live?
Kiab: I live close by with my husband and children. We are thinking father might like to come and stay with us some days when Luv is in school . . .

Many emotions and needs were expressed in this short exchange. The therapist noted that the father was well cared for. This complimented Luv as a caretaker and Neeb as a father who raised a loving daughter. The therapist also complimented the father by acknowledging the success of his children. Luv and Kiab acknowledged their father's sacrifice for them—the impact of war, migration, and loss—by showing gratitude and respect. Kiab was able to indirectly tell her father that it would be helpful to Luv for him to allow her to care for him some of the time without stating that he was a burden on anyone. The family might move into expression of more emotion, but it would be done slowly and within the family's cultural language.

Power

Experiential therapy relies on a relatively democratic view of families. Although parents must have influence over children, therapy takes on a quality of treating all family members with equal respect and concern, making room for all voices. This remains the goal but is not assumed.

⊷ ⟫

Socioculturally attuned experiential family therapists analyze power dynamics from the broadest global to the most intimate family relationships.

⊷ ⟫

Emotion and Power

Socioculturally attuned experiential therapists pay attention to how emotions are intrinsically connected to power dynamics and sociocultural context (Turner, 2007; Pease, 2012). For example, negative emotion has been found to be associated with getting less than one's fair share (Turner, 2007). Consider a family in which one of three children routinely feels overlooked compared to siblings who excel in academics or sports. This child is likely to have negative emotions about parents, siblings, and/or self. Those with greater influence and power tend to experience more positive emotions, particularly when they see themselves as getting the respect and rewards they expect and deserve. Following this example, now imagine the sibling who is amply rewarded for good grades gleefully running around the house. Getting more than we expect leads to even more positive emotions. Let's now say the athletic child unexpectedly won a spot in the state finals—eyes wide and mouth dropped open she lets out a shriek of delighted surprise. At the same time, the child who is routinely overlooked falls again into the background feeling jealous, hurt, and/or devalued in comparison. In this case, the social valuing of success in sports during childhood overrides qualities and potential (e.g., kindness, other orientation, contemplative nature) of the child who withdraws.

Overall, those with less influence and privilege tend to feel more negative emotions, including hurt, shame, guilt, and/or anger. Anger toward others tends to result from viewing others as responsible for not getting what we expect and/or feel we have earned. This can be part of our sense of entitlement. Shame and embarrassment tend to follow perceptions that we are at fault for not getting what we expect (Turner, 2007). Those who have less power may feel less worthy, turning to feelings of shame, guilt, or worthlessness. Consider the impact of unexamined gender, race or class privilege in which those with greater privilege expect more and believe at some level those who have less deserve less. Let's go back to our example of Lars and Vina. Lars has had a lifetime of male privilege. Even as a child, he experienced higher expectations being placed on him than on his sisters. These expectations sent him the message that as a male he was worth more. The deference shown him within the family (e.g., compliments for working hard, being excused after a meal while his sisters cleaned up) followed him through adulthood. Vina, on the other hand, received messages throughout her life that she was to accommodate and attune to others' needs.

Emotion and Resistance

According to Garcia, Košutić, and McDowell (2015) "emotions can fuel our social awareness and resistance to oppression, . . . prompt us to contribute, perhaps unwittingly, to oppression, [or] . . . intervene in our ability to see and resist oppression" (pp. 3–4). Power is reproduced in part through emotions that hold in place dominant systems of thinking, doing, and being. Emotions also contribute to resistance to oppression. Social movements are often associated with feelings such as anger over social injustice, love, and selfless solidarity.

↞⟶

Feelings produced through processes of marginalization and oppression, as well as those that emerge from growing awareness of power structures, can mobilize us into action.

↞⟶

This felt resistance is essential for social change just as it is essential for interpersonal change. Consider a heterosexual couple who came to therapy with their only child, Laura (age 16). Laura and her father, David, frequently engaged in verbal conflict. Laura's mother, Kim, silently disagrees with David's strict fathering and experiences her own frustrations with his attempts to control their marriage. The socioculturally attuned experiential family therapist, Latisha, engaged the family in a sculpt. The family placed themselves in the room showing David with his finger wagging at Laura who is standing up to him. Kim was behind Laura offering her support. As she was helping the family with the sculpt Latisha asked what contributed to the father being in such a position of power. Along with personality and physical size, the family identified that he made most of the money. Latisha slipped one of the platforms she kept in her office under the father, raising his height in the sculpt as she continued to explore. Laura blurted out "Because he is the man and no one will stand up to him!" Latisha took out another platform, suggesting it represented male privilege. The family began to see how both women, mother and daughter, struggled against male privilege and the valuing of money producing work over other types of work (e.g., running a family, school work, housework, relational work). This dynamic maintained the father's power but kept him from truly connecting with those he loved the most—his wife and daughter. Latisha continued to engage the family in exploring and expressing how societally supported power dynamics impacted their relationships and helped them all resist dynamics that were harmful to their growth as individuals and connections as a family.

Connection and Equity

Power is highly nuanced and deeply impacts emotional attunement in intimate relationships. According to Knudson-Martin (2015):

> When power is not equal, the more powerful partner will be less aware of the other's experience. What makes it more complicated is that people in higher power positions generally are not aware of their power; they may not even realize that others are attentive to their needs or that their interests are dominating the agenda. On the other hand, people in less powerful positions are likely to automatically take into account the desires or expectations of the more powerful. People in powerful roles (i.e., teacher, employer, physician, husband) may take for granted that others accommodate them—or become distressed when they do not.
>
> (p. 16)

For example, children with an abusive parent often become highly attuned to the parent's feelings, reading footsteps, facial expressions, and voice tone for indications of mood. Those in power often lack awareness of the damage their power causes relationships. It is not uncommon for people of color to point out how they must be knowledgeable and attuned to white people and the dominant culture to be able to successfully navigate U.S. society. White people, on the other hand, may choose to go their whole lives without listening to the experience of people of color or learning about another culture.

Imagine how paying attention to connection and equity might change the therapeutic process. For example, women often present as more emotionally expressive. In heterosexual relationships emotional descriptions of needs are often repeated to male partners, who in turn dismiss or pay cursory attention to requests. Experiential therapists work to help both partners understand and empathize with the other's feelings and needs. Consider viewing a female partner's emotional escalation as an attempt to influence a more powerful partner. She is bidding for connection and relying on empathy as a pathway to influence and/or as a way to prevent her partner from becoming upset. A socioculturally attuned experiential therapist would notice this and encourage shared power by helping the male partner learn to listen and attune to the female partner.

Third Order Change

➤←➤

Third order change involves going beyond understanding each other to understanding the impact of societal contexts on our relationships, including how societal structures support the voice and welfare of some at the expense of others.

➤←➤

Let's go back to Lars and Vina one more time. First order change might result if the therapist, Greta, were to help Vina explore her needs and set limits as a caretaker. Second order change might include Greta helping Lars and Vina understand their own and each other's frustrations, emotions, and experiences. Greater understanding and improved communication would help them both meet individual needs while negotiating a more satisfying relationship. Third order change would target understanding the broader societal context in which caring for an elder occurs. They would be able to name how caretaking and emotion work is devalued in U.S. society and most often relegated to women. They would become more overtly aware of how their relationship is affected by societal power dynamics; the power difference between an older father and younger daughter. Lars and Vina would begin to recognize how male privilege and power erodes the possibility for harmony and closeness in their relationship. Lars could become softer and more emotionally available in his later years while Vina could become more empowered in her adulthood.

Practice Guidelines

Understanding the impact of societal systems on presenting problems increases therapists' ability to attune to client experience and tailor experiential interventions. Following are four guidelines important to practicing socioculturally attuned experiential family therapy. These include honoring culturally relevant experience and expression, encouraging awareness of self and other in context, attending to the relationship between power and emotion, and promoting equity based attunement and connection.

1. Honoring Culturally Relevant Experience and Expression

Every culture has rituals, traditions, and ceremonies that promote resilience and demonstrate collective values and beliefs. These serve many societal functions, including punctuating life cycle transitions, enhancing cultural norms, or solidifying religious beliefs. Most cultures have specific religious ceremonies for a person's birth, marriage, school graduation, initiation, coming of age, marriage, and death. These rituals offer insight into culturally informed beliefs about what is appropriate at a given age, for a specific gender, or a specific religion. Rites of passages may be formal (e.g., quinceanera, sweet sixteen party, or a debutante ball), or informal (e.g., such as rites for boys like joining a gang/fraternity, drinking alcohol, having sex, driving a car, getting into a fight, or registering for Selective Services). There are also countless healing and cleansing rituals, meditation practices, and prayer rituals.

There are ample opportunities for therapists to **attune** to cultural rituals and traditions to help clients work through difficult transitions, problems, or merely connect with cultural traditions they may have lost or forgotten. Asking clients if they have cultural, personal, family, and/or religious rituals, traditions, or ceremonies may help therapists gain greater insight as to other ways of "being" in the therapy room that expand action-oriented, creative, and sometimes non-verbal forms of expression.

It is also important for therapists to **attune** to the cultural nuances of nonverbal expression and communication and to honor those forms of expression in therapy. There are many ways in which our actions express culturally ascribed ways of being. How we use silence, touch, facial expressions, movements, embodiment, and physical closeness and distance all influence our gender and cultural expression. So often, therapists unknowingly adhere to androcentric, Eurocentric, and/or Westernized beliefs about what forms of communication and expression are privileged. Being open to learning and honoring multiple forms of expression is especially important for socioculturally attuned experiential family therapists. For many, connection and understanding can be best accessed with a glance, touch, or embrace. Clients need permission and the space to use all forms of expression that honor multiple ways of knowing, being, and relating to each other across cultural and relational contexts.

2. Encouraging Awareness of Self and Other in Context

Familiarity with societal systems and power dynamics is necessary to guide therapy in ways that attend to how the most intimate experience is affected by individual, relational, and societal systems.

❧←→❧

Socioculturally attuned experiential family therapists pay close attention to societal systems and the nuances of power that block potential for growth in any and all family members.

❧←→❧

Those with greater societally assigned power are often unaware of the negative impact their power has on others. This creates pockets of stagnation for everyone involved. Consider David, a conservative Christian in a patriarchal family in which the husband/father is regularly accommodated by the wife/mother and children. Although family members and the church expect him to be a spiritual leader, the father confuses this role with a *power over* stance in which he expects to make all final decisions and have his needs met first. He is unaware of the full impact of his actions as he experiences the positive effects of being accommodated without always knowing others are yielding or bending to his will. His wife and children feel routinely dismissed and forgo many of their own needs to meet his. It is relatively simple to see how the needs of the wife and children take a back seat, potentially limiting their growth and potential.

It is less clear that this dynamic also harms David, who is unaware of the increasing emotional gap or the growth-limiting effects of being consistently accommodated by others. He is not challenged to put others first or to expand his faith by learning to truly serve, rather than control and "lead" the ones he loves. As he ages and turns toward his relationships for support and meaning, he is likely to be stunned and disappointed by the distance and resentment his behavior caused. Socioculturally attuned experiential therapists **name** inequities to help free *all* family members, including those in dominant positions, from the constraints of power imbalances, keeping in mind the well-being of all.

3. Exploring Relationships Between Power, Emotion, and Expression

❧←→❧

Societal and interpersonal power dynamics may result in some family members being heard more loudly and/or accommodated by others both in and out of the family.

❧←→❧

Those with less power may be emotionally demonstrative or shut down completely, preoccupied or guarded. As therapists work to bring forth emotional experience in the room, they need to attend to power imbalances by helping more powerful persons attune and **value** the experience of those who are less powerful, working to avoid eliciting even more vulnerability from less powerful persons. When powerful persons become more attuned, they are also better able to respond in caring and relationally accountable ways. Understanding self and other in societal context increases willingness of more powerful family members to step down from their positions and connect with others. Facing one's own privilege opens opportunities to be more accountable to loved ones, maintaining healthier interpersonal relationships.

Families must also be able to explore and support each other's experiences relative to power dynamics outside the family. Consider Sarah, who routinely experienced harassment from a male colleague at work. She and her husband, Nathan, entered therapy to find a way to deal with her growing anxiety and depression. Nathan told the therapist he had "tried everything short of beating [Sarah's colleague] up!" Sarah often came home distraught from being yelled at by her colleague or being the recipient of his unreasonable demands. Nathan responded to Sarah's emotional upset by becoming angry himself or telling Sarah what she should do. The therapist in this situation helped Nathan become more aware of societal dynamics around gender and to emotionally attune to Sarah. The situations at work and home were both embedded in gendered power dynamics, leaving Sarah with nowhere to turn where her experience and emotions could be validated. As Sarah and Nathan became more aware of gender and power, Sarah could take the lead (with Nathan's support) in reporting her colleague's behavior to Human Resources.

4. Promoting Equity Based Attunement and Connection

As the choreographer of the session, socioculturally attuned family therapists use themselves and their experience in the room to promote equity based attunement among family members.

⟵ ⟶

Mutual attunement includes willingness on the part of everyone to pay close attention to each other's experiences, not only understanding, but responding in ways that prioritize connection.

⟵ ⟶

Children may not feel heard or even have words for what they are experiencing. Less powerful persons with differing views may feel shut down in conversations and family decisions or not even be able to articulate their experience as there is no common language to legitimize their perspectives. Socioculturally attuned experiential therapists notice when those in centered, dominant positions subtly dismiss the experiences of those with less power or those on the edges of family belonging, and create experiences that **name** their realities and **value** their voices.

Attunement infers attempting to be with others, bear witness to their testimony, help them make meaning of their experience, and walk next to them in their journey. In effect, we are **intervening** by inviting family members to socioculturally attune to each other. To do this family members must be aware of the societal contexts that shape their lives and the impact of power dynamics on their relationships.

⟵ ⟶

Awareness must go hand-in-hand with the willingness and ability to tune in and effectively respond to each other.

⟵ ⟶

Consider a family living in the rural Midwest U.S. in which Lou, age 14, who was assigned male at birth, is perceiving and experiencing herself as female. When Lou's family is out of the house she tries on her sister's clothes and experiments with makeup. She shares this with no one, prays for her urges to go away, and is terrified of being found out. There is no one who talks about gender in her family or community; Lou just knows not to speak. When Lou is able to get access to the internet at school, she discovers she is not alone. She is not wrong because she has been assigned the wrong sex and gender. She now grows emotionally and intellectually alongside this liberating information, reaching out to others through the internet. Later, when she transitions and decides to tell her family, they will need to socioculturally attune to her in order for the family to continue into the future together. Parents and siblings will need socioeducation about transgender identity and rights. They will need to be able to listen to and empathize with Lou's silenced and marginalized experience. Her family will need to share emotion in ways that bring them together.

A socioculturally attuned experiential family therapist would facilitate this type of under-standing and attuning within societal context. The therapist would interrupt microaggressions such as parents asking what they did wrong. They would help the family challenge power dynamics that insinuate cisgender children are "normal" and **envision** acceptance and sup-port. As the family moves through this process the therapist might encourage them to engage in a type of renaming ritual (Brown, Dimitriou, & Dresner, 2010). Brown et al. (2010) described engaging in renaming rituals with African American youth who are "given a name at birth, and how during the struggles of childhood and young adulthood . . . may lose his/her way and need to be reminded of the name's significance to the community he/she belongs to" (p. 334). The ritual involves family and community sitting in concentric circles around the youth and stating aloud the meaning of the youth's name along with poems, songs, or other meaningful readings. Lou would have an opportunity to reflect before the community stands to affirm a new name that describes her journey and future. In our case, the therapist might encourage **transformation** by asking supportive family and friends to gather to wit-ness Lou's journey by telling stories of her strength, affirming her identity through prepared statements, poems, and music; and standing to verbally and symbolically pledge their support.

Case Illustration

Emilio presented in therapy due to feelings of sadness and confusion about his marriage. He and his wife, Mandy, had been married for 14 years. Many of those years had been difficult. He loved his wife, but she often got angry at him. He felt as though Mandy did not under-stand him or appreciate the efforts he made for her and their family. Emilio reported that most of their important discussions ended in heated arguments. He was a practicing Catholic, 32 years old, from the Dominican Republic. Mandy, who was European American, was from Dallas, Texas, and grew up Baptist. Both were college educated and wanted to raise their children as Christians. They shared values around family and education. Their therapist Leah was of bicultural descent. Her mother was from the northeast U.S. and her father was Puerto Rican. Leah grew up in Puerto Rico and was fluent in Spanish and English. She shared her clients' experience of being from a mixed cultural family. Leah asked Emilio if he would consider inviting his wife to couples therapy given that most of his concerns centered around his marriage.

The therapist began by spending time helping Mandy feel welcome. She focused on join-ing with her, asking about her life and background, and what her hopes were for the therapy process. Mandy was forthcoming but it became apparent that both Mandy and Emilio had difficulties expressing their emotions and did not openly discuss their thoughts or feelings. Mandy often responded with "I don't know" or "I'm not sure" and Emilio responded non-verbally, by just shaking his head yes or no or lifting his shoulders. After the therapist was able to understand their presenting problem and gather information about their individual and couple history, it was still apparent that they were not able to fully express themselves in session. They seemed to be stifling their responses and emotions. Neither of them reported a history of violence, substance abuse, addiction, infidelity, financial distress, personal health problems, or any other individual and contextual issue compounding their marriage. Both had jobs they enjoyed and their children, ages 4 and 6, seemed to be doing well. After the fourth conjoint session, the therapist asked if they were interested in trying an experiential and creative approach to therapy.

Honoring Culturally Relevant Experience and Expression

Given that both the therapist and Emilio were from a Latin/Caribbean culture, Leah asked if they would be interested in making a series of altars or shadow boxes for themselves as individuals and for themselves as a couple. "Altares", as they are called in Spanish, are personally handmade or assembled shrines or spaces that serve many functions, not only to spiritually honor deceased family members, but also as a way to express one's culture, relationships, and the things a person, couple, or family may value (Bermudez & Bermudez, 2002). Altares can be small movable shadow boxes, temporary shrines, such as those created for the Day of the Dead in Mexico, or more permanent shrines, such as those that occupy a small nook in homes to memorialize someone or something. Deeply rooted in Latino, Indigenous, Catholic, and Afro-Caribbean cultures, altar-making invites people to honor what they believe to be sacred, important, and meaningful, offering an opportunity to openly and publicly express those sentiments to others. In therapy, the process enables clients to express emotions and have an experience that engenders a deeper experiential level of individual and relational growth.

Emilio and Mandy made three large shadow boxes—one for each of them and one for them as a couple. They gathered things that were significant to them as individuals and as a couple and family. Per the therapist's request, they brought their boxes and the things they had gathered to therapy (e.g., pictures, prayers, figurines, small objects such as a needle and thread, pictures from magazine clippings, small action figures, perfume bottle, family pictures, candles, flags, small patches and awards, silk flowers, jewelry).

Encouraging Awareness of Self and Other in Context

Emilio and Mandy were able to talk about their shadow boxes as they created them. As the couple talked about their altars, the therapist was able to be open and transparent with her experiences growing up in a bicultural home. She also explained that she was going to assume multiple stances in their process, such as catalyst, witness, coach, investigator, supporter, etc. The therapist asked questions and made comments such as: "Tell me about the objects you brought in," "What does this mean to you?" "Where did it come from?" "What are your greatest memories about this?" "When did you become aware that this person/thing was important to you?" "As you look at your shared altar, what does this mean for you? Is there anything missing?" "What would you add or change?" "What do you want your spouse to know about this?" "What would others think if they saw this?" Asking questions helped Mandy and Emilio discuss the meaning surrounding what they were doing. Having a creative and culturally relevant process helped them talk about issues such as culture, values, traditions, wishes, and fears in ways they had not been able to before.

Exploring Relationships Between Power, Emotion, and Expression

The couple began their process by placing all of the pictures and objects on the table. The therapist asked them about what each one of the objects meant. They had a large grouping of matches, a wine cork and label, coins, rocks, plastic wedding bands, softball pictures, images of the beach, college memorabilia, concert stubs, and pictures of their children when they were born. After they discussed the objects and pictures they began to work together to place the images in the shadow box. As they worked, the therapist asked them questions about the influences that have been instrumental in helping them remain strong as couple, as well as the social forces that were negatively affecting their connection. These questions were difficult to answer; however, having the physical representation to reference helped them discuss what had caused the drifting apart and the distance and isolation they were experiencing.

As Mandy and Emilio looked at their own personal altars and shared them with each other, they began to notice important differences and similarities in what they valued. Mandy began to cry when she noticed that Emilio had a cross with flowers at the center of his altar along with images of his family and his country. Her images and objects reflected more about her individual hobbies and interests. When the therapist asked Mandy what her tears meant, she said that she realized that he missed his family and country of origin and that she was sad that she had not been able to help him stay more connected to his culture and family back home. He reassured her that it was not her fault, and although it was true he felt isolated and lonely and missed his family, he loved her very much and that she and their children were his main priority.

Seeing their individual altars and being able to talk about them in an accepting and non-judgmental way helped Mandy and Emilio express their emotions in new ways. With the therapist's prompts, they were able to openly talk about the gender and cultural scripts, including how being a man had paralyzed Emilio, preventing him from talking about the helplessness he felt and his need to connect with his wife and family of origin more often and in meaningful ways. He missed sharing celebrations and honoring his cultural traditions. Although Emilio felt powerful in his day-to-day life, he felt as though Mandy held most of the power in their relationship because she spoke English with an U.S. accent, was not an immigrant, and understood many more things about U.S. culture.

Although Mandy spoke Spanish and greatly appreciated Emilio's culture, she admitted that she honored her traditions more with their children and often compared him to "American" friends that "seemed to have it more together." She also was able to talk about how she felt the need to "give" him more power by "letting him" make important decisions, manage their finances, and "let him" win fights so that he would not feel like less of a man. The process of having honesty, trust, and vulnerability enabled them to position themselves to begin to make the couple altar together.

The couple began to identify the many social forces blocking their potential. For Emilio, it was his pride and his inability to admit that he was fearful and worried about losing Mandy. For Mandy, it was primarily the social comparisons and not honoring Emilio's culture and values. She realized that his values centered around his faith and family and her values centered around material wealth and shared experiences and traditions from her culture. They were able to talk about how power dynamics between the Dominican Republic and the U.S. promoted privileging Mandy's culture. Mandy's white privilege was a salient factor in their daily lives and relationship. They had not found ways to openly acknowledge this privilege before therapy. By both of them understanding the blocks to their potential as a couple, they began to open up and strengthen their ability to attune to each other's needs, fears, hopes, and desires, as well as goals for their marriage.

Promote Equity Based Attunement and Connection

After seeing all three altars side by side, and having the experience of making them and discussing their multiple meanings, Emilio and Mandy were able to experience themselves and their relationship in a different way. They became more attuned to one another, bearing witness to their testimony of pain, loss, regret, and their hopes for the future. The therapist guided them on this journey of self and mutual exploration and contemplation. By discussing social forces that were working against them, such as narrowly defined masculinity/machismo, immigration status, and rigid gender and cultural scripts, they were able to see how their different societal contexts shaped their lives and the expectations for their marriage and life together. Upon the completion of therapy, the couple was able to use the altars as a reminder of their process of growth.

Summary: Third Order Change

In this case, Emilio and Mandy were able to engage in third order change by going beyond understanding each other, to understanding the impact of their societal contexts. The global power dynamics and resource disparity between the U.S. and the Dominican Republic shaped many aspects of their lives, including who had more societal privilege, whose cultural practices were centered, and how they negotiated power dynamics relative to gender, language/accent, and race. Societal structures in the U.S. supported the voice and welfare of Mandy at the expense of Emilio in some ways and Emilio's male privilege supported his welfare over Mandy's in other ways. When they were unaware of how these dynamics shaped their relationship, they were more likely to assign their problems to themselves and each other as individuals. By the end of therapy they not only understood and appreciated each other's experiences more, but were able to come together to challenge oppressive societal forces on behalf of themselves, each other, and their children.

References

Banmen, J., & Maki-Banmen, K. (2014). What has become of Virginia Satir's therapy model since she left us in 1988? *Journal of Family Psychotherapy, 25*(2), 117–131.

Bermudez, J. M., & Bermudez, S. (2002). Altar-making with Latino families: A narrative therapy perspective. *Journal of Family Psychotherapy, 13*(3/4), 329–347. [Reprinted in T. D. Carlson and M. J. Erickson (Eds.), *Spirituality and family therapy* (pp. 329–248). New York, NY: Haworth Press.]

Brown, A., Dimitriou, M., & Dressner, L. (2010). Rituals as tools of resistance: From survival to liberation. In B. J. Risman (Ed.), *Families as they really are* (pp. 328–336). New York, NY: W. W. Norton.

ChenFeng, J., Kim, L., Knudson-Martin, C., & Wu, Y. (2017). Application of socio-emotional relationship therapy with couples of Asian heritage: Addressing issues of culture, gender, and power. *Family Process, 56,* 558–573.

Connell, G., Mitten, T., & Bumberry, W. (1999). *Reshaping family relationships: The symbolic therapy of Carl Whitaker.* New York, NY: Brunner & Mazel.

Fitzpatrick, K., & LaGlory, M. (2000). *Unhealthy places: The ecology of risk in the urban landscape.* New York, NY: Routledge.

Garcia, M., Košutić, I., & McDowell, T. (2015). Peace on Earth/war at home: The role of emotion regulation in social justice work. *Journal of Feminist Family Therapy, 27*(1), 1–20.

Knudson-Martin, C. (2015). When therapy challenges patriarchy: Undoing gendered power in heterosexual couple relationships. In C. Knudson-Martin, M. A. Wells, & S. K. Samman (Eds.), *Socio-emotional relationship therapy: Bridging emotion, societal context, and couple interaction* (pp. 15–26). New York, NY: Springer.

Košutić, I., & McDowell, T. (2008). Diversity and social justice issues in family therapy literature: A decade review. *Journal of Feminist Family Therapy, 20*(2), 142–165.

McDowell, T., (2015). *Applying critical social theory to family therapy practice.* New York, NY: Springer.

Napier, A. Y., & Whitaker, C. (1978). *The family crucible: The intense experience of family therapy.* New York, NY: Harper & Row.

Papp, P., Scheinkman, M., & Malpas, J. (2013). Breaking the mold: Sculpting impasses in couples therapy. *Family Process, 52*(1), 33–45.

Pease, B. (2012). The politics of gendered emotions: Disrupting men's emotional investment in privilege. *Australian Journal of Social Issues, 47*(1), 125–142.

Quek, K. M., & Knudson-Martin, C. (2006). A push towards equality: Processes among dual-income couples in a collectivist culture. *Journal of Marriage and Family, 68,* 56–69.

Roberts, J. (2005). Transparency and self-disclosure in family therapy: Dangers and possibilities. *Family Process, 44*(1), 45–63.

Satir, V. (1967). *Conjoint family therapy: A guide to theory and technique* (Rev. ed.). Palo Alto, CA: Science and Behavior Books. (Original work published 1964.)

Turner, J. H. (2007). Justice and emotions. *Social Justice Research, 20*(3), 288–311.

7   Socioculturally Attuned Attachment Based Family Therapies

An infant makes soft baby sounds, gesturing excitedly with her hands. The child's father looks into her eyes, makes similar cooing sounds, and mirrors his daughter's gestures. The baby smiles and joins her father in their shared experience. This reciprocal engagement is the essence of attachment. Attachment is an interpersonal neurobiological system that draws infants and caregivers together and serves to organize motivational, emotional, and memory processes (Siegel, 2012).

Attachment's importance was first identified by John Bowlby (1952) in a report to the World Health Organization on the effects of maternal deprivation on British children orphaned during World War II. At that time, application of the theory tended to reify heteronormative and sexist assumptions that mothers are naturally bonded with their children and that care for children should be their primary role (Franzblau, 1999). The value of bonds with other caregivers or the multitude of contextual factors that influence caregiving processes received little attention (Birns, 1999; Minuchin, 2002). Since then, attachment theory has been more broadly studied and applied across the lifespan, elucidating the complex bonds between biology, relationship, and social context (Cozolino, 2016; Siegel, 2012; van der Kolk, 2014) and even applying the theory to the relationships between animals and humans (Walsh, 2009).

Whether working with adults or children, attachment based family therapies (ABFTs) focus on strengthening the emotional connections among significant others. They begin with the premise that "needing and receiving closeness and support is the essence of being human" (Greenberg & Goldman, 2008, p. 84). There are a number of attachment based approaches to couple and family therapy. Among the best known are emotionally focused therapy (Johnson, 2004), emotionally focused family therapy (Johnson & Lee, 2000; Willis, Haslam, & Bermudez, 2016), attachment focused family therapy (Hughes, 2011), attachment based family therapy (Diamond, Diamond, & Levy, 2014), and emotion focused couples therapy (Greenberg & Goldman, 2008). Family therapists also draw widely on approaches that emphasize interpersonal neurobiology (i.e., Cozolino, 2016; Fishbane, 2013; van der Kolk, 2014) and the social construction of identity and emotion (Knudson-Martin & Huenergardt, 2010; Knudson-Martin, Wells, & Samman, 2015).

Third order change begins when therapists **attune** to clients' experiences of connection and belonging, apprehending their experience in relation to social locations and societal power.

＊←→

Families engage in third order change when they are able to overcome sociocultural processes that inhibit attachment and enhance a sense of safety and belonging in complex webs of individual, relational, and societal contexts.

＊←→

As therapists **name** the clients' contextual experience, clients feel understood and validated. They see themselves and their place in the world through a wider lens and **value** relational needs and behaviors that are often minimized or pathologized by the dominant culture. Therapists position their work to **intervene** in inequitable power processes that interfere with attachment responses and result in isolation and marginalization. The goal is to facilitate new experience that supports attachment bonds and empowers clients to **envision** choices in how they relate to others and **transform** roles and identities. In this chapter we outline five enduring family therapy concepts associated with attachment, then integrate principles of sociocultural attunement. We conclude with guidelines for socioculturally attuned practice and a case example.

Primary Enduring Attachment Based Family Therapy Concepts

Sometimes people think of attachment primarily as a personal internalized model of relating. If early caregivers were responsive, we engage with others from a secure base that enables autonomy and optimism (e.g., Ainsworth, Blehar, Waters, & Wall, 1978). If not, we approach life with caution or uncertainty. Individuals are assessed as securely attached, avoidantly attached, anxiously/ambivalently attached, or disorganized. Although these categorizations can be useful, family therapists focus on attachment as a systemic relational process across the lifespan, rather than a static individual state (Johnson, 2003).

In contrast to dominant Western culture that privileges autonomy, independence, and competition, attachment perspectives value relational needs and focus on processes around nurturing and giving care. The enduring family therapy concepts that follow help clarify the systemic, interactive nature of attachment: focus on relational process; mutual emotional regulation; reciprocity, interdependence, and responsiveness; relational security and trust; and change through emotional connection.

Focus on Relational Process

The earlier example of father and daughter illustrated the interactive nature of attachment. Let's call the child Mayuri. Attachment occurs *between* Mayuri and her significant caregivers. Mayuri has multiple caregivers. Her parents are divorced and share physical custody. They have arranged their work schedules so that each parent serves as primary caregiver three days a week. On the days they are the primary parent, each drops Mayuri off at a daycare well-staffed to care for infants. How long she is at the daycare varies, but because each parent has some control over their work schedules, they seldom leave her more than 5 or 6 hours. Both parents report confidence in the daycare providers, but experience a pull to get home to their child as soon as possible. They long to touch and hold her. Because family is important to them, they alternate Sundays with grandparents, sometimes leaving Mayuri with them and sometimes spending the time in gatherings with their large extended families.

The relational processes among Mayuri and her primary caregivers create shared meaning and experience from the moment of birth. Ed Tronick (2009), who studied the psychophysiology of emotional communication between infants and caregivers, emphasized that children are not passive recipients of adult action; rather, each actively changes the other. Staying with Mayuri and her father, let's imagine a situation similar to what Tronick's observational studies showed. As her father tries to put her to bed, Mayuri squirms and grasps his hair. She detects her father's fleeting angry facial expression and loud "Hey!" (even though it lasted less than a second). Mayuri grabs his hands and looks away. Almost immediately father recognizes that Mayuri is distressed. He changes what he was doing and begins to soothe her, stroking her hair and speaking in a soft voice. At first Mayuri remains turned away from him, but over the next 30 seconds she begins to smile and look at him. When Tronick measured biopsychological changes in similar interactions, child and caregiver impacted the physiology of the other.

Whether working with parents and young children or adolescents or with adult relationships, attachment based family therapists focus on the processes by which participants are emotionally accessible and responsive to each other. They look for how people handle their inherent relational needs. Processes such as attunement, communication, adaptation, conflict resolution, and intimacy are at the core of ABFTs. When attachment processes are working well, as with Mayuri, children learn that they can depend on others to be there for them, to notice their needs and respond in ways that affirm their experience. Parents will not always give children everything they want and there will be conflict and disagreement in all relationships, but communication will be "contingent." This means there is two way dialogue in which "the receiver of the message listens with an open mind and all of his or her senses" (Siegel & Hartzell, 2014, p. 82). Response is contingent on what was actually communicated, rather than automatic, predetermined, or disengaged.

When communication is contingent, "the quality, intensity, and timing of the other's signals clearly reflect the signals that we have sent" (Siegel & Hartzell, 2014, p. 84). When this happens, we feel "felt" or attuned to, that we are not alone. This interpersonal process shapes the neural processes by which our internal models of self-in-relation are encoded. When responses of significant others affirm our experience, we feel grounded and our sense of "self" is connected to something larger than ourselves. As with Mayuri, when there are ruptures to the immediate connection, they can be repaired. Adult experience is also emotionally present and appropriately available to children. Even at this very young age, Mayuri is learning that she has an impact upon and can influence her father and the other caregivers in her life. She learns to trust that she is safe and the world predictable, and also learns to reciprocally attune to the needs and experiences of others (Tuttle, Knudson-Martin, & Kim, 2012).

From an attachment perspective, seeking and maintaining emotional contact is at the heart of healthy development. Isolation and loss are traumatizing. Need for responsive, security-enhancing relationships continues throughout life (Knudson-Martin, 2012; Mikulincer & Shaver, 2012). The ability to move toward others in times of stress and crisis improves health and resilience (Taylor, 2002). Though adults are expected to set the tone with children, adult partners expect responsibility for the relationship to be shared (Johnson, 2004; Knudson-Martin & Huenergardt, 2010). Although early relational experiences shape an initial working model of attachment, new experiences continue to modify and elaborate internal attachment models (Johnson, 2004). Hurtful experiences of trauma, loss, and betrayal can move people from security to insecurity, and attuned mutually supportive relationships can help heal old wounds.

Mutual Emotional Regulation

Human neural systems are designed to be interdependent (Cozolino, 2016; Fishbane, 2013). In order to develop, we must exchange emotion and information through what Cozolino calls "the social synapse" (p. 19). Emotion is a signaling process that bridges self, relationships, and larger systems, telling us what to pay attention to and how to judge meaning (Greenberg & Goldman, 2008; Siegel, 2012). Through the sharing of emotion, "we participate in the way each other's brains are built, how they develop, and how they function" (Cozolino, 2016, p. 87). The interactions between Mayuri and her father are not simply behavioral events; they are also emotional processes that connect daughter and father neurologically.

Mirror neurons enable people to share affective states (Siegel, 2012). They are specialized cells in the frontal lobes that permit us to viscerally apprehend another's emotional state and intentions. They let Mayuri's father register her distress and revise his response to her almost instantaneously. Attuned interaction between parent and child allows the parent's more mature brain to shape the child's developing one. The parent tracks the child's state and temporarily aligns with it. The child feels felt and her aroused state is calmed. Over time, a healthy pattern of arousal and inhibition not excessive in either direction is established (Siegel, 2012).

Attuned communication remains significant throughout the lifespan, especially during times of stress or trauma (Bowlby, 1988; Johnson, 2004). Clinical issues often relate to how people try to manage painful emotion without adequate emotional support. Efforts to regulate tender emotions such as isolation or worthlessness can be destructive. When a parent or partner (or therapist) is not attuned to our primary emotional states, words can seem empty, reinforcing a sense of being alone. Persons with secure attachment histories are more likely to be able to autoregulate how they express emotion and respond to another with an attitude of acceptance, curiosity, and empathy (Hughes, 2009).

Reciprocity, Interdependence, and Responsiveness

Without mutual attunement and responsiveness, the innate interdependence of relationships can be unsafe. Although Mayuri's parents, Rajan and Lakshmi, are able to provide a secure base for their daughter, they were not able to do so for each other. It was not until after the separation and discovering that he needed to orient himself toward his daughter's needs, that Rajan realized how out of touch he had been with Lakshmi's relational needs and experience. He had felt secure and independent in the world, but did not attune to his wife and did not know how to respond to her fear, sadness, and anxiety during their marriage and pregnancy. Lakshmi described feeling alone and misunderstood. She could not trust that Rajan cared about her or what she needed, and after a while disengaged from him.

The neuroemotional process of shared affect is inherently reciprocal and requires symmetrical power positions (Hughes, 2009). When roles are unequal, as between parent and child (or therapist and client), the more powerful persons (parents) must follow the child's lead and intentionally open themselves to taking in the experience of other (children). When parents communicate acceptance of their child's emotion, the child experiences mutual respect and love rather than shame or disgust (Trevarthen, 2009). As children experience their parent being sensitive and responsive to them, they develop reflective functioning that helps them make sense of their own experience and that of others (Hughes, 2011). When parents also communicate the impact of the child's behavior on them, this mutual intersubjective experience promotes relational security and trust that guides the child's life with others.

Relational Security and Trust

Secure attachment bonds provide a safe haven against life's stressors (Johnson, 2002). "Simply holding the hand of a loving partner can affect us profoundly, literally calming jittery neurons in the brain" (Johnson, 2008, p. 26). If one's working model of self and other does not anticipate safety, people develop other adaptive responses. It is a matter of survival. Porges' (2009) Polyvagal theory helps explain the internal process. The vagus nerve connects the brain with other organs such as the heart, stomach, and facial muscles. It has multiple pathways. The usual instinctual response to a threat is to draw on the branch of the nerve that seeks engagement and connection to others. But when others are not expected to be safe, the other side takes over, shutting down these human connections. We may put up our guard, fight, or withdraw.

In our example, Lakshmi had originally felt safe with Rajan. Because she had not always experienced safety with others, she was selective in whom she trusted and had learned to withdraw when people did not meet her needs. Rajan had been well tended as a child, but had spent many years depending on himself in a new culture where he felt somewhat an outsider. He had not learned to tune into or depend on another. Their 3 year marriage did not provide Lakshmi and Rajan with a secure base. They were able to successfully co-parent, but depending on each other for emotional support was more difficult. Had either of them experienced physical or sexual abuse or other trauma, their dependence on each other might have felt even more risky. If one of them had been unfaithful, their sense of betrayal would likely have compounded the lack of safety and trust.

Change Through Emotional Connection

ABFTs work by creating a safe environment in which people are able to experience new responses to vulnerable emotions. "As families learn to respond to one another in ways that are supportive and nurturing . . . attachment to other family members can gradually become more secure" (Willis et al., 2016, p. 1). ABFTs are active, present-oriented approaches in which experience is heightened through intersubjective dialogue, enactments, and/or play. This enables couples and family members to experience positive physical and emotional connections that literally rewire the brain.

The therapeutic relationship must demonstrate secure attachment qualities (Hughes, 2011). Before couples or families can safely experience vulnerable emotions such as shame, loss, fear, sadness, desire, and longing for each other, the therapist must first attune to each person, seeking to understand and resonate with their underlying emotion. Therapists need to be open and genuinely engaged, including their experience of what clients present. They need to receive emotion openly and accept each person's experience. This requires the ability to co-regulate emotion accessed during the session and, to the extent developmentally appropriate, help people connect emotional responses to interactions with each other. Even young children can learn to recognize how they affect others (Siegel & Hartzell, 2014) and use play to generate solutions that connect one another and develop empathy, intimacy, and self-worth (Willis et al., 2016). Throughout the process, therapists recognize and attune to clients' affective desires and help them safely experience positive connections with each other.

Integrating Principles of Sociocultural Attunement

Attachment theory is often used within Western psychology to promote autonomy and goal achievement, e.g., that a strong attachment bond decreases a child's need to stay physically close and enables exploration (Cassidy, 2008) or that an adult can "continue pursuing other goals without having to interrupt them to engage in actual bids for proximity and protection" (Mikulincer & Shaver, 2012, p. 260). The value of the relational bonds themselves can get lost. ABFTs focus on relationships but typically remain decontextualized. ABFTs tend not to address societal influences or examine inequities in whose interests and values are being advanced. Therapists may also miss contextual factors contributing to clients' problems (Vatcher & Bongo, 2001). In this section we consider the connections between attachment processes and sociocultural contexts, explore how societal power dynamics create disparities in whose experience is attuned to and understood, and consider third order change from an attachment point of view.

Societal Context

The ability to nurture attachment bonds is not just an individual or family problem. Like many family and child advocates (e.g., Edelman, 1980, 1987), Bowlby (1988) described a dominant societal system not organized to support relational bonds:

> [In the] world's richest societies . . . man and woman power devoted to the production of material goods counts a plus in all our economic indices. Man and woman power devoted to the production of happy, healthy, and self reliant children in their own homes does not count at all.
>
> (Bowlby, 1988, p. 2)

A socioculturally attuned approach expands the lens to include the societal processes and contexts in which attachment processes occur.

Dominant Culture Assumptions and Contexts

Dominant cultural assumptions and contexts affect how theory is interpreted and applied. Attachment is likely to be viewed as a dyadic process without considering the role of other family members and social networks. We might assume that a child needs one primary caregiver. In fact, nonparental caregiving is either the norm or frequent in most societies (van Ijzendoorn & Sagi-Schwartz, 2008). In our example, Mayuri, whose grandparents immigrated to the U.S. from India, is benefitting from access to multiple caregivers.

⊷⊶

Attachment processes between two people are always connected to what is happening with other family members, as well as friends, community members, and social institutions and societal norms.

⊷⊶

For example, Rajan's parents had at first been very angry with Lakshmi. They insisted he sue her for full custody and were willing to use their considerable financial resources to carry the cost of a prolonged legal battle. Confused, Rajan turned to the pastor of his family's Christian church. The pastor was able to prevail upon the grandparents to take a different approach. His support enabled Rajan and Lakshmi to overcome anger and cordially share primary parenting. Focusing too narrowly on the parent-child relationship or the couple dyad can overlook the need for support within the larger community, and may sometimes hold individuals responsible for conditions out of their control.

We may also unintentionally hold women responsible for relational change. For example, in a recent demonstration of emotionally focused therapy, the therapist helped a man get in touch with vulnerable emotions that he did not usually express. The therapist ended by suggesting that his wife could help him manage these feelings. Though significant attachment figures should *reciprocally* play this role for each other, research shows that clinicians regularly put the burden of change on women and expect them to calm men (ChenFeng & Galick, 2015; Loscocco & Walzer, 2013). As a step toward mutual support, socioculturally attuned therapists could have interrupted this inequitable societal gender pattern by using the therapeutic relationship to support the husband in considering how his emotions might impact his wife and work with him to take responsibility for his emotion and response (Knudson-Martin & Huenergardt, 2010).

Warm personal styles might also be confused with attachment (Greenberg & Goldman, 2008). There are many ways loving and caring emotion can be expressed and experienced. For example, in Asian cultures expectations of "quiet fortitude" sometimes limit direct expression of worries or concerns so as not to burden others (ChenFeng, Kim, Knudson-Martin, & Wu, 2017). If Asian partners or family members demonstrate restrained emotional style, this does not necessarily mean less emotional attachment. Helping them share emotional vulnerabilities would still be part of an attachment based approach, but therapists would first attune to each person's sociocultural experience around expressing emotion and work slowly and gently with them, appreciating and demonstrating respect for less demonstrative styles while helping intimate partners find a process that works for them.

For example, Jessica ChenFeng drew on her shared heritage with a second generation Taiwanese American couple to help husband Brian emotionally engage with his wife Michelle (ChenFeng et al., 2017, p. 569).

Therapist: Brian, what did you notice that led you to initiate the conversation?

Brian: We got into an argument earlier that day and I noticed that I was upset about it. I kept thinking about it at work and wondered if it was impacting Michelle also . . . . I guess . . . (looking down) I felt bad about my tone of voice since I know now how much that affects her.

Therapist: And I also hear you acknowledging feeling bad. I know it's not typical for Asian American men to say things like that, especially with the experience you've shared about being put down in our American society; it's not easy to be open about what you're feeling . . . you're breaking out of gender expectations that our culture holds about being tough.

Michelle: Yah quite honestly, I'm still having a hard time believing this happened, but I'm so happy. I feel really connected to Brian for the first time in a long time.

Ideals regarding appropriate enactments of autonomy and dependence vary widely across cultures and contexts. If parents in Japan complete a child's sentence, that might be considered a sign of positive attunement linked to a secure attachment style; the same behavior in the U.S. would likely be viewed as intrusive and associated with an ambivalent attachment style (Rothbaum, Rose, Ujiie, & Uchida, 2002). In collectivist cultures, the hoped-for outcome of secure attachment would be willingness to coordinate one's needs with others; non-disruptive actions that "keep the peace" might be a sign of trust and security. In Western societies a secure person is typically viewed as one able to venture outward and take on independent tasks or roles.

Socioculturally attuned therapists would not be so quick to go along with cultural stereotypes or taken-for-granted expectations. Rather, they would help clients explore the relational consequences of cultural patterns. They would help parents consider what they would like their children to learn about engaging with others (e.g., Tuttle et al., 2012). For example, a Korean American couple brought their 5-year-old daughter, June, to therapy because they were concerned she was "disobedient and argumentative." As the therapist helped the parents attune to June's experience, they began to imaginatively take in what June was discovering about herself. Then the therapist helped the couple consider what "discovering herself" meant to them and how this fit with Korean and American ideas of how they wanted their child to relate. The therapist also attuned to the parents' shame around a "disobedient and argumentative" child, their sense that they were not good parents. After considering the sociocultural origins of their shame, the parents were more able to accept their daughter and take some pride in her independence while also clarifying which aspects of other-oriented behavior were important in their parenting.

Social Construction of Emotion

Neurobiological attachment processes are intricately intertwined with culture and context. From birth, the human brain is both internal and interpersonal, equipped to identify and feel the sensibilities of those around us (Trevarthen, 2009). What we feel is invited by particular social contexts. Rather than residing *within* an individual, emotions "link persons in the life of family and community" (Trevarthen, 2009, p. 56). When the Korean American couple mentioned earlier felt shame as parents, they were directly connected to a community of shared values and expectations that invited and gave meaning to their experience. Recognizing the contextual salience of emotion helps bring the larger societal context into the moment-by-moment of communication and interaction. And, as we'll discuss more later, our body's emotional read includes the power context; what we feel is always related to our place in the social hierarchy (Cozolino, 2016; Wetherell, 2012).

Gender and Relational Needs

The need to feel "felt," and the security and validation that comes from feeling connected to significant others is human. The creation of a gender binary that assigns people "male" or "female" at birth interferes with how relational needs are experienced, expressed, and heard (Davies, Reed, & Kim, 2016; Fricker, 2007; Knudson-Martin, 2013). In most societies attachment needs and behaviors are considered feminine. Characteristics associated with females are typically disvalued. Female experience is given less credibility and is less likely to be understood and validated (Fricker, 2007).

Many of us quickly learn that demonstrating relational qualities is not masculine. Boys and men must either disown major parts of themselves or manage the conflict between their relational selves and societal gender discourse. Masculine stereotypes encourage them to externalize vulnerable emotions and blame and objectify others. Many men come to parenting and intimate relationships without practice in intentionally focusing on others. Acknowledging dependency needs can be difficult. As in the previous example of Brian and Michelle, socioculturally attuned therapists counteract these societal gender patterns by helping men own vulnerable emotions. They expect that men can and do nurture, and actively facilitate their efforts to do so.

Similarly, touch is a vital human need for everyone. It is connected to brain development and the ability to organize emotion (Johnson, 2008). Societal messages about sex and touch may limit this aspect of attachment. Sue Johnson, who along with Les Greenberg developed emotionally focused therapy, noted that "North Americans are among the world's least tactile people" (p. 191). Males, in particular, are culturally conditioned to not seek touch. Boys are held and caressed less. In adulthood they may "funnel all of [their] attachment needs for physical and emotional connection into the bedroom" (Johnson, 2008, p. 192). People who do not feel safe to be emotionally vulnerable may seek what Johnson calls "sealed-off" sex that is focused on physical release rather than the relational bond. Their partners may feel used and objectified. Others may use sex as a way to find "solace," a way to feel reassured about attachment needs, especially when partners are not emotionally available. When sex is part of secure reciprocally attuned and responsive relationships, physical synchrony and emotional safety reinforce each other and partners can relax into mutual pleasuring (Johnson, 2008). Cultural gender stereotypes and objectifying discourse around sex interfere with indispensable non-sexual touching as well as emotionally safe and loving sexual relationships.

Class and Attachment

The ways attachment processes are theoretically described and researched tend to reflect Western middle-class values (Birns, 1999; Franzblau, 1999). Yet how people approach care giving and receiving varies considerably depending on social structure and the future they are preparing their children to enter (Lareau, 2003; Tuttle et al., 2012). Working-class parents have less control over their schedules and less income for quality daycare than the earlier example of Mayuri. The dispositions and values any of us bring to parenting and intimate relationships reflect the structured social arrangements we inhabit (Lareau, 2003).

For example, Luellen and her children were referred to therapy after her oldest son, Darnell (age 11) told a school counselor that his mother locked him in his room when he came home after curfew. Resonating with Luellen, a low income African American woman raising her boys in a neighborhood where many young men end up in gangs or victims of violence, required that the therapist attune to her emotional sense of how important it is that her sons be obedient, follow the rules. This would be necessary for them to safely negotiate racism and be successful in school. Independence and assertiveness, qualities often valued by white middle-class parents, would be risky in a world where Darnell could easily be judged as delinquent, defiant, or dangerous.

People nurture securely attached relationships across all socioeconomic strata (Birns, 1999). Members of economically disadvantaged groups often demonstrate considerable emotional resilience. For example, studies of children of Latino immigrants in the U.S. show high levels of emotional well-being and social skills (Fuller & Coll, 2010). Nonetheless, stresses such as limited economic resources, space, and time affect the structure and organization of family life (McDowell, 2015). Differences in measures of attachment security between socioeconomic contexts can usually be explained by the degree to which social environments support attachment processes (Bliwise, 1999).

Hermeneutical Justice

A core premise of attachment theory is that people develop a coherent self-narrative when their experience is attuned to and relationally validated (Siegel, 2012).

⊷⇥

The ability to make sense of one's experience may be disadvantaged when dominant cultural meanings systematically limit who can express themselves and be understood.

⊷⇥

For example, incongruence and resulting sense of isolation is likely for those who identify as gay and lesbian, transgender persons, and people who identify outside the gender binary (Davies et al., 2016; Devor, 2004). This is not simply a matter of parental criticism or rejection, it is part of the larger context in which the meanings of gender and sexuality are constructed. For example, Michael, who had transitioned from female to male about 10 years prior, sought therapy because he was anxious about a forthcoming career change. He described positive relationships with his family and a stable marriage to a woman. Yet in this situation in which he would be developing another aspect of his identity and new kinds of collaborative work relationships, he was faced afresh with what Miranda Fricker (2007) called *hermeneutical injustice*, inequities in whose experience is understood and given social credibility.

This means that the dominant culture offered little shared understanding as a resource to support his experience. According to Fricker (2007, p. 163), "it tends to knock your faith in your own ability to make sense of the world." At the start of therapy, Michael was confused by his anxiety because he anticipated his new colleagues would be accepting. But acceptance is different than *being known*. Over the years, Michael had adapted to unremitting hermeneutic isolation by disengaging from his own emotional experience. His family, partner, and friends tried to understand, but lacked collective meanings to activate mirror neurons to attune to him. Systemic obfuscation encouraged him to opt out of shared meaning making that constitutes the self (Fricker, 2007). Although outwardly friendly and socially involved, he kept an emotional distance, even from himself. Naming this as a societal problem rather than a personal deficiency helped Michael overcome some of the isolation and slowly experiment with steps he could safely take to attune to himself and others.

Lannie and Kent sought couple therapy to resolve trust issues before they got married. They told the therapist that neither was "a monogamous person" and that they wanted an "open" marriage. Collective understandings of monogamy made it difficult for the therapist to resonate with their experience, even though on a cognitive level she accepted that partners define for themselves what marriage means. Focusing on the power narratives that polyamorous partners might experience can help therapists challenge mononormativity while creating space for a variety of relational orientations. Regardless of a therapist's willingness to understand, it is important to reflect about how we respond to the effects of mononormativity (Jordan, Grogan, Muruthi, & Bermudez, 2017). The therapist had to practice "socially aware listening" (Fricker, 2007, p. 171) that proactively recognized the likelihood that her internal experience of Lannie and Kent was based on social meanings that obscured her ability to take in their issues.

Hermeneutic injustice creates lack of credibility (Fricker, 2007). People do not take in your experience as possible or making sense. Patricia Hill Collins (2000), described how black women in academia and other institutions learn to survive in a system that only recognizes knowledge and experience consistent with dominant white male culture. From an attachment perspective the isolation and assault to self are substantial.

Power

⤙⤚

Attachment is highly contextual and impacted by power dynamics, inclusion, and a sense of belonging at intimate, family, community, and societal levels.

⤙⤚

Expanding our lens beyond family puts relational bonds within systemic communication patterns that reflect and maintain societal power inequities (Knudson-Martin, 2012, 2013; Medina, 2013). What we feel, who is noticed and attended to, and the likelihood that we benefit from attuned support depends on social power processes that govern communication (Fricker, 2007).

Effect of Power on Emotion

Neural circuitry always registers our place in the social hierarchy (Cozolino, 2016). The unfolding of emotion is interactive, taking into account both attachment and power contexts (Greenberg & Goldman, 2008). For example, Ben and Liz, a white cisgender couple in their twenties with recent college degrees sought therapy because of escalating anger and verbal assaults. Just looking at behavior, it would appear reciprocal with each contributing equally to the escalation. From an attachment perspective, each was using anger to protect relational vulnerabilities. But their gender and social class locations placed them in different power positions, with very different emotional consequences.

As a male from an affluent family with parents he described as warm and loving, Ben believed himself to be "open" and "giving." He valued his relationship with Liz, but was blind to the ways he perpetuated systemic ignorance of and inattention to experience of those with less social power (hermeneutic injustice). He expected to be taken seriously and have agency over his own life. When Liz questioned him about his activities or expenditures, anger—inseparable from his power and identity positions—just seemed to erupt. He would lash out at Liz, blaming her for not trusting him, questioning her judgment and knowledge, i.e., "testimonial injustice" in which he did not take her voice or experience seriously (Fricker, 2007).

Liz, also from a loving family, but one with limited economic resources, tried to be sensitive to Ben's interests. Her roots lower in the social hierarchy taught her that silence was often safest in new settings (Medina, 2013). Her safety depended on gathering information about her environment. Like others in one-down social positions, she was almost always aware of what Ben was likely to be thinking and feeling (Knudson-Martin, 2013). Female gender discourse and contemporary relationship ideals premised on mutual respect (Silverstein, Bass,

Tuttle, Knudson-Martin, & Huenergardt, 2006) encouraged Liz to engage with Ben. She not only wanted to understand his actions and choices, in her one-down position she *needed* to understand. When Ben lashed out at her she felt hurt and even more vulnerable. Her sense of dismissal and injustice motivated angry retorts.

The emotions Ben and Liz experienced are not just personal power dynamics between them; they reflect and maintain societal power imbalances. These persistent socioemotional patterns are built into social structure and usually not obvious to participants (Wetherell, 2012). Therapists need a guiding lens that seeks to understand how a particular emotion is linked to larger societal power contexts (Pandit, Kang, ChenFeng, Knudson-Martin, & Huenergardt, 2014). They will avoid interventions that reinforce power imbalances, as would be the case if Liz, in a one-down position, is asked to express vulnerable emotions without first creating a context in which Ben is able to listen.

Effect of Power on Who Attunes

Those in higher power positions tend not to notice or attune to those with less social power. Mutual attunement is unlikely unless the more powerfully situated intentionally seek to understand and connect (Knudson-Martin, 2013). This usually is a question of *will* (Medina, 2013). Attunement requires willingness to temporarily let go of one's own perspective and take in another's. Instead, power processes invite persons in dominant positions to expect subordinates to soothe and regulate their uncomfortable emotions. Ben takes Liz's attunement to him for granted until her questions seem to challenge his identity, autonomy, and/or authority.

Third Order Change

Third order change from an attachment perspective includes awareness of the sociocultural context of one's attachment responses. Persons in powerful positions tend to focus outward rather than inward, blaming others rather than self-reflecting (Greenberg & Goldman, 2008). Their anger, intimidation, or silence becomes a way to regulate others.

⤛ ⤜

Third order change is facilitated when powerful persons become aware of their social location and intentionally attune themselves to others.

⤛ ⤜

As in Ben's case, powerful persons need to experience their own vulnerabilities and open themselves to the experience of others rather than resorting to control. People in one-down positions are likely to be silenced as they adapt in order to maintain safety and security. From an attachment perspective, Liz's eventual anger, rather than withdrawing, is an invitation or plea for Ben to engage. Instead of viewing her retorts as dysfunctional, it is helpful to recognize them as resistance to power. Tuning into the power context of her anger can raise useful awareness and self-reflection regarding how one wants to respond to unjust circumstances (Garcia, Košutić, & McDowell, 2015; Medina, 2013). As Ben and Liz become more contextually aware, his willingness to hear her anger and learn from it would be an important step.

Community and Empowerment

The impact of power on well-being extends to the community, the workplace, and the larger society. People do well when their social contexts affirm their identities and connections. Prejudice, discrimination, and structural inequalities have an insidious effect, perpetuating objectification, commodification, and exploitation in the routine ways people treat each other (Collins, 2000). Countering these injustices through third order change is more possible when people build relationships with others who understand and support them (Almeida, Dolan-Del Vecchio, & Parker, 2008).

The Latino Health Access (LHA) in Orange County, California (Bracho, Lee, Giraldo, & Prado, 2016) is an impressive example of collective empowerment. Participants in vulnerable low-income communities battle addiction, manage diabetes, stop violence, or improve children's health by building relational bonds. Their philosophy resists oppressive societal power processes "with a heart that feels love for our community and expresses that love through acts of solidarity" (Bracho et al., 2016, p. xv). Grounded in science about the effects of societal inequities on health, but prioritizing wisdom of the community, the project works through strengthening bonds and networks among neighbors. Everyone gives and everyone receives. Sarai, a *promotora* (community expert) who struggled with parenting and an abusive relationship summed up the positive impact of community bonds:

> When fear comes to me, I take a few steps back. Then I talk to others in the community and stop being afraid . . . . We belong to each other. Every day we work to create and invite people to safe, protected spaces where they can be themselves, feel stronger, overcome their fears, and be part of the solutions.
>
> (Bracho et al., 2016, p. 67)

Models like LHA support family bonds within wider webs of relationships and use those bonds to construct new knowledge, resist injustice, and create transformative change (e.g., Collins, 2000).

Practice Guidelines

❧

The goal of socioculturally attuned attachment based therapy is to develop relational connections that enable couples and families to equitably support each other in the face of life's stresses and concerns in order to engage in transformative action.

❧

The following guidelines are adapted from Wells and colleagues' (Wells, Lobo, Galick, Knudson-Martin, Huenergardt, & Schaepper, 2017) study of how SERT (Knudson-Martin & Huenergardt, 2010; Knudson-Martin & Huenergardt et al., 2015; Knudson-Martin & Wells et al., 2015) addressed the impact of gender, power, and other societal inequitable on relational safety.

1. Recognize Power's Effects on Relational Safety

When first engaging with individuals, couples, or families, socioculturally attuned therapists seek to understand how social power, the capacity to "influence how things go in the social world" (Fricker, 2007, p. 9) is reflected in how participants orient to each other and the larger environment. How likely is each to *feel felt?* Who attends to whom? How do gender and other power contexts affect responses to vulnerability? How do these patterned responses create safety for some at the expense of others? To create an equitable foundation for therapy, therapists act to balance power in ways that support emotional safety for everyone. They take in each person's perspective without unintentionally allowing more powerfully situated members to define the direction of therapy.

2. Attune to Underlying Sociocultural Emotion

Safety is enhanced as therapists actively **attune** to each person's sociocultural emotional experience (Pandit et al., 2014). Socially aware listening is facilitated as therapists attune to client emotion through a lens curious about how personal experience connects to larger societal discourses and power processes:

Therapist: It's so distressing when Liz questions you, almost as though she is questioning your judgment.
Ben: Yeah! Like she's putting me down. Like she doesn't trust me.
Therapist: What's that like for you? What does it seem to say about you as a man?

Therapists reflect an understanding and **name** clients' sociocultural experiences, explicitly linking emotions, experiences, and processes with sociocultural context:

Ben: Nobody ever questioned my dad. I don't know why she is always questioning me! Who does she think I am?
Therapist: So, when Liz questions you, you feel like you're not much of a man in her eyes. You want her to look up to you. Am I getting that right? (David nods). It makes sense to me that if you learned that men are supposed to be right, to be looked up to, that it might be pretty uncomfortable if it feels your authority is questioned.
Ben: I'm not really like that you know—not one of those men who has to be the authority.

As clients identify the social contextual nature of their emotions and feel understood, like Ben, they are more able to reflect on themselves and others.

3. Accentuate Relational Needs

Attachment based therapists look for and highlight each person's relational commitments and **values.** They look for relational strengths already present, but which may be currently hidden or overlooked. This helps those in powerful positions be willing to attune to subordinates. It also validates relational motives and skills that tend to be discredited in Western culture. A demanding and punitive father may be guided to express his love and concern for his acting out teenager. Angry teens may fear they are not loveable and long for acceptance. A couple divided by hurt may need help recognizing their dreams for love and understanding.

Identifying, **naming**, and focusing on relational needs creates a vision of what clients are working toward. As the therapist resonates with and gives voice to clients' relational foundations and dreams, they "feel safe enough to be in touch with their need for emotional connection and the positive intentions each held for their relationship" (Wells et al., 2017, p. 21). Therapists can then help clients access and express these hopes and commitments as they rebuild and develop their bonds. Individuals get perspective on how they want to engage in relationships and what to expect. Therapists may **intervene** to help clients consider how other family members, friends, work and community contexts, and societal discourses support (or not) their relational values and needs.

4. Initiate Power-Sharing Through Socioemotional Enactments

Socioculturally attuned ABFTs help clients choreograph interactions that interrupt societal power dynamics and facilitate reciprocity and mutual support. They **intervene** by supporting more powerful persons to listen and respond, express vulnerability, and take initiative in building relational connections. Therapists work with in-the-moment-process between clients, focusing on how they relate to each other and expanding underlying sociocultural emotion. Clients begin to see how they enact cultural stereotypes and power dynamics, as well as recognize when they experience connection and mutuality. It may take repeated enactments of attunement before the less powerful feel safe to ease their guard.

5. Reinforce Relational Patterns that Create Mutual Support

As clients experience relational safety, connection, and mutual support, therapists heighten and expand the moment. They encourage clients to recognize what they did to build relationship and highlight the positive relational impact of mutual attunement, vulnerability, and influence. In the process, clients are able to articulate ways they have "become more fair and reliable . . . to have a sense of shared accountability" (Wells et al., 2017, p. 24). Therapists help consolidate experiences of shared relational responsibility and connection and help clients **envision** how they will engage with each other and society going forward. Socioculturally attuned therapists will have been attentive throughout to key persons and communities that support clients' **transformation** through evolving relationship bonds and identities.

Case Illustration

Jolene (31) was referred by her midwife following the birth of Matthew (5 months). The therapist, Norma (26), a black family therapy intern who used female pronouns, invited Jolene's wife Lara (33) to the first session. Norma learned that the white, cisgender female couple had been married for 5 years, together for 9, and also had a 4-year-old daughter, Camilla. When Lara, a kindergarten teacher, gave birth to Camilla she took a year's (unpaid) maternity leave. Jolene, an advertising account manager, was doing the same now with Matthew, while Camilla was in preschool in the mornings and with Lara's mother in the afternoon. Jolene had looked forward to special time with Matthew; instead she was "losing it." She felt inadequate, incompetent, and ashamed. She was especially humiliated that Lara, who was diagnosed with multiple sclerosis (MS) when she was 20, was a "natural" mother despite coping with her MS, which included damage to the optic nerve, somewhat unpredictable balance, and occasional flare-ups.

Recognize Power's Effects on Relational Safety

As Norma began to get to know Jolene and Lara, she was interested in who attended to whom. The couple quickly described Lara as a "caregiver." Her accounts frequently included Jolene's perspective. Jolene appeared much less attentive and attuned, insisting that Lara focused too much of her time on friends and family that did not deserve her.

Lara: Like last weekend, my cousin needed a ride. Jolene was mad at me for doing that. I understand how she feels; she thinks I'm being taken advantage of.

Jolene: It's stupid! You never learn!

A pattern of unequal attunement continued throughout the session. Jolene was the beneficiary of considerably more relational care from Lara than she returned. Each woman had suffered childhood abuse and/or neglect and had worked to overcome the effect of these attachment injuries. Lara trusted that Jolene loved her and minimized the hurt she experienced when Jolene did not tune into her. She was used to soothing Jolene, helping her work through her stresses. But when she tried to help Jolene in caring for Matthew, Jolene just seemed to get more depressed.

Jolene also described feeling betrayed when she discovered that Lara had coffee with Dillon, her "first love." It had been 10 years since Lara had seen Dillon when she ran into him unexpectedly. They had coffee to "catch up." She did not tell Jolene about the meeting, fearing that it would upset her. Norma recognized Lara's secretiveness as a reaction to Jolene's "disentitled power," common among victims of child abuse (Wells et al., 2017, p. 129). Though more likely among men, this kind of power does not come from an overtly powerful position; it is connected to feeling worthless and unlovable. Yet their self-focus creates a power imbalance in the relationship.

Attune to Underlying Sociocultural Emotion

Norma conveyed deep interest in knowing and "getting" each partner's sociocultural experience. Jolene was not stereotypically "feminine," but she internalized all the societal messages about "a good mother." When she did not always feel loving thoughts toward her baby, she felt like a failure. She could not tell anyone, especially when she had been so sure she had so much love to give. The more she felt like a failure, the more isolated and withdrawn she became. Norma reflected and validated these socioemotional experiences, linking emotion to relational and societal contexts:

Norma: All your life you've known you have so much love to give.
Jolene: [When my parents abandoned me] I was on my own. I knew all I needed was a chance. I knew I would be a good mother . . . I've been a good mother to Camilla.
Norma: Even though your mother couldn't be there for you, somehow you carried this idea with you, of a good mother . . . like a dream. Do you think your dream is similar to other women's?
Jolene: I think everyone knows what mothers are supposed to do.
Norma: When I talk with mothers, almost everyone seems to feel like they're failing in some kind of way. Women get a lot of messages about all that they're supposed to do—and how loving they're supposed to be.

Jolene and Lara had spoken at length about what good mothers they would be, how they would arrange donors, how they would manage child care. They did not speak of their fears, doubts, and vulnerabilities. This was not simply because of prior attachment injuries. It was also because women receive strong societal taboos regarding expressing and sharing these feelings (Knudson-Martin & Silverstein, 2009; Mauthner, 1999).

Norma also explored the extra pressure Jolene and Lara felt to represent the LGBTQ community as "good mothers" and how all these intersected with MS disability:

Lara: I have always kept going no matter what. When my uncle molested me, when I was bullied at school because I looked funny and didn't have the right clothes, I never told anyone. I didn't let myself care. When MS came, more the same.
Norma: You've always had to keep going. It was all on you . . . and from what you've said, you always tried to make it easier for others.
Lara: I didn't want to make people uncomfortable. Didn't want to worry my mom. With MS, people don't understand. They might think I shouldn't be a mom. [shrugs and smiles] I have to keep smiling.

Accentuate Relational Needs

Norma helped the couple begin to see their relationship patterns and provided a framework of mutual care through which to understand depression and repair power imbalances. She validated and built upon the positive connections already evident in the relationship.

Norma: I see the love—how much you each value your relationship. . . . You've described patterns in which Lara is really focused on you, Jolene. I'm guessing that you want to be there for her, too. [Jolene agrees.] What's happened now and how hard it is to not feel the way you want with Matthew, it might be a good time to find a way to make the back and forth more mutual, to make the relationship a safe harbor for each of you. My hunch is that will help the depression, too.

Positively framing the couple's commitment to each other and their family helped counter societal messages that they were "less than" and not entitled to care. Conversations that connected their family experiences to larger societal contexts helped remove personal blame and develop empathy for themselves and their caregivers' situations:

Norma: What do you think it was like for your mother . . . taking care of you on her own?
Lara: She was working all the time. She was working for us. If she knew what my uncle did, what I was going through . . . I couldn't do that to her.
Norma: It seems like you had a sense that your mother was carrying a very heavy load. Even then, it seems you might have known there was injustice there. [Lara emphatically agrees.] Almost like to the rest of the world your family wasn't very important.

Initiate Power-Sharing Through Socioemotional Enactments

Jolene and Lara adapted differently to emotional insecurity. Lara worked to calm others, while Jolene kept emotional distance, unaware of how much she depended on Lara for emotional stability. Jolene had survived by not letting herself feel vulnerable. In the incident with Dillon, she did not let herself feel what it was like to need someone; instead, she tried to control Lara's relationships. She had not developed the practice of taking in what others felt or reflecting on her own feelings. Jolene loved Camilla's bubbly 4-year-old laughter and felt good when she held Camilla close. With Matthew it was different. She was on her own most of the day and he didn't respond the way she expected. The more helpless she felt, the more unlovable and unworthy she felt. Lara was moved when she witnessed Jolene's vulnerability, but neither paid attention to Lara's relational needs.

Norma developed enactments that interrupted the couple's power imbalance and expanded attachment beyond a dyad. First, she asked Jolene to reflect on what she thought it might be like for Lara when she (Jolene) was having such a hard time with Matthew. This helped Jolene move away from self-focus that not only perpetuated the power imbalance, but also maintained the feedback loop between isolation and depression (Knudson-Martin & Silverstein, 2009). In setting up the enactment, Norma first validated Jolene's despair, then drew on her commitment to Lara:

Norma: (to Jolene) It's so hard. You feel like a failure as a mother, as a person . . . I'm also wondering what it's like for Lara. You've said so clearly how much she means to you. What have you noticed? What's it's like for her to see you so down?

Jolene struggled to have a response. She wanted Lara to tell her, but Norma stayed with Jolene, supporting her to imaginatively take on Jolene's experience:

Norma: You know her. "Hard for her," you said. What's hard?
Jolene: (pauses, looks at Lara, then shrugs) Just hard, you know. I can't be easy to deal with!
Norma: You see that it must be hard for Lara. What do you think the hardest part is for her?

Norma gently persisted so that Jolene could have a successful experience of attuning to Lara. She resisted the temptation to simply ask Lara.

In a second enactment Norma asked Jolene to share a fear that she had regarding Lara. Norma asked Lara just to hear it. This was very difficult for both women, but Norma wanted Jolene to practice vulnerability in the safety of the therapy room. After Jolene took the lead in expressing vulnerability, her fear that she was not loveable, Norma helped the couple process the experience, emphasizing both the emotional risk they took and the positive consequences. This set the stage for mutual sharing of vulnerability:

Norma: This is a hard time for all of you. You both need each other; you're both vulnerable. But Jolene's pain is easier to see. And I can understand, Lara, why you don't want to add to Jolene's plate right now. But I wonder if there is a way you could check in with each other and each share a vulnerability you're feeling? Agree that you don't need to try to solve it right then, just listen.

Reinforce Relational Patterns that Create Mutual Support

Norma continued with enactments designed to help the couple risk an expanded level of emotional engagement, always paying attention to the balance of mutual care and highlighting the positive aspects of their evolving relational bond. Though it can take considerable time to rework attachment traumas (see Johnson, 2002; Wells et al., 2017), Jolene began to feel better almost immediately and each week the couple reported a more secure bond. They said that the depression and incident with Dillon were the best things that happened to their relationship. Their prior therapy had helped them develop personal responsibility, but they appreciated that this therapy validated their closeness. Instead of feeling like a set of diagnoses, they felt affirmed as mothers and partners. Conversations about mutual care and support included considerable discussion about living with MS. That Jolene wanted to share this part of Lara's life was astounding to Lara. Jolene, who had always been "private," joined a support group for mothers and quickly became one of the organizers.

Summary: Third Order Change

First order change is "common sense" but does not change the systemic ways people engage with each other. Perhaps they learn some new communication skills or how to better manage symptoms. Jolene might have taken an antidepressant or discussed her experience with a therapist. Perhaps Lara would have learned more effective strategies to support Jolene through the depression. These potentially useful steps would have been unlikely to stimulate second order change in the nature of the couple's attachment bonds with each other and their children. Their responses to each other would still reflect different adaptive responses to earlier attachment injuries. Jolene would still have received more understanding and care than Lara. Lara would have remained the competent one, able to look after herself and others even while dealing with a chronic illness.

Second order change would have resulted in new ways of relating based on increased security. If attention had been paid to reciprocity, the balance of who attuned to whom and who accommodated would have become more equal. Their strengthened bonds would have decreased anxiety around parenting and supported more flexible boundaries outside the nuclear family. They would have been more able to share response to MS. But understanding themselves in relation to the larger society most likely would not have changed. They would have still seen themselves as "survivors" creating a better life for their children. They would not have questioned societal messages about mothers. They would not have had a lens through which to see their experiences as part of societal patterns larger than their family. They would not have experienced transformation from being aware of the effects of injustice in their lives. They would not have seen how abuse, abandonment, lower socioeconomic status, disability, and "alternative" sexualities all intersected with limited credibility still accorded women (or those who act like women), or how this limited their ability to know themselves and each other and to recognize their own worth (Fricker, 2007; Medina, 2013).

Third order change for Jolene, Lara, and their children began with willingness of a straight, single, African American intern therapist to step away from her own knowing to as much as possible take in Jolene and Lara's socioemotional experience. As she took time to try to truly understand and to link her clients' experience with their social locations and societal power, Lara and Jolene began to see themselves and the world around them through new eyes. They felt validated as never before. Norma's carefully choreographed enactments helped them transform an unequal power dynamic that had not only maintained previous attachment responses, but also reproduced underlying societal messages of unworthiness. Their relatively quick transformation reflected the empowerment they felt as they began to see their experience as similar to that of others in their positions (Fricker, 2007; Medina, 2013). Jolene's leadership in a mothers' support group enacted third order change as she and Lara began to see alternative possibilities and choices in their roles as women, mothers, and community members.

References

Ainsworth, M. D. S., Blehar, M. C., Waters, E., & Wall, S. (1978). *Patterns of attachment: A psychological study of the strange situation.* Hillsdale, NJ: Erlbaum.

Almeida, R. V., Dolan-Del Vecchio, K., & Parker, L. (2008). *Transformative family therapy: Just families in a just society.* Boston, MA: Pearson Education.

Birns, B. (1999). Attachment theory revisited: Challenging conceptual and methodological sacred cows. *Feminism & Psychology, 9*(1), 10–21.

Bliwise, N. G. (1999). Securing attachment theory's potential. *Feminism & Psychology, 9*(1), 43–52.

Bowlby, J. (1952). *Maternal care and mental health.* Geneva, Switzerland: World Health Organization.

Bowlby, J. (1988). *A secure base.* New York, NY: Basic Books.

Bracho, A., Lee, G., Giraldo, G., & Prado, R. (2016). *Recruiting the heart, training the brain: The work of Latino health access.* Berkeley, CA: Hesperian Health Guides.

Cassidy, J. (2008). The nature of the child's ties. In J. Cassidy & P. R. Shaver (Eds.), *Handbook of attachment: Theory, research, and clinical applications* (pp. 3–22). New York, NY: Guilford Press.

ChenFeng, J. L., & Galick, A. (2015). How gender discourses hijack couple therapy—and how to avoid it. In C. Knudson-Martin, M. A. Wells, & S. K. Samman (Eds.), *Socio-emotional relationship therapy: Bridging emotion, societal discourse, and couple interaction* (pp. 41–52). New York, NY: Springer.

ChenFeng, J., Kim, L., Knudson-Martin, C., & Wu, Y. (2017). Application of socio-emotional relationship therapy with couples of Asian heritage: Addressing issues of culture, gender, and power. *Family Process,* 56, 558–573.

Collins, P. H. (2000). *Black feminist thought: Knowledge, consciousness, and the politics of empowerment.* New York, NY: Routledge.

Cozolino, L. (2016). *Why therapy works: Using our minds to change our brains.* New York, NY: W. W. Norton.

Davies, D., Reed, S., & Kim, L. (2016). *Attuning to trans-clients' epistemic complexity.* Poster session. American Family Therapy Academy, Denver, CO. June 17.

Devor, A. H. (2004). Witnessing and mirroring: A fourteen stage model of transsexual identity formation. *Journal of Gay & Lesbian Psychotherapy, 8*(1/2), 41–67.

Diamond, S., Diamond, M., & Levy, S. A. (2014). *Attachment-based family therapy for depressed adolescents.* Washington, DC: American Psychological Association.

Edelman, M. W. (1980). *Portrait of inequality: Black and white children in America.* Washington, DC: Children's Defense Fund.

Edelman, M. W. (1987). *Families in peril: An agenda for social change.* Cambridge, MA: Harvard University Press.

Fishbane, M. D. (2013). *Loving with the brain in mind: Neurobiology & couple therapy.* New York, NY: W. W. Norton.

Franzblau, S. H. (1999). Historicizing attachment theory: Binding the ties that bind. *Feminism & Psychology, 9*(1), 22–31.

Fricker, M. (2007). Epistemic injustice: Power and the ethics of knowing. New York, NY: Oxford University Press.

Fuller, B., & Coll, C. G. (2010). Learning from Latinos: Contexts, families, and child development in motion. *Developmental Psychology, 46*(3), 559–565.

Garcia, M., Koštić, I., & McDowell, T. (2015). Peace on Earth/war at home: The role of emotion regulation in social justice work. *Journal of Feminist Family Therapy, 27*(1), 1–20.

Greenberg, L. S., & Goldman, R. N. (2008). *Emotion-focused couples therapy: The dynamics of emotion, love, and power.* Washington, DC: American Psychological Association.

Hughes, D. A. (2009). Communication of emotions. In D. Fosha, D. J. Siegel, & M. F. Solomon (Eds.), *The healing power of emotion: Affective neuroscience, development, and clinical practice* (pp. 280–303). New York, NY: W. W. Norton.

Hughes, D. A. (2011). *Attachment-focused family therapy workbook.* New York, NY: W. W. Norton.

Johnson, S. M. (2002). *Emotionally focused couple therapy with trauma survivors: Strengthening attachment bonds.* New York, NY: Guilford Press.

Johnson, S. M. (2003). Introduction to attachment. In S. M. Johnson & V. E. Whiffen (Eds.), *Attachment processes in couple and family therapy* (pp. 3–17). New York, NY: Guilford Press.

Johnson, S. M. (2004). *The practice of emotionally focused couple therapy* (2nd ed.). New York, NY: Brunner-Routledge.

Johnson, S. (2008). *Hold me tight: Seven conversations for a lifetime of love.* New York, NY: Little Brown.

Johnson, S. M., & Lee, A. (2000). Emotionally focused family therapy: Restructuring attachment. In C. E. Bailey (Ed.), *Children in therapy: Using the family as a resource* (pp. 112–136). New York, NY: W. W. Norton.

Jordan, L. S., Grogan, C., Muruthi, B., & Bermudez, J. M. (2017). Polyamory: Experiences of power from without, from within, and in between. *Journal of Couple & Relationship Therapy, 16*(1), 1–19.

Knudson-Martin, C. (2012). Attachment in adult relationships: A feminist perspective. *Journal of Family Theory and Review, 4*, 299–305.

Knudson-Martin, C. (2013). Why power matters: Creating a foundation for mutual support in couple therapy. *Family Process, 52*(1), 5–18.

Knudson-Martin, C., & Huenergardt, D. (2010). A socio-emotional approach to couple therapy: Linking social context and couple interaction. *Family Process, 49*, 369–386.

Knudson-Martin, C., & Silverstein, R. (2009). Suffering in silence: A qualitative meta-analysis of postpartum depression. *Journal of Marital and Family Therapy, 35*(2), 145–158.

Knudson-Martin, C., Wells, M. A., & Samman, S. K. (2015). Socio-emotional relationship therapy: Bridging emotion, societal context, and couple interaction. New York, NY: Springer.

Knudson-Martin, C., Huenergardt, D., Lafontant, K., Bishop, L., Schaepper, J., & Wells, M. (2015). Competencies for addressing gender and power in couple therapy: A socio-emotional approach. *Journal of Marital and Family Therapy, 41*(2), 205–220.

Lareau, A. (2003). *Unequal childhoods: Class, race, and family life.* Berkeley: University of California Press.

Loscocco, K., & Walzer, S. (2013). Gender and the culture of heterosexual marriage in the United States. *Journal of Family Theory & Review, 5*(1), 1–14.

Mauthner, N. S. (1999). "Feeling low and feeling really bad about feeling low": Women's experiences of motherhood and postpartum depression. *Canadian Psychology, 40*(2), 143–161.

McDowell, T. (2015). Applying critical social theories to family therapy practice. *AFTA SpringerBriefs in Family Therapy.* New York, NY: Springer.

Medina, J. (2013). *The epistemology of resistance: Gender and racial oppression, epistemic injustice, and resistant imaginations.* New York, NY: Oxford University Press.

Mikulincer, M., & Shaver, P. R. (2012). Adult attachment orientations and relationship processes. *Journal of Family Theory and Review, 4*, 259–274.

Minuchin, P. (2002). Cross-cultural perspectives: Implication for attachment theory and family therapy. *Family Process, 41*(3), 546–550.

Pandit, M., Kang, Y. J., ChenFeng J., Knudson-Martin, C., & Huenergardt, D. (2014). Practicing socio-cultural attunement: A study of couple therapists. *Journal of Contemporary Family Therapy, 36*, 518–528.

Porges, S. W. (2009). Reciprocal influences between body and brain in the perception and expression of affect: A polyvagal perspective. In D. Fosha, D. J. Siegel, & M. F. Solomon (Eds.), *The healing power of emotion: Affective neuroscience, development, and clinical practice* (pp. 27–54). New York, NY: W. W. Norton.

Rothbaum, F., Rosen, K., Ujiie, T., & Uchida, N. (2002). Family systems theory, attachment theory, and culture. *Family Process, 41*(3), 328–350.

Siegel, D. J. (2012). *The developing mind: How relationships and the brain interact to shape who we are* (2nd ed.). New York, NY: Guilford Press.

Siegel, D. J., & Hartzell, M. (2014). *Parenting from the inside out: How a deeper self-understanding can help you raise children who thrive* (10th anniversary ed.). New York, NY: Jeremy P. Tarcher/Penguin.

Silverstein, R., Bass, L. B., Tuttle, A., Knudson-Martin, C., & Huenergardt, D. (2006). What does it mean to be relational? A framework for assessment and practice. *Family Process, 45*, 391–405.

Taylor, S. E. (2002). *The tending instinct: How nurturing is essential to who we are and how we love.* New York, NY: Times Books.

Trevarthen, C. (2009). The functions of emotion in infancy: The regulation and communication of rhythm, sympathy, and meaning in human development. In D. Fosha, D. J. Siegel, & M. F. Solomon (Eds.), *The healing power of emotion: Affective neuroscience, development, and clinical practice* (pp. 55–85). New York, NY: W. W. Norton.

Tronick, E. (2009). Multilevel meaning making and dyadic expansion of consciousness theory. In D. Fosha, D. J. Siegel, & M. F. Solomon (Eds.), *The healing power of emotion: Affective neuroscience, development, and clinical practice* (pp. 86–111). New York, NY: W. W. Norton.

Tuttle, A. R., Knudson-Martin, C., & Kim, L. (2012). Parenting as relationship: A framework for assessment and practice. *Family Process, 51*, 73–89.

van der Kolk, B. (2014). *The body keeps the score: Brain, mind, and body in the healing of trauma.* New York, NY: Penguin.

van Ijzendoorn, M. H., & Sagi-Schwartz, A. (2008). Cross-cultural patterns of attachment: Universal and contextual dimensions. In J. Cassidy & P. R. Shaver (Eds.), *Handbook of attachment: Theory, research, and clinical applications* (pp. 880–905). New York, NY: Guilford Press.

Vatcher, C. A., & Bongo, M. (2001). The feminist/emotionally focused therapy practice model: An integrated approach for couple therapy. *Journal of Marital and Family Therapy, 27*(1), 69–83.

Walsh, F. (2009). Human-animal bonds I: The relational significance of companion animals. *Family Process, 48*, 462–480.

Wells, M. A., Lobo, E., Galick, A., Knudson-Martin, C., Huenergardt, D., & Schaepper, J. (2017). Fostering trust through relational safety: Applying SERT's focus on gender and power with adult-survivor couples. *Journal of Couple & Relationship Therapy, 16*, 122–145.

Wetherell, M. (2012). *Affect and emotion: A new social science understanding.* Los Angeles, CA: SAGE.

Willis, A. B., Haslam, D. R., & Bermudez, J. M. (2016). Harnessing the power of play in emotionally focused family therapy with preschool children. *Journal of Marital and Family Therapy, 42*, 673–687.

8 Socioculturally Attuned Bowenian Family Therapy

In the 1950s Murray Bowen made the groundbreaking proposition that symptoms such as depression, alcoholism, or physical illness need to be understood as a dynamic process involving the family as a unit, rather than the individual. He described human behavior as part of interlocking emotional systems through which people receive information from the environment, adapt, and respond (Bowen, 1978; Kerr & Bowen, 1988). Beginning in response to Freudian theory, Bowen argued that the principles governing emotional connectedness are "written in nature" and common to all natural systems (Kerr & Bowen, 1988, p. 26). Two natural life forces are involved: those that promote self-interest and those that promote the group. These innately affect functioning across all systemic levels from the cellular to the societal.

↞ ↠

Third order change is facilitated from a Bowen perspective when clients see themselves and their concerns not only as part of multigenerational family systems, but also as part of ongoing sociocultural systems.

↞ ↠

Bowen viewed family members as needing to differentiate within a shared emotional system. For socioculturally attuned Bowenian therapists, differentiation includes being able to **attune** to the confluence of social location and family dynamics and **name** inequities and the impact of societal norms and taken-for-granted assumptions, recognizing and giving **value** to that which has been minimized or devalued by the dominant culture. Therapists help clients **intervene** in oppressive power dynamics, **envision** their lives and relationships without reactivity to dominant societal discourses and judgments, and make choices that **transform** relationships and society based on awareness of options and intentional application of one's values.

In this chapter we first explore five key aspects of family therapy based on Bowen theory and then consider how to integrate principles of socioculturally attuned therapy with guidelines for practice and a case example.

Primary Enduring Bowenian Family Therapy Concepts

Emotion is the energy that drives relationships (Bowen, 1978). Like an "emotional magnet," family members automatically respond to and influence each other (Titelman, 2014, p. 22). Differentiation of self is the core developmental process and is at the heart of therapy. It is described as the ability to "maintain emotional objectivity while in the midst of an emotional system . . . yet at the same time actively relate to key people in the system" (Bowen, 1978, p. 485). We view the following components of Bowen family therapy as central to increased differentiation and relationship functioning: differentiation of self, transgenerational patterns and transmission, flow of anxiety, maintaining emotional engagement, and therapist's family of origin work.

Differentiation of Self

A child is born. Her parents name her Arielle. Arielle is born into a web of emotional connections that predate her and extend across generations. According to Bowen theory, from the moment of birth—or even prior to birth—Arielle will experience an automatic pull toward this togetherness (Bowen, 1978; Titelman, 2014). She will also experience a natural pull toward individuality. Differentiation of self is how the tension between these two forces is managed. Arielle's development of self will move along a continuum from low to (potentially) high differentiation. On the low end is *emotional fusion* in which individual responses are highly reactive to others. On the high end is a *solid self* that enables reflective and differentiated responses. Arielle's capacity to move from emotional fusion inherent at birth to differentiation depends on the level of emotion fusion in her family of origin. It is an individual *and* family level process.

Arielle's African American family values tightly knit family bonds. In a nearby neighborhood, Eric is born. His European American family prefers more personal space and emphasizes individual achievement. According to Bowen theory their process of differentiation is the same. It begins with functioning based on automatic responses similar to emotional reactions among other life forms; for example, Carmen's horse demonstrated emotional reactivity when he would sense danger, tense up, and step around the shadow of a mailbox every time he passed one. He behaved similarly when he came to muddy puddles, even if they were only a few inches deep. He did not have the capacity to reflect on the current meaning of a shadow or puddle. He reacted not only on his experience, but from instinctual "horse" experience across generations. At this level of differentiation there is no ability to observe oneself separate from the group or context. Differentiation increases when intellectual functioning or awareness enables one to distinguish a sense of self and respond in a less reactive or automatic way.

Transgenerational Patterns and Transmission

Arielle and Eric's basic levels of differentiation depend primarily on how their families handle the intrinsic melding of family members' emotional states, i.e., their degree of fusion. It is important not to confuse emotional fusion with preferences for physical closeness and deep caring about one another. Arielle's African American family enacts family-centered values within a relatively well-differentiated family system. People in her family like each other's company and participate in many shared activities. They enjoy spirited disagreement and have lively family conversations on many topics. When faced with a crisis, such as the great-grandmother's recent diagnosis of Alzheimer's disease, the extended family discussed many options for how to share her care. Individual family members felt respected and freely reflected on what they could and could not do to help. Even though the emotional demands on the family are high, they are able to lovingly and non-reactively respond to Arielle's needs as a newborn while also helping care for their great-grandmother. Growing up in this well-differentiated family environment promotes Arielle's individual differentiation.

In contrast, Eric is growing up in a much less differentiated emotional context. Family members have never been able to tolerate differences among them. People attend family gatherings as expected and are careful not to upset each other. Eric's aunt refuses to participate. When he was born she brought a gift at a time when no other family members would be there. The conflict between this aunt and the rest of the family causes Eric's mother, Jamie, considerable distress, and she expends significant energy trying to keep the peace. She is similarly cautious about upsetting her husband (Eric's father) and often feels lonely and unappreciated. Though Eric's parents and extended family genuinely love him, the low level of differentiation in this family system is accompanied by intense intergenerational and marital anxiety. The high level of emotional reactivity will make it difficult for Eric to differentiate within this system.

Bowen theory emphasizes that emotional systems are transmitted from one generation to another. By the time Arielle and Eric are born, the emotional functioning of their family systems has been evolving for many generations and has been influenced by many factors. Because human systems are inherently social, family functioning is connected to historical sociopolitical contexts such as war, the economy, systems of stratification, privilege and marginalization, and cultural expectations. As will be illustrated in more detail later, this means that what we feel is always connected to the larger societal context. Anxiety related to these kinds of survival issues can manifest for generations outside conscious awareness (Gilbert, 2013).

Nodal events such as births, deaths, immigration, marriages, and other times when family members entered or left the family system can impact generations to come. How families respond to these stressors depends on their degree of emotional fusion or differentiation. Families who face fewer societal stressors may be able to maintain stability and basic functioning at a lower level of differentiation; however, in times of stress the intensity of the emotional fusion will increase and the capacity to respond effectively will be limited (Papero, 2014; Titelman, 2014). Conversely, some people may be stimulated to differentiate within harsh, traumatic, or inequitable situations as a part of survival and resilience. We should not assume that people living with poverty, racism, or other forms of dominance or stress are less well-differentiated than those with more privilege.

By the time Arielle and Eric become adults, their levels of basic differentiation will be relatively stable. Arielle's family has historically been able to respond to important nodal and sociocontextual issues—including the civil rights movement, job loss, and the death of Arielle's grandfather in the Vietnam War—with considerable self-awareness on the part of individual family members and the ability to support each other without sacrificing autonomy. Arielle is therefore likely to develop a well-regulated emotional system and approach adult relationships from a non-reactive, intellectually reflective position. This will help her sustain a network of supportive relationships (Kerr & Bowen, 1988).

Eric will probably experience more difficulty forming healthy and satisfying adult relationships. His historical legacy includes multiple generations in which family members responded to immigration to the U.S. with high anxiety about economic success and fitting into societal expectations of the dominant culture by which they judged themselves. No deviations from rigid roles and expectations were allowed. When Eric's grandparents lost a child to cancer, they were never able to speak of it. Since she was a child, Eric's mother, Jamie, responded to familial distress by trying to make her parents happy. This pattern is repeated in her relationship with her husband, Robert, who is frequently angry and not attentive to her. This emotional context will inhibit Eric's movements toward differentiation of self and perpetuate societal power differences between women and men.

Flow of Anxiety

According to Bowen theory, anxiety in response to interpersonal differences or life's challenges is a natural response to low levels of differentiation. An important part of assessment in Bowen therapy is to track the flow of anxiety within the shared emotional system. Not everyone is equally affected; some family members absorb and bind the anxiety in ways that allow others a greater degree of differentiation. People can bind anxiety in many ways. Some constantly seek relationships and try to please; others deny their need for relationships and keep their distance. Substance use, eating disorders, physical symptoms, and traits such as obsessiveness, grandiosity, perfectionism, aggressiveness, paranoia, hopelessness, etc. can all be ways anxiety is bound in a system, as are polarizing beliefs (Kerr & Bowen, 1988). "In general, the more anxious people become, the less constructive their responses to others tend to be" (p. 124).

When tension is high between two persons, they may deflect their anxiety by directing attention to another person or thing to stabilize the relationship. This is called *triangulation*. This happens quite naturally and may not be intentional. For example, the tension between Jamie and Robert is high. Rather than upset Robert, Jamie directs her attention to her newborn son Eric. This calms her. The connection she experiences with her son makes it possible for her to avoid addressing her unhappiness in the marriage. Eric absorbs the tension. If this pattern continues, Eric is likely to become a symptom-bearer. This is an example of what Bowen theory terms the *family projection process*; that is, the anxiety of one generation is passed to another through a series of interlocking emotional triangles. Jamie's parents absorbed the anxiety of previous generations, making it difficult for them to deal with their child's cancer and death. Jamie and her sister were part of multiple triangling processes involving their parents, their sick sibling, and grandparents. That intense anxiety continues to be present in the family emotional system today.

Bowen theory does not typically highlight sociopolitical processes involved in who absorbs anxiety in the family system and how it is expressed. It is important to note that the female's (Jamie) automatic response to the family projection process serves as the glue that keeps the family together. This reflects the intersection of a high level of systemic anxiety with socio-cultural gender norms that leave women vulnerable to carrying the emotional stress for others (Kendall-Takett, 2005). Her husband Robert responds to the anxiety with anger and emotional distance. These are relationship limiting responses invited by sociocultural norms for men.

Maintaining Emotional Engagement

The ability to maintain genuine relationships in the face of stress or turmoil is the outcome of differentiation. The Bowen clinical approach emphasizes learning to make "inner-directed" decisions from within the self, rather than "coercion or persuasion from others" (Kerr & Bowen, 1988, p. 105). The goal is to respond less on the basis of emotional reactivity and more from a *solid self* that can tolerate intense feelings and think out responses to others. Turning to her infant son when there is stress between Jamie and her husband may be a sign of emotional fusion. Others may respond to emotional fusion by neglecting or abusing others or by cutting off from them in order to maintain emotional distance (Papero, 2014). For example, Robert reactively responds with anger when his wife disagrees with him. When his son Eric cries for long periods of time, Robert has little ability to tolerate the intensity. He disengages and puts his focus elsewhere. He might react to emotion in the system by physically or emotionally abusing Eric or his wife, having a sexual affair outside the marriage, or directing all his energy and attention to work or some other activity rather than engaging with his wife and child. Low differentiation perpetuates this pattern, making it increasingly hard for him to engage.

People can increase basic differentiation by developing awareness of the emotional patterns in their lives, the contexts that invite them, and how their own reactivity contributes. This enables more choice about how one responds, reduces the anxiety in the family system, and has an impact on the emotional transmission process for future generations.

Therapist's Family of Origin Work

Therapists applying Bowen theory must work from a differentiated sense of self. This enables them to avoid emotional fusion with clients' anxiety. It requires developing a clear sense of self, knowing our place in the world, and what matters to us (McGoldrick, 2016). Like a coach, Bowen therapists are then able stay outside the system, asking questions and making observations that help clients in their own process of self-discovery. The therapist is a "witness on the sidelines . . . inspiring clients to undertake their own work" (McGoldrick, 2016,

p. 111). Containing anxiety requires a calm presence that can make it safe for people to engage in the therapeutic process.

Integrating Principles of Sociocultural Attunement

Human systems are both natural (e.g., biological) and sociocultural (Innes, 1996). Bowen purposefully viewed human behavior only as part of natural systems. He focused on what humans have in common with all life forms and biological evolution (Bowen, 1978; Kerr & Bowen, 1988). Information from study unique to humans (e.g., social sciences) was not integrated (Innes, 1996). Bowen emphasized universal principles and did not focus on how key processes such as differentiation intersected with sociocultural context or societal power dynamics. Yet because the theory emphasizes the reciprocal flow of anxiety between individuals, families, institutions, and society at large, attention to the impact of sociocultural, political, and economic systems enhances the model and increases the potential to transcend destructive patterns invited by societal inequities.

In this section we examine differentiation in societal context, why power processes are important, and how awareness of one's sociopolitical, cultural, and historical contexts can be the foundation for empowerment and third order change. We also show how recent findings from neuroscience support this expanded application of Bowen theory (Damasio, 1999; Porges, 2009; van der Kolk, 2014).

Differentiation in Societal Context

Assessment of differentiation may reflect dominant culture values and miss the merit and usefulness of togetherness, feeling based knowledge, or a focus on other. In the same vein, client perceptions and expectations may be fused with cultural discourses that limit choices and genuine human connections.

↤ →

Therapists must be cautious regarding judging differentiation. What looks like low differentiation may sometimes more appropriately be understood as the effects of discrimination and/or limited power.

↤ →

Anxiety in the Macrosystem

Bowen postulated similar emotional processes at the societal level as in organizations and families. When anxiety is high, groups within the system are isolated from each other (Bowen, 1978). People tend to take sides on issues without hearing each other (Friedman, 2007). People are "constantly bombarded" by other people's reactivity (Friedman, 2007, p. 62). Bowen noted that people or groups respond to the anxiety by scapegoating persons in subordinate positions; e.g., people of color, low income people, sexual or gender minorities, the mentally ill. Unfortunately, the theory also sometimes seemed to itself scapegoat disenfranchised populations, suggesting that their acts of resistance (e.g., protests or divorce) are a sign of emotional immaturity and that "over-lenient" public officials keep low-income people "one-down" (Bowen, 1978, p. 445). An approach more informed by critical theory (McDowell, 2015) would focus on resilience and motivation to claim a self embedded in "acting out" behavior (McGoldrick, 2016; Unger, 2015) and challenge those with more power to be open to hearing from those with less power, making it safe for them to speak, even when what they have to say makes us uncomfortable.

᠁ ← → ᠁

Societal projection processes such as discrimination, scapegoating, and entrenched power hierarchies are likely to disproportionately affect targeted or marginalized groups.

᠁ ← → ᠁

Living on a day-to-day basis at lower levels of the societal power hierarchy increases stress hormones and poorer health outcomes, even when controlling for access to health care (Lantz, House, Mero, & Williams, 2005). Societal stressors become embodied in neuroendocrine and immune systems (Sternberg, 2001). For example, people raised with fewer economic resources are more likely to get sick when exposed to a cold virus than people raised with more affluence, even when economic circumstances have improved later in life (Cohen, Janicki-Deverts, Chen, & Matthews, 2010). From a Bowen perspective these are examples of the inequitable effects of societal anxiety, in which the well-being of one group comes at the expense of another. Although living with the effects of discrimination could certainly affect the differentiation process, persons in more privileged positions are not necessarily more differentiated. Their apparent health may be a myth held in place by dependence on others to automatically meet their needs or by their positions of power (McGoldrick, 2016). It is important to consider all the intersecting factors.

For example, Julia, a lab technologist who had been working at the same hospital for over 20 years, sought therapy because she was so depressed she could barely get out of bed. Going to work produced considerable anxiety. She said she needed to learn what was the matter with her. She felt ashamed that she could not cope better and took people's teasing personally. The intense, emotional way she spoke, the questioning of her own competence, and judgmental statements she made about others all lined up to easily think of her as "poorly differentiated." But as the therapist expanded the lens to ask about the changes happening in the hospital and in medical services more broadly, a series of interlocking triangles became evident. Anxiety in the larger health care system moved to multiple levels of managers in this hospital, which increased the pressure on her team to perform an extraordinary amount of work with no mistakes in a very short amount of time, and finally led to scapegoating Julia who was different than the others in age and ethnicity and perhaps took professional standards more stridently than some of her younger colleagues.

Most likely, Julia was no less differentiated than the others in her workplace. She was targeted because anxiety in the larger system made it difficult for the workgroup to tolerate differences. But she was the one showing the symptoms and being most affected. As Julia reflected on the anxiety in the system and how various people responded to it, she was able to consider her options and develop a strategy for how to deal with it. Because her managers seemed unable to respond in ways that changed the work environment, the burden fell on Julia to change her own response, including the ramifications of possibly deciding not to work in this setting. Naming the inherent unfairness in the situation was important.

Intersection of Differentiation and Culture

As we saw in the cases of Arielle and Eric, cultural patterns intersect with emotional differentiation processes. Eric's less well-differentiated family enacts ideals of autonomy and achievement in ways that limit positive connection and adaptation. Arielle's better-differentiated family enacts the cultural ideal of sticking together to face adversity (Cowdery et al., 2009). In a less differentiated African American family, the emotional pulls toward togetherness may invite women to sacrifice their needs, resulting in somatic symptoms or depression (Astbury, 2010).

➻←➻

When differentiation is high, people are able to apply cultural values in relatively functional ways. When differentiation is low or in times of distress, cultural values can become exaggerated.

➻←➻

Takeshi Tamura (2016), a family therapist in Japan, calls this exaggeration "cultural overdose." For example, Japanese culture tells adolescents that they should achieve for the sake of family honor. According to Tamura, when anxiety is high, Japanese youth are likely to isolate themselves and avoid social situations, increasing the risk for suicide, depression, and self-harm. In the U.S., pulls toward independence may be reflected in acting out and externalizing behaviors. Adolescents may break curfews, run away, join gangs, and use drugs as a way to express independence and resist authority (Unger, 2015). Understanding these behaviors as individual pathology or family issues without taking larger societal contexts into account will miss the socioemotional experience that gives rise to them.

Tamura (2016) cited the example of a family in Korea. When the video opens, two adolescent daughters are arguing about using the computer. The mother—with some tension in her voice—tells the older daughter that she needs to shut down the computer and go to bed in a few minutes, reminding her that she has school tomorrow. When the daughter does not do this and the two girls begin to scream at each other, the mother also begins to scream and threaten the older daughter. Tamura explained that the anxiety in this household reflects societal performance expectations that make going to school highly anxious for the daughter. The resulting family conflict is triangulated with societal anxiety projection processes in a way that holds the mother responsible for the daughter's performance. Sociocultural attunement to this highly charged societal projection process requires awareness of geopolitical changes in South Korea in recent decades (Tamura, 2016).

Societal Transmission of Collective Trauma

Just as traumatic family legacies are passed on from generation to generation and affect current relationship functioning even when people are not aware of these past histories, collective historical traumas continue to perpetuate heightened anxiety and reactivity. Watson (2013) described collective nervousness that many African American people experience regarding how they appear to others. For example, she told of her experience as a black woman in a restaurant with a white friend. When a nearby table of black people were loud and noisy and rude to the waiter, she felt ashamed and embarrassed. It is unlikely that her white friend would have felt similarly shamed had the rude diners been white. Watson attributed this emotional response to the history of slavery where "if one slave got out of line, all slaves might feel the lash, or worse," and to internalized black inferiority that leaves people "on the edge . . . obsessed with how we and other blacks look, talk, and act because we were enslaved and then discriminated against for having black skin" (p. 50). The feeling of shame says more about the power context of the situation than Watson's level of differentiation.

➻←➻

It is important to recognize, acknowledge, and name realities of collective trauma and unsafe contexts. The problem may be a history of collective trauma lived out and repeated in individual lives.

➻←➻

One of our students witnessed the destructive tendency to pathologically label the individual in a supervision group at a community agency. A black mother was referred for her angry and disruptive behavior at her daughter's school. She was quickly described by the supervision group members as "paranoid." Under that label, no one asked about her experience with schools, especially schools like this one where the teachers, principal, and most of the students were white. They did not seek to understand her expectation and fear that her daughter would be treated unfairly. They could only see that her reaction to the school appeared "out of proportion" to the issue at hand.

Value of Belonging

In Bowen theory the self can never be defined separately from significant relationships and contexts (Nel, 2011). The goal is to define a "self" while staying in relationships (Walsh & Scheinkman, 1988). However, dominant Western discourses tend to value individuality and autonomy over more connected ways of relating. This bias can be seen in how Bowen theory is often presented and applied (Knudson-Martin, 1994, 1996).

⟵⟶

Socioculturally attuned therapists resist the temptation to view individual autonomy as more important than relationships.

⟵⟶

McGoldrick (2016) gave the example of how therapists may be more likely to support a decision for a wife to move to advance her husband's career than for a wife to not move in order to stay close to her sisters. McGoldrick also emphasized the importance of community for well-being and strength to resist oppressive forces of society. Sources of healing are embedded in clients' social contexts. A clear cultural or racial identity has been found to be associated with high levels of differentiation (Skowron, 2004).

Marie, a 35-year-old European American woman, strongly identified with her Christian denomination. She felt depressed and powerless in her marriage and told the therapist she wanted a more equal marriage, but also believed in the principles of her religion, including that the husband was the leader of the family. The feeling that she needed to choose between equality or her religion distressed and isolated her. As the therapist sensitively helped Marie explore her faith beliefs in relation to equality, she began to feel more connected to her religion, concluding that "God was caring—more like a woman than a man" (Silverstein, Bass, Tuttle, Knudson-Martin, & Huenergardt, 2006, p. 401). Feeling pressure to conform to the expectations of her group, a sign of low differentiation from a Bowen perspective, Marie had kept all her concerns to herself. With the therapist's encouragement, she sought a woman in the church she thought would understand. Marie returned to therapy the next week saying, "All the women in the church feel the same way I do!" As Marie explored her Christian identity, she was also more able to connect to her religion in a personal way and more genuinely engage in her church community. Marie did not need to differentiate *from* her faith; she needed to differentiate *within* it.

Value of Intuition and Feeling

Like dominant culture values that prioritize thinking and rationality, Bowen theory has also been criticized for valuing objectivity over intuition, subjectivity, and emotional expression (Knudson-Martin, 1994, 1996; Luepnitz, 1988). Bowen emphasized using the intellectual system to mediate responses to the emotional system and advocated clinical strategies that stressed cognitive awareness and distinguished thinking from feeling. Such approaches fail to acknowledge or value self-knowledge that comes through development of the feeling system and affective awareness. In so doing, they discount the experience of many women and cultures. Nouvelle, an African American nurse in her mid-thirties, described her subjective, "gut knowing:"

> I think that growing up as a person of color in this society, you develop something more instinctual and survival like. It's a different kind of smart and a different kind of sense . . . . It's much more visceral, it's much more down here [points to stomach].
>
> (Goldberger, 1996, p. 352)

When people experience a disconnect between what their bodies or experience tell them and what is expected or known in the dominant culture, they are likely to discount or silence their own knowing (Jack & Ali, 2010). Rather than a solid, unitary self, people in subjugated positions may develop a shifting consciousness in which they simultaneously perceive multiple realities (Hurtado, 1996). The ability to apprehend multiple consciousnesses enables them to make sense of the complexities in their lives and negotiate multiple and stigmatized social identities as they move from context to context. For example, Hurtado spoke of the need for women of color to navigate danger and anger to successfully manage marginality:

> There develops an intuitive sense of danger that is primarily kept at bay through anger. Putting a "bit" on anger is of primary importance for survival . . . . The challenge is to "know what you know" *and* be able to circumvent the consequences of that knowledge while being true to yourself.
>
> (p. 378)

↞—↠

A socioculturally attuned application of Bowen theory appreciates and draws from many forms of knowing.

↞—↠

It recognizes that what it means to differentiate a "solid" self depends on the power and sociocultural contexts of one's social location.

Differentiation and Societal Power Processes

The ways of relating associated with high differentiation such as direct communication, "I" statements, and ability to respect differences and deal with conflict presume relatively equal power positions. But social systems have long histories of inequality. Power imbalances are built into social structures and norms that directly connect to emotional experience and relational dynamics (Knudson-Martin & Mahoney, 1999; Komter, 1989). Stable systems are not necessarily equal systems. Power imbalances and low differentiation maintain each other.

Power Structures, Fear, and Anxiety

Societal inequities based on race, class, gender, sexuality, or other differences require emotional fusion, whereby the dominant group's interests are supported at the expense of subordinate groups (McGoldrick, 2016). Norms of the dominant culture will be privileged.

❧ ❧

Members of more powerful groups are largely unaware that members of less powerful groups accommodate them.

❧ ❧

Survival for the women of color quoted earlier required them to be attentive to the potential emotional responses of the powerful. They needed to manage their emotion in relation to the power situation. (e.g., put a "bit" on their anger). Without taking power into consideration this could seem "overly" focused on other. Instead, this attention to context is important to their well-being.

❧ ❧

Until those in powerful positions develop awareness of their dependence on being accommodated by others, they remain emotionally fused with societal power processes.

❧ ❧

Inequities inspire anxieties. A well-differentiated system would recognize and address fairness issues openly and directly. Taking "complaints" or "resistance" of the less powerful seriously and making it safe for them to speak would be a step toward increased functioning and equity. In contrast, autocratic/totalitarian leadership styles seek to contain the anxiety (Friedman, 2007). Those in positions of power maintain power through inciting fear among the less powerful. This may be unintentional through unquestioned expectations, such as when a boss expects an employee to be available for shifts any time of the day. They may also intentionally incite fear through threats, intimidation, or force; the boss may threaten employees with losing their jobs if they don't comply.

In less differentiated systems, responsibility for managing the anxiety often falls on the less powerful. For example, Bryan Stevenson (2014), a black civil rights attorney, described the anxiety he experienced early in his career when he was sitting in his car listening to music on the radio after parking near his apartment. He looked up and saw a white policeman pointing a gun at him:

> My first instinct was to run. I quickly decided that wouldn't be smart . . . "move and I'll blow your head off!" The officer shouted the words, but I couldn't make any sense of what he meant. I tried to stay calm . . . I put my hand up and noticed that he seemed nervous . . . I don't remember deciding to speak, I just remember the words coming out: "It's all right. It's okay . . . I live here." I hated how afraid I sounded and the way my voice was shaking.
>
> (p. 40)

Stevenson's relatively high level of contextual awareness helped him defuse the situation, but the unacknowledged injustice and assault to his dignity continued to impact him. When he got into his apartment Stevenson kept saying over and over again, "They never even apologized" (p. 42). Stevenson attributed his ability to think through the situation—a differentiated response—to his years of study and legal training (which his instincts told him not to disclose), but the fear and humiliation he experienced were related to his subordinate position and vulnerability because of his black skin.

Situated Emotion/Affect

Emotion occurs at the intersection of sociopolitical life and daily interactions. It is situated in a complex material and relational field never separate from a person's power position in the setting (Wetherell, 2012). The feeling of humiliation experienced by Stevenson is an example of his body reading and recording the meaning of the racial hierarchy surrounding the event. Had the same event happened to a white attorney (which in itself seems unlikely), the emotional experience of the participants would have been different, with the attorney likely experiencing indignation rather than humiliation.

※←→※

Socioculturally attuned therapists must listen for, and seek to understand, the societal contexts in which family histories are embedded in order to identify and name issues of fairness and injustice.

※←→※

What kinds of societal messages about their worth and value did they and their family members receive? What comments did they hear about people like "them"? What kinds of assumptions and stereotypes influence what people feel entitled to? How safe and protected could they feel in the outside world?

Relational Justice

Inequitable power processes at the societal level create power imbalances within couples and families. Gilbert (2006) noted that relationships with a high level of differentiation are characterized by equality. One person does not function at the expense of another. Each is open to hear and understand the other. There is direct, mutual conversation in which partners freely communicate their own thinking and each is actively engaged in listening. Power imbalances inhibit this kind of direct, mutually engaged communication and tend to be connected to societal based power differences such as gender, race, and socioeconomic status (Knudson-Martin, 2013; Mahoney & Knudson-Martin, 2009). On the other hand, relational equity facilitates increased differentiation.

To see how gendered power, differentiation, and anxiety intertwine in a heterosexual relationship, let's return to the relationship between Eric's parents, Robert and Jamie. The low levels of differentiation transmitted to each of them across generations makes it difficult for them to relate outside gender stereotypes. Like most contemporary couples they believe that their relationship should equally support each partner (Mahoney & Knudson-Martin, 2009). Robert is not aware that latent power associated with how gender is constructed means he is less likely to notice and attend to Jamie's needs and interests than she is to his (Knudson-Martin, 2015). When anxiety is high, his reactive responses escalate from obliviousness of Jamie and Eric's needs to hurtful rage and anger. These responses are most likely when he's not able to live up to societal messages that he should be competent and in charge. Jamie reacts to societal messages that it is her job to calm his tension and protect him from shame (ChenFeng & Galick, 2015). Their emotional responses to each other are directly connected to their positions in the gender hierarchy and also maintain it.

Without attention to societal power processes, it may appear that those in powerful positions are more differentiated, especially if their reactive responses appear rational rather than emotional. Increased differentiation in this case means becoming *more* attuned to others (Knudson-Martin & Mahoney, 1999). From a relational perspective holding a power position is destructive rather than helpful (Fishbane, 2011). When we expand our lens to include power differentials associated with other social locations, the intersections become even more complex. For example, if Robert were unemployed, disabled, or a person of color, the anxiety around his sense of failure might escalate even more. If Robert and Jamie were a gay couple, they may be more likely to negotiate their roles and notice power differences between them; however, their reactivity could also become even more fused as a result of social rejection and devaluation in the larger society (Richards, Jonathan, & Kim, 2015).

Empowerment and Third Order Change

In Bowen theory, increasing one's level of differentiation provides a foundation for empowerment and third order change. A socioculturally attuned approach takes very seriously Bowen's proposition that we cannot understand emotion out of context. Doing so requires intentionally weaving the connections between interpersonal neurobiology, relational dynamics, and societal power processes (Fishbane & Wells, 2015). Emotion arises as affective stimuli and social meaning simultaneously activate a broad range of neural regions in the body. Study of neurobiology helps expand our understanding of the processes involved (for family therapy focused summaries see Cozolino, 2015; Fishbane, 2013; Hanna, 2014).

The Sociocultural Brain

Bowen emphasized distinguishing thought and feeling as part of the differentiation process. More recent work shows that these two cannot really be separated. No parts of the brain are specifically cognitive or specifically emotional (Damasio, 1999). There is no such thing as a "non-affective thought" (Duncan & Barrett, 2007). This new information actually reinforces Bowen's ideas that the individual does not biologically exist and that social processes become embodied (Burkitt, 2014; Gilbert, Sapp, & Tauber, 2012).

＊←→＊

Larger societal processes are part of the nearly instantaneous neurological sequence in which the contextual and situational nature of relationships register in the body and are felt.

＊←→＊

In an effort to apply Bowen theory to women and less individualistic cultures, Knudson-Martin (1994, 1996) advocated use of visceral feeling based knowledge and movements toward healthy togetherness. These attributes tend to be less valued in the dominant Western white male culture. Porges' (2009) Polyvagal Theory of neurophysiological emotional regulation supports this expanded application. Porges described parallel paths or branches of the vagus nerve that assesses for safety. One seeks neurophysiological calming through social engagement involving facial expression, head gestures, human voice, etc.; the other impedes behaviors that support social engagement (fight or flight). From this perspective, rather than primarily using the "higher" brain to overcome the more primitive brain, differentiation would also include developing awareness of one's sensory experience and activating the social engagement system.

For example, Julia, the lab technologist described previously, was very agitated as she described what was happening at work. The therapist recognized that the part of her vagus nerve that impeded social engagement was activated. Before trying to expand systemic understanding of the situation or strategize a response to her hostile work environment, she stayed very engaged with Julia, gently reflecting resonance with her contextually inspired emotion, "It's so unfair. You know you're competent, but you feel so humiliated . . . . You just want to do your job." This empathic engagement calmed Julia's anxiety and enabled her to move into a more reflective position. The therapist then invited Julia to take some deep breaths and feel the anxiety in her body. Through a series of questions about the size, shape, color, and location of the anxiety, Julia described a psychedelic ball that flashed changing colors and pulsated from her head. In the weeks that followed, Julia found that allowing herself to recognize and feel these physical sensations was important to her empowerment process.

Critical Awareness

As suggested by Paulo Freire (1970/2000), consciousness and critical self-reflection are the first steps toward liberation and the possibility of becoming a "protagonist in one's own life" (McGoldrick, 2016, p. 4). Awareness of the system and one's role in it makes this possible. Though neglected by Freire, awareness of one's emotions and being able to intentionally respond to them is important to developing critical consciousness (Garcia, Košutić, & McDowell, 2015).

↤ ↠

A socioculturally attuned understanding of Bowen theory encourages critically examining how personal biographies are interwoven with societal relationships in the experience of feeling.

↤ ↠

Reflective consciousness always involves attuning to and engaging the bodily sensations; without them, words and the images associated with feelings and emotion are empty and meaningless (Burkitt, 2014). It is empowering to name and validate emotional experience linked to societal discourses and power (Pandit, ChenFeng, & Kang, 2015).

Differentiation from Dominant Cultural Values

Therapists need to be well-differentiated and able to intentionally counteract societal emphases on autonomy, competition, materialization, goal-directedness, and objectivity. Because the language used in Bowen theory can obscure values more commonly associated with women and less individualistic cultures, clinicians need to be aware of how their own values may have been informed by the dominant culture.

↤ ↠

Socioculturally attuned therapists consider what values they want to represent in their work, asking questions that help expose taken-for-granted societal expectations. They do this while standing aside to enable clients to reflect on the values *they* prefer and make informed choices from positions of self and contextual awareness.

↤ ↠

This is an active, not a passive role. Therapists take a clinical stance that greater equity leads to differentiation and, as Monica McGoldrick (2016), one of the first family therapists to apply Bowen theory from a socioculturally attuned perspective described, "come back again and again . . . to help clients expand their perspectives on their values" (p. 63).

Practice Guidelines

The goal of socioculturally attuned Bowenian therapy is to increase individual empowerment so that clients are able to make choices about how to respond to the circumstances of their lives. The following guidelines promote critical awareness of the systems within which one is embedded and differentiation that enables equity, flexibility, and options. They are not discrete steps, and therapy is likely to move back and forth between them. We end by considering Cloé, whose personal privacy and safety had been violated by their employer.

1. Expand Presenting Problem to Larger Contexts

When people initially seek therapy they are likely to be in an emotionally reactive state. The therapist's questions, comments, and observations help to deescalate the anxiety. The therapist builds trust and demonstrates respect through careful **attunement** that demonstrates thoughtful interest in the sociocultural and relationship contexts surrounding their concerns. In so doing, the presenting issues begin to feel more manageable. The therapist expands the conversation to include clients' social identities and locations, paying special attention to how these inform emotions and meaning. It is important to recognize and **name** the power processes in the immediate situation and validate emotional experiences related to injustices. Therapists promote optimism and hope by providing information about the process of change, emphasizing that through their work together, clients will gain perspective on their lives and the patterns and contexts that influence them, and that this will enable them to determine the direction they want to take.

2. Stabilize Immediate Situation

The process of thoughtfully discussing the client's situation and beginning to expand the context around it calms anxiety. Clients may also need to make decisions about the current stressors. Anxiety around these issues can easily pressure a therapist to solve the problem for clients and invite judgments that pathologize clients and undermine equity. Therapists need to have developed a critical contextual consciousness to help them be aware and respond justly. Emotions stimulated by clients' situations, such as anger, sadness, helplessness, or shame, provide useful information, particularly regarding the power contexts underlying the presenting issues. Being aware of one's own emotional response can help therapists mindfully determine the most appropriate and helpful action (Garcia et al., 2015).

3. Assess Differentiation Through a Relational Lens

As discussed earlier, thinking and feeling are connected. The ability to be empathic and connected to others is essential to well-being. In the process of self-discovery and differentiation, clients need to draw on and develop all of these. Because Western society privileges values such as individualism, rationality, and competition, therapists need to actively **value** feeling, intuition, empathy, and connectedness. They should encourage clients to be aware of their emotions, accept them, and use them to help clarify what is important to them (Garcia et al., 2015). They should also help clients identify and connect with people and communities that enhance their sense of belonging and support. According to McGoldrick (2016), "Clinicians and policy makers who do not consider clients' deep-seated need for continuity and belonging . . . are likely to increase the trauma of the original experience by ignoring the importance of their clients' connectedness" (p. 12).

4. Develop and Support Critical Consciousness

Bowen therapists often use genograms to map the people, places, contexts, and communities that are important in clients' lives (see McGoldrick, 2016; McGoldrick, Gerson, & Petry, 2008 for detailed guides). Questions suggested by McGoldrick, et al. begin with the immediate household and life cycle changes: Who lives there? What do they know about the problem? How do they view it? Where do other family members live? What has been happening recently? Questions expand to the current community, workplace, school settings, and to wider intergenerational, cultural, and societal contexts: What ethnic, religious, racial, trade, or professional groups do you feel part of? How was your family perceived in the community? What experiences have been most stressful for your family in the U.S.? This work may be done relatively quickly or expanded upon in depth over many sessions. As therapists help clients track family patterns over time and space, they raise questions that call automatic cultural assumptions into question and that help clients recognize and resist societal patterns that reinforce inequity.

For example, in this exchange between Monica McGoldrick (2016, p. 63) and a male client, she persisted in raising questions about his resistance to needing help:

MM: What do you think about what I am saying, that the strongest man is a collaborator, not a do-it-yourself guy who never needs anything? Do you believe that?

Client: . . . I still believe it's like my father was. You're the man of the house and take care of the family. That's it.

MM: And how did that work for him?

Client: I don't know. He did his best . . .

MM: . . . And you've always had the sense, maybe because of the "man thing," your father didn't let himself connect as much as maybe you needed . . . But my thoughts are that the rules for men have been very unfair and not worked well . . .

Socioculturally attuned therapists need to acknowledge aspects of their client's histories that have been influenced by injustice and marginalization as well as sources of resilience (Hardy & Laszloffy, 1995; Košutić et al., 2009). What sources of pride and shame are related to your culture of origin? What beliefs and dreams did your ancestors have? How have you been wounded by wrongs done to your people? How have you been complicit in wrongs done by your ancestors? What values are important now? Questions like these evolve as clients tell their stories. As the therapist listens through a sociocultural lens, new questions emerge, new stories are told, and clients develop a contextual understanding of themselves and their life choices. They may do research to learn more about the sociopolitical context of their family history.

5. Help Client Observe Own Part in the System

In this phase of therapy clients hone in on the most troubling or persistent patterns in their lives. They become observers of themselves in the present, connect current behavior to sociocultural patterns and family histories, and learn to recognize their own emotional triggers. Clients need support to tolerate the pain they may feel as they confront their sociocultural contexts and patterns that have been shaping their lives. Attention to emotions such as fear, anger, or shame arising from contextual experiences may catalyze reflective action (Garcia et al., 2015). Clients in power positions need to become aware of the consequences of their actions on others (Samman & Knudson-Martin, 2015).

As clients reflect on themselves and realistically assess their contexts, they acknowledge what they predictably do when anxiety gets high and begin to identify empowering actions they can take. People in all power positions may also experience "felt resistance" (Garcia et al., 2015, p. 5) as they consider changes that resist or disrupt established power systems and the status quo. Being aware of that anxiety and reflecting on it enables clients to shift toward action and self-responsibility. They can **envision** change and develop a plan for how they will respond differently to familiar patterns.

6. Increase Equity and Flexibility in the System

Clients are now ready to do the work of making choices, trying new responses, and developing more authentic and genuinely connected ways of relating. Instead of automatically reacting according to prior family patterns and societal stereotypes, or on the basis of one's power position, clients use knowledge of their own experience and situations to respond more intentionally. The therapist **intervenes** by serving as a coach and mirror, asking questions about what happens and challenging clients to break through societal patterns that encourage withdrawing, triangling, or other forms of reactivity. The therapist serves as an advocate for equity and flexibility, supporting all participants to expand beyond their comfort level to resist taken-for-granted pulls back to the status quo (Knudson-Martin & Mahoney, 1999).

For example, if working with Eric's parents, Jamie and Robert, the therapist would remind Robert of his desire for relationship and encourage his efforts to listen to Jamie and stay engaged rather than distance through anger or work. She'd support Jamie in her efforts to think through her choices when socioemotional triggers tell her she must keep Robert calm. The therapist would take a stand that men are able to care for children and help Robert persist when he is tempted to give up emotionally connecting with his son. As clients make movement toward increasing differentiation, their ways of relating become more flexible, less bound by fusion with sociocultural stereotypes and expectations. **Transformation** occurs as they are able to relate to each other from more equitable positions and join together to effectively resist discriminatory and marginalizing larger systems.

7. Plan Meetings with Family and Community

Bowen therapy may be conducted with individuals, couples, or families or applied in community settings such as workplaces and churches (e.g., Friedman, 2007; Gilbert, 2006). Regardless of who is involved in the sessions, the differentiation process involves thoughtfully planning and preparing for meetings with family members and other significant relationships and settings. Meetings may be part of researching information about one's family, history, and culture or steps to engaging with significant people and contexts in new ways. Ultimately, the goal is to be able to connect with one's own family history and sociocultural contexts and to build and maintain these continuing relationships from a differentiated sense of self.

Case Illustration

At the suggestion of their attorney, Cloé (aged 23) first visited Judith, a white 56 year old cisgender straight female LMFT, several weeks after discovering that their boss had installed cameras that enabled him to secretly view Cloé from under their desk. They reported that apart from a visit to their attorney, this was the first time they had left their apartment since the discovery. Judith's intake form asked several questions that helped her begin to orient to her clients' sociocultural contexts. She learned that Cloé identified as "queer" and preferred pronouns "they," "them," and "theirs." They had been married to James (age 23) for 3 years, held a BA in English literature, cited Swedish cultural background, and said religion was not important to them.

Because Judith had a daughter about Cloé's age and positioned her clinical work to counteract societal inequities, she was aware that the case raised in her feelings of both anger and protectiveness. As a socioculturally attuned Bowen therapist, she drew on awareness of these feelings to take a differentiated stance in relation to Cloé that was clear about the values that guided her work while allowing Cloé the space to define themselves.

Expand Presenting Problem to Larger Contexts

Judith began by asking Cloé about what had happened and the nature of the workplace and their relationships with people who worked there. She learned that it was a small accounting office consisting only of their employer, a white male in his 50s who appeared to be widely liked in the community and had long-standing relationships with the clients he served, a black female office manager who had worked with him for over 20 years, and a young single mother who assisted with the accounting on a part time basis. In exploring the incident, Judith assessed how the job fit into Cloé's sociocultural identity.

Cloé had felt lucky to have a full time job as an office assistant because it provided benefits and seemed more personal and flexible than larger places. They said that working for a large corporation would not fit with their values; that they and their partner James wanted a lifestyle connected to nature and the local community. Learning that their employer had violated them in this way was not only a betrayal by someone they trusted, but put into question their own judgment. They had thought of this man and the women they worked with almost as family. Their fear about leaving the apartment now was in reaction to loss of their identity as a confident person who could make their own way in the world.

Judy named the violation Cloé had experienced; that it made sense that it would call into question everything they believed about themselves. She shared her experience that when people are violated in this way, they often feel shame even though they had done nothing to deserve the assault. Cloé agreed that they were not at fault—that was why they had hired an attorney. Yet they were paralyzed, not able to trust themselves, while he [perpetrator] went about his business. Judith reiterated the unfairness and her genuine sadness and anger that this had happened to Cloé: "You did nothing to deserve this. I am so sad that this happened to you. I get angry when I hear stories like yours." This differentiated expression of the therapist's own beliefs and response to the injustice helped to set the tone for the critical self-reflection and action that their work together would inspire.

Focusing on the meaning and context of the violation started to expand the presenting issues within just a few minutes. Judy then further expanded the context by asking how their husband James reacted to the assault and about their history together. Cloé described James as "completely supportive," "angry on their behalf," and "a good listener." Cloé and James had married as young undergraduates at a small liberal arts college. James represented values different than Cloé's family of origin, who "were good, loving people that did not understand her." She and James had traveled and lived in several different places, looking for communities that were "more open and accepting" than the small town in Minnesota where Cloé had grown up. James fully supported Cloé's queer identity, which they embraced more fully in recent years. However, Cloé was still cautious about their gender identity and had "passed" as cisgender at work.

Judy sketched a brief genogram in her notes and used it to raise additional questions regarding relationships with family of origin and other significant community connections.

Judy:	You said your parents are "good people." What does that mean to you?
Cloé:	My dad's a deacon at church. My mom and dad would do anything for anyone. Dad's a teacher; Mom's a nurse. They care about people.
Judy:	How was that for you growing up? Would they do anything for you, too?
Cloé:	I always knew they loved me. I still talk with them every week. They're just so different from me. They can't understand. They know I don't go to church, but we don't talk about it.
Judy:	Have you told them about what happened?

Cloé: Not really. I told them I quit my job. When I call I ask them about their lives. It makes me feel better to talk with them, but I don't want to upset them and they'd want me to come home. Or Mom would come out here.

Judy: So you still keep connection with your parents, even though you feel you have to keep this big piece of your life to yourself. . . . Are there other people? Friends? Community here?

As the initial conversation continued, Judith picked up on key sociocultural themes and invited Cloé to expand on them. For example, Judith noted that Cloé described their parents as religious and that their intake form said religion was not important to them. She asked Cloé to say more about that. She also asked about their experience of living outside the gender binary. By the end of the first session, Judy and Cloé had developed a picture of the trauma as an assault to Cloé's identity as a queer person and a demonstration of patriarchal societal patterns that they worked hard to resist.

Stabilize Immediate Situation

Judith was concerned that Cloé had not left the house in almost 3 weeks and had mostly been sleeping. She was aware of her impulse to make decisions for Cloé. Instead, she engaged directly with them about the seriousness of the situation, inviting Cloé to think through how best to address these concerns,

Judith: I'm wondering what you think about not leaving the house for almost 3 weeks?
Cloé: I just couldn't. James is worried about me. He tries to get me to go places with him.
Judith: Are you worried?
Cloé: Not so much worried . . . I know this isn't me. I just need some time.

Judith continued the conversation with questions that contrasted Cloé's current isolation with their pattern of taking on challenges. Together they used anger at the injustice as a motivator for planning some steps to break out of the isolation:

Judith: From what you've been telling me, I get the sense that it's not like you to hole up by yourself. Is that right?
Cloé: I've always been so free, so bold. I think maybe I've been naive.
Judith: It seems more like it's the injustice to me. It's not fair that you're not able to be you . . . . How do you respond to that?
Cloé: It makes me mad! I want my life back. I don't want to be a victim.
Judith: What do you think would be a first step that you could do to take your life back?

Cloé decided that it was too soon to go out on their own, but that they would arrange to go on a hike with James on the weekend. Judith also suggested that James join them for the next session.

Assess Differentiation Through a Relational Lens

Given the family of origin history and early marriage that Cloé described, some therapists might have approached the couple with an assumption that the two were emotionally fused and needed to individuate. Judith began the couple session with a conversation about how they supported each other. She reinforced the value of James's focus on Cloé, his ability to empathize with them and to temporarily give up some of his needs to help them through this hard time:

Cloé: (to James) I worry that I'm being unfair to you. You're so willing to be there for me. And it just seems like all I can do is focus on me right now.

James: You don't need to worry about me. I just want you to get better.

Judith: Cloé, you said James was such a good listener, a real support to you. Has this been a pattern throughout your relationship?

Cloé: I think we've always been there for each other, but maybe sometimes I've needed James more than he's needed me. I think I struggle more than he does.

Judith: James, are you aware of that capacity Cloé says you have to listen and empathize with her?

James: Well I care about Cloé. And, ya, (smiles) I think I might be better at empathy than a lot of guys.

Judith: I know the give and take is a little out of balance right now. But it seems like your ability to be there for each other when you need it is a real strength.

At this point in the therapy, Judith wanted to focus on the strengths in their relationship, to see their connectedness as a foundation for healing and further differentiation. Judith also encouraged Cloé to be aware of their feelings. Rather than continuing to resist the feelings of helplessness and unfairness, Cloé decided to journal about them and make drawings based on them. They and James began to take daily walks together, while Cloé continued with therapy sessions individually. The more comfortable Cloé was accepting James's care, the more able they were to engage in the work of self-discovery.

Develop and Support Critical Consciousness

In their college classes Cloé had developed considerable critical consciousness related to oppressive societal norms and structures. Together with James they had taken active steps to avoid falling into taken-for-granted societal norms and create a life more consistent with their values. These were moves toward increased awareness, differentiation, and choice. Yet, as might be expected given their stage of life, these changes also involved some cut-off from connection to Cloé's sociocultural roots and family. In the next sessions Judith guided Cloé in continuing to explore how their response to the violation inflicted upon them related to key themes and patterns in their family of origin, culture, religion, and sociopolitical context. Through questions that challenged assumptions, expanded the focus outward, and invited reflection and integration, Judith maintained a curious and supportive partnership with Cloé.

"Men are violent and unsafe," was identified as a family and sociopolitical theme brought to the surface by Cloé's assault:

Judith: So now you think that all men are unsafe? How has that been for the women in your family?

Cloé: My mother is always telling us to be careful. Not to trust men. To be careful where you go. In her work as a nurse she has seen so many women raped or beaten.

Judith: How do you think this message that men are unsafe has affected your mother?

Cloé: My mother is very cautious. She doesn't go many places by herself. My sister is just like her.

As the conversation continued, Cloé realized that they didn't actually know much about their mother's experiences with men or the experience of women in previous generations. Their father and spouse were described as "exceptions," warm, loving, and nonviolent. Judith expanded the topic of male dominance from the family to the larger society.

Judith: You said your father is very kind. How does power work between your mother and father?

Cloé: No one really questions my father . . . . They're very traditional really.

Judith: But you question male dominance—a lot, it seems to me.

Cloé: Yeah. But it's everywhere, everywhere I look. That's why [explicative] like [employer] get away with it. Because they can!

Judith: Yeah. That's how power works, isn't it? But you're not letting him get away with it. You're taking him to court. You're holding him accountable. What else do you think is important to counter the male dominance in our society?

Framing their assault as an example of a larger system of male dominance was an important step in Cloé's ability to develop a thoughtful response to it. Several other key themes evolved as Judith continued to expand genogram work. For example, "doing good" by following a religious code was a major moral theme across multiple generations. Independence and stoicism were connected to survival and success for their immigrant great-grandparents from Sweden and continued to be valued family traits. Holding back from full engagement was a common "solution" to potentially disruptive disagreements.

Help Client Observe Own Part in the System

Cloé became better able to name the marginalization they experienced as a queer person living in a world still organized around a gender binary and male dominance. It began to make sense that they hid this identity much of the time, both because of very real societal discrimination and because family patterns encouraged only partial engagement of the self. Cloé also recognized that their sense that they should cope with the trauma of the assault primarily on their own was also part of family and cultural legacies that they had unconsciously continued. Through conversations with Judith, they began to track how their response to injustice maintained isolation.

Judith: How has the journaling about your feelings been going? What have you noticed?

Cloé: I've noticed that I am very lonely. I want to share my feelings, but I can't.

Judith: What do you think stops you?

Cloé: It just feels wrong.

Judith: Like you're breaking a rule?

Cloé: Yes! It might seem silly, but it's scary to think about telling someone what I'm feeling—even James.

Judith: How do you think people would respond? I'm guessing maybe some people would be more able to hear you than others?

Cloé: Ya. Probably. I think I just don't want to bother people. To upset them. To be a burden.

Increase Equity and Flexibility in the System

Judith began to coach Cloé in initiating a plan of action with four goals, all related to living out the family legacy of "doing good" in a differentiated way: (1) to become engaged in collective action to combat male dominance, (2) to expand safe spaces for authentically expressing their voice and identity, (3) to develop their own spiritual practices, and (4) to update and deepen their bonds with James and their family. One week they came in with an announcement that they had told their parents about the assault:

Cloé: I told my parents what happened!

Judith: Wow. That was a big step. Did it go as you expected?

Cloé: They were great! I told them that I had not told them before because I didn't want to worry or upset them. They seemed to understand that. They listened really well.

Judith: How do you think you were different in the way you talked to them?

Cloé: I had decided that I didn't care how they reacted. I just needed to be honest with them.

Judith: So you wanted them to know what was really going on with you. You wanted to be you. Were you prepared that they might not be able to handle it well?

Cloé: I thought through all that. I decided that I could handle it. I knew they loved me.

Cloé made similar changes in how they related to James, not only accepting his care, but also being more able to focus on what he needed. This change promoted more genuine equality between them:

Judith: It's interesting that you are more able to focus on James's needs now. Do you think this is because the effect of the violation at work is letting up, or do you think something else is going on?

Cloé: It's both. I always followed James's lead. I liked that he wanted to travel and live different places. I liked that he accepted me for who I am. But I didn't feel like I could disagree with him. I didn't even let myself have those kind of thoughts. So I think I also kept my distance a little bit. If I let his needs to be too important, I would have felt dominated.

Plan Meetings with Family and Community

Much of Judith's work with Cloé involved expanding their interpersonal connections and strategizing how to do this. This included being able to connect with the women they had worked with to tell them what happened and preparing to tell their story in court. Judith was always careful to recognize and validate the real dangers and stresses involved and to support Cloé in working through what responses were right for them. Another important step was volunteering in two community groups for young people. One provided support for children and adolescents questioning their gender identity; the other provided education to teenaged girls regarding sexual violence. Cloé invited James to several therapy sessions to help them work through the changes in their relationship as Cloé took a more differentiated position. In these sessions, Judith also helped James become aware of the hidden power he held in their relationship and to be able to receive disagreement from Cloé.

Cloé and James took a trip back to visit their family in Minnesota. One of the issues Cloé decided they wanted to share with their parents was their newly evolving spirituality. After the trip to visit their parents, Cloé returned for a final therapy session. They said they were surprised at how much more able they were to be themselves with their family. They realized how much they had missed being more connected to them. As a result, Cloé and James were discussing using the settlement Cloé received from [perpetrator] to start a small farm to table restaurant in Minnesota, a few hours away from their family. Cloé had initiated the idea and felt confident that they could thoughtfully work through this decision on equal par with James. Whether or not they started this business, Cloé wanted more connection with their family and was better able to engage with them even though their parents could not fully understand their identity and lifestyle.

Summary: Third Order Change

Bowen theory promotes systemic thinking. Understanding symptoms or patterns always requires going larger (McGoldrick, 2016) so that clients can see themselves, their concerns, and their multigenerational family systems as part of ongoing sociocultural systems. Third order change involves being able to critically reflect on how societal context and power processes are part of one's situation and making choices less reactive to these dominant societal discourses and contexts.

Cloé and James had begun this process. They recognized systems of systems and elected to live outside the dominant social structure as much as possible. But at their stage of differentiation, their responses demonstrated the tenacity of emotional fusion within both larger societal and family systems. Much of their resistance to dominant societal values had been reactive in nature, cut off from bonds that connected them to family and sociopolitical contexts. Cloé's differentiation work in response to the sexual assault enabled third order change; that is, greater ability to recognize and navigate complex social forces while staying genuinely engaged in their social worlds.

The clarity and sense of self that comes with third order differentiation involves awareness and respect for one's interconnectedness with the larger group (e.g., Wiseman & Papero, 2011). It may be compared to Freire's (1970/2000) idea of liberation through grassroots consciousness-raising and action. Through critical thinking and awareness of self-in-context, people discover their situatedness and how their own internalized images have been emotionally fused with dominant social systems, leaving them trapped inside a socioemotional web rather than able to make freely informed choices about their lives. Reflection on the self and the systems within which one is embedded enables transformative action. This enables awareness of community, which in turn supports increased empowerment.

References

Astbury, J. (2010). The social causes of women's depression: A question of rights violated? In D. C. Jack & A. Ali (Eds.), *Silencing the self across cultures: Depression and gender in the social world* (pp. 19–45). New York, NY: Oxford University Press.

Bowen, M. (1978). *Family therapy in clinical practice.* New York, NY: Jason Aronson.

Burkitt, I. (2014). *Emotions and social relations.* Thousand Oaks, CA: SAGE.

ChenFeng, J. L., & Galick, A. (2015). How gender discourses hijack couple therapy—and how to avoid it. In C. Knudson-Martin, M. A. Wells, & S. K. Samman (Eds.), *Socio-emotional relationship therapy: Bridging emotion, societal discourse, and couple interaction* (pp. 41–52). New York, NY: Springer.

Cohen, S., Janicki-Deverts, D., Chen, E., & Matthews, K. A. (2010). Childhood socioeconomic status and adult health. *Annals of the New York Academy of Sciences, 1186*(1), 37–55.

Cowdery, R., Scarborough, N., Knudson-Martin, C., Lewis, M., Shesadri, G., & Mahoney, A. (2009). Gendered power in cultural contexts part II: Middle class African American heterosexual couples with young children. *Family Process, 48,* 25–39.

Cozolino, L. (2015). *The neuroscience of human relationships* (2nd ed.). New York, NY: W. W. Norton.

Damasio, A. (1999). *The feeling of what happens: Body and emotion in the making of consciousness.* New York, NY: Harper Collins.

Duncan, S., & Barrett, L. F. (2007). Affect is a form of cognition: A neurobiological analysis. *Cognition and Emotion, 21*(6), 1184–1211.

Fishbane, M. D. (2011). Facilitating relational empowerment in couple therapy. *Family Process, 50*(3), 337–352.

Fishbane, M. D. (2013). *Loving with the brain in mind: Neurobiology & couple therapy.* New York, NY: W. W. Norton.

Fishbane, M. D., & Wells, M. A., (2015). Toward relational empowerment: Interpersonal neurobiology, couples, and the societal context. In C. Knudson-Martin, M. A. Wells, & S. K. Samman (Eds.), *Socio-emotional relationship therapy: Bridging emotion, societal discourse, and couple interaction* (pp. 27–40). New York, NY: Springer.

Freire, P. (2000). *Pedagogy of the oppressed.* New York, NY: Bloomsbury. (Original work published 1970).

Friedman, E. H. (2007). *A failure of nerve: Leadership in the age of the quick fix.* New York, NY: Seabury Books.

Garcia, M., Košutić, I., & McDowell, T. (2015). Peace on Earth/war at home: The role of emotion regulation in social justice work. *Journal of Feminist Family Therapy, 27*(1), 1–20.

Gilbert, R. M. (2006). *Extraordinary leadership: Thinking systems, making a difference.* Falls Church, VA: Leading Systems Press.

Gilbert, R. M. (2013). *The eight concepts of Bowen theory: A new way of thinking about the individual and the group.* Stephens City, VA: Leading Systems Press.

Gilbert, S. F., Sapp, J., & Tauber, A. I. (2012). A symbiotic view of life: We have never been individuals. *Quarterly Review of Biology, 87*(4), 325–341.

Goldberger, H. (1996). Cultural imperatives and diversity in ways of knowing. In N. Goldberger, J. Tarule, B. Clinchy, & M. Belenky (Eds.), *Knowledge, difference and power Essays inspired by women's ways of knowing* (pp. 335–371). New York, NY: Basic Books.

Hanna, S. M. (2014). *The transparent brain in couple and family therapy: Mindful integrations with neuroscience.* New York, NY: Routledge.

Hardy, K. V., & Laszloffy, T. A. (1995). The cultural genogram: Key to training culturally competent family therapists. *Journal of Marital and Family Therapy, 21*(3), 227–237.

Hurtado, A. (1996). Strategic suspensions: Feminists of color theorize the production of knowledge. In N. Goldberger, J. Tarule, B. Clinchy, & M. Belenky (Eds.), *Knowledge, difference and power: Essays inspired by women's ways of knowing* (pp. 372–392). New York, NY: Basic Books.

Innes, M. (1996). Connecting Bowen theory with its human origins. *Family Process, 35*, 487–500.

Jack, D. C., & Ali, A. (2010). *Silencing the self across cultures: Depression and gender in the social world.* New York, NY: Oxford University Press.

Kendall-Tackett, K. A. (2005). *Handbook of women, stress, and trauma.* New York, NY: Brunner-Routledge.

Kerr, M. E., & Bowen, M. (1988). *Family evaluation: An approach based on Bowen theory.* New York, NY: W. W. Norton.

Knudson-Martin, C. (1994). The female voice: Applications to Bowen's family systems theory. *Journal of Marital and Family Therapy, 20*(1), 35–46.

Knudson-Martin, C. (1996). Differentiation and self-development in the relationship context. *The Family Journal, 4*, 188–198.

Knudson-Martin, C. (2013). Why power matters: Creating a foundation of mutual support in couple relationships. *Family Process, 52*(1), 5–18.

Knudson-Martin, C. (2015). When therapy challenges patriarchy: Undoing gendered power in heterosexual couple relationships. In C. Knudson-Martin, M. A. Wells, & S. K. Samman (Eds.), *Socio-emotional relationship therapy: Bridging emotion, societal discourse, and couple interaction* (pp. 15–26). New York, NY: Springer.

Knudson-Martin, C., & Mahoney, A. R. (1999). Beyond different worlds: A "postgender" approach to relational development. *Family Process, 38*(3), 325–340.

Komter, A. (1989). Hidden power in marriage. *Gender and Society, 3*(2), 187–216.

Košutić, I., Garcia, M., Graves, T., Barnett, F., Hall, J., Haley, E., . . . Kaiser, B. (2009). The critical genogram: A tool for promoting critical consciousness. *Journal of Feminist Family Therapy, 21*(3), 151–176.

Lantz, P. M., House, J. S., Mero, R. P., & Williams, D. R. (2005). Stress, life events, and socioeconomic disparities in health: Results from the Americans' Changing Lives Study. *Journal of Health and Social Behavior, 46*(3), 274–288.

Luepnitz, D. A. (1988). *The family interpreted: Feminist theory in clinical practice.* New York, NY: Basic Books.

Mahoney, A. R., & Knudson-Martin, C. (2009). The social context of gendered power. In C. Knudson-Martin & A. R. Mahoney, *Couples, gender, and power: Creating change in intimate relationships* (pp. 17–29). New York, NY: Springer Publishing Co.

McDowell, T. (2015). *Applying critical social theories to family therapy practice.* New York, NY: Springer.

McGoldrick, M. (2016). *The genograms casebook.* New York, NY: W. W. Norton.

McGoldrick, M., Gerson, R., & Petry, S. (2008). *Genograms: Assessment and intervention* (3rd ed.). New York, NY: W. W. Norton.

Nel, M. J. (2011). Bowen theory and Zulu understanding of family. In O. C. Bregman & C. M. White (Eds.), *Bringing systems thinking to life: Expanding the horizons for Bowen family systems theory* (pp. 335–345). New York, NY: Routledge.

Pandit, M., ChenFeng, J. L., & Kang, Y. J. (2015). SERT therapists experience of practicing sociocultural attunement. In C. Knudson-Martin, M. A. Wells, & S. K. Samman (Eds.), *Socio-emotional relationship therapy: Bridging emotion, societal discourse, and couple interaction* (pp. 67–78). New York, NY: Springer.

Papero, D. V. (2014). Emotion and intellect in Bowen theory. In P. Titelman (Ed.), *Differentiation of self: Bowen family systems theory perspectives* (pp. 65–81). New York, NY: Routledge.

Porges, S. W. (2009). Reciprocal influences between the body and the brain in the perception and expression of affect. In D. Fosha, D. S. Siewgel, & M F. Solomon (Eds.), *The healing power of emotion: Affective neuroscience, development & clinical practice* (pp. 27–54). New York, NY: W. W. Norton.

Richards, J. C., Jonathan, N., & Kim, L. (2015). Building a circle of care in same-sex couple relationships. In C. Knudson-Martin, M. A. Wells, & S. K. Samman (Eds.), *Socio-emotional relationship therapy: Bridging emotion, societal discourse, and couple interaction* (pp. 93–106). New York, NY: Springer.

Samman, S. K., & Knudson-Martin, C. (2015). Relational engagement in heterosexual couple therapy: Helping men move from "I" to "we." In C. Knudson-Martin, M. A. Wells, & S. K. Samman (Eds.), *Socio-emotional relationship therapy: Bridging emotion, societal discourse, and couple interaction* (pp. 79–92). New York, NY: Springer.

Silverstein, R., Bass, L., Tuttle, A., Knudson-Martin, C., & Huenergardt, D. (2006). What does it mean to be relational? A framework for assessment and practice. *Family Process, 45*(4), 391–405.

Skowron, E. A. (2004). Differentiation of self, personal adjustment, problem solving, and ethnic group belonging among persons of color. *Journal of Counseling and Development, 82*(4), 447–456.

Sternberg, E. (2001). *The balance within: The science connecting health and emotions.* New York, NY: H. W. Freeman.

Stevenson, B. (2014). *Just mercy: A story of justice and redemption.* New York, NY: Random House.

Tamura, T. (2016). *Family therapy: East meets west.* Plenary presentation at the 2016 International World Family Therapy Congress, Waikoloa, HI.

Titelman, P. (2014). The concept of differentiation of self in Bowen theory. In P. Titelman (Ed.), *Differentiation of self: Bowen family systems theory perspectives* (pp. 3–64). New York, NY: Routledge.

Unger, M. (2015). Varied patterns of family resilience in challenging contexts. *Journal of Marital and Family Therapy, 42*(1), 19–31.

Van der Kolk, B. (2014). *The body keeps the score: Brain, mind, and body in the healing of trauma.* New York, NY: Penguin Books.

Walsh, F., & Scheinkman, M. (1988). (Fe)male: The hidden gender dimension in models of family therapy. In M. McGoldrick, C. M. Anderson, & F. Walsh (Eds.), *Women in families: A framework for family therapy.* New York, NY: W. W. Norton.

Watson, M. F. (2013). *Facing the black shadow.* (n.p.): Author.

Wetherell, M. (2012). *Affect and emotion: A new social science understanding.* London, UK: SAGE.

Wiseman, K., & Papero, D. V. (2011). How Bowen theory can be useful to people in the workplace: A conversation between Kathy Wiseman and Daniel V. Pepero. In O. C. Bregman & C. M. White (Eds.), *Bringing systems thinking to life: Expanding the horizons for Bowen family systems theory* (pp. 209–217). New York, NY: Routledge.

9 Socioculturally Attuned Contextual Family Therapy

Contextual therapists take the view that humans are fundamentally connected, indebted, and responsible to each other. Ivan Boszormenyi-Nagy devised contextual therapy as a socioethical umbrella under which other approaches may be leveraged (Boszormenyi-Nagy, 1987). The core idea—relational justice—encompasses fairness, loyalty, trust, and love. Its emphasis on "ethical demands for being aware of and responding to the needs of others" (Boszormenyi-Nagy & Krasner, 1986, p. 60) counters dominant Western ideas of utilitarian self-interest (Fishbane, 1998). Contextual therapy uniquely places justice as primary to healthy relationship functioning and personal well-being. When developed, it represented a shift from an emphasis on intrapsychic change to facilitating change in the ethical contracts between people (Boszormenyi-Nagy, 1987).

Nagy framed therapy as encompassing four levels: (1) the facts, e.g., the circumstances that impact life experience such as where one is born, key life events such as traumas, losses, and transitions, (2) individual psychology, or the meaning that individuals make of their experience and how that is internalized, (3) transactional patterns involving family communication, structures, and interactions, and (4) relational ethics—fairness in what we give to each other—as the overarching contextual framework for the other dimensions. This integrative approach invites many styles of practice and focuses on resources rather than pathology (Dankoski & Deacon, 2000; Hargrave & Pfitzer, 2003).

↞→

Socioculturally attuned contextual therapists inspire third order change by addressing how larger social contexts and societal power inequities affect the balance of fairness in people's lives.

↞→

The focus is not only on the immediate give and take among individual family members, but also on historical indebtedness at family and societal levels. From this perspective, third order change begins with **attuning** to systemic societal-level injustices under the surface of relationship patterns and **naming** unfairness in current relationships and those of prior generations. It **values** just relationships by crediting the contributions of others and taking accountability for the impact of one's actions. Therapists **intervene** in inequitable relationship patterns and help clients **envision** an ethical give and take with an eye toward **transformation** of the systemic balance of fairness across current and future generations.

In this chapter we first highlight five enduring family therapy concepts that guide contextual therapy: interpersonal consequences, balance of fairness, entitlement, intergenerational loyalty, and multidirected partiality. We then show how to apply them from a socioculturally attuned perspective and illustrate with a case.

Primary Enduring Contextual Family Therapy Concepts

In Nagy's framework, context refers to the ethical connections within which individual development and interpersonal dynamics occur (van Heusden & van den Eerenbeemt, 1987). Whether we see an individual or a family, these ethical considerations are always present. A look at the case of Barbara, a 25-year-old Anishinabe (sometimes referred to as Chippewa or Ojibwe) woman with a 5-year-old daughter, will help us understand the concepts in contextual therapy. Barbara sought therapy because she was in a new relationship with Karl, aged 32, whom she described as a "good" man that she did not want to "lose." Both the men in her previous relationships were in prison. She said she could afford one session a month from her job as a waitress and would not accept a reduction in fee. From a contextual perspective, this therapy is about what Barbara has a right to expect in relational give and take between herself and others.

Interpersonal Consequences

Nagy was strongly influenced by Martin Buber's (1958) view that personhood is founded on relationships rather than self-interest, living *with* the world rather than *in* it (Boszormenyi-Nagy & Spark, 1973; Fishbane, 1998). He viewed relationships as a dialogical process "of receiving through giving, through caring about the other" and grounded his approach to therapy in "responsibility for all those who will be affected by his or her work" (van Heuseden & van den Eerenbeemt, 1987, pp. 4–6). In Barbara's case this included her relationships with her daughter Cora and partner Karl, but also her mother, stepfather, former foster care parents, former partners, people in her community and at work, and future grandchildren.

Contextual therapists believe that what we do inevitably has consequences for others. Symptoms occur when there are violations to this foundational ethical contract (Hargrave & Pfitzer, 2003). Like many clients, Barbara had a long history of interpersonal wounds and betrayals. She "inherited" the effects of her drug-addicted mother who supported her habit through sex work and the stepfather who sexually abused her. She suffered physical abuse from her first partner, and left him when she learned she was pregnant. These relational injustices were rooted within legacies of historical injustice and trauma suffered by the Anishinabe (which means "first people") as European Americans systematically took their land and culture from them. As we will see, the consequences of the trauma inflicted upon her people continued forward through multiple generations.

Contextual therapy emphasizes that Barbara was entitled to care and respect *and* helps her be responsible for the consequences of her responses to these prior injustices. Her therapist is empathic and stresses that Barbara is not responsible for the abuse she endured. She also asks about how these previous experiences affect the way Barbara parents Cora and her ability to be a trustworthy partner with Karl. Rather than considering only pathology in her family history, contextual therapy helps her find resources that she can carry forward (Boszormenyi-Nagy & Spark, 1973; Fishbane, 2005). The work is intergenerational and seeks to rebalance fairness in these relationships, with attention to the consequences for all family members (Roberto, 1992).

Balance of Fairness

Justice is a synthesis of the reciprocity balance among family members (Boszormenyi-Nagy & Spark, 1973). This means that people must openly acknowledge the positive contributions that they have made to others and that others have made to them (Goldenthal, 1996). Nagy called this *due crediting*. This is not just a behavioral action; it includes the capacity to be sensitive to others, to see from their perspective, and "above all give care to others" (Goldenthal, 1996, p. 19). When the giving and taking of care is out of balance, the relationship is not just. Therapists must be able to name and acknowledge the unfairness and play an active role in facilitating a more equitable and ethical balance of care. Helping family members balance the ledger of fairness—who owes what to whom—is a core goal in contextual therapy.

Justice is not simply a 50-50 exchange, "I do this for you, and you do this for me." It is based on genuine care and giving what is needed in the circumstances. It means providing care when someone is sick or disabled, but also acknowledges ways those receiving may also be giving. It involves commitment to the well-being of one another over the long term. In the case of a parent such as Barbara, reciprocity is not "tit for tat"; as an adult Barbara is responsible for creating a safe and nurturing environment for her daughter. In her relationship with Karl, Barbara is entitled to mutual support (Knudson-Martin & Huenergardt, 2010).

Entitlement

All persons are entitled to care and nurturance from others. This is especially true of children from adult caregivers. Boszormenyi-Nagy used the notion of *constructive entitlement* to describe the outcome of receiving positive and responsive care. Having received care as children, we have the capacity to give care to others as adults, to pass it along. When entitlement to care is not met, the person approaches relationships from a position of *destructive entitlement*; they are owed a debt, and this may result in lack of sensitivity to others and actions that cause pain or harm. Or, as in Barbara's case, destructive entitlement may skew a person's perceptions of justice so that they do not feel entitled to care and do not expect to receive it from others. They may always do for others without receiving care in return. Either way, the balance of care in current relationships is unfair.

Sometimes destructive entitlement weakens parental boundaries such that the child must take care of the parent. Barbara had been expecting 5-year-old Cora to show care and respect for her feelings, something she was entitled to and did not receive as a child or in prior relationships with men. Although a 5-year-old can and should learn to respond sensitively to others (Siegel & Hartzell, 2003), Barbara had been expecting a level of validation from Cora that a child could not provide. When she understood this, Barbara was able to respond to Cora from a position of care rather than anger.

On the other hand, Barbara had been uncertain whether she was entitled to the care and sensitivity Karl demonstrated to her. She began to feel emotionally indebted, fearful that he would leave her if she asked or expected too much. The therapist facilitated several couple sessions that helped Karl explicitly credit Barbara with all that she gave to him, reinforced her entitlement to care, and clarified what mutual care and support would look like for them. As we will discuss in more detail later, the imbalance of expectations around care, common among heterosexual couples, was also part of Barbara's intergenerational legacy with gender, race, class, and oppression intersecting in her family history.

Intergenerational Loyalty

In contextual therapy, Barbara's current relationships cannot be understood apart from her loyalty to her family of origin. Loyalty is defined differently than we may usually think of it. Here, it is an existential bond that connects us to our origins, but may be invisible to us. According to Boszormenyi-Nagy and Krasner (1986), "it is almost synonymous with the essential irrefutability of family ties" (p. 15). We may consciously disavow or disconnect from family members but remain drawn to our indebtedness to them. It is a systemic force directed toward group survival rather than just individual character (Boszormenyi-Nagy & Spark, 1973).

Barbara left home at the age of 16 and has not seen her mother since. The doubt, uncertainty, and inability to trust that Barbara experienced when Karl demonstrated caring and treated her well are examples of invisible loyalty. She did not want to be obliged to the therapist by not paying full fee, but was unaware of the ways she unconsciously maintained loyalty/obligation to her mother and prior generations. From a contextual perspective, finding ways to express healthy filial loyalty to her parents was an important developmental task (Fishbane, 2005). It would free her to new possibilities in her own life and help her engage responsibly with Cora and Karl. It meant learning to see her mother in a broader context and giving her credit for her positive contributions to Barbara's life. In contextual therapy this process is called *exoneration*, or "lifting the load of culpability of a person who has previously been blamed for a violation" (Hargrave & Pfitzer, 2003, p. 139). Ideally, but not necessarily, it is also linked to processes of forgiveness in which love and trust are reestablished (Hargrave & Pfitzer, 2003).

Multidirected Partiality

Multidirected partiality is at the heart of what contextual therapists do (Goldenthal, 1996; Roberto, 1992). Therapists demonstrate empathy to everyone while highlighting issues of relational ethics (Sibley, Schmidt, & Kimmes, 2015). They take into consideration the relational claims of each person, whether or not they are in the room. Through the technique of due crediting, therapists highlight relational injustices that each person has experienced and acknowledge their efforts and contributions. For example, Barbara's therapist recognized and empathized with the pain and injustice she suffered as a child and in her prior relationships. However, she also brought the interests and contributions of her birth and foster parents into the room.

Contextual therapists explore the past but emphasize due crediting as a current process. The therapist asked Barbara what she learned about relationships from her foster family. Though Barbara had not previously focused on the resources this family had provided to her, it was easy for her to identify the stability and love they had offered. The value of these important contributions had been lost to Barbara due to *split loyalty*; the invisible pull of loyalty to her birth family kept her focused on what they owed her, rather than what she had actually received from the foster family. As a result, she had not maintained connection with them. When she contacted her foster parents and thanked them, they were overjoyed and still available to her.

Rebalancing trust and fairness when there are legacies of injustice such as trauma and abuse can require many sessions (Wells et al., 2017). But not always (Goldenthal, 1996). Barbara did not know much of her mother's story, but knew how to find her. The therapist and Barbara discussed what it would mean to invite her to a therapy session and the uncertainty of not knowing what to expect. Barbara was motivated to transform her life and ready to take this important step. In the intervening time her mother had done a lot of her own transformative work and was active in a 12-step program. She welcomed the opportunity to revisit her relationship with Barbara. The therapist began the one two-hour session with an assumption that there were relational resources that could be accessed. She invited the mother to tell her story, helping them look not only at what Barbara was entitled to as a child, but to hear and credit the mother's anguish at willingly giving up her child because she did not believe she could care for her. The mother recounted how her desire to get her child back had motivated her to get clean and marry an older man (now deceased) who could provide economic stability.

The role of the therapist is not neutral (Goldenthal, 1996). Therapists align with different persons at different times and use their power to help balance relational ledgers. This is an active role based on multidirected caring and empathy (Sibley et al., 2015). Barbara's therapist moved back and forth between caring and empathy for Barbara and for her mother.

She brought forward and credited the mother's story and then also brought forward Barbara's sense of abandonment when losing the foster family she had loved for 10 years. The therapist used her role to facilitate a conversation about what Barbara and her mother needed from each other now. She addressed their shared sadness at never knowing the birth father and Barbara's experience of sexual abuse, which the mother had not known. Barbara recounted how she had purposely protected her mother from knowing this because she did not want to hurt her (an example of invisible loyalty). The mother was able to acknowledge that at the time she was using Barbara to fill her own need to be a better mother. Understanding how larger patterns of societal injustice contributed to the trauma they each experienced was an important part of the process.

Exoneration of past injustice occurred as Barbara began to understand why she was not given her due and began to see her parents as real people (Fishbane, 1998). Barbara and her mother developed a plan for maintaining limited contact with each other and for Cora to know her grandmother. This was facilitated by their shared interest in reconnecting with generational legacies of injustice, community, and pride as members of the Anishinabe nation. Following this session, Barbara reported a fundamental transformation in her sense of self. She felt more comfortable with, and entitled to, a mutually supportive relationship with Karl and more confident in herself as a loving parent, while also gradually building a relationship with her mother and claiming her identity as an Anishinabe woman. The therapist's active use of multidirected partiality enabled the family to rebalance the generational ledger and intentionally redirect their responses to old wounds.

Integrating Principles of Socioculturally Attuned Family Therapy

Contextual therapy has been underutilized and understudied (Dankoski & Deacon, 2000; Gangamma, Bartle-Haring, Holowacz, Hartwell, & Glebova, 2015; Sibley et al., 2015). In part, this may be because notions such as sensitivity, integrity, and relational responsibility do not resonate with Western male dominant culture as much as ideas such as rationality, individuality, and authority (Dankoski & Deacon, 2000). The relational justice focus of contextual therapy can be expanded to clarify the impact of broader societal systems and power to enable third order change.

⥾

Justice within a family system can never be separate from justice within the larger societal context.

⥾

Societal Systems

How family members experience what they owe each other and what they are entitled to is shaped by cultural norms and values, structural inequities, and legacies of sociopolitical injustices and traumas.

Justice

Like feminists and critical theorists, Nagy suggested that therapists look beneath observable behavior to the underlying experience of justice (Boszormenyi-Nagy & Spark, 1973). The meaning and impact of a behavior can only be understood in this context. Imagine that you are watching the tape of a therapy session and see a male partner place his hand on his female partner's leg. Is this a sign of support or control? Does it represent an alternative to male dominance or an enactment of it? When a child sits quietly in a family therapy session, is this a sign of fear or trust? How do societal models of parenting or structural oppression in the community invite this behavior? What if a child is not attentive in the classroom? What aspects of family and societal justice might be involved? What dimensions of relational justice are involved when a teenaged male joins a gang? How might racial or socioeconomic justice impact this act? How do these experiences connect to gender or historical family ledgers?

Nagy emphasized the need to look beyond the immediate give-and-take to place relationship patterns in context of the ledger of indebtedness across generations and the group's history. Though he was interested in the distribution of merit across the whole relational/social system, he avoided addressing what this might look like at the societal level (Boszormenyi-Nagy & Spark, 1973; Fowers & Wegner, 1997).

◄←→►

A socioculturally attuned approach links person-to-person exploitation to structural exploitation that may be oppressing all participants.

◄←→►

As we will discuss more fully, in Barbara's case, she and her mother were both exploited through patriarchy and colonization.

Values

Unlike dominant economic systems, contextual therapy values caring work and equity. It challenges the myth of the rugged individual (Fishbane, 1998) and views justice as collaborative rather than competitive. It can be easy for persons raised in Western cultures to think of ledgers or give-and-take from a more individualistic exchange perspective. Instead of helping people negotiate "I'll do this for you and you do this for me," socioculturally attuned therapists help people approach each other with empathy rather than blame and encourage them to attune to each other and the relationship overall. Competitive mindsets and power dynamics can limit this kind of mutual attending (Knudson-Martin & Huenergardt, 2010).

◄←→►

When persons genuinely take on the experience of another, they also begin to demonstrate more responsibility for the effect of their actions on them.

◄←→►

Knudson-Martin and Huenergardt (2010) described therapy with Damon, a European American university student who considered himself a "geek" and not people-oriented, and his female partner Ellie. Though Ellie was also studying computer science, like many women she took a more collaborative approach to their relationship. The couple typified the gendered culture of contemporary heterosexual relationships in the U.S.; men enact individualism while their partners carry the relational load (Loscocco & Walzer, 2013). The couple described an incident in which Damon got angry with his aunt (with whom they lived) and walked out of the room, leaving Ellie to deal with the aunt. The therapists did not automatically accept the cultural idea than men, especially computer nerds, are not relational. Instead, they encouraged Damon to imagine what it was like for Ellie when he walked out. The therapist did not place the burden on Ellie to tell him—an approach that could reinforce the relational disparity between them; they stuck with Damon until he could take in her experience. When he did, he began to see the unfairness and was motivated to engage more equitably in the relationship.

Helping clients identify multiple cultural discourses in their lives enables more choice regarding what cultural values mean to them, which they want to enact, and how they perform them. In addition to thinking that geeks could not be people persons, Damon also believed in fairness and genuinely valued and loved Ellie. He needed help enacting these caring values that male dominant culture discouraged. We find that nearly all religions and cultures hold values related to mutual respect and fairness. Socioculturally attuned therapists help clients reflect on these values and consider how to embody them in their relationships.

Historical Injustices and Trauma

Millions of people suffer from intergenerational effects of historical injustices such as slavery, religious oppression, genocide, and colonization that systematically destroy the culture, land ownership, spiritual practices, and humans themselves (Brown, 2008). This kind of historical trauma weakens traditional cultural coping strategies and creates stress and trauma that affects present-day circumstances. Because it was not safe for disenfranchised survivors to express hostility toward the oppressors, they often internalized anger, grief, sadness, loss, shame, and inferiority that are passed on and affect the next generation (Brave Heart & DeBruyn, 1998). Groups with these historical injustices endure high rates of depression, violence, substance abuse, and suicide (Brown, 2008). From a contextual therapy point of view, when the reality of these injustices is acknowledged, it is possible to transform what they mean going forward.

Consider the effect of the cultural genocide of indigenous people on Barbara. European colonization of the Anishinabe homeland forced social changes that disrupted her ancestors' balance of life, leaving them facing death, disease, and starvation and increasingly reliant on foreign commodities (Brave Heart & DeBruyn, 1998; Brownlie, 2008). In the 19th century her people were removed from their traditional lands. Those who survived were consigned to small tracts, reservations with few resources. Women, who had held high status prior to European encroachment, found their roles and value diminished (Brownlie, 2008).

Barbara's grandparents grew up in the economically devastated conditions of one of these reservations. Her grandfather was sent to a boarding school designed to solve the "Indian problem" by teaching native children dominant culture values (Brave Heart & DeBruyn, 1998, p. 63). He was beaten for speaking his native language, not allowed to see his family all year, and labeled as a failure. As a young man he was sent to an urban relocation center where he was not prepared to succeed, developed problems with alcohol, and drifted back and forth between the reservation and the city. Barbara's mother grew up in this environment, with a father who was frequently absent and violent when he was present. She did not see jobs or opportunity for herself and felt ashamed of her heritage. At the age of 16 she left the reservation with an older man. Soon she was alone and drug-addicted, with no way to support herself.

The effects of historical injustice had been passed forward in Barbara's family and community for many generations. Barbara had grown up unaware of the strength of women and spiritual resources within her Anishinabe roots and with limited awareness of what her ancestors suffered. Naming the injustice was very important. This freed Barbara and her mother to embrace their Anishinabe identity, overcome internalized shame, and develop new life patterns that honored their shared history.

Environmental Justice

The balance of justice extends beyond the family to communities, nations, and social systems (Boszormenyi-Nagy, 1987). Nagy argued that family therapists have an ethical responsibility to contribute to survival of the planet, stating it was "therapy's ultimate mandate for humanity" (p. 321). The effects of environmental distress are not equitable. Mental health is highly correlated to where we live and our access, not only to services, but to a safe and life-sustaining environment (Hudson, 2012; Magistro, 2014). What is the quality of the air our clients breathe? Do they have access to green space? How crowded are their living conditions? Dialogue about environmental issues can help families redefine their lifestyles and priorities.

Many families have limited choice about where they live, the number of hours they work, or availability of safe and affordable green places (McDowell, 2015). Engagement in collective action is empowering. For example, as Sarah Delgado encouraged a group of homeless immigrant Latinas to reflect on how environmental factors impacted their relational functioning, the women began to expand their networks and create their own form of activism. "Many . . . stay[ed] after to talk to each other to assist with childcare and/or transportation" (Esmiol, Knudson-Martin, & Delgado, 2012, p. 581). Rather than turn injustice inward in the form of depression and hopelessness, they "grieved . . . their 'invisible' status here in America" (p. 583) and developed strategies for collective resistance and survival (see Dolan Del-Vecchio & Lockard, 2004).

◂─▸

The contributions that people from less wealthy parts of the world make to the lives of those in more affluent parts of the world is often overlooked.

◂─▸

Justice Across Cultures and Contexts

Men and women leave their families and homelands to provide services such as childcare and farm labor that promote the well-being of other people's families. Relational justice requires crediting these contributions and accountability to those who make them. For example, Rena's (heterosexual co-parent living in an upper class neighborhood) therapy focused on her depression and the effects of trauma in her life. When the therapist inquired about how she attended to her middle-school-aged daughters when she was feeling low and self-focused, Rena said that Josephina, her housekeeper from the Philippines, was "around." The therapist wondered how Josephina's contributions to the family were recognized. He asked Rena about the relationship with Josephina, her circumstances, and their agreement about her services. As a result, Rena acknowledged Josephina and developed a more equitable contract that included compensation for childcare. This was important because Josephina had been doing extra hours and shopping to make sure Rena's daughters were cared for. Her uncompensated work perpetuated societal and relational injustices. And, like many who care for children of the affluent, she had to leave her own two young children in the care of a neighbor.

Professional discourse regarding families and mental health tends to privilege science and objectivity as paths to healing and recovery. Therapists may overlook or discredit rituals and processes outside the dominant culture that may also facilitate and support relational justice. For example, once a year Hindu women in Nepal come together to participate in the Taj, where they perform dukha songs of "sadness, hardship, and suffering" through which they envision a world "where women were not the social and ritual inferiors of men" while men watch and listen (Holland, Skinner, Lachicotte, & Cain, 1998, p. 258). Valuing and expanding upon cultural mechanisms like these can help clients address and transform injustice in their lives.

Power

Societal power inequities affect whose needs and interests are noticed and attended to. This occurs in the larger society and in interpersonal communication processes. Preemptive silencing happens when people are never asked and their interests are not included in discussions (Medina, 2013). Decisions are made to develop a neighborhood, but residents themselves are not included in the discussion. Or, a family debates whether to go to the beach (which the children want) or hiking in the mountains (which the father wants). No one asks what the mother wants.

Recognizing Power Imbalances

It may be harder to notice power imbalances when people participate in communication exchanges, but their credibility and perspectives are minimized. This would happen if, in the family mentioned earlier, the mother says she has a lot of things to do and, whatever they do, wants to get an earlier start, but her concern is overlooked by the father and dropped from the conversation. Latent power (Komter, 1989) happens when participants automatically focus on the needs of the dominant person, primarily because societal norms and expectations limit the options. For example, the owner of a home has a right to sell it. Unless regulations protect renters they have no legitimate voice. Or, a family moves for the husband's job without fully considering the impact on the wife and children.

People in situations where their voice is not valued learn to keep their perspectives to themselves or find indirect ways to get what they want and need. Sometimes they eventually explode in anger. Others become depressed or resentful. Some simply stop being aware of their own needs.

↞—↠

In order to facilitate relational justice, therapists need to assess the power context of communication patterns.

↞—↠

For example, Kirstee Williams (2011) described her work with a female couple in which one, Michelle, had an affair. Michelle's partner Nicole was older, made substantially more money, and judged Michelle's "emotional" communication style as "immature" (p. 524). Michelle's affair was an indirect response to the power imbalance. "Naming the power difference enabled them to come face to face with the ways their differing societal power positions interfered with attaining their egalitarian ideals" (Williams, 2011, p. 524).

There are differences in how people see fairness, depending on their power location. Those in higher power positions tend not to notice that others attune to them and accommodate their needs. They may not feel powerful (Kimmel, 2011). Women are likely to feel more gratitude for the contributions of male partners than men do for women's contributions (Coltrane, 1996; Matta & Knudson-Martin, 2006). Promoting relational ethics requires that therapists' observations and questions make these subtle power dynamics and their relational effects visible.

Therapist Power

Multidirected partiality does not mean neutrality (Dankoski & Deacon, 2000). Contextual therapists care equally about all participants, but are prepared to use their power to temporarily "side with one person" in order to help create more balanced relationships (Goldenthal, 1996, p. 11).

◂—▸

From a socioculturally attuned perspective, therapists need to be accountable for which values they promote and how their actions affect relational justice.

◂—▸

Research shows that if therapists are not intentional about positioning themselves to help undo power imbalances, their actions often maintain unjust power relations, e.g., they may follow the interests of the dominant partner or speak as though the relationship is equal when it is not (Ward & Knudson-Martin, 2012).

Third Order Change

Like other family therapy models, contextual therapy draws on systemic understandings and interventions that include second order change in transactional patterns, e.g., change in the rules by which the relationship operates. Contextual therapy places this work within a larger ethical context—how individuals are responsive and accountable to relational connections beyond themselves (Boszormenyi-Nagy & Krasner, 1986).

◂—▸

Socioculturally attuned contextual therapy seeks third order change in which family members see themselves not only as connected and ethically responsible to each other, but also see their relationships and loyalties in context of their societal position and are accountable to the wider community.

◂—▸

A third order shift in consciousness provides family members with perspective on their social situations and ethical responsibilities and increases their ability to make intentional choices about how their actions contribute to posterity and the systemic balance of fairness. For Barbara, this meant she saw her own life in the larger scheme of history and actively engaged with her mother and Karl and their community in ways that help restore gender and cultural justice. They were able to intentionally promote the kind of future they want for Cora and society by balancing the ledger of fairness within their own relationship, in parenting, and in their relationships to the wider society.

Therapists are also accountable about the impact of their interventions and the values they reinforce (Melito, 2003). They are answerable to how their clinical actions help undo societal inequities or reinforce them. The following practice guidelines help socioculturally attuned contextual therapists facilitate third order change.

Practice Guidelines

Socioculturally attuned contextual therapy expands the relational ethics lens to include the sociopolitical context of intergenerational family processes. Goals go beyond symptom relief or behavioral change to love and trust grounded in a balance of fairness. As noted earlier, therapists are not neutral; they actively position their interventions to catalyze justice.

They are likely to engage as many family members as possible, including extended family and family of choice. The seven guidelines below are interconnected and inform clinical decisions and therapist actions throughout the course of therapy.

1. Practice Multidirected Sociocultural Attunement

As therapists seek to understand and **attune** to each person's sociocultural experience and empathize with it, clients feel felt (Pandit, Kang, ChenFeng, Knudson-Martin, & Huenergardt, 2014; Sibley et al., 2015). This sets the stage for family members to also experience empathy for one another, to acknowledge the hurts and injustices each has experienced, and to begin envisioning potential pathways to healing (Sibley et al., 2015). Identifying the societal contexts that give rise to expectations and feelings helps reduce blame and opens family members to each other's experience. They become more willing to be accountable for the effect of their actions on others.

2. Discuss Sociohistorical Context/Background

Socioculturally attuned contextual therapy focuses on justice as the bridge between the past and the future (e.g., Hargrave & Pfitzer, 2003). Therapists help clients explore and **name** the sociopolitical context of their family legacies. They want to know about the effect of historical events such as war, immigration, and economic conditions, as well as the family's ethnic background and position relative to others in the community. How was the family treated and regarded by others? What messages did prior generations receive about their value and worth? How might these have been related to social identities such as gender, sexuality, religion, race, ethnicity, or ability? As therapists and clients collaboratively create a sense of these sociocultural contexts, it becomes possible to develop empathy and/or understanding of parents and prior generations. People begin to see themselves as a transformative link in the evolving family and sociocultural history.

3. Identify and Acknowledge Unfairness

Socioculturally attuned contextual therapists assess the balance of fairness within relationships and social experience. Through observation and questioning, they track the giving and receiving care across generations and within intimate relationships. When people have suffered injustice, in their families and/or as part of societal processes of power, privilege, and oppression, having the unfairness recognized, **valued**, and witnessed is empowering (Weingarten, 2003). **Naming** the ethical violation is an important aspect of healing. Socioculturally attuned contextual therapists look for and explore experiences of societal level violence to the self and to one's group. We use violence broadly here to refer to direct physical attack and witnessing death, etc. to the insidious effects of continued disparagement, invisibility, or limited access to economic and other valued resources.

4. Assume People Want to Give

Societal discourses around autonomy and competitiveness can mask or pathologize people's desire to give to and support others. People who have been hurt by injustice and are owed care sometimes find it difficult to give to others, and people in power positions may not notice what others need. Contextual therapists know that at our core, people want to give to others and **intervene** accordingly. They approach each family member with these expectations and, without minimizing hurts they may have caused, also ask about ways that each has been, or would like to be, helpful. Conversely, it is a great gift to know how to receive, and not just give. By graciously receiving a gift, we are giving a gift in return. Identified patients/persons, i.e., those who have been defined as the problem, are invited to give as well as take. If the therapist is attuned to this process between give and take, then clients will be able to recognize relational goals and name interest in another's well-being. This shifts focus away from pathology toward resources each can provide others. Importantly, the giving of care is validated and honored rather than overlooked or framed as a problem. This shift in toward a relational perspective actively counters models of human nature based primarily on self-interest.

5. Encourage Due Crediting

Once naming and validation of harm and injustice have been clearly acknowledged, therapists encourage due crediting; e.g., giving the other credit for positive contributions to one's life and to the relationship. This must never seem to positively connote abusive or harmful behavior, but it does involve seeking to find genuine contributions (Goldenthal, 1996, p. 68). For example, Reuben had a history of relationships that ended because he was not able to make a long-term commitment such as marriage. He, his current partner, and their therapist all agreed that his ongoing experience since childhood of needing to care for and protect his mother due to her bipolar diagnosis made commitment to intimate partners feel emotionally risky. The therapist credited his entitlement to care from his mother, especially as a child:

Therapist:	(after Reuben described his childhood anxiety about his mother's needs) You were just a child. You needed her to be there for you. All children do.
Reuben:	I know. It's not her fault. She did her best.
Therapist:	She did her best, but she wasn't able to mother you the way I imagine she wanted to, the way you had a right to be parented.
Reuben:	She tells me she's sorry. But it's still a one way street you know. It's still about what she needs from me.

After more dialogue that explored and validated Reuben's right as a child to an adult he could count on to look after his needs and also being careful to credit ways he also experienced abandonment from his father, the therapist then moved the conversation to ways his mother had given to him:

Therapist:	We know your mother wasn't able to parent you the way she would have wanted to . . . . I'm curious, though; I'm guessing there are also things she *has* given to you. Do you have any ideas about what those might be?
Reuben:	She loved me! I always knew that! I still know that. She tells me all the time.
Partner:	You're so loving. That's what I love about you. You got that from your mother. I see that.

Both aspects of due crediting are key to rebalancing Reuben's relationships going forward; crediting what he deserved or was entitled to, but also acknowledging what he did get. Because mothers tend not to be credited and are frequently blamed for their children's problems (i.e., mother-blaming), helping Reuben acknowledge and credit what his mother did give him was an important social justice intervention.

6. Encourage Accountability

Contextual therapists raise issues of responsibility and accountability regarding the consequences of what clients say and do on others. For example:

Therapist: It makes sense that you would hold yourself back a bit from commitment. How do you think your holding back affects [partner]?

Reuben: She doesn't like it. But I tell her I just need time.

Therapist: (persists with effect on partner) What do you think it is like for her?

Socioculturally attuned therapists are also attentive to how relational accountability intersects with societal power dynamics. Reuben's sense of destructive entitlement from his family of origin combined with societal gender entitlement (Wells et al., 2017). The therapist helped him explore gendered power in his relationship, intentionally interrupting societal messages that say women are responsible for making relationships work or calming men's emotions:

Reuben: (regarding partner) She needs to be less defensive. I need to be able to have a conversation without her getting reactive. We can't solve anything when she's upset.

Therapist: It sounds like you're putting all the responsibility on her. What do you think you could do to make it safer for her to engage?

After conversation about the potential positive effect Reuben could have on how his partner communicated, the therapist directly raised the issue of societal based gender injustice:

Therapist: A lot of men I work with have a hard time staying present when their partners are upset. They have a hard time really wanting to hear her. Is that something you're aware of?

Reuben: Ummmm. Yehhh!

Therapist: What do you think society teaches men that gets in the way of being there for a partner?

7. Focus Forward

As clients develop fuller understanding of the sociopolitical and interpersonal contexts of their parents and communities, they are freed from invisible loyalty to the past and past injustices. Socioculturally attuned contextual therapists help people be intentional about how they want to interrupt the impact of family and societal injustice, what they **envision** going forward for themselves, their children, and posterity. This opens space for **transformation**.

Case Illustration

Let's return to Rena, the mother with the housekeeper from the Philippines. About a year prior, Rena (45), a heterosexual woman of Jewish descent, moved to the Midwest from the East coast when her husband Gideon (53) was relocated by the airline for which he was a pilot. Daughters Anah (12) and Ellen (11) went to a small private school. Rena sought therapy with Peter, stating that she battled depression due to a trauma history and that before the move she had seen a therapist twice a week for 7 years. She had tried several other therapists in the new community but was not satisfied with any of them. Peter, a 55-year-old European American who earned his LMFT after an earlier career in pharmaceutical sales, was the single parent of three teenagers following his wife's death 2 years earlier.

Peter approached Rena's case with the conviction she would be better able to manage depression and the effects of trauma if therapy focused on these as part of a larger set of ethical relationships. He was aware that his wife's death and his earlier career change highlighted for him the importance of being accountable to one's relationships and values and deepened his commitment to and hope for future generations. Though Peter was careful to distinguish his personal history from Rena's, as a socioculturally attuned contextual family therapist, he actively positioned his clinical actions to advance relational and societal justice.

Multidirected Sociocultural Attunement

Although Peter typically invited all involved family members to attend the first session, in this case he first met individually with Rena because she was so clear that she was looking for a therapist who would support her. He wanted to begin to know her and demonstrate multidirected partiality toward the well-being, interests, and perspectives of other family members as well. His questions focused on what family members needed from each other and what they were able to give. He also clarified what Rena needed from him and what each was willing to give to the therapeutic process. Peter began by letting Rena know that what she suffered was wrong, that she was entitled to better:

Peter: (after Rena described an overview of the history that brought her to therapy) You have endured so much! People have hurt you and treated you unjustly. A teacher who was supposed to support your dignity and growth, sexually harassed you. Young men you thought were friends brutally assaulted you, and your first husband raped you. And no one seemed to care or notice. No one should be treated like you have been! You were entitled to teachers and friends who supported you and a husband that cherished you. You had a right to expect others—your parents, your friends, the school—to stand up for you. And you didn't receive that.

Rena: (softly) No one has ever said that to me before.

Peter: You have suffered unfairly. I work from the idea that everyone needs loving and supportive relationships—in their families and also in their schools and communities. I see many people who live with the effects of the trauma and injustice they suffered. I see them turn the impact of these legacies around to create a better future for themselves and those they love, and to make the world a better place. Does this fit with what you're looking for?

Rena: Absolutely! You seem to understand how hard it is. I think I could work with you.

In this statement, Rena conveyed that the therapist offered her what she felt she was owed: understanding and safety. Peter then introduced the idea that Rena also owes others, especially her children.

Peter: I would like to work with you. I'm wondering also how your girls are doing? How what we do here will affect them?

Rena: They're doing OK. The move has been hard for them. Their new school is kind of hard to break into. You know how kids are.

Peter: I imagine that you want to be there for them, make their transition easier. What do you think they need from you?

With this line of questioning, Peter established from the very beginning that he sees Rena's therapy connected to the give and take between her and others, to what she is entitled as well as what she owes others. He also laid the foundation for exploring inequity in her marriage and extended family relationships:

Peter: How about your relationship with Gideon? How does he attend to what you need?

Rena: (tears) Gideon is gone so much. And he's under a lot of stress. Pilots in their 50s have to prove they're healthy enough to fly. When he gets home he needs to relax.

Peter: It sounds like you try to be aware of Gideon's stress and what he needs. Is he aware of yours?

Rena: I don't know. Maybe sometimes. I try to be careful not to upset him.

Peter also learned that Rena had limited connections with her parents, her two brothers, and their families. She perceived that they did not care about her, except in the most perfunctory of ways, such as attending family events and observations. Peter's response also showed multidirected partiality to them and to the family's ethical commitments to each other:

Peter: What do you think your family is missing out on by not knowing you better?
Rena: They don't know me at all really. They never did!
Peter: I imagine there is a lot of you that you wish they could know. I wonder what has gotten in the way?
Rena: (shrugs) Who knows? They always seemed more concerned about what others would think than about me.
Peter: That must have been very hard, especially for a child. . . . As an adult now, do you have any idea what would have made them so concerned about making a good impression on others?

Discuss Sociohistorical Context/Background

In the next session Peter began a discussion of the sociohistorical context of Rena's relational experience and the traumas she suffered.

Peter: What was it like for you growing up in [East coast city]?
Rena: I was always kind of lonely. Kids teased me about my curly hair. I tried to keep in the background.
Peter: You said on the intake that you are ethnically Jewish. Were there other Jewish kids? Do you think they teased you because you were Jewish?
Rena: There were only a couple of other Jewish kids in my school. I know there were other neighborhoods with lots of Jewish people, but not where I lived. I was embarrassed that I looked different and we didn't celebrate Christmas like the other kids.
Peter: How was your family connected to the Jewish community?

As this line of conversation continued, Peter learned that Rena had always felt isolated. Though her working-class family had lived in the same house all her life and were considered "respectable" by the neighbors, they seldom engaged socially with them. Her family did not practice Judaism or participate in the large Jewish Center in a nearby community. Peter also asked about gender:

Peter: What messages about being a girl did you receive from your family and school?
Rena: That I was supposed to be pretty . . . but I wasn't. I had a funny nose and unruly hair. I was skinny. Most people in my school didn't have expensive clothes, but the girls dressed cute, you know? I was always plain. My parents didn't allow short skirts or makeup.

Peter began to see that Rena found herself alone and in a one-down position at school. He explored more about this experience and asked where she found support:

Rena: I had a friend, Erin. She didn't have friends either. Nobody liked her. My parents didn't like her; they didn't like her values and Erin's mom didn't care where she went.
Peter: What did you value about your relationship with Erin?
Rena: I could just be me. She listened to me . . . sometimes. She made me laugh.

Peter asked about the sexual harassment from a teacher, placing this in context of her social location:

Peter: Being with Erin must have been a relief. You didn't have to be on guard. She accepted you. I can see why Erin was important to you. School was a pretty unsafe place for you. You were teased. You felt like an outsider and didn't fit what it seemed girls were supposed to be like.

Rena: (tears) If it wasn't for my friend Erin, I don't know what I would have done.

Peter: You said a teacher sexually harassed you. What happened?

Rena had been surprised when the male music teacher asked if she would like to help him with the music and instruments. She had never been singled out in a way that felt special before. When he started making comments about her body and sexual innuendos, she didn't know what to do. Erin told her it was nothing to be worried about; it was what men did. Rena felt uncomfortable but did not dare stop working for him. Her parents had seemed so pleased that she had been selected for this honor; she never told them how painful it was being with him. Several years later, when assaulted by multiple teenage boys at a party, she didn't tell anyone, not even Erin.

Peter also began to explore what Rena knew about her parents' history. She knew both came from families that immigrated to the U.S. from Poland shortly before World War II, when it became apparent that it was increasingly dangerous for Jewish people. Because her family seldom talked about the past, she did not know much about their experience growing up at this time in history, only that both families scraped by with very limited economic resources and were grateful to be alive. Peter wondered aloud what it must have been like for them and how their experiences may continue to affect them:

Peter: I wonder what it was like to grow up in families who left everything they knew and loved? I wonder how people treated your grandparents when they got here and what it was like to raise young children in a place where they were considered foreigners? This must have affected your mother and father and how they parented you.

Rena: I don't know. I never really thought about it. (reflective pause) Maybe that's why my parents were always so worried about what other people thought, why my dad just seemed to keep his head down and keep going.

Peter: You're probably right. I think it might be helpful to know more about this history.

Identify and Acknowledge Unfairness

Rena entered relationships from a position of destructive entitlement. In other words, she brought a ledger of unfairness from the past with her. The trauma and injustice she experienced as a result of bullying, harassment, and rape were not separate from, and were intensified by, her marginalized female, economic, and Jewish identities. Her family had responded to the historical trauma of the Jewish Holocaust by keeping quiet and trying not to call attention to themselves in their new homeland. Stripped of their economic wealth, living in a neighborhood with few Jewish people, and not knowing what to expect, they avoided close affiliation with their neighbors and kept their Jewish identities quiet. As Rena learned more about her personal and family histories and shared it with Peter, he took care to name the injustice:

Peter: The injustice done to your family can never be repaid. Your grandparents ran for their lives and for the lives of their children. They faced discrimination and poverty not of their making. . . . You needed people to protect and look out for you.

Peter helped Rena recognize how these past injustices contributed to inequity in her relationships with men, including messages she received about her worth:

Peter: All those ideas about how girls are "supposed" to look, how do you think they have disadvantaged you or put you at risk?

Rena: They made me think I was ugly, that I wasn't worth much. So I didn't expect much.

Peter: Do you think this is still true with Gideon? That you don't expect much?

Peter suggested Gideon join some of their sessions. This enabled both Rena and Gideon to recognize and name the inequity in their marriage, an inequity perpetuated by differences in social class and economic resources, as well as gender. The disparity was present from the beginning of their relationship:

Gideon: I was attracted to Rena because she seemed so pretty and so vulnerable. Just being with her made me feel good!

Peter: How did she make you feel good?

Gideon: She was there for me. She liked to be with me and do the things I like to do. She was a great listener! She still is.

Rena said that she was attracted to Gideon because he was stable; he knew what he liked and was "mature." She said she was surprised he would be interested in her. He came from a higher SES family, had economic security, and (in her mind) could have his pick of women. Recognizing a likely disparity, Peter began to explore their balance of give and take:

Peter: Gideon, you said you were attracted to Rena because she was a good listener and liked to do things with you. How does this work in your relationship now? Are you a good listener for her?

Gideon: (pauses) Hmm. I'm tired when I get home. She usually asks me what I'd like, how my trip went.

Rena: I try to focus on him. He deserves it. It would be nice if he listened to me, but my life isn't very interesting.

After more fully exploring this imbalance and Rena's need and right for care and attention, Peter named the inequity and asked Gideon if he'd be interested in knowing more about Rena's life.

Peter: Gideon, you really appreciate the care and attention Rena gives you. It seems like a pattern has developed where she focuses on you. When you come home she stops what she was doing and tries to be there for you. She doesn't have the sense that you're also interested in her. You've gotten used to her tending to you. Is this a pattern that you'd be interested in changing, that you could be there for her as well?

Gideon: Of course. I love Rena. She just never seems to have anything to say.

Peter: I think Rena has a long history of learning that people, especially men, aren't very interested in what she has to say. How do you think you could make it safer for her, how could you show her that you're interested?

Note that in this example, accountability for change was directed first toward Gideon, because he was the beneficiary of the imbalance.

Assume People Want to Give

Peter began with the assumption that Gideon cared about his wife and would want to help create a more fair balance of give and take. Rather than primarily seeing Rena individually, Peter encouraged couple sessions. This act of commitment to Rena and their marriage on Gideon's part was an important step in rebalancing the ethical ledger. In the past, frequent individual therapy sessions helped to fill the void in her life, but could not correct the imbalance of relational fairness that sustained Rena's depressive symptoms. Both partners began to look forward to the couple sessions, in large part because Peter recognized and highlighted their love and concern for the other, even when the going was tough. For example, one day the couple came in very distressed. Gideon was visibly angry; Rena was pale and silent. She seemed almost invisible in the room and surely her past injustices had been triggered. Peter joined with Gideon around his desire to be there for Rena:

Peter: (to Gideon) I don't know if I've ever seen Rena look so scared. I know you're angry. I can see that. I also know how much you love Rena, that you don't want to hurt her, that you want to be there for her . . . . What do you think happened that made her so scared right now?

Acknowledging Gideon's relational resources helped him calm and engage in the process of working through the situation. It helped reassure Rena that she had not lost his love.

Peter also assumed that Rena and Gideon loved their daughters and wanted to provide a safe and loving environment for them. He regularly asked about their well-being and included their concerns in their sessions. He also suggested several family sessions and one with Rena and the girls. These sessions included the premise that the girls had something to give:

Peter: (to Anah and Ellen) We've been talking a lot about what you need from your parents. That's important. And I'm guessing you also want to give to them. What do you think you have to give that might make it easier for your mother?

When asked, the girls showed considerable insight into their mother and seemed energized to think that they could help her:

Ellen: Mom really loves flowers! I could pick them from the garden and bring them to her. That would make her feel cared about.

Anah: I think mothers don't get cared about very often. Mom feels better when I tell her about my day and I ask her about hers. But I forget to do that. I should do that more often.

Peter also assumed that Rena's parents, who were in the late 70s, also wanted to give and that Rena would want to give to them.

Encourage Due Crediting

Rena had spent most of her life focusing on what she had missed. Crediting her parents for what they had already given to her was an important part of her healing. Rena was grateful that both her parents were still alive and that she could tell them in person. She experienced an important internal shift when she understood that her parents had always cared deeply about her and tried to protect her in the ways they knew. She looked forward to visiting them and her brothers and called them more frequently. Rena acknowledged the courage and sound judgment her grandparents demonstrated in leaving Europe before it was too late and how their immigrant experience was an act of love. She was surprised by how willing her parents were to talk to her about their lives when she asked.

Encourage Accountability

In addition to providing support and validation for what Rena was owed, Peter encouraged her accountability and responsibility to others from the very first session. He helped Rena develop strategies to stay engaged with her daughters even on down days. Rena discovered that this outward focus often helped her feel better. She learned to be accountable for what she expected from Gideon, her children, and her parents. As her understanding grew that she was entitled to receive love and care, that she was worthy, Peter also encouraged her to be intentional in how she wanted to relate to others and what she wanted to contribute, not only to her own family, but to the future.

Focus Forward

Understanding the effect of past injustices in her life and rebalancing the give and take in her marriage and with her children helped Rena move from hopelessness to optimism for the future. She made conscious choices about how to respond to her Jewish legacy and the isolation her family experienced as a result of the Holocaust and immigration. She became involved in Bend the Arc, which is a Jewish Partnership for Justice, where she learned how to advocate for the values she cared about. She also joined a knitting group at the Jewish Community Center that provided friendship and conversation in her new community and she volunteered for a committee at her daughters' school. She and Gideon took advantage of the many beautiful parks in their area, hiking as often as they could. Though still on anti-depressant medication, Rena was working with her physician to lower the dosage, with the expectation that she may not need to continue them over the long term.

Summary: Third Order Change

Rena's case illustrates how contextual therapy can catalyze third order change that transforms historical injustice and indebtedness to create an ethical balance in current and future relationships. The therapist positioned his work to be accountable to values of fairness and responsibility to others, actively engaging with clients in ways that moved away from dominant culture ideals of self-interest to our responsibilities toward others. This intentional shift on the part of the therapist was the result of third order change in how he viewed his professional role and responsibilities, with a focus on how the effects of his work ultimately affect the next generation and which societal values are transmitted. He recognized choices in how systems operate and that his actions were not neutral in what kind of social world he was supporting. This reflective stance served as an overarching lens through which Rena and her family could see themselves as a transformative link between the past and the future.

The therapy moved from a focus on individual pathology to the underlying relational and societal injustice and uncovered family members' desire to give. As they began to see their connections to social structures and sociohistorical events, they recognized how these had limited their responses to each other in ways that perpetuated isolation, loss, and trauma. Naming the injustice and unfairness while also crediting what family members had given each other enabled "exoneration," or starting fresh, so that they could envision an ethical balance of fairness and transform their ways of relating to each other and the wider community based on awareness of systemic choices. They moved from isolation to love, connectedness, and social action.

References

Boszormenyi-Nagy, I. (1987). *Foundation of contextual therapy: Collected papers of Ivan Boszormenyi-Nagy, M.D.* New York, NY: Brunner/Mazel.

Boszormenyi-Nagy, I., & Krasner, B. R. (1986). *Between give and take: A clinical guide to contextual therapy*. New York, NY: Brunner/Mazel.

Boszormenyi-Nagy, I., & Spark, G. M. (1973). *Invisible loyalties: Reciprocity in intergenerational family therapy*. New York, NY: Harper & Row (reprinted by Brunner/Mazel, 1984).

Brave Heart, M. Y. H., & DeBruyn, L. M. (1998). The American Indian holocaust: Healing historical unresolved grief. *American Indian and Alaska Native Mental Health Research, 8*(2), 56.

Brown, L. S. (2008). *Cultural competence in trauma therapy: Beyond the flashback.* Washington, DC: American Psychological Association.

Brownlie, R. J. (2008). "Living the same as the white people": Mohawk and Anishinabe women's labour in Southern Ontario, 1920–1940. *Labour/Le Travail, 61,* 41–68.

Buber, M. (1958). *I and Thou* (R. G. Smith, Trans.). New York: NY: Charles Scribner's Sons.

Coltrane, S. (1996). *The family man: Fatherhood, housework, and gender equity.* New York, NY: Oxford University Press.

Dankoski, M. E., & Deacon, S. A., (2000). Using a feminist lens in contextual therapy. *Family Process, 39*(1), 51–66.

Dolan-Del Vecchio, K., & Lockard, J. (2004). Resistance to colonialism as the heart of family therapy practice. *Journal of Feminist Family Therapy, 16*(2), 43–66.

Esmiol, E., Knudson-Martin, C., & Delgado, S., (2012). How MFT students develop a critical contextual consciousness: A participatory action research project. *Journal of Marital and Family Therapy, 38,* 573–588.

Fishbane, M. D. (1998). I, thou, and we: A dialogical approach to couples therapy. *Journal of Marital and Family Therapy, 24*(1), 41–58.

Fishbane, M. D. (2005). Differentiation and dialogue in intergenerational relationships. In J. Lebow (Ed.), *Handbook of clinical family therapy* (pp. 543–568). Hoboken, NJ: Wiley & Sons.

Fowers, B. J., & Wegner, A. (1997). Are trustworthiness and fairness enough? Contextual family therapy and the good family. *Journal of Marital and Family Therapy, 23*(2), 153–169.

Gangamma, R., Bartle-Haring, S., Holowacz, E., Hartwell, E. E., & Glebova, T. (2015). Relational ethics, depressive symptoms, and relationship satisfaction in couples. *Journal of Marital and Family Therapy, 41*(3), 354–366.

Goldenthal, P. (1996). *Doing contextual therapy: An integrated model for working with individuals, couples, and families.* New York, NY: W. W. Norton.

Hargrave, T. D., & Pfitzer, F. (2003). *The new contextual therapy: Guiding the power of give and take.* New York, NY: Brunner-Routledge.

Holland, D., Skinner, D., Lachicotte, W., & Cain, C. (1998). *Identity and agency in cultural worlds.* Cambridge, MA: Harvard University Press.

Hudson, C. G. (2012). Disparities in the geography of mental health: Implications for social work. *Social Work, 57*(2), 107–119.

Kimmel, M. (2011). *The gendered society* (4th ed.). New York, NY: Oxford University Press.

Knudson-Martin, C., & Huenergardt, D. (2010). A socio-emotional approach to couple therapy: Linking social context and couple interaction. *Family Process, 49,* 369–386.

Komter, A. (1989). Hidden power in marriage. *Gender and Society, 3*(2), 187–216.

Loscocco, K., & Walzer, S. (2013). Gender and the culture of heterosexual marriage in the United States. *Journal of Family Theory & Review, 5*(1), 1–14.

Magistro, C. A. (2014). Relational dimensions of environmental crisis: Insights from Boszormenyi-Nagy's contextual therapy. *Journal of Systemic Therapy, 33*(3), 17–28.

Matta, D., & Knudson-Martin, C. (2006). Father responsivity: Couple processes and the co-construction of fatherhood. *Family Process, 45*(1), 19–37.

McDowell, T. (2015). *Applying critical theories to family therapy practice.* New York, NY: Springer.

Medina, J. (2013). *The epistemology of resistance: Gender and racial oppression, epistemic injustice, and resistant imaginations.* New York, NY: Oxford University Press.

Melito, R. (2003). Values in the role of the family therapist: Self determination and justice. *Journal of Marital and Family Therapy, 29,* 3–11.

Pandit, M., Kang, Y. J., ChenFeng J., Knudson-Martin, C., & Huenergardt, D. (2014). Practicing socio-cultural attunement: A study of couple therapists. *Journal of Contemporary Family Therapy, 36*(4), 518–528.

Roberto, L. G. (1992). *Transgenerational family therapies.* New York, NY: Guilford Press.

Sibley, D. S., Schmidt, A. E., & Kimmes, J. G. (2015). Applying a contextual therapy framework to treat panic disorder: A case study. *Journal of Family Psychotherapy, 26*(4), 299–317.

Siegel, D. J., & Hartzell, M. (2003). *Parenting from the inside-out: How a deeper understanding can help you raise children who thrive.* New York, NY: Jeremy P. Tarcher/Penguin.

Van Heusden, A., & van den Eerenbeemt, E. (1987). *Balance in motion: Ivan Boszormenyi-Nagy and his vision of individual and family therapy.* New York, NY: Brunner/Mazel.

Ward, A., & Knudson-Martin, C. (2012). The impact of therapist actions on the balance of power within the couple system: A qualitative analysis of therapy sessions. *Journal of Couple and Relationship Therapy, 11*(3), 221–237.

Weingarten, K. (2003). *Common shock: Witnessing violence every day.* London, UK: Dutton Adult Penguin Group.

Wells, M. A., Lobo, E., Galick, A., Knudson-Martin, C., Huenergardt, D., & Schaepper, J. (2017). Fostering trust through relational safety: Applying SERT's focus on gender and power with adult-survivor couples. *Journal of Couple & Relationship Therapy, 16*(2), 122–145.

Williams, K. (2011). A socio-emotional relationship approach to infidelity: The relational justice approach. *Family Process, 50*(4), 516–528.

10 Socioculturally Attuned Cognitive Behavioral Family Therapy

Cognitive behavioral therapy (CBT) refers to a range of problem focused approaches that address the reciprocal influences between thoughts, feelings, and observable behavior. With roots in behavioral psychology, early models emphasized a linear analysis of stimulus-response patterns, goal setting, and behavior modification strategies. The addition of the cognitive component in the 1970s emphasized how people's thoughts or ideas about a situation impacted their responses. Many found these approaches too linear and focused on individual pathology to fit with systemic and relational approaches. In what has been called "the third wave" of behavior based therapies (Hayes, Luoma, Bond, Masuda, & Lillis, 2006) a variety of new, more contextually focused approaches emerged. These newer approaches (e.g., dialectical behavior therapy, acceptance and commitment therapy) include attention to how the context of a situation informs behavior and strategies that help people be more emotionally present, aware of their situation, and able to make intentional responses.

Though most CBT approaches still tend to focus primarily on individual experience (Craske, 2010), cognitive behavioral family therapy (CBTF) (e.g., Dattilio, 2010; Epstein & Baucom, 2002) was developed to deal with the more complex, systemic ways family members' underlying belief systems, emotional responses, and behaviors influence each other.

⟵ ⟶

Socioculturally attuned CBF therapists create third order change by attuning to systems of systems that maintain problematic relational sequences.

⟵ ⟶

Socioculturally attuned CBF therapists **name** unjust societal schemas and cognitive distortions and help clients **value** what society may minimize or overlook. They **intervene** by coaching clients to track and interrupt inequitable patterns, **envision** alternatives, and take **transformative** actions. In this chapter we first briefly review five enduring family therapy concepts related to CBFT then illustrate how therapists can integrate principles of sociocultural attunement and a shift to third order change.

Primary Enduring Cognitive Behavioral Family Therapy Concepts

CBT begins with the premise that troublesome behaviors, emotions, and thoughts are acquired, at least in part, through learning and experience and thus can be changed (Craske, 2010). The goal is to help people identify problematic emotional, behavioral, and cognitive sequences and replace them with more adaptive ones. When applying this process within a systemic framework (CBFT), five concepts are particularly foundational: mutual behavioral reinforcement, schemas, cognitive distortion/incongruent thinking, relational patterns of thought, emotion, and behavior, and therapist as coach.

Mutual Behavioral Reinforcement

According to learning theory, the consequences of an individual's behavioral response have an effect on its future occurrence (Craske, 2010). So if a child cries when a mother leaves and the mother responds by giving the child attention and delaying her leaving, the child may be more likely to cry the next time the mother leaves. CBF therapists focus on these kinds of observable patterns of interaction and the ways in which family members serve as *both* stimulus and response for each other. Integrating Bandura's (1973) ideas of continual social reinforcement with the systemic notion of circular causality, one person's behavior becomes the prompt for another's. Thus the CBF therapist would not only focus on the mother's impact on the child's behavior; she would also be interested in how the child's behavior impacts the mother.

CBF therapists are interested in how mutual behavioral reinforcement cycles influence family communication and problem-solving patterns. They have not necessarily attended to how interlocking patterns within relationships are connected to larger sociocultural processes. For example, they might not ask how the mother's response is related to sociocultural expectations about mothering or gender inequalities in family life and the workplace.

Schemas

The notion of schemas is central to how cognition is linked to behavior (Beck, 1967; Dattilio, 2001). Schemas are "deeply rooted cognitive structures and beliefs that help define a person's identity in relation to others" (McKay, Lev, & Skeen, 2012, p. 9). They are experienced as taken-for-granted "truth" about the world and our role in it. Schemas are acquired from repeated messages about the self as we engage in social situations. They organize the huge quantity of information in the environment into meaningful patterns that help us predict the future (Dattilio, 2005; Farrar & Goodman, 1990; Welch-Ross & Schmidt, 1996). Schemas are tied to emotion and thus serve as triggers for behavior. Maladaptive schemas such as the belief that others are unreliable, will harm you, or won't meet your needs are often connected to early childhood experience (McKay et al., 2012).

Schemas such as beliefs that one is inferior, unlovable, different, inadequate, or superior and deserving are examples of how core beliefs about the self affect how one approaches relationships and responds to others. If your internal truth is that you need to put the needs of others over your own, then when someone is upset you will likely feel guilty. But if your internal truth is that you are entitled to having your needs met, you may respond with anger if someone seems to ignore you. These fundamental orientations to others arise within a person's web of relationships and societal contexts such as gender, culture, race, ethnicity, socioeconomic status, sexual orientation, and other relevant social locations that inform our position relative to others (Silverstein, Bass, Tuttle, Knudson-Martin, & Huenergardt, 2006).

Though schemas are considered relatively stable over time, they evolve as we travel through life, go to school, engage in the workforce, move across cultures, and utilize technology (e.g., video games, television, movies, the internet). For example, children in the same family may have very different schemas based on their experiences at school. One child may develop a sense of herself as competent and the world as supportive and responsive; another may see himself as picked on and view the world as a hostile place where he has to fight for recognition or respect.

Cognitive Distortion/Incongruent Thinking

An important idea in CBFT is that family members perceive and interpret each other based on relatively stable internalized schemas that provide roadmaps for how to respond (Dattilio, 2005).

The problem is that these schemas tend to be inflexible and create distortions in thinking and attributions that create distress and conflict. For example, conclusions may be drawn about a family member's behavior without knowing all the facts or circumstances. Information about another may be taken out of context so that when a man makes a decision without consulting his female partner, she believes he doesn't care about her. Behavior of a family member may be overgeneralized, magnified, or minimized as in when a woman raises a concern and her female partner responds, "I can never do anything right!" or "I am worthless." Tunnel vision may develop so that we see only what we expect or want to see. A father may not notice his son's substance abuse or aggressive behavior because he sees him as living up to standards for masculinity that he admires.

How family members perceive each other affects their interaction. As they interact they not only create perceptions, but also see what they expect to see, filtering out information that does not fit. For example, Frank's schema suggests that Judy should be available when he wants her attention. He does not notice Judy's schedule or what her needs are and acts upset or disappointed when she is not available. In turn, Judy starts to see Frank as demanding and self-centered. Because her schema tells her she must satisfy him and keep the peace, she accommodates quickly to him in order to avoid conflict and keeps her resentment to herself. Frank sees their relationship as comfortable and is not aware that she experiences him as selfish.

After interacting together over many years, couples and families develop shared beliefs, or family schemas (Dattilio, 2005), e.g., "we can't upset Dad," or "it's best to keep our thoughts to ourselves." Entrenched ideas about how each member behaves and how a family functions and solves problems are foundational to the way a family operates. Oftentimes these are helpful, such as when children learn that sharing their feelings is expected and welcomed or when partners expect each other to share their concerns and are responsive to them. Schemas can also become rigid, restricting the interpretation of events and limiting choices and flexibility (Dattilio, 2005). CBF therapists focus on how schemas can create distortions and omissions in thinking that affect family communication processes (Baldwin, 1992; Baucom, Epstein, Sayers, & Sher, 1989). They have not always considered how these "distorted" ways of thinking may reflect shared sociocultural schemas that support some people's interests over others' and perpetuate societal inequalities; for example, how Frank and Judy's behavior reflects and maintains power differences between women and men.

Relational Patterns of Thought, Emotion, and Behavior

Family therapists typically do not believe it is possible to separate one person's patterns of thought, emotion, and behavior from the relational systems within which they are embedded. They are likely to be interested in breaking down or deconstructing the patterns of beliefs, attributions, and experiences that create and perpetuate destructive relationship patterns. In the case of Frank and Judy, the therapist would help the couple identify how each person's schema connects to their core beliefs about coupling and family life and how these guide their assumptions about how to behave and what they can expect from the other. Each will have brought their own schemas about relationships from their families of origin, and these will have been impacted by their life experiences (Dattilio, 2001). For example, even though Frank's mother had a full time job, she organized her schedule so that she was always home before her husband. When Frank was in college, the conversation among his male peers emphasized female availability to meet guys' needs. Anger was an accepted male emotion. Judy observed more mutuality between her parents and had learned to put relationships first. When Frank did not seem to notice her needs, her schema of self and others was challenged, leaving her hurt and surprised. When Frank got angry, her idea that she should preserve relationships influenced her to respond in ways that would calm him and, in the process, silence her concerns.

When people form adult relationships, they also create a union of their beliefs as they interact and respond to each other. This combination of ideas and life experiences becomes the family of origin schema passed on to their children (Dattilio, 2005). The family schema includes the beliefs, experiences, and perceptions of all the family members and evolves over time as circumstances and experiences change and new family members enter (e.g., birth or marriage) or leave (e.g., death or divorce). Individual cognitions thus reflect shared experience across multiple systemic levels. Judy and Frank (and their children) are now part of each other's cognitive, behavioral, and emotional systems. Though not always addressed by CBF therapists, sociocultural and community systems within which families are embedded are also embodied in the moment by moment of each family's relational processes (Knudson-Martin & Huenergardt, 2010). Judy and Frank have unwittingly enacted a model of male dominance that is now part of their own and their children's relational schema.

Shared schemas guide how we derive meaning from interpersonal experience and serve as important underlying organizational mechanisms for communication and relational/family interaction. This may help explain why Rusovick (2009) found that in their early months of attraction, heterosexual partners described finding themselves in the other; they reported a sense of sameness, of shared understanding into which the other fit and through which they recognized themselves. Because society and cultures are constantly changing, our shared schemas also continuously evolve. Just the other day Carmen overheard a 6-year-old say to his brother, "When you grow up, do you want to marry a boy or a girl?" This statement reflected a societal-informed schema about himself and others and what he can expect in life that had clearly been passed on to him by the people around him and legal changes in the U.S. that made this option possible.

Therapist as Coach

CBFT is described as collaborative (Craske, 2010; Dattilio, 2010). The image of a coach is a good metaphor for the CBF therapist role. CBF therapists are likely to begin by educating clients about the approach and some of the key concepts, such as automatic thoughts, core beliefs, etc. They engage clients in the process of observing repetitive patterns of thought, behavior, and emotion. For example, they might ask Frank and Judy to identify and record their automatic thoughts about each other and to note how each thought influenced their responses to each other. The therapist might then engage with them in a functional analysis of their interaction, pinpointing problematic schema formations that are leading to cognitive distortions. Like a coach, therapists work with clients to identify clear goals with specific objectives for change. They then work to develop homework assignments and/or communication and problem-solving exercises that will help clients attain their goals. The therapist is a facilitator and educator that helps couples and families take new perspectives and try new approaches to familiar situations.

CBF therapists draw on a range of interventions to help clients reach their targets. One way they do this is by highlighting and challenging thinking errors. Though these thinking errors can differ among family members, cognitive distortions are often shared. Both Judy and Frank may assume that the burden for regulating emotion in the family falls on Judy; that it is her job to keep Frank calm. Or perhaps Frank's masculinity-informed schema leads to the idea that if someone loves him, they will always do what he wants and not question him. Years of shared interaction have confirmed this perception and he and Judy may now share aspects of this idea. The therapist may help the couple challenge this belief, consider alternative cognitions that might produce different responses, and help them develop a plan to change this interaction. The process requires active participation and motivation for change on each participant's part. CBF therapists help keep therapy focused on defined goals, help clients create an agenda for each session, and provide useful information. The therapist may help family members practice good expressive and listening skills, facilitate conversation about their interlocking communication patterns, and/or develop contracts with each other.

Because CBF therapists play active educational and structuring roles in the process of therapy, their actions and input to therapy have a major impact on whether or not clients learn to see their problems as manifestations of individual deficits or as connected to sociocultural systems and the associated power processes.

↞→↠

Therapists help determine whether or not new relational alternatives generated in therapy replicate and maintain societal inequities or promote equity and justice.

↞→↠

Integrating Principles of Sociocultural Attunement

Practicing socioculturally attuned CBFT begins by taking stock of one's own conceptual frameworks about reality. Therapists must make sense of the vast and often conflicting ideas, experiences, values, and beliefs that inform how we understand and work with individuals, couples, and families, i.e., our schema of schemas (Parker & McDowell, 2017).

↞→↠

Socioculturally attuned therapists begin with the view that social schemas are inseparable from personal and family schemas; they organize therapy in ways that attend to power dynamics inherent in creating and maintaining these schemas.

↞→↠

Contextual Nature of Schemas

Even ideas integral to CBFT, such as the value of having goals or that people can and should take active steps to shape the direction of their lives, are linked to Western social schemas prizing individual autonomy and an orientation to the future. Learning to recognize how our own social schemas implicitly organize what we see is an ongoing process, with some social schemas easier to recognize than others.

↞→↠

Shared social schemas are so deeply embedded into every level of society that they tend to be almost invisible to us; they are so taken for granted that we often don't see how they shape and organize us.

↞→↠

Societal schemas shape the experience of self and relationship from a very young age. A major error in thinking typically occurs at birth when children are assigned a gender category based on the appearance of their genitals (Welch-Ross & Schmidt, 1996). This creates and reinforces the idea that there are two distinct gender groups and that people must fit into one or the other. Parents, caregivers, and other children believe in these binary differences and relate to children in ways that anticipate and reinforce them, even though the biological differences between male-identified and female-identified babies are minimal (Eliot, 2009). For example when parents expect a male child to be more active, they are likely to encourage and reinforce energetic behavior while being more apt to calm a female child.

The idea that there are two distinct genders and that these are somehow an essential part of a person's nature are part of a whole system of relating that informs identity and prescribes behaviors based on one's assigned gender. This gender system limits the allowable options for everyone and disregards and/or renders invisible a much wider range of experience. Societal gender schemas also typically presume heterosexuality as seen in a tee shirt for a male infant that reads "chick magnet." The slogan not only implies heterosexuality, but carries power differences in the construction of gender by characterizing females as diminutive. When a child does not fit this message, he learns that he is different, inferior, or incompetent.

Heteronormativity and patriarchal gender systems tend to reinforce each other. Thus parents of a young boy whose behavior seems "feminine" (e.g., sensitive, submissive, emotional) might worry that he will "grow up to be gay" and experience the negative effects of homophobia. Though the parents would be confusing sexual orientation with gender, this is a societal level error, not just a personal one. In order to optimally support their child, the parents may need help distinguishing the real effects of not conforming to societal gender schemas and how to advocate for their child from their own unhelpful fears and beliefs (Malpas, 2011).

The impact of social schemas on families and family therapy involves the broadest levels of social, economic, and political arrangements. When therapists **attune** to core beliefs within clients' schemas, there is nearly always opportunity to examine how these connect to societal norms and values that reflect and maintain larger social systems. For example, Tony, a heterosexual working-class father of three, sought therapy to address impulsive behavior that he described as "sabotaging his relationship." As he and the therapist detailed the sequence of thinking and feeling surrounding this behavior, his acting out was connected to core beliefs that "family men had to give up their creativity to keep a job." Rather than see this as simply a reflection of Tony's individual distorted thinking, the therapist engaged him in examining and **naming** the values and structure of the workplace, societal expectations for men around work and family, and how these affected his personal schema and relational well-being.

Behavior-shaping schemas based on capitalism narrowed both Tony's actual and perceived options. As a smart but not formally educated man, he experienced little validation for his independent thought or expectation that his contribution would be valued. Yet he also received many societal messages that as a man in the U.S. he *should* have a measure of power and individual choice. The effects of patriarchy, capitalism, and democracy came together in his schema in ways that were inherently contradictory. The idea that men have to give up their creativity to keep a job reflects Tony's low-status role in the workplace hierarchy. Yet the cultural measures by which Tony judged himself also included values such as free choice and entitlement to respect that reflect and maintain the privilege of the dominant group; i.e., white, upper-class, able-bodied, heterosexual, cisgender privileged adult males. As Tony became more aware of the impact of sociocultural schema on his behavior, he experienced less self-blame and resentment and was able replace destructive impulsive behavior with intentional actions that improved both his work and family life.

Patriarchy also requires males to develop characteristics that will allow them to take power over gendered positions congruent with traits valued in capitalism (McDowell, 2015). Men are thus trained to respond to others within a hierarchical schema of how relationships work (Tannen, 1994). In Tony's case, this meant he was supposed to comply with orders and policies delivered in a top-down fashion while at work and then take a leadership role in his family. These hierarchical relationship schemas left him feeling disconnected both at home and work. As he learned to recognize how these societal schemas impacted him, he was able to give more **value** to the relational role he wanted with his children and better understand his frustrations at work in order to develop strategies for how to respond.

Conflicting societal messages also place women and girls in a cognitive bind. They are socialized to develop a more relational schema (Jordan, 2009; Tannen, 1994). They are expected to emotionally attune to others, yet also learn that thoughts and logic are valued over emotions and intuition. Even though relational skills are institutionally and historically devalued, if women do not demonstrate them they are likely to be viewed as shrill, cold, uncaring, or self-centered. Holding a stereotypic female schema inherently requires accepting a less valued societal position in order to be desired or accepted.

Power and Social Schemas

Therapists need to **name** whose interests are reflected in the social schemas embedded in their clients' schemas. For example, African American family therapist Marlene Watson (2013) tells the story of her grandmother who said, "I was never pretty like my sister Brazolia. She was the pretty one. I was black and ugly" (p. 1). Though a black women, her schema of self and others reflected the societal framework that people with darker skin are inferior (i.e., colorism). Social schemas generally promote the cultural capital (Bourdieu, 1986) of the dominant group by privileging how *they* think and what *they* do while marginalizing the cultural capital and schemas of other groups. Like Marlene's grandmother, people often unwittingly adhere to schemas that reflect and support unjust social arrangements in their communities, living conditions, work settings, and intimate relationships. For example, systems of patriarchy that privilege "male" values such as competition, rationality, and autonomy and minimize "female" qualities such as cooperation, emotional expression, and caring for others (Jordan, 2009) are widely reflected in family structures in which women continue to do the majority of housework while their needs and interests are overlooked (Knudson-Martin, 2013).

‣‹→

Power processes in the broader society tend to be reflected in the power dynamics within intimate and family relationships.

‣‹→

CBF therapists should not assume that each family member contributes equally to creating the family schema or that each feels equally free or entitled to express their thoughts. For example, in the previous case of Frank and Judy, the entire family operated according to schemas that privileged Frank's experience and caused everyone else to avoid saying or doing things that might upset him. Judy's relationally-oriented schema from her family of origin, her experience as a woman, and more egalitarian models of marriage were subsumed over time by Frank's schema of male power and entitlement, even though he was largely unaware of his expectations or how Judy and the children accommodated him. Expecting Judy to challenge her schema-driven thoughts before Frank adjusted his would be difficult given Frank's inherent power in the family system (Knudson-Martin, 2015). In some relationships, encouraging a less powerful voice to express herself could be dangerous.

Prejudice and Discrimination as Cognitive Distortion

Prejudice is a form of cognitive distortion (Parker & McDowell, 2017). Societal messages about the deficits and inadequacies of non-dominant groups are integrated into our schemas along with those promoting the superiority of other groups. Those in marginalized groups are described in negative or less valued terms while positive attributes are associated with members of the most privileged groups; as when some people are thought to be smarter, more athletic, and better looking than others.

Though based on inaccurate thinking, processes surrounding prejudice maintain existing systems of power and privilege and support the idea that exceptions to our social schemas (e.g., the "poor" kid who becomes wealthy) are primarily dependent on individual motivation and hard work. CBF therapists can easily become induced into promoting these prejudicial systems.

‹←→›

If therapists are not intentional about expanding their lenses beyond individual and family schemas they will likely label problematic symptoms as individual deficits or flaws in thinking.

‹←→›

For example, consider a therapist working with a teen who is a member of a low socioeconomic group and identified as having a behavior problem. If he helps the youth recognize his belief that "I will fail no matter what I do" as distorted thinking without exploring the societal messages that tell him he is a failure, then the youth will see only himself as the problem—or he will resist therapy—and the systemic nature of prejudice remains unchallenged.

Prejudices are collectively enacted and maintain systematic discrimination throughout society. Social norms, laws, policies, and precedents result in unequal access to social influence and material resources (Jones, 1997).

‹←→›

Those in dominant groups tend to internalize positive messages about themselves such that their schema of self and other includes little or no awareness of their privilege that accrues based on group membership.

‹←→›

In the U.S. this enables middle-class white males to view their economic success and achievements as the outcome of individual hard work (i.e., myth of meritocracy). This is a cognitive distortion based on a partial truth; while hard work is important, the contribution of other social supports and access to relevant knowledge and resources is overlooked (Parker & McDowell, 2017).

Like the African American grandmother we discussed earlier, persons in marginalized groups frequently internalize negative messages about their group. These destructive ideas adversely shape beliefs about personal worth and abilities. For example, a woman may view herself (and be viewed by others) as too emotional to make good decisions. Two social schemas are involved here: one says that men are more capable leaders than women; the other privileges intellect over emotion. Moreover, this kind of systematic distortion (i.e., prejudice and internalized oppression) results in discrimination that maintains the dominant social structure. That is, leaders of an organization are more likely to be male and, regardless of who fills the position, expected to disavow empathy in order to put the success of the institution over the needs and well-being of workers. These social schemas also tend to denigrate those who receive welfare as unfairly "living off others," while viewing upper-class wealth made from the work of those in the middle and lower classes as fair.

Social schemas that support established larger systems are reflected in the attitudes, values, and behavior of individuals and families. For example, in the U.S. the economic system depends on willingness of people in the middle and lower classes to work hard, which is reflected in how values play out within families. Family members may be in conflict over what work counts, whose work is more important, and so on. The tendency to value paid work over family work is directly linked to societal schemas connected to capitalism

(Folbre, 2001). These schemas likely contribute to the power Frank holds in his family and Judy's tendency to accommodate his work schedule.

Impact on Equity and Well-Being

Socioculturally attuned CBF therapists should be alert to and **intervene** in the impact of societal schemas that suggest who is worth more—who deserves what and why. Considerable research shows that the quality of people's health in the U.S. depends on their race, socio-economic class, gender, sexual orientation, age, and ability (Center for Disease Control and Prevention, 2013). Those with lower socioeconomic class have higher rates of both psychiatric and physical illness (McCulloch, 2001). Racial minorities experience more illness and higher rates of mortality than the racial majority (Beals et al., 2005; Jones, 1997; Williams, 1997). Women are more likely to experience anxiety and depression than men (National Institute of Mental Health, 2014) and lesbian, gay, bisexual, and transgender (LGBT) youth are two to three times more likely to attempt suicide (Garofalo, Wolf, Wissow, Woods, & Goodman, 1999) and be homeless (Conron, Mimiaga & Landers, 2010; Kruks, 1991).

⟊

Client symptoms should always be examined in relation to their location in larger systems of stratification, power, privilege, and oppression as well as the patterns of thinking and doing that perpetuate prejudice and discrimination.

⟊

Deidre, a white single mother of four, was referred to a community clinic for depressive symptoms. At first, Deidre appeared difficult to engage and somewhat hostile. When the therapist expanded assessment of the presenting issues to include the sociocultural context, Deidre became more engaged. The therapist learned that the family was living in a homeless shelter, the children needed to get to three different schools, and no school buses served the shelter. Deirdre feared that she was at risk of losing her children if they were late for school again.

Deidre's automatic thoughts were that it was hopeless to deal with the school system and that she was a failure as a mother. Even so, she did not give up. She made an appointment to see the school official monitoring her case, but returned feeling defeated and even more fearful. Applying a systemic view, the therapist and Deidre could **envision** more equitable possibilities by visiting the school together. The therapist's role was to work with the school official to identify the patterns of thinking (i.e., prejudices and oppression) within the larger system that made it difficult for the official and Deidre to find a more adaptive solution. This enabled a **transformative** systemic shift in thinking and a more workable plan. Though Deidre continued to address her role as a mother, her depressive symptoms improved almost immediately. If the therapist had focused the therapy primarily on developing more positive thoughts about herself and ways to be more organized in preparing the children for school, Deidre would have continued to internalize ideas that she alone was responsible for her children's success or failure and the school system would continue to see her as a problem parent.

Third Order Change

The possibility of third order change depends on seeing the systems one is embedded in and envisioning alternative options and choice. In fact, most cultures are complex and people enact cultural models in many different ways. For example, a study of heterosexual couples in Iran found that they drew on multiple societal schemas when describing their relationships and there appeared to be considerable diversity in how Iranian couples integrated and responded to potentially contradictory societal schemas (Moghadam & Knudson-Martin, 2009). Though the powerful impact of male-dominant social norms was evident as women reported ways husbands could use the law to limit where they went, others spoke of values inherent in Islam that promoted expectations of mutuality and respect for women and described them manifested in their marriages. The authors concluded that couple and family therapists should help clients explore religious, cultural, and legal values and ask what their faiths or cultural norms teach about justice and respect rather than assume that these social schemas are not open to reflection or able to be enacted differently.

↔→

Conflicts inherent in social schemas are common and create openings for third order change.

↔→

For example, a couple's power dynamics might be influenced by the deeply embedded expectations one or both hold about who has the right or is more qualified to make major decisions (patriarchy) alongside the expectation that each should have equal voice (democracy). Although these contradictions can be the source of cognitive distortion, they are also potential fertile ground for developing more adaptive relationship patterns. People are usually not aware of the impact of contradictory societal schemas in their lives. When these are made visible they have more choice. For instance, though most heterosexual couples fall into taken-for-granted gender schemas that promote unequal relationship patterns (Mahoney & Knudson-Martin, 2009), if Frank is asked whether he thinks Judy's needs should be important, he is likely to draw on beliefs regarding equality and say they are.

The ability to transform destructive patterns is enhanced when people are aware of the multiple values inherent in their social schemas, the consequences of each, and whose interests these represent and maintain. A study found that when therapists identify and validate men's relational schemas *and* also immediately help them track the impact of their behavior on a partner, men are more likely to begin making behavioral changes that reflect relationship equality rather than patriarchy (Samman & Knudson-Martin, 2015).

↔→

Though it is not easy to step outside dominant social schemas, practicing from a socioculturally attuned perspective can lead to more options and third order change.

↔→

Practice Guidelines

The following five practice guidelines help family members recognize commonly held societal schemas, track their effects on their relationships, and develop alternative relationship models that work better for them (Parker & McDowell, 2017). It is helpful to note that they are not always implemented sequentially and may move fluidly back and forth over the course of the therapy.

1. Identify Problematic Schemas

Socioculturally attuned CBF therapists systematically gather information about how client families function, identifying the schemas and cognitive distortions that contribute to concerns that brought the family or couple to therapy.

⊷⊷→

Socioculturally attuned CBF therapists look to the larger context to help pinpoint societal schemas that underlie problematic behavior, provide contextual meaning to family interaction, and affect the way family members perceive and impact each other.

⊷⊷→

Figure 10.1 provides questions that can help guide therapists' initial assessment of potential sources of societal schemas that contribute to the problematic schemas affecting each client.

2. Track Patterns at Multiple Levels

CBF therapists help family members track how their thoughts, feelings, and behaviors are part of circular interactional patterns that include multiple family members. In this process, they make explicit how problematic schemas underlie the targeted emotions and behaviors. Tracking patterns provides an opportunity to begin to discuss the beliefs and ways of making meaning that guide family members' expectations of each other and make the thinking behind the behaviors visible. Socioculturally attuned therapists approach this task with interest in how the patterns they are identifying are part of cultural, historical, and sociopolitical processes and seek to expand and contextualize them (Pandit, Kang, Chen, Knudson-Martin, & Huenergardt, 2014). As the therapist develops questions and hypotheses that clarify the repetitive patterns and cognitive distortions, family members begin to see themselves responding to each other and develop interest in the source of the schemas influencing their relationships. Therapists use a variety of techniques to visualize these patterns of influence, such as the downward arrow technique (Beck, 1995) (see Figure 10.3).

Source of Societal Schemas	Therapist Listens For
Place	In what kinds of contexts is the client embedded? How have they changed over time? How much mobility possible?
Gender	What societal messages about gender has the client internalized?
Socioeconomic Status	How do socioeconomic status and economic situation impact schema of self and other?
Sexual Orientation	How have societal messages about sexual orientation influenced client's internalized identity and expectations about life cycle?
Sociocultural Location	How do client's culture, religion, age, race, ethnicity, and disabilities impact schema of self and relationships?
Larger Systems	How do client relationships with legal structures (immigration, justice system, and so on) impact their schema of self-worth and agency?
Social Power	How much personal, interpersonal, and institutional power does the client experience as a result of their societal position?
Societal Position	What overall messages about self in relation to others are perpetuated by client's position in societal context?

Figure 10.1 Sources of societal schemas and influence. From "What does it mean to be relational? A framework for assessment and practice," by R. Silverstein, L. B. Bass, A. Tuttle, C. Knudson-Martin, and D. Huenergardt, 2006, *Family Process, 42*(4), p. 399. Adapted with permission.

3. Connect Individual, Family, and Societal Schemas

Therapists must be intentional in helping families become aware of the ways they are enacting commonly held societal schemas. When family members see themselves caught in patterns larger than themselves rather than as simply something wrong with them, their experience is less pathologized (Pandit et al., 2014). Once thoughts, feelings, and behaviors are identified, there are many ways therapists can help people explore the underlying assumptions or values that societal schemas impose on them and how these impact their behavior. Video clips from movies or psychoeducation groups can be helpful sources of consciousness-raising conversation. Therapists can recognize societal schemas embedded in clients' automatic thoughts and directly identify them and track their consequences in the relationship. For example, when a woman says that her thought was that she didn't want to upset her male partner, the societal idea that "women should protect men's emotions" could be named as a societal expectation and its consequences on her and the relationship identified. A column for messages from society can be added to a thought record (see Figure 10.4.). Opportunities to critically reflect on the connection between personal, family, and societal schemas from a meta-perspective are empowering (Hernández, Almeida, & Dolan-del Vechhio, 2005). Figure 10.2. provides examples of questions that can help make this link.

4. Commit to Alternative Relationship Models

As consequences of destructive societal schemas are linked to the sequence of thoughts, emotions, and relational patterns, family members become interested in other options. Values associated with alternative ways of relating can be explored. In acceptance and commitment therapy, family members are able to take more ownership of the values that they want to guide their life (McKay et al., 2012). Recognizing how their reactions to each other have been connected to restrictive and/or inequitable societal models decreases self-blame and makes it more possible to label barriers, observe impulses to act with old schema coping behaviors, and develop values-based strategies to move beyond them. To help overcome the power of dominant societal schemas, therapists provide leadership in engaging family members

Sample Questions to Link Personal, Family, and Societal Schemas
1   The idea that [insert distorted individual thought] is interesting. Where do you think you learned [insert parallel societal stereotype or expectation]? How did/does [your family] enact this pattern?
2   I noticed that when [interpersonal trigger] you responded by [insert societally stereotyped or inequitable behavior]. What thought was going on for you right then? Is the idea that [client answer] common among other [relevant social group] that you know?
3   The idea that [cognitive distortion] is really causing you to [problematic behavior]. How do you suppose this kind of idea has affected other people [or men, women, etc] in our society? How do you think this idea has emerged in history? How does the thought that [distorted societal idea] affect others in your family?
4   When you feel [troubling emotion] what thoughts about yourself as a [relevant social group/role] pop up for you? What messages in society encourage this thought? What expectations about [social role] do you take in? What parts of yourself do you have to keep hidden? How does this impact others?
5   How do others in your community view [problematic behavior]? What moral codes or societal expectation are tied to your [distorted thought]. Who in society benefits when you think this way? How did you learn to think this way? How has this kind of thinking affected your family/relationship?

Figure 10.2 Sample questions to link personal, family, and societal schemas.

in examining and experimenting with relationship models that support the well-being of all. They support couples and families in envisioning an agreed-upon plan for change.

5. Create Behavioral Change Based on New Schemas

Core schemas of self and other are very persistent. Clients are now ready to actively engage in an intentional process of responding to each other based on the new schemas to which they have committed. This requires activities that help each of them recognize when problematic emotions and thoughts arise and to do something different. The therapist may provide education about practices that help enable this kind of behavioral change. For example, they may teach mindfulness skills to facilitate emotional regulation (McKay, Wood, & Brantley, 2007) or strategies to face emotions rather than avoiding them. The therapist helps family members and partners track their new responses to each other and identify how they overcame the old emotional cues and thoughts and the pieces involved in enacting something new. They will need to provide support and guidance that enables people to persist even when powerful emotions and old thoughts arise. Part of the coaching role is to remind people of the values and goals they identified and help families develop homework activities that keep the new relational schemas visible, such as a communications checklist or values intentions worksheet (see Figure 10.5). Accepting the power of old personal, familial, and societal schemas can paradoxically help face and transform them (McKay et al., 2007; McKay et al., 2012).

Case Illustration

Jared (35) and Wendy (29), a European American heterosexual working-class couple married for 8 years, sat straight, their bodies stiff as they described the concerns that brought them to the marriage and family therapy training clinic. They said that about the only time they talked was when they were "fighting about the boys." Aaron (aged 13) did not want to go to school, Jason (aged 12) got into fights, and they feared that Dillon (aged 9) worried too much about all of them. Wendy reported feeling "depressed" and "exhausted all the time." Their therapist, Claudia, a Latina family therapy graduate student, aged 35, was also a married heterosexual woman and mother of a toddler. As the session began, Claudia noted that the couple seemed nervous and approached her as an authority. Jared said that he "wanted to learn what he was doing wrong."

Claudia was aware that the couple's subservient orientation to her was very different from how she had learned to approach authorities in her relatively affluent home. She was mindful that her context for parenting was likely to be very different from this family's. She checked her own feelings about Wendy having become a mother at such a young age and, while mostly experiencing awe for how anyone could manage this, she was also conscious of some judgment beneath the surface that Wendy "should have planned her life better" and recognized this as part of what she had learned was important in order to be successful. When she did not plan, Claudia felt inferior, less than. She had been especially careful to avoid the stereotype that Latinas get pregnant at a young age. This self-reflection helped Claudia orient herself to the couple with respectful curiosity about how they made meaning of their responses to each other and an interest in how the world around them influenced their schemas.

Identifying Problematic Schemas

Claudia wanted to get background information about the family's context and the factors that might influence their personal and family schemas. She also wanted to engage the couple in an exploration of their interactional patterns and begin to develop hypotheses about the sequence of thoughts, emotions, and behaviors causing distress. After she gave the couple hope and a vision of how change could occur by describing the process of therapy, she explained that problems were often related to living in environments that created toxic and distorted ideas about ourselves and how we relate to others. She invited the couple to describe the problem that brought them to therapy.

When Jared said he was frustrated and didn't know what to do, she asked questions that helped to detail his view of the problem: "What happens? Who does what? What thoughts go through your mind?" She was especially interested in understanding the context in which he felt so helpless. Jared described fights between Wendy and the boys. He would raise his voice and tell the boys to stop arguing with their mother, but this did not help and seemed to make Wendy even more upset. When Claudia asked him what he did when his efforts didn't help, Jared replied that he felt "useless" and usually "gave up." Using the questions in Figure 10.1 as a guide, Claudia recognized his feelings as connected to societal schemas that create the distorted expectation that men must always be competent and in charge.

Turning to Wendy, Claudia was aware that not all voices in a relationship come from equal positions and made sure to not automatically follow Jared's definition of the problem and to instead invite another perspective: "Jared says that it's upsetting to see you and the boys fighting and to feel useless in making the fighting stop. That's his point of view. What do you see as the problem?" Wendy described being worried about the boys and needing to protect them. She was quick to praise Jared, who was not the birth father, for being there for them. Claudia asked questions to detail what happened from Wendy's point of view and began to establish a picture of how her responses connected to Jared's. For example, Wendy repeatedly spoke of how indebted she and the boys were to Jared. When Jared would yell at the boys it triggered thoughts in her that she had no right to expect much of him. They began to pinpoint Wendy's underlying schemas about self and others—that it was not safe to trust anyone and that she was worthless if she upset a man. Claudia wondered how these personal schemas connected to larger sociopolitical systems and how these impacted what happened within this family.

Claudia immediately began to widen the lens to learn more about the societal contexts surrounding their problems and expanded upon this in the next session. She asked about the neighborhood they lived in, their experience with school, economic, and legal systems. She asked about how others had viewed their families growing up and what they learned about things like gender, social class, and sexual orientation. She encouraged reflection about how these affected their expectations and responses. Together, using questions like those illustrated in Figure 10.2, the therapist and couple began to pinpoint a troublesome sequence in which the emotions and automatic thoughts generated around parenting resulted in responses that distanced them from each other and increased arguments with the boys.

Tracking Patterns

The boys were invited to several sessions to further track interactional patterns. Claudia helped the family observe their responses to each other, systematically detailing how each served as triggers for the others. For example, when Wendy said that 12-year-old Jason was getting in fights at school and needed to change his behavior, Jason told her to back off. Dillon, age 9, came to Jason's defense and 13-year-old Aaron rolled his eyes. When Wendy raised her voice and repeated her concern, telling Jason that fighting was dangerous and would get him in trouble, Jason directed an angry curse toward her. Jared told him to respect his mother.

The therapist guided the family in identifying each person's automatic thoughts and reactions, making visible a behavioral sequence they could all recognize and bringing new awareness regarding their situation. Underneath Jason's reaction was the idea that if he did not fight, he would never be respected at school; that he would not survive. Aaron anticipated increased distress between his parents that he could do nothing about and squelched his fear that Jared would leave the family by telling himself he didn't care. Dillon broke into tears, saying that Mom should leave Jason alone; that she was making everyone unhappy. Wendy became visibly depressed, a reaction supported by the idea that she was worthless because she failed to keep all members of the family safe and was upsetting them. Jared physically pushed his chair back saying, "I give up." The therapist helped clarify the desire for family members to be able to express disagreements and still love each other. All agreed that helping Mom and Dad stay connected to each other during times of stress was a primary goal.

In couple sessions, Claudia helped Wendy and Jared create a downward arrow diagram to visualize the connection between their contexts, core schemas, and responses to parenting. As illustrated (Figure 10.3), parenting was connected to core schemas about self-worth and gender for both parents. When the boys acted out or were distressed, Wendy experienced an almost automatic cascade of thoughts connected to the societal idea that "women's worth is defined by men." This led to the irrational thought that "she is worthless if the children upset Jared." Jared reacted to underlying societal schemas regarding male leadership that in the end translated to the distorted idea "that for him to be a man Wendy had to keep the boys in line and doing well." The couple readily recognized these thoughts as errors that did not really represent how they viewed parenting or their relationship with each other, but escalated in times of stress.

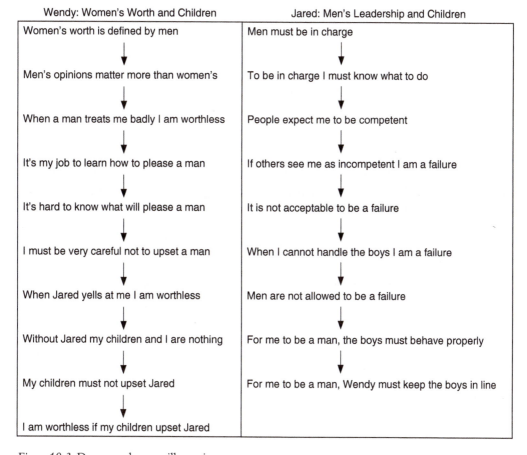

Figure 10.3 Downward arrow illustration.

Connecting Individual, Family, and Social Schemas

Claudia helped the couple develop strategies to observe their own behaviors, recognize when they were being triggered, and identify their underlying automatic thoughts. They discussed situations that happened and what they noticed. As they talked, they created thought logs that included the triggering event, feeling, thought, response, and associated societal expectation. An example is illustrated in Figure 10. 4. Expanding the pattern to detail how their environment contributed to the family pattern helped Jared and Wendy feel understood and validated and more able to approach their problems without blaming themselves or each other.

For example, the high cost of housing in their urban area meant that they could not afford to own a home near Jared's work even though he had to drive 3–4 hours every day. Claudia asked questions that helped the couple examine taken-for-granted assumptions about owning a home and how this societal-driven need was related to social schemas about class and economics that made owning a home a measure of personal worth and success, especially for Jared.

They discussed how the schools in their neighborhood suffered from limited resources and Wendy's fears about violence on the school grounds. When she saw Jason fighting, she feared that he was taking on male models of violence that triggered her own experience with men. They also examined the racial composition of schools and how as parents of white children their fears might be related to racial stereotypes and biases regarding children of color. They began to consider how to talk about racial issues with their sons without perpetuating discrimination and irrational racist fears.

Wendy was especially concerned for Aaron's safety, as he had recently told his parents that he thought he might be gay. They examined each parent's responses to these safety concerns

Triggering Event	Thought	Feeling	Societal Schema	Response
Wendy: School calls because Aaron is not in school	School is unsafe I'm a bad mother	Guilt Worthlessness	Stereotype that black kids are violent and hate gay kids Schools judge parents	Call Jared to ask him to talk to the school
Jared: Wendy calls me at work	The guys think I'm a "wuss" My boss might see	Embarrassment Anxiety	Men shouldn't let women "hang on them" Work and family should be separate.	Anger at Wendy. Refusal to call the school
Wendy: Asks Jason to turn down the music and do his homework	Jared's worked hard; the noise will upset him I can't even get Jason to do his homework	Guilt Worthlessness	Women need to calm men Mothers are responsible	Yells at Jason that he won't be able to go to the party unless he does his homework
Jared: Jason calls Wendy "bitch," slams his door, and turns up the music	Wendy is too controlling I'm entitled to some peace and quiet	Anger Anger	Boys should not be over-protected Work is a man's priority; he should be able to relax at home	Yells at Wendy, "Why are you always over-reacting?" and goes out

Figure 10.4 Thought log with societal schemas.

in light of internalized societal ideas about masculinity, sexual orientation, and appropriate behavior for boys. Though both parents said they accepted Aaron's sexual orientation, they needed help examining how internalized homophobia limited their ability to engage with Aaron and support him. Jared, who already felt unsure and disengaged from his role as a father, was especially at a loss regarding how to develop a relationship with a gay son.

Wendy, who became a mother at 16 and had lived in a world dominated by poverty and male violence prior to meeting Jared, felt extraordinarily grateful for his financial support. They examined how her ideas about herself were influenced by societal schemas that valued people based on their income and limited what people with little money felt entitled to. Jared, who was brought up in a middle-class family with a physically violent father and adamantly resisted using physical force, discovered that he was left with no positive model for how to engage with the family and focused most of his personal identity on work. Jared began to recognize how his anxiety at work was linked to underlying societal schemas that valued his performance at work more than his relationships and caused him to resist missing work for family matters, but take time from family to "go out with the guys" after work. Wendy came to see that part of her depression was internalized anger at the unfairness in their relationship and gendered and classist ideas that, though she desired more emotional closeness with Jared, said she was not entitled to it.

Commit to Alternative Schemas

Jared and Wendy began to have a sense of the systems of schemas influencing them. They saw how the schemas into which they had been socialized, together with their prior life experiences, generated automatic thoughts and emotions that triggered behaviors that added to their stress, increased conflict, and created emotional distance. To achieve their goal of staying connected even in the face of conflict, they not only needed to change the way they communicated, they needed to identify and commit to a new relational schema. Because societal schemas limit the options people are able to envision, the therapist gave them a handout illustrating a model of relationship based on equality and mutual support (Figure 10.5) and used

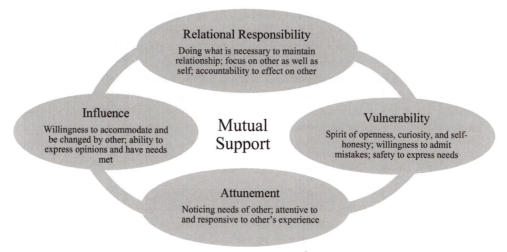

Figure 10.5 Model of mutual support. From "Bridging emotion, societal discourse, and couple interaction in clinical practice," by C. Knudson-Martin and D. Huenergardt, in C. Knudson-Martin, S. K. Samman, and M. A. Wells (Eds.), *Socio-Emotional Relationship Therapy: Bridging Emotion, Societal Context, and Couple Interaction* (p. 6), 2015, New York, NY: Springer. Adapted with permission.

it as a guide to help them examine and identify values that were important to them. She also engaged them in conversations about ideals they wanted to model and support for their boys as they form relationships and participate in social systems outside the family.

With Claudia's encouragement and support, Wendy and Jared made a list of the values to which they wanted to commit. They detailed what behaviors based on these alternative schemas would look like and the ideas that needed to be challenged to attain them. For example, they decided they liked the idea of shared relationship responsibility. This meant they had to resist societal schemas that said women needed men but men didn't need women, that women were responsible for raising children, and that men always had to have the answers and be competent. They wanted to know Aaron as a person and not just accept him as "gay." This meant they had to relate outside gender and sexual binaries and stereotypes. Jared wanted to learn to have a father-son relationship with him. Overall, they wanted to organize their family more around relationships and less around economic measures of success and to equally support the well-being of every family member.

Creating Behavioral Change Based on New Schemas

Though Wendy and Jared did not have the time or comfort with writing to keep regular thought records at home, they created a special place to keep logs from sessions easily accessible. They also found it helpful to tape a copy of the model of mutual support where they could see it. Wendy and Jared showed the diagram to the boys and told them they were trying to model a new way to respond to each other. The therapist also helped the couple practice letting themselves sit briefly with their stressful emotions, recognize them, and name the family and societal messages underlying them. This made it easier to respond differently. When the couple reported triggering events that resulted in the old cycle, Claudia coached them in identifying new responses that would help them attain their goal of staying connected during times of stress.

One of the most transformative sessions included the boys. Claudia guided a conversation about masculinity between them and Jared. Jared spoke of what he had learned about the destructiveness of needing to be "in charge" and how he had not really learned how to focus on others in the family. He told Aaron that he wanted to not let his fears about homosexuality limit their relationship. With Claudia's encouragement, Aaron was able to risk sharing his ideas about what he'd like from his father. Witnessing this event between her husband and sons helped Wendy solidify a new schema about men, women, parenthood, and her worth. Claudia asked her to share these ideas with her family. The family examined the list of values they had previously made in terms of both the progress they had made and the new challenges they gave themselves. They had learned to take a meta-perspective on societal schemas and were moving into third order change, intentionally developing a new shared family schema less constrained by inequitable and limiting societal messages and structures.

Third Order Change: Summary

Socioculturally attuned CBFT is well suited to the process of third order change. The approach encourages people to raise consciousness about societal influences on their thoughts and how these are connected to their emotions and interactions. Couples and families can recognize the impact of societal inequities in their lives and decide to create more just relationships and challenge discriminatory social distortions and prejudices that maintain them.

In the case of Wendy and Jared, first order change occurred when Wendy learned to pause and be aware. She was able to recognize that the extent to which she worried about upsetting Jared was problematic. She began to respond in ways that helped her feel better about herself and the marriage. Second order change occurred when Wendy and Jared redefined their shared family schema to include more options for who does what. Family members no longer held Wendy responsible for everyone else's behavior. Third order change occurred as they began to develop social awareness, to consider the systems of systems (Ecker & Hulley, 1996), and began to see how their life was organized around prescribed roles.

Wendy and Jared no longer automatically followed societal norms and expectations. They still experienced times of conflict and confusion, but their response to the conflict was different and brought them together as they reminded themselves of the societal schemas they were resisting. If automatic thoughts from earlier schemas were triggered, they recognized their oppressive nature and were able to draw on a different view of the world. Though not all families may make such fundamental shifts in their lives, the ability to see multiple sets of societal schemas and make choices in relation to them is transformative.

References

Baldwin, M. W. (1992). Relational schemas and the processing of social information. *Psychological Bulletin, 112*(3), 461–484.

Bandura, A. (1973). *Aggression: A social learning analysis.* Upper Saddle River, NJ: Prentice Hall.

Baucom, D. H., Epstein, N., Sayers, S. L., & Sher, T. G. (1989). The role of cognitions in marital relationships: Definitional, methodological, and conceptual issues. *Journal of Counseling and Clinical Psychology, 57*(1), 31–38.

Beals, J., Novins, D. K., Whitesell, N. R., Spicer, P., Mitchell, C. M., & Manson, S. M. (2005). Prevalence of mental disorders and utilization of mental health services in two American Indian reservation populations: Mental health disparities in a national context. *American Journal of Psychiatry, 162*(9), 1723–1732.

Beck, A. T. (1967). *Depression: Clinical, experimental, and theoretical aspects.* Philadelphia: University of Pennsylvania Press.

Beck, J. S. (1995). *Cognitive therapy: Basics and beyond* (1st ed.). New York, NY: Guilford Press.

Bourdieu, P. (1986). The forms of capital (R. Nice, Trans.). In J. Richardson (Ed.), *Handbook of theory and research for the sociology of education* (pp. 46–58). New York, NY: Greenwood Press.

Center for Disease Control and Prevention (2013). *CDC health disparities and inequalities report—United States, 2013.* Retrieved from https://www.cdc.gov/mmwr/pdf/other/su6203.pdf.

Conron, K. J., Mimiaga, M. J., & Landers, S. J. (2010). A population-based study of sexual orientation identity and gender differences in adult health. *American Journal of Public Health, 100*(10), 1953–1960.

Craske, M. G. (2010). *Cognitive-behavioral therapy.* Theories of psychotherapy series. Washington, DC: American Psychological Association.

Dattilio, F. M. (2001). Cognitive-behavior family therapy: Contemporary myths and misconceptions. *Contemporary Family Therapy, 23*(1), 3–18.

Dattilio, F. M. (2005). The restructuring of family schemas: A cognitive-behavior perspective. *Journal of Marital and Family Therapy, 31*(1), 15–30.

Dattilio, F. M. (2010). *Cognitive-behavioral therapy with couples and families: A comprehensive guide for clinicians.* New York, NY: Guilford Press.

Ecker, B., & Hulley, L. (1996). *Depth oriented brief therapy: How to be brief when you were trained to be deep and vice versa.* San Francisco, CA: Jossey-Bass.

Eliot, L. (2009). *Pink brain blue brain: How small differences grow into troublesome gaps.* New York, NY: Mariner Books.

Epstein, N. B., & Baucom, D. H. (2002). *Enhanced cognitive-behavioral therapy for couples: A contextual approach.* Washington, DC: American Psychological Association.

Farrar, M. J., & Goodman, G. S. (1990). Developmental differences in the relation between scripts and episodic memory: Do they exist? In R. Fivush & J. A. Hudson (Eds.), *Knowing and remembering in young children* (pp. 30–64). New York, NY: Cambridge University Press.

Folbre, N. (2001). *The invisible heart: Economics and family values.* New York, NY: The Free Press.

Garofalo, R., Wolf, C., Wissow, L. S., Woods, E. R., & Goodman, E. (1999). Sexual orientation and risk of suicide attempts among a representative sample of youth. *Archives of Pediatrics and Adolescent Medicine, 153*(5), 487–493.

Hayes, S. C., Luoma, J., Bond, F., Masuda, A., & Lillis, J. (2006). Acceptance and commitment therapy: Model, processes, and outcomes. *Behaviour Research and Therapy, 44*(1), 1–25.

Hernández, P., Almeida, R., & Dolan-del Vechhio, K. (2005). Critical consciousness, accountability, and empowerment: Key processes for helping families heal. *Family Process, 44*(1), 105–119.

Jones, J. M. (1997). *Prejudice and racism* (2nd ed.). New York, NY: McGraw-Hill.

Jordan, J. (2009). *Relational-cultural therapy*. Washington, DC: American Psychological Association.

Knudson-Martin, C. (2013). Why power matters: Creating a foundation of mutual support in couple relationships. *Family Process, 52*(1), 5–18.

Knudson-Martin, C. (2015). When therapy challenges patriarchy: Undoing gendered power in heterosexual couple relationships. In C. Knudson-Martin, M. A. Wells, & S. K. Samman (Eds.), *Socio-emotional relationship therapy: Bridging emotion, societal context and couple interaction* (pp. 15–26). New York, NY: Springer.

Knudson-Martin, C., & Huenergardt, D. (2010). A socio-emotional approach to couple therapy: Linking social context and couple interaction. *Family Process, 49*(3), 369–384.

Kruks, G. (1991). Gay and lesbian homeless/street youth: Special issues and concerns. *Journal of Adolescent Health, 12*(7), 515–518.

Mahoney, A., R., & Knudson-Martin, C. (2009). The social context of gendered power. In C. Knudson-Martin & A. Mahoney (Eds.), *Couples, gender, and power: Creating change in intimate relationships* (pp. 17–29). New York, NY: Springer.

Malpas, J. (2011). Between pink and blue: A multi-dimensional family approach to gender nonconforming children and their families. *Family Process, 50*(4), 453–470.

McCulloch, A. (2001). Social environments and health: Cross sectional national survey. *British Medical Journal, 323*(7306), 208–209.

McDowell, T. (2015). *Applying critical social theories to family therapy practice*. New York, NY: Springer.

McKay, M., Lev, A., & Skeen, M. (2012). *Acceptance and commitment therapy for interpersonal problems*. Oakland, CA: New Harbinger Publications.

McKay, M., Wood, J. C., & Brantley, J. (2007). *The dialectical behavior therapy skills workbook*. Oakland, CA: New Harbinger Publications.

Moghadam, S., & Knudson-Martin, C. (2009). Keeping the peace: Couple relationships in Iran. In C. Knudson-Martin & A. Mahoney (Eds.), *Couples, gender, and power: Creating change in intimate relationships* (pp. 255–274). New York, NY: Springer.

National Institute of Mental Health. (2014). *Women and depression: Discovering hope*. Retrieved from http://www.nimh.nih.gov/health/publications/women-and   depression-discovering-hope/index.shtml

Pandit, M., Kang, Y. J., Chen, J., Knudson-Martin, C., & Huenergardt, D. (2014). Practicing socio-cultural attunement: A study of couple therapists. *Journal of Contemporary Family Therapy, 36*(4), 518–528.

Parker, E. O., & McDowell, T. (2017). Integrating social justice into the practice of CBFT: A critical look at family schemas. *Journal of Marital and Family Therapy, 43*(3), 502–513.

Rusovick, R. M. (2009). Discourse and identity: Socially constructing heterosexual attraction. (Unpublished doctoral dissertation).

Samman, S. K., & Knudson-Martin, C. (2015). Relational engagement in heterosexual couple therapy: Helping men move from "I" to "we." In C. Knudson-Martin, M. Wells, & S. K. Samman (Eds.), *Socio-emotional relationship therapy: Bridging emotion, societal context, and couple interaction* (pp. 79–91). New York, NY: Springer.

Silverstein, R., Bass, L. B., Tuttle, A., Knudson-Martin, C., & Huenergardt, D. (2006). What does it mean to be relational? A framework for assessment and practice. *Family Process, 45*, 391–405.

Tannen, D. (1994). *Gender and discourse*. New York, NY: Oxford University Press.

Watson, M. F. (2013). *Facing the black shadow*. (n.p.): Author.

Welch-Ross, M. K., & Schmidt, C. R. (1996). Gender-schema development and children's constructive story memory: Evidence for a developmental model. *Child Development, 67*(3), 820–835.

Williams, D. R. (1997). Race and health: Basic questions, emerging directions. *Annals of Epidemiology, 7*(5), 322–333.

11 Socioculturally Attuned Solution Focused Family Therapy

Solution focused family therapy (SFFT) evolved from the work of Steve de Shazer, Insoo Kim Berg, and their colleagues during the early 1980s in the U.S. at the Brief Family Therapy Center (BFTC) in Milwaukee, Wisconsin. Those at BFTC developed a collaborative, eco-systemic approach that assumes families have the solutions they need to solve problems (Lipchick, 2002). SFFT shares a number of tenets with other brief systemic models, including a focus on the here and now, the assumption that change can happen quickly, understanding problems from a relational, interactional perspective, and the idea that small change can lead to more significant desired change. Its reliance on a social constructivist, post-structural framework also aligns SBFT with postmodern models such as collaborative and narrative family therapy. Commonalities with these models include not pathologizing clients, viewing the therapist and clients as co-constructing reality through therapeutic conversations (Chang & Nylund, 2013), taking a highly collaborative relational stance in therapy, and recognizing clients as the experts of their own lives.

SFFT is more about creating change than about understanding problems. Consider parents who enter therapy with their 4-year-old child who is having angry outbursts. The therapist acknowledges the problem, but assumes the child does not always have outbursts. She asks parents about places in which outbursts don't occur, questions the family about times when outbursts are less severe, and searches for times when the child starts to have an outburst but quits. As a solution focused brief therapist, she puts her energy into what works. She helps the family determine what is different about their thoughts, feelings, behaviors, and interactions during times when the problem is not occurring, i.e., when the family is engaging in pre-ferred behaviors and interactions. She works together with the family to identify and amplify solutions that have been overlooked, avoiding hypothesizing about the cause of the problem, e.g., that the parents don't have enough control, the child is expressing pent up feelings, the child is caught in marital conflict. SFFT relies on the idea that change is always happening and there are always times when presenting problems don't occur or at least aren't as severe (Thomas & Nelson, 2007).

＊←→＊

Socioculturally attuned solution focused family therapists encourage third order change when they help families choose and amplify solutions that support equitable and just relationships.

＊←→＊

This way of working includes expanding conversations to encourage family members to **attune** to each other's experiences in the family and broader societal context. Engaging all family members in **naming** and **voicing** their experience in relationship to societal systems and power dynamics enhances the family's collective expertise of their own lives. This process itself **intervenes** in power dynamics that give some members of the family more voice and influence. In essence, clients are invited to imagine or **envision** the miracle of family and societal change and take steps toward **transformation** by identifying and amplifying strengths that support equitable relationships.

In this chapter we describe enduring family therapy concepts and practices related to SFFT and offer a set of guidelines for socioculturally attuned practice. We share a case illustration to demonstrate how to create third order change by integrating societal systems and attention to power into solution focused practice.

Primary Enduring Solution Focused Family Therapy Concepts

Although no family therapy model is without theoretical underpinnings, SFFT is more about language than theory; about asking the right questions at the right time. That said, SFFT is often misinterpreted as simply a set of techniques. Therapists who too rigidly and quickly move from one solution focused question to the next often overlook relevant informa- tion, e.g., undisclosed problems and experience, feelings, meaning-making, and relational dynamics. Therapists who avoid problem stories can leave clients feeling they have not been heard, putting at risk a meaningful collaborative therapeutic relationship. The focus on what to do may be reassuring and seem rather simple at first. Without deeper understanding of the approach, however, it is easy for therapists and clients to miss opportunities for finding strengths and solutions within the rich tapestry of life that extends from the most intimate thought and feeling to the broadest complex societal system.

There are many guidelines for working from a solution focused stance that are beyond the scope of this chapter and published elsewhere (e.g., Berg, 1994; de Shazer & Dolan, 2007; Nelson & Thomas, 2007; Lipchick, 2002; O'Hanlon & Rowan, 2003; Selekman, 1997; Walter & Peller, 1992). Following we share the hallmarks of SFFT, including resolute attention to the use of language, a collaborative stance in which therapists rely on clients' strengths and expertise, careful construction of therapeutic goals, and finding and amplifying exceptions.

Use of Poststructural, Social Constructivist Language

In SFFT, therapists and clients work together to construct meaning in ways that help solve problems. All therapies rely on language, but SFFT pays particular attention to the use of language from a social constructivist and poststructural perspective. De Shazer and Berg relied heavily on Austrian British philosopher Ludwig Wittgenstein's understanding of language games to create change through therapeutic conversations (Bidwell, 2007; de Shazer and Berg, 1992; de Shazer, 1997). From this perspective, words without specific referents are fluid and boundaries around them (i.e., what they are and are not) can become easily blurred. This is helpful in SFFT because it allows therapists to participate in the co-construction of meaning in ways that can make problems more solvable. This is particularly important to the process of moving away from being defined by problems. Take as an example a white middle-class father, Daniel, who entered therapy after his wife has been incarcerated. His only child, Maya, is 10 years old. They entered therapy after the school called Daniel to tell him that Maya had been getting into fights. Their therapist, Aziza, was an upper-middle-class, Arab American Muslim, who identified as a heterosexual woman.

Aziza: So tell me about why you came in today.

Daniel: Maya has been having fights at school. She never used to be aggressive but since her mom went to prison, she hasn't been herself.

Aziza: I see, so your mom is in prison now?

Maya: Yes and I hate it! I want her to come home.

Daniel: So do I, but it doesn't help for you to be aggressive! (turns to therapist) I know she is depressed, but she can't take it out that way.

Aziza recognized Daniel's description of his daughter as aggressive and depressed as contributing to the stuckness of the problem. She responded to Daniel's statement in a way that began to shift meaning from Maya being defined by characteristics or qualities of aggression and depression to Maya experiencing those states. She encouraged Daniel to describe specific observations that lead him to conclusions about his daughter.

Aziza: What tells you Maya is feeling depressed?

Daniel: She is irritable and spends most of her time alone in her room. She also cries a lot.

Aziza: So Maya, your dad has seen you crying a lot and spending a lot of time in your room. You are feeling sad?

Maya: Of course I am. My mom is in prison and everyone knows it!

Aziza: The kids at school know?

Daniel: Her best friend told a few of the kids and now they all know.

Aziza: That must be difficult and upsetting, Maya.

Aziza began to move away from the father's description of his daughter as being aggressive and depressed in favor of moving toward a co-construction of the problem as Maya feeling upset and sad because she is going through a difficult situation. Aggressive and depressed are terms with fluid boundaries that give way to the equally fluid but more solvable and transient problems of upset and sad. Changing the description of the problem affects meaning and alters future interactions.

It is important not to immediately accept problems as clients understand and present them. The therapist in this situation worked with the family to contextualize the problem. SFFT has been critiqued for failing to place problems in social context (Dermer, Hemesath, & Russell, 1998), however contextualizing language, meaning, and experience is a basic premise of this model. As we argue later in this chapter, there is room to expand the context further without abandoning the core of how language should be used to co-create solvable problems and well-designed goals.

All questions shape meaning, including what therapists expect by asking them. SFF therapists carefully use questions to inspire the expectation for change. Questions are open-ended, often using words like "when" and "will." A SFF therapist is likely to say "Tell me about a time when . . ." rather than "Has there ever been a time when . . .?" and "What will it look like when . . ." rather than "What would it look like if . . .?" Let's jump ahead in the therapeutic conversation with Daniel and Maya.

Aziza: Tell me about times when you feel sad or upset about your mom when you are at school but you don't get into a fight?

Maya: I don't know. I guess when the teacher is looking at me.

Aziza: So when the teacher is looking at you, you decide to do something different? What do you do?

Maya: I just think "don't get in trouble" and keep my head down.

Aziza: Really? You are able to keep your head down and remind yourself not to get into trouble?

Maya: Yeah, I guess.

Aziza: How about other times when you feel sad or upset about your mom at school but you don't get into a fight?

Maya: When I am with my friend or I see my dad is there to pick me up.

Aziza: So when you are with your friend or getting ready to be with your dad you don't start a fight? I am curious about that. What is it like for you to be with your friend or your dad? How does that help?

Maya: I don't know. I guess I know they care about me.

These questions demonstrated Aziza's belief that change is possible and exceptions are already occurring. Maya's strengths began to emerge. In time, Aziza and the family discovered that Maya is someone who cares deeply about others, appreciates close caring relationships, and has the ability to resist acting out her feelings. This questioning continued until Maya, her father, and the therapist had a clear plan for how and when to amplify the exceptions they identified.

The types of questions most frequently used in SFFT include miracle questions, scaling questions, and coping questions. There are volumes written about why and how to ask these and other types of questions (e.g., de Shazer & Dolan, 2007; Lipchick, 2002; O'Hanlon & Rowan, 2003; Selekman, 1997; Walter & Peller, 1992). What follows here are some comments about the foundational role these questions play as interventions in the practice of SFFT.

According to de Shazer and Dolan (2007) the miracle question serves several important functions. First, it is useful in setting goals. If the therapist asks something like "If you wake up tomorrow to a miracle, and the problem is solved . . .?" or "How will we know when the problem is solved and we are done with therapy?" they are inviting clients to imagine solutions. Asking questions like "What will each of you be doing differently?" or "If we had a movie of your family when this problem is resolved . . .?" or "What will each of you notice . . .?" help the therapist and family understand the current impact of the problem and descriptions of solutions. Second, the miracle question provides an emotional experience. Through imagining, clients can experience some of what it will be like after they make the desired change. Imagining is a powerful tool that motivates us and gives us hope in everyday life. Third, the miracle question sets the stage for finding exceptions. Clients' descriptions of what will be different provide them and the therapist with clues—specific feelings, behaviors, thoughts, interactions—that are likely already occurring to some degree at least in some contexts. Finally, miracle questions help clients move from digressive stories (i.e., what has or is getting worse) to progressive stories (i.e., what has or is getting better).

Once the therapist and clients establish goals, scaling questions are used to assess progress toward goals and focus on exceptions (de Shazer & Dolan, 2007). Scaling questions send the message that the problem isn't static—that there are times when the problem is less present and/or solutions are more accessible. For example, a therapist might ask a couple questions like "On a scale of 1–10, with 1 being not giving each other the benefit of doubt at all and 10 being really giving the other the benefit of doubt (one of the clients' goals), where were each of you on the scale when the fight broke out? How about times when you were getting along? Or when during the week did you notice you gave the other or they gave you a little more benefit of the doubt (e.g, going from a 5 to a 6)?" These types of questions imply that clients have control over giving each other the benefit of the doubt and that at times they do just that. They help explore the connection between giving each other the benefit of the doubt and getting along. Scaling questions can also be used to help clients describe their inner world of emotions (de Shazer & Dolan, 2007; Lipchick, 2002) which can then be connected to what is happening relationally.

Typically therapists use scaling questions around exceptions that reflect positive goals (i.e., what is happening rather than what is not happening). This following example demonstrates a slightly different way to use scaling questions to identify and deal with emotions. Although SFFT relies heavily on moving toward positive goals (i.e., what is rather than what isn't), it can be helpful at times to make space for unwanted emotions. Let's go back to Daniel and Maya:

Aziza: So Maya, if I had a big thermometer that went from the floor to the ceiling, and the bottom is not sad at all and the top is as sad as you can ever imagine (uses hand gestures to describe the thermometer), how sad are you right now?

Maya: About here (holds her hand up to about the middle of the imaginary thermometer).

Aziza: What do you notice when you are about this sad (uses hand gesture to show the point in the thermometer Maya indicated)? What do you usually do?

Maya: I just maybe read a book or watch TV.

Aziza: How does your dad know when you are this much (hand gesture to same spot) sad?

Daniel: I know she is about that sad when she gets quiet and won't talk to me.

Aziza: What helps you go from here (on the imaginary thermometer) to here (a little lower on the thermometer)?

Maya: Maybe when Dad and I play a game or Grandma comes over.

Aziza: So when you and Dad play a game or Grandma comes over you feel a little better. What do you do differently when you are a little less sad? When you are playing a game or spending time with Grandma?

Maya: I don't know . . . maybe talking and just having fun.

Aziza: O.K. So when you are talking to Dad or Grandma and having some fun you are not quite so sad. Dad, what are you doing differently at these times Maya is talking about?

Daniel: Well I guess I am talking more too, having some fun. It is nice when my mom comes over. It gives me someone to talk to.

Aziza: Helps you feel better too?

Aziza was able to assess the current level of sadness. She would likely want to compare that to the previous week and carefully investigate what was better if the sadness had lessened. The series of questions helped the family and the therapist identify a solution they are already using, i.e., talking to each other and having some fun. In the future, once the family has had enough time to talk about sadness, Aziza might want to change the scale to one indicating a positive outcome like happiness rather than sadness.

Finally, coping questions (Lipchick, 2002) are used when clients can't identify exceptions to a problem. There are times when problems are so overwhelming that it is hard to even imagine life without them. For example, a client who is devastated over the loss of a child is likely to feel hopeless about ever feeling anything but sadness and loss. In these situations, SFF therapists ask coping questions such as "How have you been able to keep breathing?" or "How have you managed to just get from one day to the next?" or "What keeps you going?" This often reveals rich and meaningful information about strength and resilience that can be built on over time. Answers such as "I have to keep going for my other children," "I turn to God every minute of every day," or "I know my child would want me to" point to strengths such as a sense of duty, parental integrity, fierce determination, and unwavering faith that can be further explored. At other times when no exceptions can be identified, the therapist might simply ask the family to "do something different" (de Shazer & Dolan, 2007).

Collaborative Therapeutic Relationships

The therapist may be the expert in the process of therapy, but clients are experts of their own lives (Anderson & Goolishian, 1992). SFF therapists recognize that each client is unique and avoid assuming they know what clients need based on theory or clinical experience. Therapists take a "not knowing" (Anderson & Goolishian, 1992), unassuming, tentative stance so they are always in the position of learning from clients (Thomas & Nelson, 2007). Past clinical experience is used as a last resort, when clients are stuck and unable to imagine solutions. At these times, SFF therapists may tentatively contribute something like "I don't know if this is helpful, but a lot of people I work with who are in your situation tell me . . ." (Lipchick, 2002). Clients take on an active role in discovering exceptions through examining thoughts, feelings, behaviors, and interactions along with the therapist. When clients say "I don't know" the therapist believes them and helps them discover what was previously out of their awareness.

Successful SFFT depends on therapists genuinely believing clients have what they need to solve problems. Therapists need to be authentically hopeful, curious, respectful, and positive (Thomas & Nelson, 2007). SFF therapists are deeply committed to believing in and finding strengths, which helps them persevere when clients doubt their own abilities to overcome problems. Therapists who successfully use this model not only ask the right questions, but listen deeply to clients. They allow clients time and space to share problematic stories so that they are truly heard. Problem stories also offer therapists opportunities to explore strengths including how clients got through hard times. Although there is a clear focus on solutions, exceptions are embedded in both problem and solution patterns. SFF therapists can track problem patterns in order to notice exceptions in and out of sessions. For example, a common problem pattern for a couple might be to immediately distance when they start to have conflict. In this case the therapist would want to notice times when a couple stayed engaged whether or not clients are aware of these exceptions. The therapist might say to a couple "I noticed just now that you stayed in the room, in the conversation even though you both became angry. How were you able to do that?" The couple might respond with "It is because you are here," which only speaks to motivation. The therapist would press further: "I understand you are motivated to do something different when you are in therapy and I am sitting with you, but I am still really interested in *how* you were both able to stay in the conversation." This is not a simple question and would most likely take the couple and therapist some time to unravel.

Therapists must enter clients' worlds—the way clients make meaning—to cooperate with them on solutions. What other models see as resistance is viewed as therapists not cooperating the way clients expect or need. The therapist gently leads from behind. Although most SFF therapists consider customers for change to be those who share a goal for change and are willing to do something about it, many invite all family members to treatment to recruit as many customers as possible to help resolve problems.

SFF therapists, having faith in clients' strengths, connect deeply and authentically with all members of a family and inspire expectation for change through their own unwavering optimism (Lipchick, 2002). Therapists join with clients in part through compliments and seeing the best in clients; however, compliments are genuine rather than paternalistic. For example, a therapist would be taking a one-up patronizing stance by saying something like "That is so amazing, good for you for not giving up!" but an authentic stance when saying something like "I notice that you don't give up easily on what is important to you and your family; that you are tenacious and determined."

Focusing on Client Goals

It is not accurate to assume the therapist simply accepts the goal as first delivered by clients. The therapist plays a highly instrumental role by facilitating the process of helping clients develop workable goals that meet a variety of criteria. This requires exploring clients' experiences, the meanings they make of their situation, their opinions of each other, their sometimes conflicting hopes and dreams, their past struggles, and, as we will introduce further along in this chapter, their sociocultural context.

There are six criteria for a well-defined solution focused goal, including: being stated in positive form (e.g., what will be vs. what won't be), referring to process (e.g., I will be getting out of bed, looking for work vs. I will have a job), being in the here and now (e.g., get along better vs. get married someday), addressing the right level of specificity (e.g., I want to be more efficient vs. I want to get my filing done on time), being within the client's control (e.g., I want to follow through on rules and consequence vs. I want my son to do his chores), and using the client's language (e.g., you want to get along as a family vs. you want to function better as a family unit) (Walter & Peller, 1992). To clarify, the therapist attends to client language throughout therapy while actively engaging in co-constructing new language and meaning. In the example of Daniel and Maya, Aziza would not accept as a goal the first explanation of what the client is after. Aziza would have made a mistake if she had said:

Aziza: So tell me about why you came in today.

Daniel: Maya has been having fights at school. She never used to be aggressive but since her mom went to prison, she hasn't been herself.

Aziza: So fighting at school is a problem? Do you agree with your dad, Maya?

Maya: Yes.

Aziza: What do you want Maya to do instead of fighting, Dad?

Daniel: I just want her to get along with the other kids.

Maya: Duh Dad. Like I don't want the other kids to like me.

Aziza: So both of you want Maya to get along better with the kids at school? Tell me about times when you do get along, Maya.

In this scenario, the therapist accepted the definition of the problem too quickly, without exploring what was going on in the family or hearing Maya's story about her mother being incarcerated. The goal is positive, refers to process, is in the here and now, and uses the father's language. Although it is not fully in the client's control, the family and Aziza could certainly revise it to cover what Maya can actually do to better get along with other kids. This type of goal could be instrumental in finding exceptions to fighting as the therapist pursues what getting along looks like, what each person is doing, and so on. Aziza could ask the miracle question "Suppose tomorrow on the bus on the way to school you find a magic wand that will suddenly make it so by the time you get to school you are getting along with everyone, what will you be doing differently? What will you notice?" This might lead to specifics like smiling rather than frowning and letting it go when kids tease her about her mom. The problem with this goal is that it is not at the right level of specificity. It too narrowly defines the problem. It also includes only one member of the family, inadvertently implying the child is the problem and missing opportunities for more significant systemic change. Notice the difference in the type of goal that can be set after exploring the problem more fully:

Aziza: O.K. So when you are talking to Dad or Grandma and having some fun you are not quite so sad. Dad, what are you doing differently at these times Maya is talking about?

Daniel: Well I guess I am talking more too, having some fun. It is nice when my mom comes over. It gives me someone to talk to.

Aziza: Helps you feel better too?

Daniel: Yeah. It has been hard on me too and on my mom. Well of course on Maya's mom especially. We all worry about her.

Aziza: Sure, it has been hard on everyone—everyone worries. It sounds like it helps though when you talk to each other and stop every once in a while and remember to have fun?

Daniel: Yeah I guess so.

Aziza: Maya, how about at school, what helps you get along with everybody as often as you do?

Maya: Sometimes I don't think about it. Maybe I am having fun with my friends or doing school work.

Aziza: I will be interested in knowing more about times you start to think about it or start to worry but decide not to and times when you are thinking about it but manage not to get into fights . . . but right now I am wondering if you are both saying that it is important to take a break from thinking and worrying about Mom sometimes.

Here the therapist builds on exceptions that include having some fun and not worrying to ask the family to consider the idea that they can take a break from the problem. This implies that the problem is not always occurring and points toward further exceptions.

Daniel: I suppose it doesn't help any of us to just dwell on it. I know Maya's mom wouldn't want that. We need to start getting back to normal.
Aziza: Maya what does your dad mean when he says "getting back to normal?"

Aziza picks up and repeats Daniel's statement about getting back to normal. This prospective goal uses the client's words and has the potential to meet the criteria required to co-construct a well-defined, solution focused goal.

Maya: I don't know . . . maybe doing things we used to do, wrestling, watching TV together, eating dinner at the table . . . just normal stuff.
Aziza: So as a family you would like to get back to normal? As normal as you can be given what's going on? Maybe at school too?
Maya: Yeah. Everywhere. I just want to get back to normal.
Daniel: I know her mom wants that too.

Aziza didn't force a goal or accept the first idea that came along. She kept talking with the family until the right type of goal emerged. This goal is at the right level of specificity. It may seem broad at first glance, but "back to normal" serves as an umbrella goal under which many more specific interactional solutions can be identified. This is a goal that has a solution embedded in it because it refers to a time when the problem did not exist while still taking into account the family's difficult situation. This goal is also helpful to everyone and includes all of the family in the solution. Finally, the goal makes sense as the family is identifying what many families report, i.e., that maintaining family routines in a crisis enhances resilience.

Discovering and Amplifying Exceptions

Exceptions to any problem can be found, created, or imagined and focusing on the positive helps nudge clients in the direction of desired change. SFF therapists are continuously operationalizing goals and identifying anything that clients do that moves them toward desired outcomes. They encourage doing more of what is working and examine how clients are able to do things differently when change is spontaneous. Let's continue with our example of Daniel and Maya. Aziza would want to identify what is included in "back to normal," trusting that the family knows what this will take even if they can't immediately describe it and have the strength and resilience to accomplish this goal.

Aziza: So Dad and Maya, let's imagine that we are meeting for the last time because we all agree that you are as back to as normal as you can be until Mom gets home. What will we notice? What will each of you be saying? Better yet, let's say you bring in a movie to show me how things are back to normal. What will we see you doing in the movie?
Maya: We will be talking and laughing. Dad would be tickling me.
Daniel: Maya would be coming home saying she had a good day at school.

Aziza follows these more global statements like a good day at school with specific, observable behaviors.

Aziza: The two of you will be talking and laughing more. You will be wrestling and tickling and Maya will have good days at school? (therapist repeats replacing the word "would" with the word "will" moving from hypothetical to expected change)

Daniel: Yes. And Maya won't be so sad all of the time.

Aziza: And you, Dad?

Daniel: Well I suppose I wouldn't be so sad either.

Aziza: So what will you both be feeling instead of so sad? (looking for the positive vs. absence of negative)

Daniel: Maybe less worried about Maya's mom being okay.

Aziza: So less worried and sad. Tell me about times now when you are a little less worried and sad. (continues to use this language because it still seems most meaningful and useful to client)

Daniel: I think when I remind myself that Maya's mom will be all right. That we will get through this.

Aziza: You have been through other difficult things in your life? (looking to transfer solutions from one context to another)

Daniel: Yes. My father died a couple of years ago. Maya was really sick when she was a baby.

Aziza: (lowers voice speaking more slowly) How did you remind yourself that you could get through those hard times? That things would be all right?

Daniel: (tears up) I just told myself that I could do it. That I wasn't alone and that eventually things would get better.

Aziza: How are you teaching your daughter to have that kind of courage and deep optimism as she is going through her first really hard time?

Daniel: I think I could do better. (turns softly to daughter) Sweetie, things are going to be all right. Your mom is safe and will be home by next summer. We can make it. She wants our lives to be as normal as we can make them while she is gone.

Maya: (quietly) I know Dad. I'll be all right.

Toward the end of the session:

Aziza: So I am wondering if you would be willing to do an experiment this week? It seems like you both want things to be as normal as possible and that you agree you can get through this. Would you be willing to do something every day that will reassure the other that things are going to be O.K.? You know something normal! (all laugh)

Now we have some exceptions that are related to the goal, can be used across contexts, are relational, and within the clients' control. The therapist knows enough about the problem to notice exceptions when they may be out of the family's awareness. Aziza would also be keen to watch for exceptions that occur in session. For example, if Maya, Daniel, and Daniel's mother are in a session and the therapist notices them teasing each other, she might say "Is teasing each other one of those things that you normally do?"

Integrating Principles of Sociocultural Attunement

SFF therapists support social equity by challenging power dynamics between clients and therapists, seeing clients as experts of their own lives, and taking a collaborative, power-sharing stance. SFF therapists also serve as activists when they avoid pathologizing clients, refusing to focus on problem-saturated descriptions and labels. It logically follows that the better clients and therapists understand the societal context, the better they are able to use language to solve problems. Yet, as Chang and Nylund (2013) noted, "While a respectful solution-focused therapist would not shut down conversations about larger cultural constructs, SFT would not go there by default" (p. 73). Why not? Solution focused therapists ask "how and when", but rarely "why." The concern is that asking why questions sends clients and therapists looking for the cause of problems within individuals or families (Thomas & Nelson, 2007). So why ask "why" at a societal level?

⤛ ⤜

Socioculturally attuned solution focused family therapists help clients access personal and contextual strengths and resilience by integrating critical awareness of societal context and power dynamics.

⤛ ⤜

Solutions in Societal and Cultural Context

SFFT is based on social constructivist and post-structural thought, which centers the relationship between culture, societal context, and meaning. Solutions to problems emerge from cultural and social frameworks which both expand and limit possibilities. Cultural groups within societies collectively generate solutions over time. This long list includes things like rituals that help mark change or deal with loss, acts of resistance through the use of language and song, and rules that support caring family relationships. Cultural and societal norms are not apolitical, however, as they advantage some over others. Those with greater influence in societies have greater impact on meaning-making. According to Bidwell (2007), "social constructionist theory does not necessarily reject an underlying 'reality'" (p. 73). Uneven influence over meaning-making has real material consequences including access to adequate healthcare and housing, level of food security, influence in the legal system, and so on. Although SFFT is well-suited for practice across cultures and societies due to social constructivist underpinnings, therapists and clients will be limited in imagining and discovering solutions if they fail to realize the potentially restricting aspect of unexamined cultural frameworks and societal systems. The question is how we do this without imposing a theoretical framework on our clients.

A number of scholars have advocated integrating Paulo Freire's (1970/2000) approach to raising critical consciousness using dialogue, reflection, and action into the practice of family therapy (Korin, 1994). There are several points of convergence between Freirean ideas and SFFT. Chief among these is the belief that people are the experts of their own lives. Like SFF therapists, Freire viewed emancipatory education as helping people become aware of what they already know. Although SFF therapists focus primarily on clients' expertise of themselves and each other (what they know works to eliminate their problems), Freire focused on encouraging people to recognize their expertise of their environment and societal context. A main difference is that SFFT aims to help people *discover* what is helpful on a personal and interpersonal level. Emancipatory education aims to help people *uncover* societal realities so they are in a better position to take action necessary to improve their lives. What they know about themselves and the world is transformed by an understanding of the reality of broader cultural and societal dynamics. These may seem in theory like small points or major impasses to doing socioculturally attuned solution focused therapy. Raskin (2010) addressed this seeming impasse between consciousness-raising and constructivist counseling as follows:

> From a constructivist vein, consciousness-raising must be reconsidered. Instead of seeing it as something that brings people into direct contact with extra-linguistic reality [what is

real outside of meaning imposed through language], consciousness-raising is *consciousness-raising-within-a-tradition*. This shift encourages social justice therapists to continue their work, but with a subtle and important difference. Rather than seeing themselves as dispensers of a higher truth, they are asked to settle for seeing themselves as advocates of a particular framework for living. They invite clients to try on their preferred discourse with the idea that perhaps it might open new avenues of understanding. At the same time, they remain cognizant . . . that every discourse (their own included) sometimes oppresses and at other times liberates.

(p. 252)

꘏ ꘏

Inviting clients to explore societal forces that affect their lives can increase potential solutions and encourage discovering and amplifying a broader set of exceptions.

꘏ ꘏

SFF therapists are above all pragmatic—willing to explore what works. They rely on asking poignant questions and avoid getting caught in theoretical word games. In practice, it is not so difficult to imagine integrating social and cultural awareness. Take for example Janise, an African American single parent living on low income who is struggling with being the mother she wants to be while she pursues a college education. A SFF therapist is likely to ask Janise questions about where she lives, who is in her life, what social support systems she has (e.g., church, peers at college), interactions between family members, and so on. The therapist would work to co-create a goal that is in positive form, for example "being the mother I want to be" in spite of her challenging situation. The therapist would then help Janise operationalize what this means and explore times when she is able to do so, e.g., complete her school work while parenting, act according to her values and beliefs, enjoy being with her child.

A socioculturally attuned SFF therapist would extend the context and word questions in ways that would help Janise and the therapist become more aware of the effect of her societal context. Questions might include, "You mentioned that most of your peers at school are single, middle-class, white students. What is your experience in that context? How do you make sense of the racial and social class dynamics?" As Janise and the therapist uncover the impact of oppressive sexist, racist, and classist educational and other societal systems, Janise would be able to make new meaning of her situation. This would not alleviate her financial stress or the racism, sexism, and classism she is faced with on a daily basis, but would expand potential solutions and better acknowledge existing strengths. Solution focused questions that follow might include things like "How do you think black women have historically been able to survive and thrive when there has been so much working against them?" and "How have you been able to do this for so many years? Be successful in school and still be a caring mother in spite of the racism and sexism you experience? With so few financial resources?" These questions would help Janise move from the broader context, including strengths black women in her situation have historically shared, to her own strengths and solutions.

꘏ ꘏

Clients and therapists can move from seeing the client as having unique solutions to a private problem to being part of a collective with both common and unique solutions to a shared public problem.

꘏ ꘏

Language and Power

The relationship between language and power in socioculturally attuned SFFT takes us back to the beginning—to de Shazer's (1997) reading of Wittgenstein, who postulated that meaning associated with words emerges only when used and heard in context (Pitkin, 1972).

↞—↠

Socioculturally attuned solution focused brief therapists critically analyze discourse as it unfolds in therapeutic conversations, attending to words, tone, body language, and emotion to understand how power shapes meaning.

↞—↠

This includes attention to the role of power and context in how problems are understood and goals are identified. We might think of socioculturally attuned SFF therapists as routinely engaging in a type of informal critical discourse analysis in order to understand how group power dynamics are part of the context in which meaning is made and social arrangements are reinforced. According to van Dijk (1999) critical discourse analysis "focuses on (group) relations of *power, dominance* and *inequality* and the ways these are *reproduced* or *resisted* by social group members through text and talk" (p. 18).

Let's explore how societal context and power dynamics impact meaning embedded in even the most seemingly simple questions and solutions. Suppose a therapist echoes a remark by a family that the mother "is a strong woman." This won't evoke the same image or description for all of us, but for many of us it means something like "she can endure a lot" or "she can stand up for herself and won't take being put down." The meaning of the statement is inseparable from gendered power dynamics. SFF therapists must attend closely to meaning to ensure questions and solutions support social equity. The therapist might follow with questions like "You mention that you see your partner as a strong (woman/man/person). Can you describe what you mean? What do you and others notice that leads you to describe them in this way?" These questions open space for discussing gender and other power dynamics using specific, here and now examples. If being a strong woman includes enduring a lot or not taking being put down, questions that follow would include identifying how a client is able to stand up to others as well as what is happening relationally that requires standing up to others.

Third Order Change

Third order change occurs when the experience of all family members is fully explored within their sociocultural context. Slowing the process of imagining values, solutions, expanding what is both possible and preferable to include equitable relationships, mirrors the model's expectation of collaboration between therapist and clients. When offered space to do so, families and therapists can envision, identify, and amplify *just* solutions. This requires extra steps to ensure what has been silenced can be named and voiced; that therapists intervene to encourage families to develop the willingness to respond to each other; and exceptions are noticed and amplified that encourage transformation toward *just* relationships within and beyond the family.

Practice Guidelines

Following are four guidelines for practicing socioculturally attuned SFFT. These include inviting clients to explore the societal context in which they live, considering equity when setting goals, broadening the search for solutions to the wider societal and historical context, and discovering and amplifying just solutions.

1. Invite Clients to Explore Societal Context

Socioculturally attuned SFF therapists invite clients to examine the relationship between societal context and presenting problems in order to expand possibilities for solutions and support equitable relationships. This is done in ways that are in keeping with the rest of the model. Therapists need to have the social awareness to know where to look and what to ask, but not assume they know the social reality of clients' lives. Therapists and clients explore social dynamics together engaging in mutual conscious raising. It is assumed that each family has a unique relationship to its societal context and therapists must **attune** to their specific situation. In other words, societal context plays out differently across families and the therapist must take a stance of inquiring to help families explore context as integral to the meaning they make of the world, including how they relate to each other.

2. Consider Equity in Co-Constructing Client Goals

Socioculturally attuned SFF therapists work with families to ensure goals include as many members as possible and support relational equity. Imagine asking a few well-placed questions in addition to the typical miracle question such as: "So you have described that when this problem is gone all of you will be communicating more. I am curious about how you **envision** each of you being heard by the others. Whose voice will carry the most influence and be heard the loudest? Who is likely not to be heard or have as much influence in conversations?" and/or "What will it look like when you all have the influence you need to feel heard and get your needs met?" As clients answer these questions, they are likely to negotiate goals that include attention to power dynamics. The therapist might **name** the impact of the family's societal context by asking questions like "What will be the difference between how males and females are heard in your family?" or "How will this be the same or different from your experience in the rest of your lives?" Socioculturally attuned SFF therapists continue to check with clients about the impact of goals relative to their relational power throughout the course of therapy.

3. Broaden Search for Solutions to Wider Context

Culturally attuned SFF therapists broaden the search for solutions by **valuing** the wider social and historical context. This includes working with clients to identify collective resistance and resilience. Clients are encouraged to consider the exceptions of their ancestors, those in their social identity groups, and those whom they admire. Having ancestors who maintained their humanity even when enslaved, practicing a religion in spite of discrimination, or being part of a group that continues to practice cultural traditions in spite of colonization and attempted genocide are examples of the power of the collective. Individuals within these collectives are also important sources for exceptions (e.g., a grandmother who completed college in spite of getting married, a father who continued anti-war protests even when serving in the military). Exploring these resources often exposes shared characteristics, or solutions, that can be amplified. Questions might include: "In what ways are you like your grandmother?" and "How have the many generations of your religion been able to stay faithful in spite of discrimination?" and "How have you been active in keeping cultural traditions going?"

4. Identify and Amplify Just Solutions

Therapists and clients work collaboratively to identify and amplify exceptions. They expand available solutions and then choose from possibilities. Each member of the family is asked to identify exceptions and prompted to do more of what works. Socioculturally attuned SFF therapists add a step to this process by **intervening** to ensure that what works is just; that exceptions which are amplified are those that all members of the therapeutic system agree support, or at least don't interfere with, relational equity. Equity is supported in all relationships, e.g., relationships in the workplace, social groups, and religious communities. Socioculturally attuned SFFT pay constant attention to societal stereotypes and systems of discrimination and oppression. Consider a male client answering a question such as "What seems to help the two of you get along better?" with "When she listens to me!" Of course listening to each other helps most of us get along, yet few therapists would proceed with "So do you agree that listening to your husband helps the two of you get along better?" It would not be uncommon, however, for a therapist to say something like "So do you both agree that you get along better when you listen to each other?" A socioculturally attuned SFF therapist again takes a few extra steps toward **transformation**, resisting the temptation to gloss over the power imbalance indicated in the original statement. The therapist might ask the husband "So you would like your wife to listen to you. What does that mean for you? How do you know when she is listening to you? How does she know when you listen to her?" and then ask the wife "What do you think he means when he says he wants you to listen to him? How do you know when he is listening to you?" and so on. Socioculturally attuned SFF therapists ensure that family members do not act in ways that oppress or limit each other's strengths and solutions. Rather, the therapist would work with the family to ensure equitable relationships that support the well-being of all members.

Case Illustration

Tina, age 40, emigrated from Taiwan to the U.S. when she was 25 and married a European American man, David, age 39. Most of her family still lives in Taiwan, including her parents and two siblings and their children. Her nephew, Eric did not do as well as the family hoped on the Taiwanese national Form III exam at the end of junior high school and was placed in a less than desirable high school. The likelihood of Eric passing college entrance exams in Taiwan loomed over the family. Eric's parents also wanted Eric to become more fluent in English than was possible in compulsory English language courses and costly after school programs. Simply put, like most parents, they wanted their child to have opportunities for a better life. The extended family collectively decided Eric would live with Tina and David to attend high school and college in the U.S.

Within months of arriving, Eric had become isolated, spending most of his time in his room. Try as they might, Tina and David were not successful in drawing Eric out to be an active member of their family. David had become irritated with Eric's seeming unwillingness to contribute to basic family chores. David complained to Tina about Eric leaving his dirty plate on the table or having to be asked to gather his dirty laundry week after week. Eric had also become increasingly unhappy with his aunt, whom he expected would be there to help him more than she was. Tina was caught in the middle, feeling burdened by her brother's expectation that she would take on the responsibility of raising her nephew and worrying she was burdening David with her family problems.

Eric felt lost in the U.S., unable to speak the language fluently or understand the culture. He was not making friends at school, relying on communicating mainly with his aunt and playing video games with kids back home whenever he got the chance. Tina and her sister-in-law talked daily about Eric and how Tina and David might help him adjust. Things did not improve, however, in spite of their efforts. Eventually Tina asked Eric's parents for permission to take him to therapy in the U.S. Tina was referred by one of her friends to a Taiwanese American family therapist, Alice, who worked from a solution focused framework.

Invite Clients to Explore Societal Context

The therapist explored the relationships between David, Tina, and Eric, including how they saw the problem within their societal and cultural context. Eric described his Aunt

Tina as "not having Chinese thinking." He expected his aunt to offer him more guidance, help him more with daily decisions, monitor his homework, and instruct him in what she expected him to do around the house. Eric respected his aunt as his elder but there had been little connection between them before he arrived in the U.S. David wanted Eric to be more independent and thought by now he should be able to see what needed to be done and take responsibility for his own schoolwork. David and Eric agreed they expected Tina to be the bridge between them. Following is an excerpt from their therapy conversation:

Alice: So Tina, you mentioned that you are sort of a bridge between Eric and David. Also between your family here and your family in Taiwan?

Tina: Yes I guess I am. I want to support my brother and nephew but also want to make sure David doesn't have to take on my whole family.

Alice: So trying to bridge what everybody needs?

David: She is the one everybody goes to. She is the bridge for Eric too.

Alice: Eric, you go to your aunt when you need something, or don't understand something about being here?

Eric: Yes. My aunt helps me the most.

Alice: So Tina is the bridge because she knows both countries—knows how to think Chinese and to think U.S. How do each of you think gender might also play into this on both ends of the bridge? To Tina's role in helping everyone understand each other?

Alice continued to help the family explore the transnational contexts which were impacting their daily lives and each of their contributions to helping the family adjust before moving on to co-constructing goals. It was evident that Tina was expected to take on the most responsibility for cultural translation. As a Taiwanese American woman living with a European American man, she had been the one to culturally accommodate. David did not put equal effort into bridging the cultures, unknowingly expecting Tina would take on this burden. Gender dynamics were also at play as Tina's husband, brother, and nephew all expected her to solve family problems.

Consider Equity in Co-Constructing Client Goals

After exploring cultural and societal context, Alice was in a better position to co-construct equitable goals. The family went on to talk about what it will look like when they no longer need a bridge or a cultural translator. They agreed that one of their goals was everyone learning to live in two cultures at once.

Alice: When you have all adjusted to living together in two cultures, what will we notice? What will you see each other and yourselves doing differently?

David: Eric will be talking to us more, spending more time trying to make U.S. friends . . . contributing to the household without always being asked . . .

Alice: And what will you be doing differently, David?

David: Maybe not going to a therapist every time I don't understand Eric or don't like what he is doing?

Alice: Tina, what will you be doing differently when you are no longer taking on most of the burden of being the bridge or translator in the family?

In this excerpt, David begins answering the miracle question with what he wants from Eric. Alice continues to ask questions that will co-construct a goal that encourages equal participation and holds everyone equally accountable for change. The conversation continued in this way until all members of the family and the therapist co-created the goal of everyone working together to learn how to live in two cultures at the same time. The goal was then carefully defined and described. This might include recognizing when cultural norms and values are at odds, making room for multiple traditions, and learning key words in both languages. This goal challenged the inequity of those in the most marginalized cultural positions (i.e., outsiders from the less globally powerful Taiwan) needing to be the ones to adjust to those in the most centered and dominant cultural positions (those in the most privileged group in the more powerful host country). Likewise, contributions were expected to be equal among all genders.

Broaden Search for Solutions to Wider Context

Alice searched for exceptions by identifying ways David and Tina were already able to live together and adjust to living in two cultures at once. Exceptions included each of them explaining cultural differences to their families, negotiating different values, beliefs, and cultural practices, and thinking about cultural differences rather than assuming the worst when differences arose between them. Alice also asked about Eric's willingness to come to a new country, his ability to navigate school, and times when he was aware of cultural differences. Alice also helped the family draw from collective successes. These included drawing from the rich history of Chinese and Taiwanese people in the U.S., including how they coped with discrimination and cultural difference. It also included stories of those like Tina who found ways to successfully live in the U.S. without losing connection to core cultural values or family in her home country.

Identify and Amplify Just Solutions

The therapist in this case was careful not to promote or amplify solutions that worked for some but were not just for others. For example, asking Tina to continue to work harder than the rest of the family to bridge the two cultures may have worked and in fact had been working to some extent, but was not a just solution. Alice could reasonably assume that amplifying unjust solutions would lead to further problems later on. Identifying and amplifying just exceptions and solutions included times when David and Tina talked together with Eric to help him interpret differences in U.S. and Taiwanese culture. It also included times when David worked to understand and support Taiwanese cultural beliefs, values, and practices in ways that matched Tina's work to learn about and fit into European American culture. Alice helped the family amplify times when David and Eric spent time together and when Eric went to David for help and David advised Eric.

Summary: Third Order Change

Third order change occurred in this family when there were major shifts in how they saw the world and the problems they were having within this expanded view (Ecker & Hulley, 1996). The family was able to consider more possibilities for how to organize their relationships when they were able to take a meta-view of culture and transnational power dynamics and gender across two societies. This helped them realize the impact of these broad social arrangements on their most intimate relationships and to make more conscious choices about how they wanted to live. The therapist invited the family into third order change by asking questions that placed their lives within cultural and societal context.

The family continued to work on bridging two very different cultures in a single household, but now did so from a perspective that broadened options. They could more consciously share the burden of living in two cultures rather than Tina having to do all of the cultural accommodating. They developed a more critical view of the relationships between countries and the tendency for one partner's culture and gender to dominate the other. Third order change made it impossible to automatically assume the prescribed and stereotypical roles of a female cultural outsider who must learn to live in the U.S. and a white U.S. male who married an accommodating Asian female. This arrangement was now one of many possibilities that Tina and David could choose for their lives together and with Eric.

References

Anderson, H., & Goolishian, H. (1992). The client is the expert: A not-knowing approach to therapy. In S. McNamee & K. J. Gergen (Eds.), *Therapy as a social construction* (p. 25–39). London, UK: SAGE.

Berg, I. K. (1994). *Family-based services: A solution-focused approach.* New York, NY: W. W. Norton.

Bidwell, D. R. (2007). Miraculous knowing: Epistemology and solution-focused therapy. In T. S. Nelson & F. N. Thomas (Eds.), *Handbook of solution-focused brief therapy* (pp. 65–88). New York, NY: Haworth Press.

Chang, J., & Nylund, D. (2013). Narrative and solution-focused therapies: A twenty-year retrospective. *Journal of Systemic Therapies, 32*(2), 72–88.

de Shazer, S. (1997). Some thought on language use in therapy. *Contemporary Family Therapy, 19*(1), 133–141.

de Shazer, S., & Berg, I. K. (1992). Doing therapy: A post-structural re-vision. *Journal of Marital and Family Therapy, 18*(1), 71–81.

de Shazer, S., & Dolan, Y. (2007). *More than miracles: The state of the art of solution-focused brief therapy.* New York, NY: Hawthorn Press.

Dermer, S. B., Hemesath, C. W., & Russell, C. S. (1998). A feminist critique of solution-focused therapy. *The American Journal of Family Therapy, 26*(3), 239–250.

Ecker, B., & Hulley, L. (1996). *Depth oriented brief therapy: How to be brief when you were trained deep and vice versa.* San Francisco, CA: Jossey Bass.

Freire, P. (2000). *Pedagogy of the oppressed.* New York, NY: Bloomsbury. (Original work published in 1970).

Korin, E. C. (1994). Social inequalities and therapeutic relationships: Applying Freire's ideas to clinical practice. *Journal of Feminist Family Therapy, 5*(3/4), 75–98.

Lipchick, E. (2002). *Beyond technique in solution-focused therapy.* New York, NY: Guilford Press.

Nelson, T. S., & Thomas, F. N. (Eds.). (2007). *Handbook of solution-focused brief therapy.* New York, NY: Haworth Press.

O'Hanlon, B., & Rowan, T. (2003). *Solution oriented therapy for chronic and severe mental illness.* New York, NY: W. W. Norton.

Pitkin, H. (1972). *Wittgenstein and justice.* Berkeley: University of California Press.

Raskin, J. (2010). Constructing and deconstructing social justice counseling. In J. Raskin, S. Bridges, & R. Neimeyer (Eds.), *Studies in meaning 4: Constructivist perspectives on theory, practice and social justice* (pp. 247–276). New York, NY: Pace University Press.

Selekman, M. (1997). *Solution-focused therapy with children.* New York, NY: Guilford Press.

Thomas, F. N., & Nelson, T. (2007). Assumptions and practices within the solution-focused brief therapy tradition. In T. S. Nelson & F. N. Thomas (Eds.), *Handbook of solution-focused brief therapy* (pp. 3–24). New York, NY: Haworth Press.

van Dijk, T. A. (1999). Critical discourse analysis and conversation analysis. *Discourse & Society, 10*(4), 459–460.

Walter, J., & Peller, J. (1992). *Becoming solution-focused in brief therapy.* New York, NY: Brunner/Mazel.

12 Socioculturally Attuned Collaborative Family Therapy

Collaborative practices (Anderson, 1997), also known as the collaborative language systems approach (Anderson, 1993, 1995) and the postmodern collaborative approach (Anderson, 2012b), attend to listening and responding to a client's narratives in a skillfully attuned manner. Leaders in the field of family therapy, including Harlene Anderson, Harry Goolishian, Lynn Hoffman, Tom Anderson and Peggy Penn, were instrumental in developing these practices. Collaborative family therapists are known for taking a humble, unassuming "not-knowing stance" and examining multiple narratives and perspectives in order to create new meanings and possibilities. Those who engage in collaborative practice contend they may be experts in shaping the clinical process, but clients are always the experts of their own lives (Goolishian & Anderson, 1992; Monk & Gehart, 2003).

Anderson asserted that working from a collaborative stance is a philosophy of life in action. She (1997, 2007) stated that the postmodern understanding of knowledge and language is at the heart and soul of therapy and referred to this philosophical stance as a way of being in relationship and conversation. Anderson postulated that it is a "a way of thinking with, experiencing with, relating with, and responding with the people we meet in therapy" (Anderson, 2007, p. 43). Collaborative practices are seen as a generative way of being *with* people, not a typical model of therapy (Shotter, 2005).

+←→+

Collaborative practices encourage third order change through generative dialogue that expands possibilities for more equitable relationships in families and society.

+←→+

Third order change in the context of the collaborative approach means **attuning** to external forces that affect our ability to engage, work toward understanding, and respond with humility and compassion. It also requires **naming** what is unjust or has been overlooked and intentionally sharing space and voice as collaborative conversational partners. Collaborative practices **value** and acknowledge the worth of what has been ignored, minimized, or devalued. Therapists **intervene** through questions and transparent statements that support relational equity and disrupt oppressive power dynamics. They create space with clients to imagine and **envision** and **transform** relationships to achieve more "just" alternatives.

In this chapter, we identify core enduring concepts of collaborative practices and then integrate the tenets of socioculturally attuned family therapy into the practice of collaborative therapy. We illustrate these ideas by sharing a case example of a Latino family in crisis due to the deportation of their son. Our aim is to demonstrate an application of socioculturally attuned collaborative family therapy, integrating a rich understanding of the influence of sociocultural systems.

Primary Enduring Collaborative Family Therapy Concepts

In the following, we describe what we believe are enduring concepts of collaborative practices, including: reality is socially constructed through language, therapy is a dialogic process between conversational partners, therapists assume an unassuming, humble, not-knowing stance, and therapy is a mutual endeavor toward possibilities.

Reality is Socially Constructed

Social constructionists assume that knowledge and meaning are constructed through interactions between people. It is impossible to "know" outside of context (Rosen, 1996). Words do not have meaning in and of themselves. They derive their meaning from the contexts in which they are created. Language is more than just the words and gestures that are expressed or performed between people. Meaning emerges from the cultural practices that define and shape our interactions. It is through historically and culturally located language that we construct the manner by which thoughts, feelings, and behaviors are produced and understood. (McNamee & Gergen, 1992; Monk & Gehart, 2003).

The hope is that therapists' words and body language convey to clients that they are valued as unique persons and not as representations of a type or group. Collaborative therapists exude the belief that those with whom they meet are important and have something worthy to say and worthy of hearing. They are able to meet clients without judgment of past, present, or future and the therapist does not have a hidden agenda. Anderson (2007) stated that the key word for this way of practice is *with*; a process that is participatory and mutual rather than hierarchical and dualistic (Anderson, 2007; Anderson, 2012b). In collaborative processes, all persons come together as equal partners in the construction of meaning and possibilities. Language and therapy is a "talking with" in a non-interventive conversation (Anderson, 1999).

Conversational Partners

Collaborative therapists assume clients will be collaborators or co-investigators. Therapists assume the position of collaborator before meeting or knowing anything about clients (Guilfoyle, 2006). They engage clients in a shared conversation that generates new meanings— "different way[s] of understanding, making sense of, or punctuating one's lived experiences" (Anderson, 1997, p. 109). As a consequence, each person experiences a newness that emerges from the dialogue and leads to problem dissolution and a greater sense of agency.

At the most basic level, the primary aim of the therapist is to facilitate a conversation in which all persons are fully engaged and heard by each other (Mills & Sprenkle, 1995). This dialogic process is the primary "intervention," inviting clients into a conversation in which the therapist explores conversational streams that arise in different relationships and situations. The pacing of the conversation is often slower than other conversations in order to allow space and time for inner dialogues to shape and take new forms. Through the subtle shifts of inner and outer dialogue, each person's perspective and experience of the problem shifts (Monk & Gehart, 2003). It is not possible to predict how the story will unfold or how it will end. The dialogical process is an intentional, generative, dynamic mutual activity that feels distinct from other forms of language, such as a discussion, debate, or simply chitchatting (Anderson, 2007).

Therapists facilitate a process that keeps all voices in motion and contributing to the conversation. The therapist models honesty and sincerity, helping clients be receptive to hearing and engaging in each other's stories. All clients should feel equally important, that their version of the narrative is as important as that of any other. Therapists are intentional about not siding with any one particular person, by showing they are "for" all persons simultaneously.

These dialogical conversations create different ways of understanding, making sense of, and/or punctuating one's lived experiences.

Humility and Uncertainty

Taking a not-knowing stance is one of the most important, and also potentially misunderstood, aspects of collaborative practices. Collaborative therapists walk a tightrope between understanding and not understanding, knowing and not-knowing. The not-knowing stance does not mean that the therapist doesn't know. That would be impossible. It means that the therapist brackets or suspends what they believe they know, so that new understandings can emerge (Anderson, 2012b). Attending to clients' local knowledge and their lived experience is at the core.

Working from this stance creates space in which participants continuously challenge assumptions and open up to untapped potential and new possibilities. This means welcoming multiple and sometimes contradictory narratives. The therapist suspends any commitment to a particular outcome or agenda other than that which has been jointly determined by all involved. This frees the therapist from imposing an agenda and opens space to collaboratively create new interpretations. Therapists are always informed, knowledgeable, prepared, educated, well-trained, and knowing. The stance of not-knowing is about having the courage and humility to remain in a respectful, unassuming, learner position.

Expanding Possibilities

Meaningful conversations that *open* space for possibilities are central to the work of collaborative therapy. Possibilities unfold when both clients and therapist are in the moment and open to being influenced. The dialogic process invites participants to influence and be influenced, to shape and be shaped by the interaction, and to mutually co-create meaning. This egalitarian relationship should not be authoritarian or imposing. The therapist is careful not to reproduce predetermined meanings. It is through this rich process that the *not-yet* said or heard meanings can emerge (Guilfoyle, 2003). If the therapist is open to the process of therapy unfolding in the ways it needs to, it is possible that an isomorphic process can occur in the lives of both clients and therapist.

Being open to possibilities, instead of dogmatically holding on to predetermined scripts, paths, and "shoulds," enables participants to explore paths that are better suited for their lives, contexts, and preferred ways of living and being. Being open to possibilities in and out of therapy can open doors to what was previously limited or constrained. Comments such as "I have never thought of that before," "I could not have imagined my doing something like this before now," "No one has ever mentioned this to me in this way," or "That goal seemed impossible to achieve," reflect clients' experiencing space opening for new realities to emerge.

Integrating Principles of Sociocultural Attunement

Hare-Mustin (1994) said therapy can be like a mirrored room in which a therapist and client can only openly discuss what is reflected in the dialogue between them. When this happens, freedom to discuss what is unsaid becomes constrained. If the therapist or clients feel unable to address larger social issues (i.e., racism, classism, xenophobia, homophobia, sexism, etc.) because the client has not brought these discourses into the room, then systemic change is not possible. Hare-Mustin suggested that it is the responsibility of the therapist to develop consciousness about larger systemic issues and invite these topics into the room so that these social forces do not remain silent. Socioculturally attuned collaborative therapists open these dialogues.

This section focuses on ways in which societal context and power shape and influence dialogic processes in and out of therapy. Through clinical examples, we demonstrate how to intentionally weave principles of sociocultural attunement into the fabric of the collaborative approach, specifically examining practices that lead to transformational change.

Societal Context

We see no inherent conflicts in working from the collaborative approach while attending to larger structural and systemic forces in therapy.

⊷ ⇥

Socioculturally attuned collaborative therapists engage in conversations with a heightened awareness of sociopolitical and contextual issues.

⊷ ⇥

Socioculturally attuned collaborative therapists acknowledge that culture shapes and constrains local meaning making (Anderson, 1997; Anderson & Goolishian, 1988; Monk & Gehart, 2003). They do not know until they are in the conversation what sociocultural issues will arise. Given that conversations unfold in unique and collaborative ways, it is impossible to predict which contextual factors will become meaningful in the dialogue.

In the following we offer an example of what this type of conversation might sound like. We do this understanding that our collaborative colleagues do not typically rely on conversational techniques or offer examples of dialogue to describe their philosophical stance. Consider Morgan, who presented to therapy with an expressed desire to transition from male to female.

Morgan:	I always felt different.
Therapist:	What do you mean? Would you be willing to tell me more about feeling different?
Morgan:	I guess I just felt different . . . . I was always teased and mocked at school for the types of clothes I wore, especially my old shoes.
Therapist:	(curious about the societal context around the notion of "old shoes") Old shoes?
Morgan:	It was humiliating, especially in middle school. We would mostly shop at the thrift store and garage sales . . . (long pause) I hated going with my mom—I was embarrassed. I didn't fit in at school and my parents were struggling too hard to help me.
Therapist:	I am curious about what you said about your parents struggling too hard to help you. Would it be okay to talk more about that?
Morgan:	Sure. Maybe I sometimes resent them, but I get it. They grew up with nothing and they tried really hard. They never had enough money. They both had crappy jobs. I wanted nice things but then I also felt bad when they had to work so hard to get them. Sometimes I kind of felt guilty.
Therapist:	Yeah, that seems really hard growing up without enough money with your parents working so hard.

Morgan was struggling financially and felt at risk for being evicted from their apartment. The therapist may have initially thought that the conversation would focus on Morgan's feelings around the desire to transition; however, the therapist realized as the conversation progressed that Morgan was concerned about their financial situation and struggled with resentment toward their parents.

The larger social constraints of poverty and classism were influencing Morgan's current struggles. As Anderson (2012a) suggested, we are born, live, and are educated within mostly invisible grand knowledge narratives, universal truths, and dominant discourses in societal contexts that we take for granted. The grand narratives of meritocracy and the intersection of gender and poverty affected Morgan's sense of self and relationship with their parents. It was essential that the therapist was able to remain "experience near" and engage as a conversational partner, gently examining the larger forces that impacted Morgan's life.

Therapist:　How do you think those "old shoes" and all the struggle you have been through about not having enough affects you now?

Morgan:　Well, I hate to say this, but I feel like I got ripped off somehow. I wasn't given a lot to build from like my friends and the kids in college. And I always work so hard and still feel like I'm broke all the time. I can never seem to just make it. And I know that people discriminate against me because I'm queer, especially at work. It just sucks all the way around.

Therapist:　Sucks all the way around . . . hmm . . . . Would it be okay to help me try to understand what that means for you? Can you say more about that?

The therapist continues to stay with Morgan, walking with them closely through their experience through the effects of societal context.

⋆←→⋆

Given that grand narratives have so much power and authority in society, they seduce us into practices that can distance others and create dissonance for ourselves and our preferred ways of being.

⋆←→⋆

In addition to the grand narratives clients have about their lives, as therapists we also have grand narratives about ourselves, our work, and our profession. The names we use to describe the profession of family therapy as well as the politics and economics of diagnoses are important grand narratives. For example, our field is often referred to as "mental health," "behavioral health," and "behavioral medicine," among others. These names were constructed by larger social systems and have been used to define the practice of "psychotherapy." Socioculturally attuned collaborative family therapists remain vigilant about how these dominant narratives define them and their work, recognizing the potential of these narratives to constrain possibilities and position therapists to impose professional knowledge on clients. Therapists are sometimes in the position of serving as gatekeepers (as in the example of Morgan who could not proceed with transitioning without therapist approval) or agents of social control, e.g., court referred therapy.

Grand societal narratives affect how people know themselves, construct their problems and solutions, and participate in therapy. For example, a therapist might diagnose Morgan with Gender Dysphoria to get approval for hormone treatment and insurance coverage. The diagnosis itself implies there is something wrong with Morgan rather than something wrong with a society that rigidly adheres to a dichotomous view of gender. Morgan might be anxious about that, not knowing who might see the diagnosis and how this could impact their living situation (e.g., housing and employment). A socioculturally attuned collaborative therapist would name injustices embedded in the medical context and engage Morgan in conversations to ensure they have the opportunity to carefully navigate difficult decisions.

As therapists, we must remain vigilant about how and why we support or reject grand narratives. These narratives have a direct effect on how we engage as conversational partners. We must be aware of how factors such as racism, classism, sexism, and homophobia affect ways clients engage as conversational partners (Ashbourne, Fife, Ridley, & Gaylor, 2016), and transparent in making connections between clients' experiences and the larger sociocultural context.

◂╾➤

Socioculturally attuned collaborative therapists do not remain neutral about the ways clients are affected by social inequality; they invite these perspectives into the dialogue.

◂╾➤

It is important to understand that as conversational partners, therapists have a responsibility to bring a voice to the dialogue (Cheon & Murphy, 2007). In fact, clients may misinterpret silence as collusion with larger dominant discourses. Let's consider a therapist who listens intentionally, respectfully, and quietly for a long period of time as a client speaks of his religious beliefs. The client becomes notably anxious as the therapist continues to affirm minimally, with an "uh huh" and slightly nodding his head. The client is left unsettled because he feels vulnerable in sharing his experience and feelings and the therapist's level of engagement does not match that of the client; exaggerating his position of power by remaining silent. His silence is disconcerting and confusing to the client because he does not know where the counselor stands in response to what he disclosed. The process needs engaged equitable conversational partners, each contributing to the dialogue in proportionate and transparent ways.

Socioculturally attuned collaborative therapists are transparent with their concerns about the impact of societal structures on dialogical processes and how these realities may limit possibilities generated in clinical dialogue. A study conducted by D'Arrigo-Patrick, Hoff, Knudson-Martin, and Tuttle (2017) examined how therapists handle possible tensions between collaborative practices and addressing social justice. These researchers found that collaborative therapists brought issues of fairness and the larger context into clinical conversations by asking questions that place social justice at the forefront while staying close to client experience, e.g., "Could it be that racism plays a role in what you are experiencing?" Their findings led them to the conclusion that the distinction between activism and collaboration is a false dichotomy. Therapists reported balancing raising these issues with maintaining relationships with clients. We believe this balance is more easily negotiated when therapists have a clear picture of the sociocultural context in which their therapeutic relationships are situated.

Culture is created and expressed through language, narratives, and social discourses (Laird, 2000). These narratives are both private (e.g., internal thoughts and processes) and public (e.g., as when we are talking to another person). We put our cultures into action through interactive processes that define ourselves and others.

◂╾➤

Socioculturally attuned collaborative therapists must attend to the relationship between the nuance of words, meanings, intonation, utterances, pauses, silences, and dominance.

◂╾➤

Cultural categories and language can justify stereotypes, power-over acts of violence (e.g., gay-bashing), and cultural atrocities (e.g., ethnic cleansing, femicide). Conversely, compassionate words and the act of *listening* are important ways to enter people's lives by creating space for them to be heard. Language acquires meaning from how we use it in our relationships, not just in what we think our words represent (Strong, 2002).

＊←→＊

It is important to be mindful of the ways in which our social locations and intersecting identities affect the nuances among conversational partners within a collaborative relationship.

＊←→＊

How people communicate and participate as conversational partners depends in part on their cultural values and social location. Laird (2000) asked, for example, "How is *this* person performing culture?" (p. 106). We add, "How is this person or myself performing the inter-sections of gender, heteronormativity, middle-class, whiteness, etc.?" Dominant discourses ascribe certain performances based on cultural norms (e.g., masculinity and femininity), which limit the possibilities generated. Socioculturally attuned therapists bring multiple possible perspectives or stories into the conversation (Ashbourne et al., 2016).

Let's consider Don, a white Jewish man in his late sixties known in the community for his collaborative practices with queer couples. He agreed to work with Tony and Gabriel, a gay Latino couple in their late twenties seeking help for Gabriel's "low sex drive." Upon meeting the couple, Don asked questions not simply to get answers, but in ways that allowed him to participate in the conversation in a curious way, responding to multiple perspectives, and to stay close to what had been said.

Don: Thank you for being here. I am eager to learn about what you both hope to accom-plish by the end of our conversation? What would be most helpful for you to leave with today?

Gabriel: I want to tell Tony something I just discovered about myself. I want him to under-stand me and be O.K. with what I have to say.

Don: Would that be alright with you Tony? Is there something specifically you would like to see happen today, in addition to what Gabriel is wanting for your first session?

Tony: No, I'm good. I just really want to focus on what Gabriel wanted to talk to me about. I know it has been weighing heavy on his mind.

As a consequence, Gabriel disclosed to Tony that he thought he was asexual. He told Tony that he did not know he was asexual until he began to read more about it. Everything he read about it matched his perception of himself.

Don: Thank you for sharing that with us Gabriel. I am curious about what meaning this new identity has had for you personally, as well as for your relationship?

Gabriel: I feel liberated from my "fake self." I have always felt like I was playing a part; like I was performing being a man, which meant being sexual. I want to be loving and giving with Tony and share my life with him, but I am tired of pretending to be a man in that way.

Don wanted to contribute to and expand the conversation to include the possibility of addressing the impact of societal context on the couple.

Don: Could it be that social pressures and notions of masculinity and culture affected your desire to conform to those expectations?

Gabriel: For sure! No one understands it. All my brothers, my dad and uncles, and friends are tough macho guys. They are always gay bashing and saying shit about women and "faggots" and "culeros" (derogatory and vulgar term in Spanish for gay men). It's exhausting and infuriating. I know that Tony is the only one who truly understands me. That is why I love him so much. I love you enough to be honest with you Tony. I want to be fair to you.

Gabriel and Tony were able to engage in a generative dialogue that helped them understand each other and how they needed to redefine their relationship. The societal context in which they and most of us live, does not support asexuality as an acceptable orientation for an attractive, Latino man in his late twenties, who is in a monogamous, committed relationship. Gabriel told Tony that he loved him and was attracted to him and wanted to continue to share their lives together, but that he did not want to hold him back sexually. His sense of self as a sexual person was a part of him that did not feel authentic. Don gently invited questions into the discussion such as "Could it be that . . .?" and "I am curious about how . . .? These type of questions help examine how the larger societal context influenced Gabriel's thoughts and feelings about his sexuality. Both partners identified and talked about their experiences within multiple societal contexts and grand narratives in ways that helped them navigate and language their evolving relationship; expanding their meaning making and engaging in a generative process that moved them both forward.

Power

Socioculturally attuned collaborative family therapists are aware of the ways power is relational and contextual. Our power within any given context heavily influences the ability to engage in specific discourses or have voice to say what we need and want to say or to make the changes we would like to see.

↞ ↠

A thoughtful consideration of any relationship must include how the greater societal context informs interactions and the power dynamics embedded in those contexts.

↞ ↠

Socioculturally attuned collaborative therapists position themselves in relation to their own knowledge of societally based power processes along with clients' culturally informed perspectives and life experience. They ask questions that elicit cultural values of mutual respect, reciprocity, and shared commitment to relationships (Knudson-Martin, 2013). These therapists recognize that clients enter therapy with perceptions of themselves that reflect their positionality based on systems of oppression and/or privilege.

Let's consider Nasheema, a woman who presented for therapy because her parents were worried about her increasingly alternative lifestyle (i.e., had many tattoos, facial piercings, wore mismatched old clothes, dyed hair) and was not doing well in college. Nasheema admitted that she was frustrated with college and not knowing what she wanted to major in or what she wanted for her future. She enjoyed her job at a coffee bar and worked 20 hours a week. Her parents were both professionals and her siblings were academically and professionally "successful." Nasheema was the youngest of three and had never felt as though she fit into her family. Although she had been afforded many privileges and felt loved, she did not understand why they pressured her so much to do well in college and have a career. She claimed to not feel depressed or concerned about any other area of her life except for school and her parent's troubled and concerned reaction to her current situation. Her therapist, Renee, who was in her fifties, *appeared* to reflect many of the same values and beliefs as

Nasheema's parents. It would have been easy for both of them to maintain positions that held each other in a negative light; ones that confirmed societal notions of power and privilege. However, Renee created the space in which Nasheema could authentically express herself.

Renee: You mentioned that you feel as though you don't measure up to your family's expectations of you. What do you think they are worried about?

Nasheema: They worry that I won't be able to support myself financially. They worked hard to give us a certain lifestyle with lots of opportunities and I think they see me as throwing it all away by not taking advantage of the life I have been given. I feel like they see me as a bum, even though they would never say it. I can feel it. And it makes it worse that my sister and brother are so perfect. They worry about me too. They are total preppies and all they care about is their nice things and expensive vacations. I don't care if I don't become something big.

Renee: I see. So to become something big, you have to make a lot of money and live a certain way? Can you help me understand that better?

Nasheema: That's right. It is like if I don't meet their expectation that I am a failure in their eyes.

As the dialogue unfolded, they began to disentangle how power is embedded in cultural and societal scripts. Renee asked her if she would be interested in learning more about the ways they both embraced, rejected, or reinforced certain culturally supported discourses. They brought up many issues; specifically those related to social status, education, work, success, image, alternative lifestyles, familial expectations, youth, and aging. Nasheema told Renee that it felt reassuring to know where Renee stood on certain issues and that she was frank about her stereotypes about people with tattoos; a bias and prejudice Renee was not proud to admit. They discussed how Nasheema began to feel as though certain possibilities were being blocked due to her appearance and beliefs and that she felt judged for reasons that did not fit her perception of herself. She perceived herself as a kind, caring, thoughtful, creative, and helpful person. She said others saw her as bum, living aimlessly without purpose. Renee stayed "experience near," continued to be transparent about her own thoughts, and asked questions that helped Nasheema make meaning of her experiences within multiple contexts of power and disempowerment.

Socioculturally attuned collaborative family therapists are keenly aware that we are all influenced by social forces that directly affect our sense of, and actual, agency to advocate for ourselves and others, as well as the ability to imagine equitable relationships. Renee had to position herself in her understanding of power dynamics. She had to understand the nuances of complex systems in which many of us, to varying degrees, are blocked from at least some possibilities due to institutional, structural, and systemic oppression, while others benefit from membership in dominant groups, including ties with those who have the greatest sociopolitical and economic power. Nasheema had ties with people with societal power, such as her family and friends growing up, but their disapproval of her "lifestyle" did not enable her to fully benefit from her association with them. Examining these power dynamics helped Nasheema navigate what she wanted for her life while remaining connected to her family.

Another point to consider is the therapist's position of power. Regardless of the therapist's aim to "flatten the hierarchy" or have a collaborative relationship, therapists *do* have power (Larner, 1995). Larner stated that power, knowledge, and influence are intricately intertwined in the very experience of therapy and in the client's expectations of change. He challenged therapists to consider the wider social context in which a 'not-knowing' or 'non-intervening' conversation takes place, pointing to Derrida's philosophy that, while power is socially constructed, it is also real. Many therapists prefer to "flatten the hierarchy," however this remains their decision in a social context in which the professional role of therapist holds power.

‹‹—››

In the end, therapists must hold themselves accountable for their own power and for promoting shared power and equitable relationships among family members.

‹‹—››

Power is part of all social relationships (Guilfoyle, 2003). The idea that participants in a therapeutic dialogue are equal and power-free can obscure our understanding of power dynamics in therapy. Not all perspectives are equally heard or have the same weight in shaping conversations and reality claims. Just because multiple people are in conversation, including in a family therapy session, being in the same space doesn't grant equal voice or satisfaction with the process and outcome. We agree with Guilfoyle (2003) who asserted that mutual construction does not occur in the absence of power. In fact, it is the ethical obligation of socioculturally attuned collaborative family therapists to promote fairness among family members.

‹‹—››

A potential trap of the collaborative approach is the genuine belief that we equally co-construct reality. This stance can be mediated with critical consciousness.

‹‹—››

The ability to manage power varies based on a person's social location and diverse intersections of their identities. For example, it can be especially difficult for women, the very young or the very old, ethnic, racial, or sexual minorities, and others from discriminated or marginalized groups, to experience power in cultures in which they are not part of the dominant group. Specifically referring to ourselves as collaborative therapists, supervisors, and educators requires being in a powerful position and making a choice to embrace a not-knowing, unassuming stance to "flatten the hierarchy," downplay, or share power. As a young Latina professor who was the first in her family to graduate from college, Maria remembers how choosing to take a one-down position when teaching a doctoral level class worked against her. Although it was her preferred stance, she did not have the social, cultural, or material capital to take this stance. Students and other faculty mistook her feminist, collaborative, and collectivistic stance as a stance of really not knowing, instead of one representing a position of power that she chose to share with others.

If persons in positions of power are not members of a dominant group, then they may not have the position of privilege to downplay or share their power with others. This aspect of power and privilege may be overlooked by some collaborative therapists. According to Tatum (1997), there is no equal influence. She asserted,

> Dominant groups, by definition, set the parameters within which the subordinates operate. The dominant group holds the power and authority in society relative to subordinates and determines how that power and authority may be acceptably used . . . the dominant group has the greatest influence in determining the structure of the society.

(p. 23)

Third Order Change

⧉←→⧉

Without a consciousness raising, action-oriented, socioculturally attuned perspective, therapists risk replicating larger sociopolitical systems and beliefs that support social inequity and injustice.

⧉←→⧉

In socioculturally attuned collaborative family therapy, dialogue generates third order transformational change, including being able to recognize and navigate the social forces in one's life in more empowered ways. For example, if we benefit from cumulative advantage, then it is important that we acknowledge our privilege and situate our success and our ability to assert ourselves or take action with confidence. Conversely, it is also important to recognize the material consequences of social inequalities, cumulative disadvantage, and other barriers due to a person's social location, as well as institutional and structural systems of discrimination and oppression. Third order change includes consciousness and action; a form of transformative praxis that increases our ability to challenge systems that impede our ability and the ability of others to overcome adversity.

Practice Guidelines

Next we share guidelines for practicing socioculturally attuned collaborative family therapy. The following five guidelines are partially informed by D'Arrigo-Patrick and colleagues (D'Arrigo-Patrick et al., 2017), who conducted a study to examine how social justice based therapists navigate critical and postmodern theories in their practice.

1. Assume a Critically Informed Stance

A critically informed stance requires therapists to bring critical consciousness to their work. On the one hand, socioculturally attuned collaborative therapists must know about the larger systems and sociopolitical context. On the other, they must remain curious and **attuned** to how these larger systems affect each individual in each family. Perils of not critically examining broader social contexts leave families vulnerable to therapists inadvertently supporting the status quo, including unequal and damaging family power dynamics. The process of developing critical consciousness is ongoing. Cultures and societal systems are always changing. If attunement is a way of being and we never fully arrive at understanding, then we must surrender to the idea that we will never fully arrive at being a socioculturally attuned therapist.

⧉←→⧉

The critical knowing stance is every bit as important as taking a not knowing stance. This allows socioculturally attuned collaborative therapists to engage in liberatory processes while maintaining deep humility.

⧉←→⧉

2. Participate with Transparency

Transparency in clinical work requires that socioculturally attuned collaborative therapists be willing to have an open stance regarding what informs lines of questioning and curiosity, be intentional about situating our interest in social issues based on our own experience, and be forthcoming with clients about the lens that shapes our distinctive approach. Therapists **value** all client voices and experiences. Clients value this open stance in which socioculturally attuned collaborative therapists reveal what informs their questions and curiosities. A therapist might say things like, "I see you as the expert on your own life because you live it. I will often share my thoughts and reactions to what you say, but my hope is that our conversations will help you all decide what is best for you and what you want for your lives." Socioculturally attuned collaborative therapists might also say things like "I will often ask questions and share my thoughts and reactions to what you are saying, but if I notice something that seems unfair or a statement about what you *should* do that may be coming from the outside or bigger society, I will ask you about it."

3. Remain Socioculturally Experience Near

Sociocultural experience near means that therapists understand clients in relation to larger societal contexts. As seen in the earlier examples, therapists are attuned to the way clients describe the impact of social issues. Therapists remain intentional, ensuring that questions attend to social issues as they directly relate to clients' experiences in their daily lives. This practice is instrumental in **naming** what is unjust or has been overlooked and intentionally sharing space and voice as collaborative conversational partners.

←→

The greater our ability to be curious about what happens for each one of us at individual, interpersonal, social, economic, and political levels, the greater our ability will be to walk closely alongside others.

←→

Broadening our lens increases the possibility of sharing connection with others that is simultaneously personal and sociopolitical. A socioculturally attuned collaborative therapist's personal experience is expanded by awareness of the experience of others across diverse social contexts. For example, Don, the therapist who worked with Gabriel and Tony, reflected on his own performance of gender within his cultural framework and became curious about what asexual identity and experience might be like in other cultural and religious contexts and from various economic backgrounds. Don also found himself able to be more flexible in his own sexuality as a white male.

4. Attend to Culture and Power Differences in Dialogical Processes

←→

Socioculturally attuned collaborative therapists are acutely aware of how power shapes dialogical conversations and ensure marginalized and subjugated voices are valued and responded to in ways that support equity.

←→

Attending to the ways in which power and culture intersect in the therapeutic process can lead to **transformational** processes that profoundly affect the ways people engage with each other within their families and the communities in which they live. With this in mind, collaborative therapists must carefully assess how a person's identity and social location affects their ability to be a collaborative partner across multiple contexts, as well as with the therapist in the course of therapy.

For example, it is well known that cultural scripts inform power dynamics. They may seem so natural that they may be taken for granted and invisible to clients and therapists (Knudson-Martin, 2013). Imagine how a younger person, who was taught to respect her elders, not to contradict or challenge what she is hearing, and to let the older person have the last word would engage in the therapeutic process. The therapist might merely think that her client is being shy or respectful and may not be fully aware of the gender, cultural, and social scripts around age, hierarchy, and respect. Socioculturally attuned collaborative therapists will work hard to be attentive to the ways in which speakers are *positioned* in discourse.

The following illustrates how the therapist helps identify how persons are positioned in the clinical context. Her clients were a mother and an adult daughter who sought family therapy because of the mother's concern about her daughter's distance in their relationship.

Therapist: I notice that your mom and I were doing most of the talking, even when we both paused for you to talk. Is this how you are with other people? Is there something that I am doing or saying that is shaping our dynamic?

Daughter: No. I don't know. I think I am just shyer around older people. It's hard for me to open up, I guess. I just want to say the right thing so that it doesn't upset them or make them feel like I am arrogant.

Therapist: Arrogant? That's interesting. I am wondering if this worry about being perceived as arrogant could be influenced by the way you were raised. Sometimes we receive messages about how young people should interact differently with others based on their age. Is this something that is true for you?

Daughter: Yes. I feel like I just need to be quiet and listen when adults are talking. That is what it means to show respect. That is weird for me to say that. I guess I am an adult now too.

Therapist: So, even though you are an adult, for you, being quiet and listening to older adults is a way to show respect. (daughter nods) Thank you for helping me understand that. Although your mom and I are both older, it will be so helpful to us both, I think, if you could say what is on your mind. I'd like to honor your voice in this process as well. (turns toward mom) I am wondering if you would like to hear more from your daughter?

Mom: Yes! I need to know what she is thinking. I know that she is shy, but I feel like as she has gotten older we need to be able to be more like friends. Sometimes I feel like I don't know her at all. I want her to know me better too. She grew up too fast!

The mother and daughter in this example were struggling with messages they were taught about power dynamics due to hierarchies within parent-child relationships. As her daughter got older, the mother wanted her daughter to assume a more adult, peer-like relationship with her. The daughter felt awkward doing so given that she was taught to not participate as an equal partner. The therapist and the mother had more power in the room than the young woman, which also played out in their dynamics. As the therapist positioned herself and helped make the process overt, space was created for the daughter to assume more power so that they could speak more freely and come together as dialogical partners in the process. The therapist was alert and recognized how power and culture intersected to create their dynamic. Power is available to people on the basis of their positions within discourses that are culturally and socially, not individually, constructed. These sociocultural discourses serve as a context for relationships and local practices (Guilfoyle, 2003; Knudson-Martin, 2013).

5. Use Inquiry to Promote Equity

Inquiry as **intervention** involves asking instead of telling clients about the effects of social issues, and allowing oneself to be led more by curiosity than by theory. Socioculturally attuned collaborative therapists bring attention and awareness to larger contextual issues through the questions they ask. For example, rather than telling clients "This is a gender issue" they might ask "How might gender be affecting your experience?" Or they may introduce voices from outside the therapeutic milieu, such as "A lot of women talk about this . . ." or "There is some research on gender and equity you might be interested in. Would you like to hear about it?" Therapists are free to draw on any and all discourses that are relevant and potentially helpful. A collaborative, not-knowing stance means being curious and asking questions and making statements that support relational equity and, by the very nature of asking the questions, disrupts oppressive power dynamics embedded in larger sociocultural systems and social structures. Socioculturally attuned collaborative therapists recognize that questions are never neutral or without purpose. They are intentionally moving us toward equitable practices. Conversations are generative as well as agentive, enhancing the ability to **envision** new realities.

Next, we discuss a case in which the therapist was working from a socioculturally attuned collaborative approach. Within the case illustration we highlight the practice guidelines provided above. As is true throughout this book, the names and other identifying information were changed to protect the participants' anonymity.

Case Illustration

In a small community, less than 10 miles from a large university in a southern U.S. state, families were awakened early on a Sunday morning by law enforcement loudly yelling and banging at their doors. Startled and scared, families opened their doors to armed agents from the Immigration Customs Enforcement (ICE) Enforcement and Removal Operations (ERO) team, many of whom had identified themselves as parole officers or police just minutes before. That morning, 14 men were handcuffed and taken from their homes in front of their terrified children, spouses, other family members, and friends. At least five others were detained locally three days after the raid, as part of ICE's "Cross Check" operation that ultimately picked up 2,059 individuals across the U.S. in five days (Department of Homeland Security, 2015). Most of those detained following the raid opted for "voluntary departure," leaving behind traumatized, disrupted families and communities. In the days that followed, members of the community responded by providing economic, legal, logistical, and emotional support to these already marginalized families. Pamela was one of the local bilingual, licensed family therapists who responded to the community crisis. She was a trusted member of the community, originally from a Latin American country and raised in the U.S.

During the months following the raid, Pamela met with several families, including the Garcia family. Pamela was given their phone number by a community liaison who lived and worked in their community. When Pamela called, Mr. Garcia stated that he was requesting help for his family, especially for his wife who was having an "ataque de nervios" (nervous breakdown). Ms. Garcia was especially in crisis, crying uncontrollably, unable to sleep or eat, and completely at a loss as to how to help her son who had been deported. Her grief was immense and her husband did not know how to help her. She was also the primary provider for their family due to her husband incurring a back injury at work, for which he could not receive medical attention. Their eldest child, who was 20, was taken from their home, held at a detention center for months, and eventually deported back to his country of origin.

Assume a Critically Informed Stance

In a "both/and" manner, Pamela was intentional about maintaining a not-knowing stance while simultaneously maintaining an acute awareness of the larger sociocultural issues affecting this family. First, and rightfully so, there was mistrust of strangers within this community. To be invited into a home was indeed an honor. Pamela was aware that entering the family's home was a stance of embracing uncertainty and humility. This stance would be true for any therapist working in someone's home, but especially in the case in which there was an obvious social class difference; with the family representing an oppressed group and the therapist representing a dominant group. In this case, the home was in a mobile home community of Latinos, mostly with mixed legal status. Although the therapist stated that she grew up in a "humble home," her current social status rendered a visible difference due to her education and assimilation in the U.S. In Spanish, the literal translation of someone who is from a lower socioeconomic status is "*una persona humilde*" (a humble person) and their home is a "*un hogar humilde*" (a humble home). Pamela had the critical consciousness and cultural awareness to sense that she was perceived as someone who represented the dominant group in a society (i.e., light skin, spoke English as her dominant language, was highly educated, and a documented Latina). This self-awareness helped her be mindful of her position of power in relation to theirs.

Her stance of humility helped her acknowledge and honor *their* positions of power. For example, she asked them to address her by her first name, and not doctor, and she was mindful of the ways she could position herself as a collaborative partner. For Latino culture, this stance would represent having an awareness of the values of hierarchy, which are based on social status, age, and gender, among others. It is also based on *respeto*/respect, which is not based on material wealth, but instead, earning respect due to treating others in a personal and respectful manner (Bermudez, Kirkpatrick, Hecker, & Torres-Robles, 2010; Falicov, 1998; Garcia-Preto, 2005). Honoring a family in their home and accepting their hospitality was an important way in which Pamela remained socioculturally attuned to how social class and cultural norms intersect. She was also careful to note how their ways of expressing themselves reflected larger narratives that were stripping them of their power.

As their time together continued, it became apparent to Pamela that Mr. Garcia was blaming himself, instead of larger forces, for what happened to his son. He stated that he had an intense sense of guilt because he opened the door for the ICE agents and he was later told that he did not have to open the door. Because he respects authority, he did not know that he could resist the unlawful entry of the agents if the door was closed. He said, "*fue mi culpa, yo les abrir la puerta.*" (It was my fault, I opened the door.) Pamela asked questions that helped him consider the larger forces that led him to believe that he had to open the door. "Could it be that you did not feel like you had a choice? That you believed you were doing the right thing?" she asked in Spanish. He said he was taught to obey authority and when they said "Open the door!" that is what he did. So in a way yes, maybe he felt like he was doing the right thing. He added, that because he and his son had the same name, he thought they were looking for him. He was confused and then so upset that they took his son instead of himself.

Pamela tried hard to remain experience near, especially as they discussed the larger contextual factors affecting the Garcia family. They lived in a southern state in which there is a history of institutionalized discrimination, racism, and oppression against people of color. Latinos were the latest target, with white supremacy groups gaining momentum using anti-Latino propaganda. The therapist was able to acknowledge their pain and struggle and discuss how larger sociocultural forces influenced their family disruption (e.g., immigration policy in the U.S., anti-immigrant sentiment in the South, hostility and discrimination toward dark skinned, low income, and non-English speaking Latinos). Although they were loving parents and providing a stable home for their children, the effects of poverty, Mr. Garcia's health problems, and gang culture surrounding their home negatively affected and limited their access to alternatives. Mr. Garcia told Pamela, "*Queríamos una mejor vida para nuestros hijos, y siento que si estamos mejor aquí, pero nos duele sentir que en el país que tanto queremos, nos rechazan constantemente. Es difícil vivir así.*" (We wanted a better life for our children, and I feel like we are better here, but it hurts to feel, that in a country that we love so much, that we feel rejected constantly. It is hard to live this way.)

Both parents were also struggling with feelings of regret and doubt. They blamed themselves, but also felt angry at their son because they felt he was actively going against the way in which he was raised, i.e., to be a good person and Christian. They were strong Catholics who had religious shrines and candles lit in their home and prayed for their son's safety. They said he was with his "bad friends who drank too much," which ultimately led him to drive while under the influence of alcohol, get arrested, and get in trouble with the law.

Ms. Garcia: (crying and shaking her head) He knew better than that. We raised him to do the right thing. He knew he couldn't put himself and others at risk, but he felt like he was helping his friends. They drank too much and felt like they couldn't drive. He was the one that drank the least. They are all so young and just weren't thinking! He should have not been with them. We told him to stay away from them. They just cause trouble. Now they are free and my son is gone and we can't help him!

Both of the parents were very upset that he was near the end of his probation when he was detained. His mother was also angry at the authorities and felt as though her son was treated unjustly due to being Latino, undocumented, and from a low socioeconomic status. Her son had no prior record or legal problems. The parents were loving, kind, responsible, and insightful. They were a cohesive family. Their frustration stemmed, not only from their self-blame and doubt, but also from the injustice they experienced due to their marginalized social status.

Their youngest daughter Evelyn was also able to gain a greater consciousness about how her family was affected by her brother's detention and deportation. Evelyn, who was 10 years old, was deeply grieving the separation from her brother and was traumatized by the way he left. Pamela had to carefully measure her words, especially given that Evelyn was present for most of their time together. She wanted to help her contextualize what happened, in a way that she could understand. Pamela told her, while her parents listened,

Pamela: Evelyn, I'm so sorry this happened to your brother and your family. He didn't deserve to be handcuffed and treated like a criminal. He is not a criminal. It wasn't his fault that he didn't have the papers that he needed to be here legally. Does that make sense to you? (Evelyn nodded yes). For those of us who are not born in the U.S., we have to have special papers that say we can be here legally. Not having the legal papers does not make someone a bad person or a criminal.

Pamela then turned to the parents and said,

Pamela: The way I see it is that your son had rights, and like many of us, you didn't know what those rights were—like not opening the door to authorities without a warrant for an arrest. You were not aware of your rights. I can't see how it's your fault.

They were able to have a frank dialogue in which the Garcia family felt heard and validated, while also understanding how their problem was situated within the larger social context. This critical stance would not mean as much without participating in an authentic and transparent manner. For many Latinos, being treated with respect and connecting in an authentic and transparent manner is a core cultural value that transcends social class and other forms of hierarchy.

Participate with Transparency

The therapist maintained a critical perspective of the context that shaped the lived experience of the Garcia family and their community. She listened carefully in an open, affirming, collaborative manner as the Garcias described the impact of larger structural, societal, and institutional realities. Pamela was clearly aware of her power in relation to the Garcias. She was a light skinned, documented Latina, reared in the U.S., who spoke English fluently. She held two advanced degrees and the many privileges associated with her social status and social location. Her stance of humility, self-reflexivity, and transparency was vital to earning respect and being considered an insider/outsider that was well-intentioned and could be trusted to help. She remained transparent and had an open stance in terms of what informed her questions and was intentional about situating her interest in social issues, i.e., her social justice and equity based family therapy approach, especially with Latinos. She also talked about how her work was situated in her own experience of being Latina and having undocumented family members.

Pamela: Like many Latinos in the U.S., I also have family members that are undocumented. I know it's hard for them, but life is good for them too; much better than it was for them back in our home country. They feel so fortunate to be in the U.S. and are doing OK, but it is hard for them sometimes. They have to work so hard physically to make ends meet. I sometimes feel guilty for having privileges that they don't have, especially for my education and the opportunities it has given me.

Pamela was also open about the reason she was there helping them. She was a family therapist who had devoted much of her energy to helping Latino families. This was her way of giving back. It hurt her to see how Latinos were treated for just wanting to have a better life. She was living the "American dream" in ways they couldn't. Pamela worked hard to remain honest and transparent. This leveraged her position to work with them as conversational partners and to share her power. She was intentional about using her position of power and privilege to help them in ways that others could not. She could only do this by fully being present and carefully attending to what was most important to them.

Remain Socioculturally Experience Near

As the therapy progressed, Pamela remained socioculturally experience near by being attuned to each family member's emotions and the ways they were affected by what happened. She attended to the specific ways in which they described and felt the impact of the effects of their son/brother being taken away, held in a detention center for months, and being deported to Mexico, a place where he did not have a strong grasp of the language and felt like an Americanized outsider. Pamela was also mindful of being experience near when attending to the child's (Evelyn's) narrative and her description of what happened. Pamela was careful not to make assumptions about how she was interpreting the events about what happened. She let Evelyn explain things in her own words and asked questions directly related to what she said. She tried to remain near to Evelyn's lived experience, not just her parents' or their experience in general. When asked about what this was like for her, Evelyn responded by saying in English,

Evelyn: I miss my brother. He was so funny and nice.
Pamela: I'm so sorry about what happened to your brother. I can tell that you love him very much. I believe you when you say he is funny and nice. Is there something that you have here at home that can help you feel close to him while he is away—something that can make you smile and remember the things he said and did to make you laugh?

At that point she ran to her room and got a stuffed animal. Pamela asked if she thought it was a good idea to hug her stuffed animal when she wanted to feel him close. She smiled and said yes and hugged it tight with tears in her eyes.

Attend to Culture and Power Differences in Dialogical Processes

Throughout their time together, Pamela remained attentive to how the various intersections of culture and power between them affected their communication as dialogical partners. As with many Latino families, the father held a lot of power, but he seemed somewhat unconventional in that he seemed equally responsible for the emotion work in the home. He initiated the therapy sessions, attended to his wife's needs, and was very active in seeking help and being resourceful for his family. His wife was also very active, but less so, given her greater language barrier and the extent of emotional crisis she was experiencing. The parents spoke very little English and did not have the means to hire a lawyer to help them help their son. Pamela also assessed how their different positions of power affected their sense of agency to mobilize them out of their crisis state. This was especially true when their son was in the detention center and they didn't know how to help him.

Pamela made every effort to not replicate oppressive practices and to treat the family as an equal partner, even though from a societal standpoint, she had more power and voice. Being undocumented immigrants with limited economic resources dictated the course of their son's and family's life. Pamela was mindful that this family felt as though their son had been forced to accept a new life and that their sense of personal agency was taken from them. They felt they had to accept the reality that their son, who had lived in the U.S. since he was 4 years old, did not know another place called home other than the U.S. His use of Spanish was limited and he hardly remembered his life in Mexico prior to immigrating to the U.S. His mother was distraught and did not know how her son could survive living in Mexico, especially going back to the violent, crime-ridden neighborhood where his grandmother lived.

After a few meetings, they felt comfortable enough with Pamela to ask her if she would be willing to talk to their son in Mexico. They were worried about his well-being and wanted Pamela to offer some comforting words of hope. They also wanted her to encourage him to see things in a more positive light. They knew it was hard for him, but he was also living with his grandmother, which had the potential to be positive for them both. He was trying to be a source of support to her in the midst of his own crisis, but Ms. Garcia said that her son seemed too depressed and angry to make it more positive. Although they called him daily, they were very concerned about him. He had been recently assaulted by young men wanting to steal his phone and shoes and to hurt him. He was able to escape, but he was injured and shaken by the experience. He felt as though he had lost all his sense of power. He was having a terrible time adjusting and missed his life with his family. Ms. Garcia handed Pamela the phone and she and their son were able to talk for a while. Pamela explained who she was and why she was there. She tried to be encouraging and asked questions about his well-being, what he wanted to do while he was there, and how he thought his family could help him. His parents were surprised that he talked as much as he did. They said their son was usually closed off emotionally and it was unusual for him to talk to others about himself.

After talking with the son, Pamela encouraged his parents to help him see the unexpected possibilities and to consider his strengths that could help him optimize his experience there—he spoke English well, had a high school education, and a home with his grandmother. He had access to resources that others did not have. These resources gave him power in his new cultural context in ways that he could not fully understand at his young age. By attending to how their experiences seemed to affect their sense of power, Pamela remained aware of how her own power could help them gain access to internal and external resources during this time of crisis.

Conversely, she had to remain vigilant about how her position as a "helper" could potentially replicate exploitative or oppressive practices for the family. When asked what she did specifically to not further oppress this family, she stated that she tried to remain mindful about her position of power, but that it was impossible to completely guard against this potential risk. This was especially important given that she worked with them as a volunteer and they did not have clear goals or parameters set for working together. The Garcias asked Pamela to help them, but given that they were not paying for her services and they were meeting in their home, the potential for boundaries to be crossed and for vulnerable persons to feel exploited remained a potential threat. Pamela said she thought remaining self-aware and setting clear expectations that their work would be short-term until the immediate crisis had subsided, helped protect them from unintended exploitation. Nonetheless, remaining socioculturally attuned to how culture and power intersect within multiple contexts was essential for promoting equity through their dialogic and inquiry processes.

Use Inquiry to Promote Equity

As mentioned previously, inquiry involves asking questions that lead people to examine the effects of social issues, as well as engage in dialogues that promote relational and social equity. Pamela talked with each family member to draw on any and all discourses that were relevant and potentially helpful. She asked questions about their sources of empowerment (e.g., church, family, neighborhood, and friends) and disempowerment, (e.g. the legal system, Mr. Garcia's health, gangs in their neighborhood, and lack of work due to health problems). They were able to name the specific things that were added stressors, as well as the things that gave them peace. They repeatedly mentioned their faith, so Pamela asked them more about it.

She noticed that they had a large image on their wall of *La Virgen de Guadalupe*, the Virgin Mary, the patron saint of Mexico. Along with this large image, they had flowers and a burning prayer candle. They mentioned their church often and Pamela used their faith based language in her inquiry. For example, she asked in Spanish, "*Creen que con el favor de Dios que van a poder reestablecer su equilibrio y sentirse fuerte de nuevo?*" ("Do you think that with the grace of God that you will be able to regain your sense of equilibrium and feel strong again?") *Qué es lo que más urgentemente quieren pedirle a la Virgen para que puedan salir de esta situation y seguir adelante en paz?*"("What is it that you most urgently feel like you need to ask the Virgin [blessed Mother] to help you get out of this situation and to move forward in peace?") Pamela's questions about the Virgin Mary helped the Garcia family rally their faith to disrupt the immense feeling of powerlessness that had overtaken them. The process helped them limit the extent to which the larger system and grand narratives of deportation had power over them individually and as a family. They had resources, especially in each other and their faith.

Pamela met with the Garcia family for six sessions. In the larger culture, the Garcia family had very little power; however, Pamela intentionally engaged with them as equitable collaborative partners. She met them in their home—a place where they were stripped of their power, sense of safety, and belonging. By being a guest in their home, Pamela was able to be in a space with the family in which *they* held the most power. The in-home family therapy was a unique opportunity for the therapist to be there in ways that neither Pamela nor the family could have predicted. The Garcias had never attended therapy and it would not have been accessible to them given their limited resources and the extreme shortage of Spanish speaking therapists in the area. Pamela was able to be *with* them and to be an important resource the family needed to regain their sense of agency in an oppressive system. She continued to volunteer her time, be a source of support and encouragement, and connect them to community resources related to health, finances, and legal aid. With a focus on activism through countering injustice, Pamela was able to help the family disrupt and challenge dominant ideologies and practices that kept them immobilized with fear, grief, and despair and to help them move forward with a greater sense of resilience and hope for change.

Summary: Third Order Change

From a socioculturally attuned collaborative perspective, third order change for the Garcia family meant that they were better able to recognize and navigate the social forces creating crisis in their lives. This necessitated a gentle, consistent, supportive response that enabled the family to increase their consciousness and their ability to restore their sense of well-being. The therapist was able to integrate a critically conscious approach to family therapy with a humble, not-knowing stance, while simultaneously responding to the family's crisis with knowledge and resources. Throughout the course of therapy, the therapist was able to remain *with* the family in a collaborative stance, while being mindfully countering injustice.

Remaining collaborative from a socioculturally attuned lens, the therapist in this case continuously engaged with the Garcia family in critical inquiry. Through this dialogic process, the Garcias felt more empowered to address their unjust situation by acknowledging and challenging racism, discrimination, and vulnerability due to lower socioeconomic and undocumented status. The ability of the therapist to respond during a time of crisis, to be with and genuinely support the family, helped them regain their sense of hope and the courage to imagine possibilities.

References

Anderson, H. (1993). On a roller coaster: A collaborative language systems approach to therapy. In S. Friedman (Ed.), *The new language of change: Constructive collaboration in therapy* (pp. 323–344). New York, NY: Guilford Press.

Anderson, H. (1995). Collaborative language systems: Toward a postmodern therapy. In R. Mikesell, D. O. Lusterman, & S. McDaniel (Eds.), *Integrating family therapy: Family psychology and systems therapy*. Washington, DC: American Psychological Association.

Anderson, H. (1997). *Conversations, language, and possibilities: A postmodern approach to therapy*. New York, NY: Basic Books.

Anderson, H. (1999). Reimagining family therapy: Reflections on Minuchin's invisible family. *Journal of Marital and Family Therapy, 25*(1), 1–8.

Anderson, H. (2007). The heart and spirit of collaborative therapy: The philosophical stance—"a way of being" in relationship and conversation. In H. Anderson & D. Gehart (Eds.), *Collaborative therapy* (pp. 43–52). New York, NY: Routledge.

Anderson, H. (2012a). Collaborative relationships and dialogic conversations: Ideas for relationally responsive practice. *Family Process, 51*(1), 8–24.

Anderson, H. (2012b). Collaborative practice: A way of being "with". *Psychotherapy and Politics International, 10*(2), 130–145.

Anderson, H., & Goolishian, H. A. (1988). Human systems as linguistic systems: Preliminary and evolving ideas about the implications for clinical theory. *Family Process, 27*(4), 371–393.

Ashbourne, L. M., Fife, K., Ridley, M., & Gaylor, E. (2016). Supporting the development of novice therapists. In S. St. George & D. Wulff (Eds.), *Family therapy as socially transformative practice: Practical strategies* (p. 41–55). New York, NY: Springer.

Bermudez, J. M., Kirkpatrick, D., Hecker, L., & Torres-Robles, C. (2010). Describing Latino families and their help-seeking experiences: Challenging the family therapy literature. *Contemporary Family Therapy, 32*(2), 155–172.

Cheon, H. S., & Murphy, M. J. (2007). The self-of-the-therapist awakened. *Journal of Feminist Family Therapy, 19*(1), 1–16.

D'Arrigo-Patrick, J., Hoff, C., Knudson-Martin, C., & Tuttle, A. (2017). Navigating critical theory and postmodernism: Social justice and therapist power in family therapy. *Family Process, 56*, 574–588.

Department of Homeland Security. (2015). *2,059 criminals arrested In ICE nationwide operation* [Press release]. Retrieved from http://www.dhs.gov/news/2015/03/09/2059-criminals-arrested-icenation-wide-operation

Falicov, C. J. (1998). *Latino families in therapy: A guide to multicultural practice.* New York, NY: Guilford Press.

Garcia-Preto, N. (2005). Puerto Rican families. In M. McGoldrick, J. K. Pearce, & J. Giordano (Eds.), *Ethnicity and family therapy* (2nd ed.) (pp. 183–199). New York, NY: Guilford Press.

Goolishian, H. A., & Anderson, H. (1992). Strategy and intervention versus noninterventions: A matter of theory? *Journal of Marital and Family Therapy, 18*(1), 5–15.

Guilfoyle, M. (2003). Dialogue and power: A critical analysis of power in dialogic therapy. *Family Process, 42*(3), 331–343.

Guilfoyle, M. (2006). Using power to question the dialogic self and its therapeutic application. *Counseling Psychology Quarterly, 19*(1), 89–104.

Hare-Mustin, R. (1994). Discourses in the mirrored room: A postmodern analysis of therapy. *Family Process, 33*(1), 19–35.

Knudson-Martin, C. (2013). Why power matters: Creating a foundation of mutual support in couple relationships. *Family Process, 52*(1), 5–18.

Laird, J. (2000). Theorizing culture. *Journal of Feminist Family Therapy, 11*(4), 99–114.

Larner, G. (1995). The real as illusion: Deconstructing power in family therapy. *Journal of Family Therapy, 17*(2), 191–217.

McNamee, S., & Gergen, K. J. (Eds.). (1992). *Therapy as social construction.* Thousand Oaks, CA: SAGE.

Mills, S. D., & Sprenkle, D. H. (1995). Family therapy in the postmodern era. *Family Relations, 44*(4), 368–376.

Monk, G., & Gehart, D. R. (2003). Sociopolitical activist or conversational partner? Distinguishing the position of the therapist in narrative and collaborative therapies. *Family Process, 42*(1), 19–30.

Rosen, H. (1996). Meaning-making narratives: Foundations for constructivist and social constructionist psychotherapies. In H. Rosen & K. T. Kuehlwein (Eds.), *Constructing realities: Meaning-making perspectives for psychotherapists* (pp. 3–51). San Francisco, CA: Jossey-Bass.

Shotter, J. (2005). "Inside the moment of managing": Wittgenstein and the everyday dynamics of our expressive-responsive activities. *Organization Studies, 26*(1), 143–164.

Strong, T. (2002). Collaborative "expertise" after the discursive turn. *Journal of Psychotherapy Integration, 12*(2), 2188–232.

Tatum, B. (1997). *"Why are all the black kids sitting together in the cafeteria?: And other conversations about race.* New York, NY: Basic Books.

13 Socioculturally Attuned Narrative Family Therapy

Narrative family therapy (NFT) is informed by postmodernism. The model employs a social constructionist stance that focuses on strengths and honors clients as experts of their own lives. Therapists take a collaborative, hopeful approach with clients to discover previously unrecognized possibilities. Therapists help clients re-author their lives in ways that allow them to overcome problems. In their groundbreaking book, *Narrative Means to Therapeutic Ends*, Michael White and David Epston (1990) drew on the work of Foucault and Derrida to outline tenets of NFT. They asserted that as human beings, we story our experiences and in doing so ascribe significance to events in our lives as a means of expression. The metaphor of story helps us consider problems as thin descriptions of our lives that have been co-written by social, cultural, and political contexts (Freedman & Combs, 1996). According to White (1995), we live by the stories we tell about ourselves and others tell about us.

In narrative practice, people are separated from, not defined by, problems. Change is not focused on solving the problem, but on creating new variations and thickening stories that no longer support the problem. Therapists assume clients have the abilities, skills, desire, and competence to overcome problems. Preferred narratives highlight these abilities and skills in ways that help clients live out their values. A common narrative process involves deconstructive listening and questioning, externalizing the problem from the person, making oppressive discourses evident, and reconstructing preferred stories that allow for well-being in the present and expanded possibilities in the future (Freedman & Combs, 1996).

⟵⟶

Third order change in socioculturally attuned NFT bridges the gap between critical theories and postmodernism. It involves families understanding how societal forces serve to create and support narratives, impact intimate relationships, and affect material realities.

⟵⟶

This includes exploring the relationship between dominant discourses, marginalization, oppression, and privilege. Socioculturally attuned narrative therapists must recognize, and help family members **attune** to sociocultural dynamics that give rise to the problem. Attuning to ways in which some (family members and/or groups) are supported and draw power from the societal context at the expense of others (family members and/or groups) paves the way to envision and create more equitable relationships.

The therapist encourages just relationships by helping family members **name** problematic and oppressive societal and familial power dynamics. As family members discuss the effects of problematic societal discourses in their lives, the therapist ensures all perspectives, including the most marginalized, are **valued** in therapeutic conversations. Therapists also help clients determine what they value. Therapists structure their inquiry to **intervene** in problematic or inequitable relationships and help families **envision** more just alternatives as preferred narratives. Therapists encourage preferred, alternative stories that center just relationships, helping families take steps toward **transformative** action to free themselves from uninvited or imposed sociorelational contracts (e.g., gender norms, male privilege, patriarchy, colorism, ableism, and heteronormativity).

In this chapter we describe key features of NFT. We illustrate how therapists can integrate principles of sociocultural attunement and offer practice guidelines. We then share a case illustration in which a young woman and her family bravely stood up to resist oppressive forces that fueled feelings of victimization and vulnerability. Our aim is to demonstrate an application of socioculturally attuned NFT that integrates societal systems and attention to power in ways that can enhance possibilities for third order change.

Primary Enduring Narrative Family Therapy Concepts

There are many rich and unique aspects of NFT. We share here what we believe to be primary enduring concepts, including the idea that reality and meaning are socially constructed, therapy is generative and time-oriented, people are not defined by problems, the life of the problem can be deconstructed, and preferred narratives can be co-created that positively affect the future.

Reality and Meaning are Socially Constructed

The foundational principle of NFT is that reality is socially constructed, constituted through language, and organized and maintained through narratives (Combs & Freedman, 2004; Freedman & Combs, 1996; Wheeler, Avis, Miller, & Chaney, 1989). We make meaning based on reflections of our experiences in the contexts of our families, communities, and cultures (Berg, 2009; White, 2002). Although we might individually or collectively believe that our reality (or someone else's) is most true, narrative therapists assert that there are multiple truths and perspectives as well as endless ways of organizing and creating meaning in our lives. Narrative therapists are acutely aware that a person's context serves to create, maintain, and strengthen the life of the problem, as well as provide a source of preferred narratives. Narratives are informed by a plethora of sources, including relational dynamics, culture, contextual influences, interpersonal or internal conflicts, family of origin patterns, gender scripts, and reactivity, to name a few.

Consider Ava (age 24) and Rob (age 23) who entered therapy when Ava began to feel uncertain about their relationship. Ava grew up in a middle-class family with her white mother and stepfather. She was 6 years old when her mother married her stepfather and had two sons. Her Haitian father was unaware of her birth and not part of the family's life. Her extended family never talked about her race, but treated her with less deference than her two brothers. This angered her mother, who would continually tell Ava how beautiful she was and remind her that "we are all the same." Rob grew up in a white middle-class family that had almost no contact with people of color. His parents assumed a "color blind" stance, teaching Rob and his brother to treat everyone with respect. Among many other narratives, the couple shared a white liberal story about race being meaningful (socially constructed as real) yet not consequential (discoursed in a way that obscures white privilege).

According to White (2007),

> many of the people who seek therapy believe that the problems in their lives are a reflection of their own identity or the identity of others . . . a reflection of certain "truths" about their nature and their character or about the nature and character of others.
>
> (pp. 24–25)

Dominant and constraining narratives impact how others see us and become further entrenched when social scripts are internalized, e.g., internalized sexism, racism, classism, ageism, or homophobia. Continuing our example, Ava and Rob's relationship was influenced by narratives of race and gender of which they were largely unaware. Ava described Rob as good-looking, athletic, and smart. Rob stated Ava was the most amazing woman he had ever known. When they shared the story of how they met they beamed with hope and excitement. Rob described Ava as being carefree, kind, and loving. Ava described Rob as being responsible, generous, and protective. Rob's family told their friends they were delighted that he had found such a "lovely girl," and Ava's family jokingly commented that now maybe Ava would "settle down."

Narrative therapists focus on understanding and responding to the lived experience of each family member within all societal contexts. They intentionally attune to clients' words, narratives, stances, and responses to the forces that maintain problematic discourses as well as those that give life to preferred narratives. White (1995) argued the meanings derived through this interpretative process are not neutral. They have real effects and consequences in our lives. One's narrative emerges within sociocultural relational discourse and determines those aspects of our lived experience that get expressed and those that get silenced, which in turn shapes our experiences and interactions. In our example, Ava's racial and gendered experience had been silenced for a lifetime. As a child, she was left trying to make sense on her own to navigate her identity as a biracial female, uncertain and unable to speak about how this social location affected her daily life in school, church, home, and the community. Rob was unaware of his male privilege and how this along with his identity as a "non-racist" white person contributed to silencing Ava as an adult. In effect, problems occurred when narratives too narrowly defined Ava and Rob's identities and dominant societal narratives (e.g., race doesn't matter; nowadays men and women are equal) were at odds with their lived experience.

Narrative family therapists engage clients in the process of re-authoring their stories through deconstructive listening and questioning. They ask questions about multiple viewpoints rather than searching for facts. They open space for considering alternative, subjugated stories and experiences (Carr, 1998). Narrative family therapists don't re-author clients' lives, but they must "be acquainted with many possible stories about life" (White, 2007, p. 82) to help clients re-author their own lives. To do this, Narrative family therapists listen carefully with the understanding that stories have many possible meanings. They are on the watch for gaps in the story; moments, experiences, actions, and explanations that are ambiguous or don't fit into how problems are storied and identity is constructed. They ask clients to fill in details about unique outcomes inviting the construction of alternative stories and/or amplification of subjugated stories. Let's listen in on the conversation between Ava, Rob, and their therapist, Wanda.

Wanda: So Rob, you said your family is very open and accepting of difference. I am curious how you know that.

Rob: Well like my parents never objected to our relationship (glancing at Ava). In fact they love Ava!

Wanda: Ava I am wondering what you think Rob means?

Ava: That I am not white.

Wanda: And your family? What do they think about you being "not white"?

Ava: I think my mom has been through a lot with my grandparents . . . but I know they love me. My mom has been my biggest cheerleader.

The story that was emerging between the lines was one of Ava being "not white" but the extended families "not minding." This is a powerfully dominant racist discourse that shaped their daily lives and relationship. Wanda's tasks as a narrative therapist included helping Ava and Rob unearth, examine, deconstruct, and re-author the meaning of race/racism (as well as gender and other stories) and challenge the effect on their relationship. Wanda recognized Ava and Rob's lives as multi-storied and engaged them in the process of choosing preferred narratives to increase their agency in making meaning, which in turn increased possibilities for the future. It is through more complex and robust stories, in this case including stories about recognizing, navigating, challenging, and overcoming racism and sexism, that we can be our best selves, generate new possibilities for relationships, and realize better futures (Blanton, 2005; Combs & Freedman, 2004).

Therapy is Time-Oriented and Generative

White (2007) used the concept of maps to help clients explore parts of their life stories that have not been previously acknowledged. According to NFT, temporal notions of past, present, and future can be carefully assessed and mapped to understand the terrain of one's life; where we have been and where we are going. Events in our lives are seen as linked across time by themes, creating plots. Events that are included in our life stories tend to fit within plot lines while contradictory events are left out.

Clients tend to enter therapy when stories about themselves and/or others become problem-saturated. Repeated definition of who we are over time can create "I am" discourses, or identity stories, that can be particularly resistant to change. For many of us, narratives about ourselves began before we were born and are shaped by our families and the contexts in which we live. We are expected to live out family legacies, cultural scripts, and social expectations. These narratives and experiences shape our worldviews and dictate what we deem to be normal. They are often internalized and entrenched in such a manner that it is difficult to imagine other possibilities. Going back to our example, Ava and Rob had very different stories about belonging in their families. Ava was constantly aware that her presence in her family of origin was from a chapter that would have otherwise been closed. Ava's mother and birth father had a brief affair that would have become an inconsequential footnote in the plot line of Ava's mother's life-before-marriage if the affair had not produced a child. Rob's nativity story was one of two birth parents waiting anxiously after trying to have a child for several years; his arrival signaling the start of a family.

NFT is considered generative because it encourages clients to construct preferred narratives that eliminate problems and create more positive futures. White (2007) promoted the idea of "experience-near definitions of the problem" (p. 40) which focus on the particulars of each client's experience. This helps the therapist and clients get to know unique and intimate details of problems and their effects. By doing so, therapists are in a better position to point out what is absent but implicit, broadening the story beyond the problem to explore what is important and valuable that is being overlooked in problem-saturated stories. Therapists listen deeply and carefully to narratives to identify words, expressions, and experiences that do not fit with pejorative, harmful, or destructive dominant discourses. Through deconstructive listening and attuning to dominant narratives, therapists notice what gives the problem power and search for unique outcomes that support alternative, preferred narratives. This space allows clients to notice times when the problem is not present and what or who helped them act or respond differently. This distance is important in order to increase one's sense of agency and decrease the effects of the problem. Having an understanding of how to situate one's self within multiple contexts and in a temporal dimension (past, present, future) is essential to moving toward preferred narratives.

People are not Defined by Problems

Unique to NFT is the idea that the problem is the problem. Instead of viewing a person or a relationship as pathological, dysfunctional, or defective, narrative therapists contend that persons are separate from their problems. By seeing the problem as separate, we are better able to understand how the problem affects us and our relationships. Although we may feel like a problem lives inside us, (depression, anxiety, addiction, stress, worry), narrative therapists contend that it is the problem-saturated belief or narrative that has become dominant in our lives. For example, a person may struggle with cancer, diabetes, HIV, bulimia, alcoholism, or schizophrenia, but a person is not those things. The illness, condition, or problem does not and should not define the person or relationship. When clients see themselves as separate, they are able to see the life of the problem and their relationship with it from many angles, perspectives, and contexts. More importantly, this process helps create the space for new and preferred narratives to emerge (Freedman & Combs, 1996; Parry & Doan, 1994; White & Epston, 1990).

Externalizing weakens the problem's power, allowing clients to enact agency by facing and defeating or weakening the effects of the problem. For example, by personifying the problem, clients are able to see how the problem can bully, manipulate, coerce, seduce, trick, punch, or kick us around. These acts of violence, power, and control can be so gripping that they inhibit us from exercising our own power, free will, and agency. Clients claim power for the first time or reclaim power that has either been lost or diminished due to the effects of the problem. This process permeates all aspects of the clinical process, from beginning to end, and is essential to understanding the forces that block preferred narratives or envisioned solutions to come forth and thrive (Bermudez, Keeling, & Carlson, 2009). The process of externalization is nuanced and can happen in many ways. It can involve one person, several people within a family, and/or an entire community (White, 1988–1989; White & Epston, 1990). Most commonly, the process involves naming, objectifying, and personifying a problem through a metaphor.

Beginning clinicians often think of externalization as a technique or an intervention; however, it is more accurately understood as a way of thinking and talking that invites a therapeutic process, generative stance, or philosophy (McGuinty, Armstrong, Nelson, & Sheeler, 2012; Payne, 2006; Roth & Epston, 1996). Furthermore, a novice might be tempted to simply accept and externalize whatever clients identify as the problem when they enter therapy without fully exploring narratives. In our example, Ava's definition of the problem as "uncertainty about the relationship" could be adopted and externalized as the problem without taking time to fully explore the situation. This would have inadvertently contributed to Ava being viewed as the one with the problem. On further inspection, Ava's uncertainty was guiding the way; shedding light on the problems the family was struggling with, including racism and sexism. In fact, Ava's willingness to question was one of her strengths that had been repeatedly overlooked. Questioning and uncertainty would go on to take a central role in the couple's re-authored preferred narrative. Let's listen in again.

Wanda:	I am curious about this uncertainty and questioning . . . did you notice that when you were a kid?
Ava:	Sure. I was always uncertain about whether or not I really belonged in the new family. I kept wondering if it was because I looked different or my step-father wished my mother hadn't been with my birth dad before him, or if it was because I was the only girl . . .
Wanda:	So lots of exploring what might be going on . . . what wasn't being talked about.
Ava:	Yeah. I am good at that right? (glances with a smile at Rob)
Rob:	(chuckles) You are. She questions everything! I guess I just always accept things at face value.
Wanda:	So Ava is the one who takes on the job of figuring things out and, finding ways to talk about them?

Ava:	I guess so.
Wanda:	Makes sense . . . particularly when you are faced with so many unspeakables.
Ava and Rob:	That's a good way to put it!

Wanda now has agreement about how to language the problem and can move on to externalize "unspeakables". Racism, white privilege, gendered power dynamics, and unwanted pregnancies are all among what is unspeakable. Externalizing questions might include things like, "What do these unspeakables look like?" "Where do they mostly live?" "Who else do they affect and who is affected the most?" "How do you know unspeakables are nearby?" "Who else notices them?" and "When did unspeakables begin to interfere with your relationship?"

Deconstruct the Life of the Problem

Another enduring concept in NFT is the notion that problems have power and problem-saturated stories need to be understood well in order to diminish or dismantle a problem's power. Rather than supporting pathologizing, deficit based, internalized descriptions of problems, narrative therapists separate people from problems with the firm belief that problems will be eliminated when stories about our lives and consequent actions no longer support problems. As noted above, White (2007) argued for the importance of paying close attention to the particulars of the problem, engaging in "experience-near" conversations that help clients and therapists get to know the detailed effects of the problem. Therapists assume a role or clinical posture as a witness or audience whose goal is to be drawn into the story in ways that lead to externalizing the problem, uncovering alternative stories, identifying unique outcomes, and re-authoring preferred life stories and/or relationships with the problem. Therapists walk alongside clients noticing the damaging effects of problem stories as well as unique outcomes when clients are able to resist or exist without the problem.

Consider how Wanda might engage with Rob and Ava to map the problem "unspeakables." Wanda might use a whiteboard to draw a diagram of the problem and how it affects individuals and relationships (see Figure 13.1).

Wanda:	How do these unspeakables affect your relationship with your family?
Ava:	It just feels awkward sometimes, like we all know something but just can't talk about it. Makes me feel like there is something to be ashamed of.
Rob:	I guess it is like if we don't talk then it doesn't exist. If we ignore differences or stuff from the past it will just go away.
Wanda:	But it doesn't?
Rob:	No. I think it makes us tense sometimes and worried.
Ava:	Definitely uncertain of our relationship.
Wanda:	Like if we can't even talk about these things they must be big!
Ava:	Yes. I feel silenced a lot . . . maybe even invisible sometimes.

Once the problem is mapped, Wanda can encourage Rob and Ava to fight against its effects, which in turn are keeping it alive. For example what is unspeakable leaves Ava feeling silenced; therefore breaking the silence challenges the problem. Talking about race, gender, white privilege, and other unspeakable dynamics provides avenues for talking about difference, power, and negotiating their relationship within social context. Not talking about these dynamics fuels Ava's uncertainty as she is not able to address "make it or break it" aspects of her relationship with Rob and their families. In turn uncertainty fuels what is unspeakable as it increases anxiety over talking about real issues.

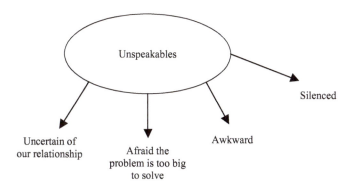

Figure 13.1 Diagram of externalized problem.

Co-Create Preferred Narratives

Key to narrative practice is the idea that dominant stories can restrict our ability to see ourselves from a broader perspective in relation to our problems. A client's problem-saturated story can become so heavy that it makes it hard to see or identify non-problematic aspects of identity and positive outcomes (White & Epston, 1990). In the process of therapy, both clients and therapists attempt to identify events, thoughts, feelings, and actions that counter the dominant story, building alternative stories by repeatedly identifying moments when the problem is not as pervasive and intrusive (Aniciete & Soloski, 2011). These alternative stories serve as gateways for new meanings to emerge that help clients change their relationship with the problem. This process allows therapists to capture thick descriptions of preferred narratives by telling and retelling stories that more richly describe clients' lives (Berg, 2009; Freedman & Combs, 1996; White & Epston, 1990). These new alternative discourses come to life, gaining strength and momentum as clients move toward their goals by taking necessary positive action (Aniciete & Soloski, 2011).

Narrative family therapists listen deeply as they search for experiences, values, and meaning that counter problem-saturated stories and help co-create preferred narratives. These may be mere traces in the form of hopes, dreams, and intentions; moments when values and actions support subordinated stories of strength. Therapists remain committed to being curious, gathering support to thicken and more richly describe new or previously subjugated preferred narratives. This shift from the problematic to the preferred narrative happens by searching for unique outcomes. The concept of unique outcomes is similar to the solution focused idea of exceptions to the problem (de Shazer, 1991). It differs, however, in the emphasis on helping clients see when they are able to resist the negative or problematic influence of the problem (White, 1993; White & Epston, 1990).

In our case example, Wanda talked with Rob and Ava about how as a couple they had already begun to challenge unspeakables of racism that can cause trouble in interracial relationships. The part of their story that was challenging existing social relationships and insisted on being uncertain until these issues could be addressed, needed to be thickened as an alternative plot. They agreed on the ideal of race and gender equality but without being able to really talk about these things, they succumbed to a white male-privileged liberal stance of maintaining inequity by acting as if equality already existed. Furthermore, Rob's acceptance of things at "face value" may have been, at least in part, a function of his unspoken white male privilege.

Understanding the landscape of identity and the landscape of action are important processes that lead clients toward preferred narratives and desired outcomes. The landscape of identity "emphasizes the irreducible fact that any renegotiation of the stories of people's lives is also a renegotiation of identity" (White, 2007, p. 82). For example, contrast the landscape of Ava's identity if she sees herself as a biracial woman from an unwanted relationship vs. a racially aware feminist. The landscape of action refers to concrete steps that must be taken through intentional thoughts, actions, and interactions, to bring preferred narratives to life in strong, tangible, and lasting ways. Following Ava, this might include her openly discussing race and gender equity and talking more openly about her birth father. That said, not all actions are possible in all contexts. People will still respond to her based on the color of her skin. There are societal and structural limits to action that can be taken on preferred narratives.

There are many ways to explore and amplify unique outcomes. For example, "remembering conversations" call on past relational knowings that contradict clients' dominant narratives that help elicit preferred, alternative stories. Those conversations thicken the preferred narrative and give it a stronger life in the future. According to White (2007),

> re-membering conversations provide an opportunity for people to revise the memberships of their association of life: to upgrade some memberships and to downgrade others; to honour some memberships and to revoke others; to grant authority to some voices in regard to matters of one's personal identity and to disqualify other voices.
>
> (p. 129)

A narrative therapist might ask, "Who in your life would not be surprised that you are now graduating from college?" This re-membering brings forth those individuals who team up with the client to thicken the plot of the preferred narrative. Definitional ceremonies (White, 2007), rituals, performances, art, creative expression, dance, letters, ceremonies, certificates, and the telling and retelling of the preferred narrative are also ways in which we can strengthen the life of the narrative that supports preferred ways of living, being, and relating to others. Bruner (as cited in White and Epston, 1990, p. 11), stated that "life experience is richer than discourse. Narrative structures organize and give meaning to experience, but there are always feelings and lived experience not fully encompassed by the dominant story." Any experiential way of performing or telling the new narrative gives it more power.

Integrating Principles of Sociocultural Attunement

The underlying postmodern assumption that reality is socially constructed has been embraced by most narrative therapists, however a number of scholars have noted the dialectic tension and limitations of this framework from a critical lens (Agger, 1991; McDowell, 2015; Miller, 2000; Slott, 2005). Many postmodern, including narrative, therapists question critical social theory as relying on a grand theory or singular truth claim. In turn, many critical social justice-oriented therapists argue postmodernism relies too heavily on relativism. This can obscure injustice as a matter of pluralistic, equally valid perspectives, disregarding the real material consequences of social inequity. Although narrative philosophy and practice are strongly situated in multicultural work (Laird, 1998), narrative therapists who neglect to attend to systems of power, privilege, and oppression, risk maintaining the status quo by failing to address the power these societal structures have over their clients' lives and agency.

In this section we attempt to bridge these competing discourses by exploring the application of critical postmodernism in socioculturally attuned NFT. According to Boje (2001) "critical postmodern is definable as the nexus of critical theory, postcolonialism, critical pedagogy and postmodern theory" (p. 433). Critical postmodernists join social constructionists in acknowledging that language does not reflect an objective reality and is not neutral. Both postmodernists and critical postmodernists agree that the social construction of knowledge (i.e., what we believe to be true) impacts and is impacted by power (Slott, 2005). Family therapists working from postmodern, critical, and critical postmodern perspectives typically share an ethical stance of promoting social justice, even though they may work toward this goal in varying ways (D'Arrigo-Patrick, Hoff, Knudson-Martin, & Tuttle, 2017).

Societal Context and Discourses of Resistance

Socioculturally attuned narrative family therapists are keenly aware of how complex, interconnected social, structural, cultural, political, and economic realities contribute to unequal division of labor and resources, as well as uneven influence in decision-making and agency within and across all societies. These dynamics influence what we deem normative and ideal, how we make sense of thoughts, feelings, and behaviors (Freeman & Lobovits, 1993, Tilsen & Nylund, 2016), the ways we are treated and/or mistreated, and how we idealize or pathologize ourselves and others (Neal, Zimmerman, & Dickerson, 1999). Societal systems may be maintained, justified, challenged, and/or transformed by language systems, which play a significant role in promoting and/or resisting them.

‹‹–›

Socioculturally attuned narrative family therapists assume dominant discourses are among many competing and interrelated discourses for which there is greater or lesser social support.

‹‹–›

Support for discourses is garnered in a number of ways including establishing and protecting truth claims (e.g., this is how it is) and/or appealing to one's interests, beliefs, and/or values (e.g., this is how it should be). When discourses are at odds, hybrids are formed. New stories emerge in the epistemological borderlands within and between global, societal, and familial contexts. For example, in the U.S. dominant discourses of democracy and capitalism are at times congruent and at times conflicting (McLaren & Farahmandpur, 2001). Contested interpretations of these value based ideologies inform the broadest (e.g., Supreme Court decisions about same sex marriage, laws banning hate crimes, banking deregulation) to the most intimate (e.g., our relationships with money, who we listen to) public and personal decisions. Spinoff discourses that have emerged as a result of the inherent incongruence of these and other dominant discourses include the myth of meritocracy, prosperity theology, and colonial narratives of eugenics that associate skin color and phenotype with evolution.

Let's consider more closely the myth of meritocracy. Meritocracy is the belief that success is awarded to those who are most qualified and work hard enough to be successful (McNamee & Miller, 2004). The belief that anyone can "pull themselves up by their own bootstraps" is an attractive story about fairness and equal opportunity in democratic, capitalist societies. This myth is contrary to democratic ideals, however, as it serves those with greater social advantage (e.g., those with white privilege, male privilege, abilities privilege) by obscuring the racism, sexism, ableism, and nationism that maintain their advantage. In the U.S., women, ethnic minorities, and immigrants earn significantly less and are promoted less often and more slowly than those who have white privilege and male privilege (Patten, 2016). The socially constructed discourse of an equal playing field (democratic ideal) in a system that requires some to be at the economic bottom (capitalism) draws attention away from the inherent conflict of these narratives by placing the problem squarely on those who have suffered lifetimes of cumulative disadvantage (Merton, 1988). Unearned advantage and unfair disadvantage are justified as earned and fair.

The aim of socioculturally attuned NFT includes helping clients deconstruct dominant discourses that maintain problems, co-create new narratives, and take action in support of preferred narratives. It also includes exploring with clients collective discourses of resistance to socially unjust dominant discourses.

⊶ ⊷

Just as all discourses are acts of collective meaning-making, dominant discourses and discourses of resistance are shared narratives.

⊶ ⊷

These various discourses are not seen simply as a smorgasbord of personal choices, but as value-driven propositions which we cast our votes for or against. When dominant discourses go unnoticed as natural, inevitable, or assumed right by nature of their widespread support, we at best inadvertently cast a vote in favor or fail to vote against what may not align with our values, best interests, experience, or epistemology. Again, therapists must "be acquainted with many possible stories about life" (White, 2007, p. 82), and we argue this includes discourses of resistance to which clients can be introduced. Consider the impact discourses of resistance might have on our couple, Ava and Rob. Wanda might introduce them to websites for multiracial families (e.g., Project RACE), invite Rob into a men's group that actively challenges male privilege and patriarchy (e.g., National Organization of Men Against Sexism), and/or offer titles of books (e.g., bell hooks readers on race and gender). All of these resources are sites of collective resistance in which meaning that challenges oppressive dominant discourses is socially constructed. They are also sites in which collective action is organized.

Dominant discourses may privilege some members of families over others, contributing to relational inequity. Socioculturally attuned NFT attunes to conflicting narratives within families. This includes exploring who is supporting them and why, as well as how narratives may benefit some over others. Therapists carefully attend to ways in which certain family members are valued by each other, by society, or by other important people and contexts in their lives. Again considering Ava and Rob, the narrative of Rob as being a non-racist white man inadvertently placed the burden of change on Ava by masking Rob's accountability for white male privilege.

Culture and (De)Colonization

Socioculturally attuned NFT aligns with decolonizing frameworks. Colonialism refers to a process in which dominant group cultural practices, ideologies, and beliefs are centered as more right and true. The ideologies, beliefs, and cultural practices of non-dominant groups are subjugated and actively interrupted. This privileges dominant groups by centering their cultural capital (Bourdieu, 1986) to create and maintain colonizers' advantage.

Colonizing forces seek to destroy or trivialize indigenous cultures while those being subjugated resist their lifeways being lost or forgotten. Consider the Indian Schools in the U.S. during the 20th century in which Native American children were removed from their families to attend boarding schools where their native language and cultural practices were banned for the sake of forced assimilation.

⊶ ⊷

Socioculturally attuned NFT adds an emphasis on the concept of space as prominent alongside the concept of time, recognizing the impact of spatial and material realities in relationship to lived experience.

⊶ ⊷

Continuing with the example of Indian Schools, native children were forced into and not allowed to leave dominant cultural spaces in which their cultural practices, food, clothing, hairstyles, language, and worldview were intentionally subjugated. An emphasis on space is in itself a decolonizing act as the temporal epistemology of the West and Global North is privileged in most therapy. For example, therapists typically consider only one dimension of space over a single lifetime. This is in stark contrast to many indigenous concepts of space existing simultaneously across multiple dimensions and time existing in nonlinear fashion. We would add that stories are not always depicted in spoken or written words, as noted in our case illustration at the end of this chapter. Meaning is also co-constructed in ways that are nonverbal, expressive, and performative.

What we commonly think of as culture, i.e., socially constructed shared systems of meaning and agreed-upon knowledge, may be fairly monolithic or highly contested and diverse. Those most culturally centered share the greatest cultural capital and therefore enjoy the greatest social capital or social advantage (Bourdieu, 1986). What is culturally centered is not stagnant, but ever-changing in constant contest. Cultural values and beliefs as well as how we perform culture through everyday actions tend to reflect the dominant group's epistemological framework, often at the expense of those in subordinate or less privileged groups. Earlier in this text, we introduced what Fricker (2007) called *hermeneutical injustice*, referring to inequities in whose experience is understood and given social credibility. This concept refers to more than fitting in culturally and having our thoughts, feelings, and behaviors validated as culturally appropriate.

⤙ ⤚

It is difficult to make sense of one's experience when there is no language; no discourse through which it can be described. Not only are experiences outside of dominant cultural discourses marginalized by others, they are often marginalized within us—kept secret and foreign to who we think we should be.

⤙ ⤚

Power and Subjugation

How we think and talk about power is important. Foucault argued that power produces, through knowledge claims, what we assume to be real or true. This includes what and who we think of as normal or not normal. The concept of power that has been most influential in postmodern family therapy is associated with subjugation via identity and definition. This includes the effects on our lives of how others define us and we define ourselves (particularly in relationship to problems), and the power therapists can impose through their institutionalized role as experts who have the authority to define clients. For example, Schnarch (2009), who emphasized the importance of intimacy during sex, publically encouraged the practice of eyes-open sex. This idea may be helpful for some couples. The problem, however, is that once an expert asserts a truth (e.g., eyes-open sex is healthier, preferred) those for whom this truth does not fit (those who prefer eyes-closed sex) are problematized. A quick look through internet blogs of those now worrying about keeping their eyes open during sex provides evidence of the power experts have in creating realities that may inadvertently support subjugation.

In other words, the power problem most narrative therapists set out to solve is that of being subjects of objective, scientific, or modern knowledge that defines who we are for ourselves and others. This has been revolutionary in the practice of family therapy. At the same time there is a risk of creating another grand narrative or truth claim by too narrowly and certainly defining what power *is* or *is not*. When we make claims such as "power is everywhere," we run the risk of engaging in the very definitional process Foucault resisted. That is not to say that power isn't everywhere, but that we might be better served by saying something like "When we think of power as being everywhere . . ." This type of statement suggests a view from somewhere (we) and that there are other perspectives ("when we think of power as"). This is particularly important in socioculturally attuned NFT as it provides a congruent theoretical perspective by which to acknowledge the lived experience of Foucault's second type of subjugation, i.e., dependence and control.

By expanding the notion of subject beyond the limits of definition and identity, we are better able to acknowledge the material consequences and lived experience of social and relational processes of oppression. Take, for example, a mother who removes herself and her children from a physically abusive male partner. Her social label and identity may be that of a single mother whose children are being raised in a broken home. Family members' identities are then deficit based and determined by divorce. A new narrative might support a family identity as liberated and whose members fought for their freedom. This is a powerful narrative, however there are still real material consequences to raising children with one income (typically 80% lower for females), dealing with restraining orders and custody battles, and getting calls from the school where teachers now frame the children as having problems at home.

Foucault assumed that resistance is present wherever there is power. Deconstructive listening and co-constructing preferred narratives are foundational to resisting the subjugating effects of defining self-as-problem. Socioculturally attuned narrative family therapists pay close attention to the effects of definitional power as well as dynamics of dependence and control. This includes noticing who takes up more space in relational contexts; who gets to talk, who talks most often, whose words have more influence, and whose role in the relationship is most valued. It also includes actively interrupting power-over in support of just and equitable relationships. This extends the therapist's value stance of disrupting subjugating dominant discourses to disrupting local, intimate performances of power that are supported by (but not entirely explained by) and support (but are not entirely responsible for) social and familial discourse.

Let's consider Marvin and Rose who have been married for nearly 50 years. Although they seem to get along well, Marvin frequently teases Rose about what she eats (policing her body and food intake), makes jokes when she gets lost or forgets something (storying her as less competent), and refers to her as his "old girl" (diminishes both her gender and age). Discourses that subjugate women are of course still present and were particularly dominant during this couple's lifetime. These intimate performances of power both reflect and support dominant discourses about gender, yet are performed by specific people within specific relationships and contexts. Their performance of power is shaped not only by social discourse, but by the couple's personalities, family of origin backgrounds, independent financial resources, relationships with children and grandchildren, and so on.

Third Order Change

Within the context of the therapeutic relationship, there are varying levels of transformative change that clients experience. As discussed in Chapter 2, therapists often challenge their clients to create second order change rather than first order change, as second order change focuses on altering systems of interactions. Second order change in narrative therapy occurs when clients reclaim their lives from dominant stories, which in turn transforms their narratives and their relationships.

⤛—⤜

Third order change raises social awareness, helping clients view dominant narratives with a sociopolitical lens. Once clients are able to notice how societal forces are perpetuating dominant discourses and contributing to problems, they are better prepared to navigate and resist their effects.

⤛—⤜

Through a socioculturally attuned framework, narrative therapists are able to name, explore, and deconstruct the influence of societal structures of oppression, such as racism, heterosexism, sexism, ableism, etc., with their clients. Questions that aim to deconstruct oppressive societal discourse might include: "How do you think homophobia is influencing the dominant view you have of yourself?" "In what ways has racism played a role in what is bringing you to therapy?" "How does sexism operate in your life?" "If ableism could speak to you, what kind of messages do you think it would be saying about your worth as a person? A partner? A friend?" "If your most empowered, best self were able to stand up to classism, what would you want it to understand about you?"

Practice Guidelines

The following five practice guidelines help family members recognize the impact of societal systems of power and oppression on not only how they story their lives, problems, and preferred narratives, but also on the material realities of their lives. It is helpful to note that they are not always implemented sequentially and may move fluidly back and forth over the course of the therapy.

1. Expand the Map to Include Sociopolitical Structures

Socioculturally attuned narrative family therapists **attune** to not only the influence of social discourse, but to the impact of societal structures in their clients' lives. They expand the map of the problem to **name** complex, interconnected social, structural, cultural, political, and economic realities that contribute to unequal division of labor, resources, influence, and agency within families and communities. Dominant discourses remain central in the work of deconstructing problem narratives and reconstructing preferred narratives. What is often less clear is the understanding of problems and possibilities within societal contexts and social structures that constrain agency and afford access to opportunities based on the many intersections of social location/group membership (e.g., race, class, gender, sexual orientation, nation of origin, abilities, religion, etc.). Expanding the map to examine larger social structures such as patriarchy, white privilege, and structures that control and maintain wealth and power helps therapists understand a person's or family's sense of agency and mobility within the larger sociopolitical terrain.

2. Deconstruct Power-Embedded Relational Inequity and Name Injustices

Socioculturally attuned narrative family therapists collaborate with clients to deconstruct dominant discourses that are at odds with their lived experience. Therapists loosen the grip of problematic narratives and help open space to link discourses to relational dynamics that may give or take away power. This includes identifying how shared narratives support unjust intimate relationships as well as how divergent narratives within families serve to create and maintain problematic power dynamics. There is a recognition that what is "preferred" may be contested across individual, family, and cultural narratives. For example, a narrative supporting male privilege may be preferred by some members of the family, while a narrative supporting gender equity may be preferred by other members of the family or all members some of the time. In other words, narratives, including preferred narratives, serve a role and must be considered relative to negotiating power in intimate relationships.

Additionally, the therapist is cognizant of the notion that having a preference is a privilege. For many, having a preferred narrative is constrained by the effects of limited financial means and restrictive social location due to specific intersections of race, gender, age, sexual orientation, nationality, religion, etc. A socioculturally attuned narrative family therapist is mindful of bias embedded in the notion of a "preferred narrative," carefully assessing for conflicts and compatibility within and across multiple narratives. These narratives, preferred or otherwise, may reflect contesting societal discourses and/or be sources of individual struggle and family conflict.

3. Explore Values Embedded in Narratives

As problem-supporting discourses are challenged, new narratives emerge that are in many ways value-driven propositions. Helping individuals and families identify, clarify, and negotiate **values** is critical to developing preferred narratives that support the well-being of all involved. For example, one parent may value autonomy and independence more highly than collective care. How they narrate their child's journey through life and problems will be impacted by these values. A father may complain that his son should have launched and been on his own by his early twenties while a mother appreciates his ongoing concern and care for the family. These are potentially very different storylines to which therapists may add their own valued position (e.g., launching in early adulthood is healthy, the mother is holding the son back to meet her own needs, the couple can't stand alone and are triangulating the son). Additionally, not all values have the same weight and power in society. It may be less apparent for a narrative therapist to determine which narratives reflect values that are supported or not supported by the dominant group in a society. These factors can remain unexamined unless the therapist is carefully attending to the implicit values embedded in the client's and their own narratives.

4. Support Relational Equity and Disrupt Oppressive Power Dynamics

Socioculturally attuned narrative family therapists pay close attention to how power is performed; what people do in relation to others, the types of influence they exert, and the consequences of relational inequity. They would be curious about how the performance of power is permitted, accepted, followed, or applauded based on a person's social location. The therapist would encourage transparency about these dynamics by asking deconstructive questions, **value** each person's voice, and help clients understand the effects of how power is enacted on each individual and the family. For example, questions that disrupt patriarchy, colorism, or sexism would focus on how inequity influences and supports the life of the problem. Clients are invited to deconstruct social and familial narratives that privilege and story unequal adult relationships as being natural, inevitable, or preferred. The therapist intentionally introduces possibilities for co-constructing new narratives that support relational equity, irrespective of culture. In every society in which systemic and culturally sanctioned injustice toward a particular group or person is enacted, there is active resistance. Socioculturally attuned therapists **intervene** by disrupting narratives that fuel oppression, inequity, and relational injustice. We are able to help clients strengthen **transformative** narratives that amplify voice and resistance.

5. Thicken Stories of Resistance and Resilience

A mistake many therapists make is taking a generalized view of culture, believing that gender or race should not be challenged because they are culturally prevalent. Therapists who fail to challenge injustice in any cultural or societal context inadvertently support those in dominant positions at the expense of those being oppressed. For example, although patriarchy is enacted in most societies, most would agree that the abuses enacted due to patriarchy, such as violence, femicide, torture, bullying, rape, and victimization should not be supported. It is important to create the space for subjugated narratives of resistance so clients can **envision** preferred liberation based narratives.

Sites of power and oppression are also sites of resistance. Where oppression occurs so do forms of resistance, small and large, internalized and externalized, overt and covert. When resistance is understood by a therapist, couple, family, or society as problematic, injustice is likely to be reified. For example, if someone resists oppression by becoming withdrawn or depressed, therapists must recognize that the problem is the oppression, which in turn feeds the life of the depression. If a therapist views depression as the problem in and of itself, there is a risk that the oppression may be inadvertently supported. New narratives must align with the lived experience of the person enacting resistance. **Naming** what is unjust and identifying resistance to oppression can be liberating, opening possibilities to begin more strategically addressing power dynamics.

Socioculturally attuned narrative family therapists excavate sites of resistance to uncover and amplify resilience. Narratives of resistance include moments when clients find ways to hold on to their values, strengthen their resolve, endure in spite of oppression, and so on. What is often explored on this personal level is tied to collective resistance and resilience. Discourses of resistance (e.g., women's movement, queer rights and discourses, fatosphere, i.e., online community for fat acceptance) are introduced as shared narratives that challenge and **transform** dominant oppressive discourses and social practices. Likewise, collective resilience among those with whom we identify over time (e.g., black ancestors, Native communities) thickens individual and family stories of resilience and resistance.

Case Illustration

This case involved family therapy with mother (Raquel) and father (Aldo), adult daughter (Ana), and their advocate (Carla). Ana was referred from a center for survivors of sexual abuse to Gabriela at Latino Family Services. Gabriela was a third generation bilingual U.S. citizen of Mexican descent. The family did not speak English, did not read or write in Spanish, were undocumented immigrants from Peru, and Ana was deaf and mute. Ana had the support of a close and loving family. She was the oldest of four siblings. Her family cared for her, but she was also responsible for caring for her family by cooking, cleaning, taking care of her siblings, and being a good companion to her mother. She had a very close relationship with her mother, who was her translator and voice. Ana had never been in a romantic relationship, had outside friends, or gone anywhere without her family. Her inability to hear kept her homebound and completely dependent on her parents. Carla was a social worker and advocate who was a kind and committed member of the therapeutic team. She was an important resource for the family, as she would often drive them to sessions, the women's shelter, the police station, and court. Carla was in a more powerful social position and the ideal advocate for the family. Although Ana was facing many challenges, she seemed eager to be in therapy and was engaged in the clinical process from the start.

Expand the Map to Include Sociopolitical Structures

Gabriela worked hard to join with Ana and help her feel comfortable. During the first session much of the time was spent talking to her mother to gather information and find ways to non-verbally connect with Ana, e.g., as much eye contact and signs of empathy as possible. What became apparent is that Ana and Raquel (Anna's mother) had their own sign language. Raquel was Ana's primary support person and translator who effectively relayed the therapist's messages. Gabriela would say things like, "Please tell her that I am so glad she is here and that she is so brave for wanting to tell her story and wanting to move forward in her life in a positive way." Then Raquel would tell Ana with a series of signs that were unique to them.

Ana was sexually assaulted multiple times by a family member who lived near them. Raquel was experiencing secondary trauma. She would uncontrollably cry when she felt

Ana's pain and the rage she felt toward her abuser. Given that Ana could not verbalize or write her story, Gabriela asked her to draw a picture of anything Ana wanted her to see. Gabriela looked at Ana to show empathy in response to everything Raquel disclosed about what happened and why they were there. By the end of the first session, it became apparent that Ana could express herself through images, which became the means of conducting socioculturally attuned NFT.

Deconstruct Power-Embedded Relational Inequity and Name Injustices

Art can be used as an experiential means to deconstruct problematic narratives, increase a client's sense of agency, and re-author preferred narratives (Bermudez et al., 2009; Carlson, 1997; Keeling & Bermudez, 2006). In this case, Gabriela used a storyboard technique to help Ana tell her story for herself. Before beginning, Gabriela met with Raquel and Aldo as Ana's parents to ask if it was acceptable to proceed with this way of working. Gabriela told them that she would stop at any point if she assessed that the process was not helpful or was harmful for Ana. They both agreed that it would be a good process and gave consent for Gabriela to meet with Ana alone to offer privacy and encourage empowerment relative to her experience of abuse. Raquel checked in at the beginning and end of each session. Raquel's presence was important, although Ana did not show any signs of distress when her mother was not in the room.

The first goal was to join with Ana and attune to her and her world by demonstrating an attempt to understand and respond to her experience. This was done by learning Ana's signs for emotions. For example, Ana and her mother explained the sign for sadness; which was a sign of a broken heart with her hands; fear, which was her acting as if she were shivering; joy, smiling with her hands on her chest and a thumbs up; peace, which was her pointing to God with prayerful hands or hands on heart; and frustration, feeling overwhelmed and anxious, which was her pointing to her head, shaking it with a sad face.

This process of attunement led to Ana naming the injustice that had occurred in her life. Her voice would have been easy to silence, but her will to be heard was more powerful than her inability to hear, speak, or write. Through the course of therapy Ana told Gabriela what happened through a total of 18 drawings, each one representing the sequence of events. The therapist would motion with her finger in a forward circle as if saying, "and then what happened?" and Ana would draw what happened on a new sheet of paper, which Gabriela numbered and kept in order. Gabriela honored Ana's language, way of knowing, and telling of her own story. Although Ana did not know the name for rape, sexual assault, or abuse, with the help of Gabriela, she was able to name the abuse through her images, her expression of emotion, and the participation of her mother and advocate.

Explore Values Embedded in Narratives

Through the process, Gabriela and Ana's parents demonstrated that they valued Ana and were able to acknowledge her worth. This was paramount in the midst of larger familial, societal, and cultural systems that tended to minimize or discount Ana altogether. Carla (the advocate) also valued Ana and served as a witness to her pain and survival, as well as to her telling and retelling the preferred narrative of strength and courage. The concern and respect demonstrated by the therapist, advocate, and her family communicated to Ana that she was loved and that her family was doing all that they could to keep her safe. Their values of family connection, respect, and resilience gave them strength and fueled their bravery to both seek resources for Ana and take legal action to keep the perpetrator and his wife away from her. Through the course of therapy, Gabriela supported the family's values of love and cohesion, as well as the emerging narrative of Ana as a survivor rather than a victim.

Support Relational Equity and Disrupt Oppressive Power Dynamics

Gabriela actively intervened to disrupt oppressive power dynamics and support relational equity throughout the therapeutic process. As noted elsewhere, it is common not only for the testimony of those in less powerful social positions to be dismissed (Tatum, 1997), but for their experience itself to be subjugated (Fricker, 2007). By walking alongside Ana as she told and re-told her story through images and helping Ana share her story with her family and advocate, Gabriela helped Ana give voice and credibility to her experience and be heard. Together, Ana, Raquel, Aldo, Carla, and Gabriela were able to disrupt the power dynamics that privileged Ana's perpetrator, a documented, middle-aged man, with a good job and financial stability. He and his wife had threatened to have the family deported if they told the authorities about the rapes. Ana and her family did not shrink in the face of these threats and were able to seek the support of the advocate and the sexual assault center. The disruption of power dynamics was also reflected in a picture Ana drew of herself destroying plants and flower bushes her perpetrator and his wife had given her as gifts by throwing them on their front door. This act of resistance, which she initiated on her own, demonstrated her strength and ability to stand up to her oppressor.

Halfway through the storyboarding Ana, Raquel, and Gabriela were able to co-create a space to imagine and envision a better way of life for Ana. Her preferred narrative depicted images of her standing next to her mother with both of them holding hands with arms in the air, as if triumphant. As White and Epston asserted (1990), with every performance of a new narrative, we gain valuable experience at re-authoring our lives. By paying close attention to the aspects of lived experience that fell outside of the dominant story, Ana and her family were able to discover important resources for generating and regenerating her preferred narrative as it emerged with ever greater strength and life.

Thicken Stories of Resistance and Resilience

It was moving for Gabriela, as well as the family, to witness the transformation that took place. They collaborated to make what was imagined real. Gabriela asked them to do a family sculpture showing how they were when they were in the grips of the fear, grief, and despair, followed by one depicting how they felt now in light of their courage and strength as a non-verbal way to thicken the new narrative. On the day of the last session, Raquel committed to helping Ana learn American Sign Language which would help her connect with others, make friends, and open herself to an adult world. Raquel and Aldo also created an art space for Ana at home so that she could create artwork to give as gifts or sell to earn her own money.

Lastly, Aldo, Raquel, and Carla committed to renewing the restraining order to help Ana continue to feel more protected. Ana and her family united to stand up to the effects of Ana's abuse by also standing up to the marginalization and oppression they experienced at a societal level. The process was empowering for everyone involved, even her younger siblings. As a final ritual, Gabriela asked Anna what she wanted to do with the drawings and she motioned with a big smile on her face that she was going to bury them in her backyard. She decided to keep the last image of her and her mother feeling triumphant.

Summary: Third Order Change

In this case, first order change occurred when the therapist found ways for Ana to communicate through drawings. This made second and third order change possible. At a second order change level, Ana moved from an unwanted, disempowering narrative of being a victim to that of a survivor. Her decision to learn sign language would provide ongoing second order change as she was learning to connect with others outside the family for the first time. Third order change occurred in several ways. Ana had never felt understood by anyone but her mother. The veil of silence that surrounded her left her particularly vulnerable to *hermeneutic injustice* (see Chapter 7). In other words, it is likely Ana felt accepted by her family, but not really known until she had an avenue through which to tell her story. Telling her story also offered her a way to know herself better, as she, for the first time, put into pictures what she experienced, thought, and felt. Ana and her family were well-versed in the narrative of deportation and anti-immigration in the U.S. When the therapist and advocate offered discourses and sites of resistance, e.g., sex abuse shelter, police station, court, Ana and her family were able to re-narrate their social experience to one in which allies and rights as a victim of crime were acknowledged and action was taken.

References

Agger, B. (1991). Critical theory, poststructuralism, postmodernism: Their sociological relevance. *Annual Review of Sociology, 17*, 105–131.

Aniciete, D., & Soloski, K. L. (2011). The social construction of marriage and a narrative approach to treatment of intra-relationship diversity. *Journal of Feminist Family Therapy, 23*(2), 103–126.

Berg, S. (2009). The use of narrative practices and emotionally focused couple therapy with first nations couples. In M. Rastogi & V. Thomas (Eds.), *Multicultural family therapy* (pp. 371–388). Thousand Oaks, CA: SAGE.

Bermudez, J. M., Keeling, M., & Carlson, T. S. (2009). Using art to co-create preferred problem-solving narratives with Latino couples. In M. Rastogi & V. Thomas (Eds.), *Multicultural couple therapy* (pp. 319–343). Thousand Oaks, CA: SAGE.

Blanton, P. G. (2005). Narrative family therapy and spiritual direction: Do they fit? *Journal of Psychology and Christianity, 24*(1), 68–79.

Boje, D. (2001). Carnivalesque resistance to global spectacle: A critical postmodern theory of public administration. *Administrative Theory & Praxis, 23*(3), 431–458.

Bourdieu, P. (1986). The forms of capital. In J. G. Richardson (Ed.), *Handbook of theory and research for the sociology of education* (pp. 241–258). New York, NY: Greenwood Press.

Carlson, T. D. (1997). Using art in narrative therapy: Enhancing therapeutic possibilities. *The American Journal of Family Therapy, 25*(3), 271–283.

Carr, A. (1998). Michael White's narrative therapy. *Contemporary Family Therapy, 20*(4), 485–503.

Combs, G., & Freedman, J. (2004). A poststructuralist approach to narrative work. In L. Angus & J. McLeod (Eds.), *The handbook of narrative and psychotherapy: Practices, theory, and research* (pp. 137–155). Thousand Oaks, CA: SAGE.

D'Arrigo-Patrick, J., Hoff, C., Knudson-Martin, C., & Tuttle, A. (2017). Navigating critical theory and postmodernism: Social justice and therapist power in family therapy. *Family Process, 56*, 574–588.

de Shazer, S. (1991). Putting difference to work. New York, NY: W. W. Norton.

Freedman, J., & Combs, G. (1996). *Narrative therapy: The social construction of preferred realities.* New York, NY: W. W. Norton.

Freeman, J. C., & Lobovits, D. (1993). The turtle with wings. In S. Friedman (Ed.), *The new language of change* (pp. 188–225). New York, NY: Guilford Press.

Fricker, M. (2007). *Epistemic injustice: Power and the ethics of knowing.* New York, NY: Oxford University Press.

Keeling, M. L., & Bermudez, M. (2006). Externalizing problems through art and writing: Experience of process and helpfulness. *Journal of Marital and Family Therapy, 32*(4), 405–419.

Laird, J. (1998). Theorizing culture: Narrative ideas and practice principles. In M. McGoldrick (Ed.), *Re-visioning family therapy* (pp. 20–36). New York, NY: Guilford Press.

McDowell, T. (2015). *Applying critical social theories to family therapy practice.* New York, NY: Springer.

McGuinty, E., Armstrong, D., Nelson, J., & Sheeler, S. (2012). Externalizing metaphors: Anxiety and high-functioning autism. *Journal of Child and Adolescent Psychiatric Nursing, 25*(1), 9–16.

McLaren, P., & Farahmandpur, R. (2001). Class, cultism and multiculturalism: A notebook on forging a revolutionary politics. *Multicultural Education, 8*(3), 2–14.

McNamee, S. J., & Miller, R. K. (2004). *The meritocracy myth*. Oxford, UK: Rowman & Littlefield.

Merton, R. K. (1988). The Mathew effect in science, II: Cumulative advantage and the symbolism of intellectual property. *Isis, 79*, 606–623.

Miller, L. J. (2000). The poverty of truth-seeking: Postmodernism, discourse analysis and critical feminism. *Theory & Psychology, 10*(3), 313–352.

Neal, J. H., Zimmerman, J. L., & Dickerson, V. C. (1999). Couples, culture, and discourse: A narrative approach. In J. M. Donovan (Ed.), *Short-term couple therapy* (pp. 360–401). New York, NY: Guilford Press.

Parry, A., & Doan, R. E. (1994). *Story re-visions: Narrative therapy in the postmodern world*. New York, NY: Guilford Press.

Patten, E. (2016). *Racial, gender wage gaps persist in U.S. despite some progress*. Retrieved from http://www.pewresearch.org/fact-tank/2016/07/01/racial-gender-wage-gaps-persist-in-u-s-despite-some-progress/

Payne, M. (2006). *Narrative therapy* (2nd ed.). Thousand Oaks, CA: SAGE.

Roth, S., & Epston, D. (1996). Consulting the problem about the problematic relationship: An exercise for experiencing a relationship with an externalized problem. In M. F. Hoyt (Ed.), *Constructive therapies 2* (pp. 148–162). New York, NY: Guilford Press.

Schnarch, D. (2009). *Passionate marriage: Keeping love and intimacy alive in committed relationships*. New York, NY: W. W. Norton.

Slott, M. (2005). An alternative to critical postmodernist antifoundationalism. *Rethinking Marxism, 17*(2), 301–318.

Tatum, B. D. (1997). *"Why are all the black kids sitting together in the high school cafeteria?": And other conversations about race*. New York, NY: Basic Books.

Tilsen, J., & Nylund, D. (2016). Cultural studies methodologies and narrative family therapy: Therapeutic conversations about pop culture. *Family Process, 55*(2), 225–237.

Wheeler, D., Avis, J., Miller, L. A., & Chaney, S. (1989). Rethinking family therapy training and supervision: A feminist model. In M. McGoldrick, C. Anderson, & F. Walsh (Eds.), *Women in families* (pp. 135–151). New York, NY: W. W. Norton.

White, M. (1988–1989, Summer). The externalizing of the problem and the re-authoring of lives and relationships. *Dulwich Centre Newsletter*, 3–20.

White, M. (1993). Deconstruction and therapy. In S. Giligan & R. Price (Eds.), *Therapeutic conversations* (pp. 22–61). New York, NY: Norton.

White, M. (1995). *Re-Authoring Lives: Interviews & Essays*. Richmond, South Australia: Graphic Print Group.

White, M. (2002). Addressing personal failure. *International Journal of Narrative Therapy and Community Work, 2*, 17–55.

White, M. (2007). *Maps of narrative practice*. New York, NY: Norton.

White, M., & Epston, D. (1990). *Narrative means to therapeutic ends*. New York, NY: W. W. Norton.

14 Integrated Equity Based Approaches to Family Therapy

As we approach this final chapter, we ask what it means to be a socioculturally attuned family therapist. What overarching mindsets, skills, or competencies are needed? Previous chapters illustrated how attention to the larger societal context and a power analysis may be applied to facilitate third order change that promotes equity; a paradigm shift in relationship to sociocultural systems that expands possibilities and enables transformation. *Any* model or approach can be practiced through this socioculturally attuned lens (Figure 14.1). It requires therapists to be aware of the influence of sociocontextual forces, intentional regarding clinical choices, and accountable for how what we do reproduces or transforms harmful inequities.

We are inspired by Salvador Minuchin (2017), legendary family therapist, teacher, and social justice advocate, who argued that the person of the therapist is an instrument of change:

> as I got more experience it became clear that the techniques by themselves weren't all that useful. It was therapists themselves who were the instruments of change, and to be effective, they had to recognize the way they were part of the system and the process in the therapy room, not just a neutral observer.
>
> (p. 37)

Many therapists today draw on multiple family therapy models and/or practice evidence based approaches. Minuchin's words do not negate the value of these models; they remind us that any clinical encounter is more than a set of skills and what we do is never neutral.

In this chapter we review guidelines that socioculturally attuned therapists apply regardless of the model they use and then look at three integrative approaches that center social equity as essential to change: SERT, the CCM, and just therapy. We offer these with an eye toward the future, encouraging clinicians to move forward in creatively developing equity based practice, not *instead* of other models but *with* them.

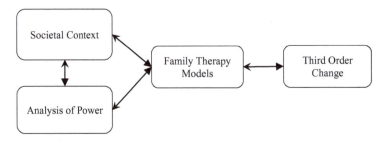

Figure 14.1 Socioculturally attuned family therapy framework.

ANVIET: Transtheoretical Guidelines for Equitable Practice

The six transtheoretical guidelines first described in Chapter 2 and listed in Figure 14.2 accomplish a central mission—to disrupt inequalities in social relationships that are largely invisible, taken for granted, or assumed natural, and to open options for relational systems that equitably support the health and well-being of all. Because awareness typically precedes action and transformation (Freire, 1971/2000), we present the six guidelines in the order most likely to be effective: attune, name, value, intervene, envision, and transform. In practice, they are interconnected and used in varying ways across each phase of therapy.

Attune to Context and Power

Therapists using each of the models described in this book intentionally attune to the connections between the larger social context and clinical issues from the very beginning of therapy. This is critical. A study of how therapists practice sociocultural attunement (Pandit, Kang, ChenFeng, Knudson-Martin, & Huenergardt, 2014) found therapists internalized a guiding lens that led them to explore the connections between the emotions, behaviors, patterns, and ideas expressed in session and sociocultural processes. This lens prompted an internal dialogue regarding how societal discourses and power structures might underlie client behavior and expressions. The lens also guided what therapists reflected back to clients and the questions they asked in order to help create a sociocultural interpretation that resonated with client experience.

Client resonance was key. Sociocultural attunement occurred when clients appeared to feel understood; therapists "got" their sociocultural experience. When this happened "clients expanded their level of disclosure, showed more emotion, became more relational in conversation, and physically connected with therapists; i.e., nodding, maintaining eye contact" (Pandit et al., 2014, p. 524). For example, when a therapist recognized and reflected a disabled woman's guilt because she could not care for her children "the way a mother should" as sociocultural, the woman "began to tear up, nod, and share her struggles and fears about not being a 'good mother'" (Pandit et al., 2014, p. 524). If clients did not resonate and instead avoided eye contact, disagreed, looked confused, changed direction of the conversation, or told the same story again, therapists did not abandon their sociocultural lens. They modified their questioning/reflecting until client resonance was achieved.

The goal of attunement is to not only understand the sociocontextual factors involved in a particular case, but to *apprehend* and emotionally resonate with how they connect to clients' experience (D'Aniello, Nguyen, & Piercy, 2016). A study of senior family therapists known

---

□ **Attune**: Understand, resonate with, and respond to experience within societal contexts.

□ **Name**: Identify what is unjust or has been overlooked—amplify silenced voices.

□ **Value**: Acknowledge the worth of that which has been minimized or devalued.

□ **Intervene**: Support relational equity—disrupt oppressive power dynamics.

□ **Envision**: Provide space to imagine just relational alternatives.

□ **Transform**: Collaborate to make what is imagined real—third order change.

Figure 14.2 Transtheoretical guidelines that create third order change.

for addressing social justice issues found that they tend to be transparent with clients about what they see through their sociocultural lens, use inquiry rather than telling to bring these concerns to the foreground, and stay close to client experience when exploring sociocultural issues rather than using abstract concepts (D'Arrigo-Patrick, Hoff, Knudson-Martin, & Tuttle, 2017). Another study found that novice therapists often felt compelled to address "the presenting issues" before applying a sociocultural lens (O'Halloran, Dunford, Kim, & Knudson-Martin, 2017). If this happens, underlying inequities persist as therapy unfolds. Socioculturally attuned therapists *begin* by expanding the lens.

⤝⤞

Attending to all perspectives may seem like simply good therapy, but beneath-the-surface sociocultural power dynamics easily shape what gets identified as the clinical focus.

⤝⤞

For structural therapists, attuning to sociocultural context means joining the family system through a deep understanding of their sociocultural world, including economic, social, symbolic, and cultural capital in the family map. Attachment based therapists seek to attune to the effects of sociocontextual power processes on the ability of family members to experience relational safety. They want to know how social power is reflected in the ways family members orient to each other, in how likely each is to *feel felt*, and in how they respond to vulnerability.

Socioculturally attuned therapists recognize and attend to how power dynamics are part of clients' experiences and are reflected in session. They do not allow more powerfully situated members to define the direction of therapy. As they help families track problematic sequences, cognitive behavioral therapists are aware that not all voices in a relationship come from equal positions. For example, when a father says that the problem is that the mother and the boys fight, and the family seems ready to agree to this problem, socioculturally attuned therapists invite other perspectives before determining the problematic sequence.

Name Injustice

⤝⤞

How we talk about clinical concerns matters.

⤝⤞

In the process of "naming" we select some experiences or ways of knowing and directly or implicitly link them to possible feelings and actions (St. George & Wulff, 2014). What therapists listen for, highlight, and name is not neutral and carries the weight of professional privilege (Hernández-Wolfe, 2013; Paré, 2014). When unfair or unjust circumstances and expectations are overlooked or minimized in clinical discourse, individuals are pathologized and clients blame themselves without connecting their troubles to larger conditions (St. George & Wulff, 2016). Socioculturally attuned therapists guide the conversation to name unfair or unjust circumstances and amplify voices whose experiences are likely to be silenced.

St. George and Wulff (2016) offered an example from their work in Canada. A middle-class biracial stepfamily sought therapy because their 16-year-old daughter had been caught lying and stealing. The parents had "developed a stern attitude of discipline using accusation, yelling, and punishment . . . as well as 'giving up' on their daughter" (p. 3). When the therapist attuned to the social context around this family's struggles, the daughter said she "didn't care what people at school said" and the parents described comments by co-workers and people at school that "mixed race families were always trouble" and "innuendos about blended families." Comments like these shamed the parents and led them to believe *they* were bad parents, exacerbating (or perhaps even causing) the family pattern of control and defiance. Naming the biases and the discrimination the family experienced expanded the conversation beyond the therapy room and enabled them to more thoughtfully address their responses to societal expectations and each other.

Similarly, when the Bowenian therapist in Chapter 8 helped the client name the assault by their employer as an example of a larger system of male dominance, they were better able to respond to the trauma in ways that supported increased differentiation rather than fear, doubt, and self-blame. Socioculturally attuned solution focused therapists ensure questions and solutions developed through a collaborative process name equitable goals. As with all models, naming is most effective when using here and now examples such as "What will you be doing differently when you are no longer taking on most of the burden of being the bridge or translator in the family?"

Value What is Minimized

Socioculturally attuned therapists acknowledge the worth of that which has been minimized or devalued in the dominant social structure and use these values and practices to promote healing (Hernández-Wolfe, 2013). By so doing, the therapeutic process begins to counter social inequities and sets the stage for transformation.

⤝ ⤞

Socioculturally attuned therapists develop special radar for ferreting out and highlighting strengths that dominant cultural and power processes mask.

⤝ ⤞

These include almost any strength associated with females or with cultures that place less emphasis on individuality and competition, such as caring for others, empathy, accommodating to preserve harmony, or prioritizing family and relationship bonds. They also include the skills and mindsets needed to survive with few economic resources or with physical disabilities.

Let's imagine a male client who sought help for depression. He has internalized an identity as "not assertive enough" and was recently overlooked for a promotion at work. He feels like a failure, like he doesn't fit. Rather than agreeing with the dominant culture assumption that what matters is that he learn how he can better assert himself or promote the products he is selling, the therapist asked questions about other aspects of his identity and listened for culturally minimized strengths.

Therapist: It sounds like there is a strong force for you to be assertive, to press your product or stand up for yourself. I'm wondering about the other side—when you are there for others. Does that happen?

Client: I think I am there for others a lot. That's always been important to me, you know. But I need to learn not to do that so much, to be more aggressive.

Therapist: It seems like being there for others is a pretty important thing. Have you seen ways that that's been good in your life, or has made life better for others?

Validating this client's capacity and desire to support others countered patriarchal expectations that men should lead or dominate others. The therapy enabled him to feel good about himself, improve his relationship with his wife, and develop career goals that did not require him to discount the value of focusing on others. His depression dissipated.

Therapists also absorb dominant cultural values. The ability to recognize and explicitly value that which is socially marginalized or does not fit into dominant expectations requires reflective practices on the therapist's part. For example, an African American therapist presented a case in supervision. The client was a 28-year-old African American woman who lived with her mother and younger siblings and helped support them. The therapist initially defined the client's problem as a lack of differentiation from the family of origin, stating that she was sabotaging her own growth for the sake of the family. Despite her own identity as a black woman, she evaluated her client through an individualistic lens promoted in academia and treatment systems. A socioculturally attuned approach would have been to explore and honor the client's ties to her family before automatically focusing on her autonomy. The therapist would be aware of how easily obligations to others can be discounted and create space to value and reinforce them.

Intervene in Power Dynamics

Positioning therapy to disrupt oppressive power dynamics and support relational equity takes active intervention. This does **not** mean that therapists need a directive stance toward therapy. Rather, they use their facilitative role to recognize when societal power dynamics are at play and use interventions that interrupt and challenge inequitable power while empowering clients to create ways to transform them. For example, in the chapter on socioculturally attuned narrative family therapy, the therapist used art with a deaf and mute undocumented young woman from Peru to create stories of strength and resilience that enabled her to stand up to a powerful documented family member who threatened to have her deported if she told authorities about being raped.

A strategic therapist might recognize symptoms like depression as resistance to societal power processes such as racism, classism, and sexism and counter injustice through strategies that call forth and highlight strengths of less powerful persons while encouraging the more powerful to focus on others. The therapist in the Bowen chapter helped Cloé, who identified as queer, not automatically follow their male partner's lead. The therapist facilitated conversations where Cloé risked expressing their ideas and needs and James was supported in taking them in.

Envision Just Alternatives

It is not enough to identify injustice or power inequities. Therapists need to provide space to imagine just relational alternatives. A task analysis found heterosexual couples dealing with infidelity *only* moved toward equity when therapists invited them to envision alternatives to gender stereotypes (Williams, Galick, Knudson-Martin, & Huenergardt, 2013). For example, they suggested enactments in which powerful partners initiate relational repair or asked partners to discuss what shared responsibility for maintaining the relationship would look like for them (an alternative to the idea that this is a woman's job).

When clients' social identities are marginalized, they may blame themselves for their problems—"I am lazy," "I have low-self-esteem," or "I have anger problems." Interventions into power dynamics will begin from the premise that these self-referents are examples of how persons located outside the dominant culture have been colonized by it (Hernández-Wolfe, 2013). A socioculturally attuned cognitive behavioral therapist would help clients recognize the root of these thoughts, notice when they are being triggered, and envision a new response. A socioculturally attuned structural family therapist would explore the family rules and patterns around these ideas, help family members link these to the effects of social structures, and use enactments to encourage potential alternatives.

Transform to Make the Imagined a Reality

Third order change results when what is imagined is made real. Socioculturally attuned family therapists collaborate with clients by being responsively persistent (Sutherland, Turner, & Dienhart, 2013). They keep bringing clients back to sources of strength and equity in their lives that enable their preferred vision of themselves. In Nagy's contextual therapy, socioculturally attuned therapists help people be intentional about their response to family and societal injustice, what they want to see going forward for themselves, their children, and posterity. They encourage and support clients' commitment and accountability to these ethical values, giving due credit and care to each other.

Socioculturally attuned family therapists help clients identify and solidify the changes they are making. They help clients see themselves as part of larger systemic processes and consider how others may respond as they make third order changes that resist dominant norms. They help clients develop social supports and strategies to sustain them, not only within their families, but in their communities and social networks.

‷←→‷

From a socioculturally attuned perspective, making change real is not just an individual or family process, it is systemic change in how we engage in social worlds.

‷←→‷

Integrative Approaches That Center Social Equity

Each of the following clinical models explicitly integrate principles of socially just practice with multiple family therapy theories. Each assumes that just relationships within families, communities, and the larger society are essential to positive therapeutic change (Hernández-Wolfe, 2013; Knudson-Martin & Huenergardt, 2010). They view presenting issues in relationship to larger sociopolitical social contexts and take an ethical stand that if therapy does not attend to larger context issues, we simply help people adapt to unjust circumstances or collude with existing power structures. Each draws on familiar family therapy concepts from multiple models, while also expanding the clinical lens in ways that target transformation at societal as well as interpersonal levels. In various ways, they challenge or restructure mainstream assumptions about the therapist's role and boundaries of the therapeutic relationship.

Socio-Emotional Relationship Therapy

SERT is designed to allow therapists in any setting—from community agencies and private practice to hospitals, health clinics, and employee assistance programs—to position their work to counteract social inequities, particularly as they are replicated and enacted or transformed within individual identities, intimate and family relationships, as well as in schools, the workplace, and other social systems. This approach was developed by Carmen Knudson-Martin and Douglas Huenergardt (2010, 2015) through action research with a team of doctoral students at Loma Linda University in Southern California. Through live observations of their clinical work, they developed a model for working with gender, culture, and societal power as they play out in the moment-by-moment of therapy with diverse clientele (Knudson-Martin et al., 2015).

SERT integrates attention to neurobiology, social constructionist thought, and social action (Knudson-Martin & Huenergardt, 2010). The therapeutic encounter is positioned to resist and disrupt inequitable societal power processes in order to create new experiences that promote just relationships that mutually support each member. There are three phases: (1) *positioning* to establish an equitable foundation for therapy, (2) *interrupting* the flow of power, and (3) *practicing* to facilitate alternative neuropolitical experience.

Attune

SERT begins with the premise that emotion arises in societal context. Therapists attune to sociocultural emotion. For example, when a male partner erupts in fits of rage, the therapist seeks to identify and attune to societal messages that prompt this response. Perhaps he has internalized expectations that he is supposed to be in charge and competent and instead feels incompetent and disrespected. Therapists connect the clients' visceral experiences to cultural meanings and societal power contexts. Each person feels "felt." In the previous example, the client begins to feel understood as the therapist explores his sociocultural context and connects with the pressure he feels: "No wonder you feel upset. You experience pressure every day to perform, to know what you're doing . . .(client affirms). What is it like for you as a black man working in a mostly white field?"

Name

SERT therapists identify and name power imbalances. Giving voice to societal discourses around client emotions and interactions (as previously), makes clients feel less judged or blamed and more receptive to recognizing how societal inequities play out in their relationships:

Therapist: What happens when all that pressure comes into your relationship?
Client: I wish she would just give me some slack! Get off my back!!

Here the SERT therapist is careful to name the relational equity:

Therapist: (softly) So, you end up not able to focus on her or what she needs, not able to respect her. You've been treated unfairly and now you're treating [partner] unfairly.

Value

SERT explicitly values mutual support and relationship qualities that tend to be overlooked or minimized in the dominant culture. Assessment and interventions are guided by four relational processes that provide a model of equality, i.e., "the Circle of Care": mutual vulnerability, mutual attunement, mutual influence, and shared relational responsibility (Figure 14.3). The model counteracts social processes that place responsibility for maintaining relationships on the less powerful by expecting them to accommodate, keep the peace, etc.

Intervene

SERT interventions interrupt unequal power dynamics. They are often experiential, supporting those in more powerful positions to take in and acknowledge how they have hurt their partners and inviting them to express vulnerability and relational desires, attune to their partners, be influenced by them, and actively take on responsibility for the relationship. Therapists take care to validate the experience and contributions of less powerful partners. They avoid making the already more vulnerable continue to carry the primary relational burden. In the earlier example, rather than asking the partner to tell him what it is like for her when he says she's "on his back," SERT therapists would first encourage *him* to imagine what it is like for her; i.e., facilitate a new experience in which he initiates the connection.

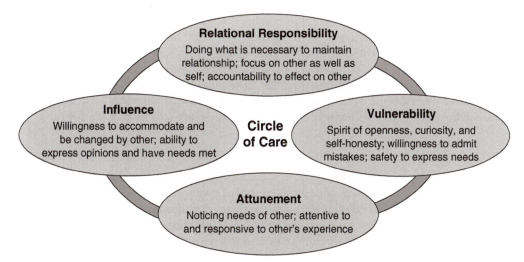

Figure 14.3 Circle of Care. From "Bridging emotion, societal discourse, and couple interaction in clinical practice," by C. Knudson-Martin and D. Huenergardt, in C. Knudson-Martin, S. K. Samman, and M. A. Wells (Eds.), *Socio-Emotional Relationship Therapy: Bridging Emotion, Societal Context, and Couple Interaction* (p. 6), 2015, New York, NY: Springer. Used with permission.

Envision

Rather than a set of skills that therapists teach, the Circle of Care is a guiding framework from which clients envision what enacting it would mean in their situation (Knudson-Martin & Huenergardt, 2015). Mutual support can look different in varying societal contexts. The idea is that when underlying societal power processes are interrupted, clients in all social locations are able to consider options and have more choice about how they interact with each other and the larger society.

Transform

SERT therapists help clients experiment with and practice new ways of relating based on mutual support. They believe all people hold relational desires and abilities, but that societal and interpersonal processes interfere with their ability to attain them. The therapeutic encounter is a place where people are empowered to develop alternatives to dominant social discourses and transform previously taken-for-granted social inequities. Originally developed to work with couples, the concepts also help individuals and families reposition themselves in relation to larger societal processes.

The Cultural Context Model

Rhea Almeida and her colleagues developed the CCM as a way to address the connection between justice and family therapy. CCM expands therapeutic models to include non-related persons in the change process (Almeida, Dolan-Del Vecchio, & Parker, 2007). Rather than work with only a single therapist, CCM reduces the dependency between clients and therapists by engaging them in cultural circles composed of community members concurrently with individual, couple, or family therapy as needed. Clinicians work as a team. The clinical milieu is designed to consider healing a community endeavor rather than an individual one.

Attune

Therapists working from CCM attune to families' presenting issues in context of historical and current processes of privilege and marginalization. They initiate conversations that help clients begin to consider the problems they are facing against the backdrop of intersecting sociopolitical processes such patriarchy, capitalism, racism, heterosexism, and ableism. A first session may be structured to ask questions that raise potential areas of power and privilege: How much money do you earn? Who makes decisions? How are household and family-care responsibilities distributed? How is your workplace organized? (Almeida et al., 2007).

Name

Raising critical consciousness is important in CCM. After an initial intake session all clients participate in 6–8 week same-gender social education groups that help them become aware of the social, political, and cultural influences in their lives through reflection on handouts, film clips, music, poetry, and readings. Power and control wheels around domestic violence, homophobia/heterosexism, gender oppression, and racism, colonization, and imperialism help guide the discussion. Groups are divided by gender and typically include a range of intersecting social locations and presenting issues. Partners and family members attend the gender groups with which they identify. They may also do genogram work to help see and name how larger contextual forces have been part of historical family processes.

Value

As people grasp how societal systems of domination and subjugation affect their lives (critical consciousness), two other values follow and organize clinical work (Hernández, Almeida, & Dolan-del Vechhio, 2005). The first is *accountability*. It "begins with acceptance of responsibility for one's actions and the impact of those actions on others" (Almeida et al., 2007, p. 14). But it also requires reparative action; e.g., actions that demonstrate empathic concern for the well-being of others. The other value is *empowerment*. A person gains empowerment through accountability. For example, a man and his family are all empowered when he is accountable and takes actions that promote "power with" rather than "power over."

Intervene

Most of the clinical work in the cultural context happens in ongoing cultural circles. These are based on the work of Freire (1971/2000). Culture circles move therapy from an individual process to a community effort. Culture circles include other clients as well as volunteer helpers and a team of therapists. Members of the culture circles help each other resist "norms that maintain hierarchies of power, privilege, and oppression" (Almeida et al., 2007, p. 15). Members support each other toward accountability and empowerment. Therapists help connect presenting problems with social realities that maintain them.

Envision

Reparative measures require that clients be able to envision alternative actions that promote just relationships. Almeida et al. (2007) offered the example of Frank, a white, middle-class corporate executive who shared how culture circles increased his awareness and helped him create a new vision of how to engage more justly with his wife:

> When I began coming to the group here, I slowly realized that I had a lot in common with these other men. I realized that these sponsors are here for a purpose, that they are

much farther down the road than I am . . . . There was Stan [another white man in his late fifties, a physician's assistant]. He asked me detailed questions about my financial situation and the role that my wife played in the economic management of our lives. Even more surprising to me, Stan then offered details of his own and his family's financial life. I never imagined talking to anyone about my finances in such detail and most certainly not to a stranger I had known just a few weeks. Our conversations and his respectful suggestions gave me a small window into the possibilities here.

(p. 101)

Transform

Culture circles do not just raise possibilities; members hold each other accountable to them. Actions may be personal like an accountability letter written to family members one has abused or collective action in which some members use their privilege to counter injustice. Hernández et al. (2005) described such an example:

> David, an African American college student, was stopped by university police and his car was impounded. This harassment was part of the police's profiling endeavor. A group of Caucasian men supported him financially to obtain legal counsel. They assisted him in suing the police department and supported his settling out of court.
>
> (p. 14)

Creating communities of resistance and support is one of the transformative outcomes of the CCM.

Just Therapy

Just therapy expands conventional therapy boundaries by engaging extended families, working within cultural and spiritual practices, and extending the clinical role to include collaboration with community projects and efforts to transform social policy (Waldegrave, 2009). Just therapy was developed at the Family Center in Wellington, New Zealand, to connect clinical practice to the impact of colonialism on the Maori, Pacific Islander, and Pakeha (European) families that comprise their community. Founders Kiwi Tamasese, Charles Waldegrave, Flora Tuhaka, and Warihi Campbell (2003) saw that much of what brought people to them related more to poverty, unemployment, housing, sexism, and racism than within the families themselves. They directed agency resources to community projects and social research and action.

The term "just" is used in two ways (Waldegrave, 2003). First, the structure of the treatment system is designed to reduce institutional power of the dominant European culture in order to create more equitable or just outcomes. Second, "just" (or simply) therapy demystifies the therapeutic process to value and welcome skills, experience, and knowledge that emerge out of communities. Therapy is viewed as a sacred exchange. People come, deeply vulnerable, with problem-centered stories. The task of the just therapy team is to offer alternative meanings that inspire resolution and hope.

Attune

Every aspect of agency structure and clinical process is structured to attune to power differences among cultural and gender groups, "Rendering power to those who have been denoted as powerless" (Tamasese & Waldegrave, 2003, p. 138). Agency leadership is dispersed among cultural sections to protect cultural equity. Family group conferences are used to attune and respect cultural resources and views of extended family members in creating safe spaces for children (Waldegrave, 2009).

Name

The just therapy team names injustices such as having no control over a situation, e.g., in housing or the language a child is made to speak. Whenever possible, they honor families' survival and management practices. For example,

> I just want to say how impressed I am with how you manage your household budget. It is very tough today with all the demands for food, rent and kid's needs, and it requires a lot of responsible decision making. You do that very well. I see a lot of families and there are not many that I reckon can manage their budgets as well as you do. That is a great contribution to your family. You guys have a very able mother.
>
> (Tamasese & Waldegrave, 2012a, p. 14)

Value

The just therapy team measures the quality of their work against three values (Tamasese & Waldegrave, 2012a). The first is belonging. It refers to the essence of identity, to who we are, our cultured and gendered histories, and our ancestry. The second is sacredness. It refers to the deepest respect for humanity, its qualities, and the environment. The third is liberation. It refers to freedom, wholeness, and justice. Accountability to these values at the organizational level is fostered through caucus groups based on gender and culture. Reflection is required for both dominant and marginalized groups. Responsibility to stop certain behaviors or discriminating practices rests with the dominant group (Tamasese et al., 2003).

Intervene

Just therapy does not use universal interventions. Rather than the professional world of the therapist defining the problems and the cures, therapists view themselves as invited to bring their skills into families' cultural worlds. They use metaphors and rituals of the culture and identify sources of resilience and social capital. Figure 14.4 illustrates a "Tree of Life" exercise (Ncube, 2006) that helps build self and collective efficacy and social capital. Therapists craft questions that help transform perceived failure into seeds of resistance, often drawing on the wisdom and resources of earlier generations.

Self and Collective Efficacy Tree of Life Exercise
❑   Roots: Who are your people and places of belonging?
❑   Trunk: What are your strengths? What things can you do?
❑   Branches: What are your hopes and dreams?
❑   Leaves: Who are the people close to your heart?
❑   Fruits: What are the gifts you've been given by others?

Figure 14.4 Tree of Life exercise. Influenced by The Tree of Life narrative approach of Ncazelo Ncube (REPSSI) and David Denborough (Dulwich Centre Foundation). See http://dulwichcentre.com.au/the-tree-of-life/. This approach was in turn influenced by the work of Anne Hope and Sally Timmel.

Envision

The just therapy team supports the emergence of new knowledge and paradigms among family members and encourages cultural capacity building. Waldegrave (2003) offered an example of the team's reflection to a Samoan immigrant family whose children were assigned to a State Home. The therapist conveyed appropriate cultural respect to the parents while also supporting accountability. This excerpt from a larger statement addressing each member of the family helps them envision themselves and their future positively:

> (to father) Sami, the team have heard today from you, and all the members of your family, about your changes. They know that you know just how dangerous your drinking has been to the family. Your family can smile again now that you don't come home drunk. Because you have succeeded in this, your children and your wife are not afraid of you like they used to be . . . (to all) you are beginning to trust each other and the team knows that all of you know this is the start of good and happy family life.
>
> (pp. 46–47)

Transform

At the microlevel, families transform problem-centered visions of themselves to create new meanings that inspire hope and resolution. At the macrolevel, staff and community become involved in projects that promote social and economic well-being. The goal of one such project is to restore well-being and resilience to families, children, youth, elders, and villages in Samoa severely impacted by the September 2009 tsunami (Tamasese & Waldegrave, 2012b). The project addressed outcomes such as appropriate and affordable housing re-established, water and electricity supplies connected, and young people returning to school, as well as looking out for each other and drawing on positive and liberative elements of culture.

Conclusion

All family therapy approaches can be equity based. Thoughtful integration of principles of sociocultural attunement expands the foundational concepts and practices of family therapy that we deeply value. The field of family therapy has progressed into an era of better understanding of the impact on individuals and families of sociopolitical contexts at local, national, and global levels. We are faced with new ethical and practical challenges in a diverse world in which families are increasingly impacted by power and resource differentials. As a field we better understand the negative impact of oppression, and the consequences of interconnected social location on real material circumstances that impact family life. There are some members of the field who argue that we have to choose between promoting social justice and doing clinical work. There is no disconnect for us. Clinical work must integrate foundational, tried, and true family therapy clinical practices with intervening to promote equitable relationships to help solve everyday problems. In many ways we are back to the beginning of family therapy, revisiting those early theorists who placed families and our work with families in social context. We are back, however, with a new collective consciousness. As a field, we can name injustices that were previously felt but not languaged. We started the chapter with a recent quote from Minuchin. We end with a quote from another legendary founder, Cloé Madanes (2008):

> I have come to see that family injustice is the root cause of pathology and that for therapy to be effective, it must bring justice to the family. Sometimes injustice comes from outside the family and then the therapist must work on bringing justice from society to the family.

References

Almeida, R., Dolan-Del Vecchio, K., & Parker, L. (2007). *Transforming family therapy: Just families in a just society*. Boston, MA: Allyn & Bacon.

D'Aniello, C., Nguyen, H., & Piercy, F. (2016). Cultural sensitivity as an MFT common factor. *American Journal of Family Therapy, 44*, 234–244.

D'Arrigo-Patrick, J., Hoff, C., Knudson-Martin, C., & Tuttle, A. R. (2017). Navigating critical theory and postmodernism: Social justice and therapist power in family therapy. *Family Process, 56*, 574–588.

Freire, P. (2000). *Pedagogy of hope*. New York, NY: Continuum. (Original work published 1971).

Hernández, P., Almeida, R., & Dolan-del Vecchio, K. (2005). Critical consciousness, accountability, and empowerment: Key processes for helping families heal. *Family Process, 44*(1), 105–119.

Hernández-Wolfe, P. (2013). *A borderlands view on Latinos, Latin Americans, and decolonization: Rethinking mental health*. Lanham, MD: Jason Aronson.

Knudson-Martin, C., & Huenergardt, D. (2010). A socio-emotional approach to couple therapy: Linking social context and couple interaction. *Family Process, 49*(3), 369–386.

Knudson-Martin, C., & Huenergardt, D. (2015). Bridging emotion, societal discourse, and couple interaction in clinical practice. In C. Knudson-Martin, M. E. Wells, & S. Samman (Eds.), *Socio-emotional relationship therapy: Bridging emotion, societal context, and couple interaction* (pp.1–13). New York, NY: Springer.

Knudson-Martin, C., Huenergardt, D., Lafontant, K., Bishop, L., Schaepper, J., & Wells, M. (2015). Competencies for addressing gender and power in couple therapy: A socio-emotional approach. *Journal of Marital and Family Therapy, 41*(2), 205–220.

Madanes, C. (2008, December 11). *Part 2*. [Video file]. Retrieved from https://www.youtube.com/watch?v=u6F_zKB7S9Y

Minuchin, S. (2017, January). Systems therapy: The art of creating uncertainty. *Psychotherapy Networker*. Retrieved from https://www.psychotherapynetworker.org/blog/details/1099/the-art-of-creating-uncertainty

Ncube, N. (2006). The tree of life project: Using narrative ideas in work with vulnerable children in Southern Africa. *International Journal of Narrative Therapy and Community Work, 1*, 3–16.

O'Halloran, E., Dunford, K., Kim, L., & Knudson-Martin, C. (2017). Learning to apply social justice: Studying SERT. Poster presentation. American Family Therapy Academy, Philadelphia, PA. June.

Pandit, M., Kang, Y. J., ChenFeng J., Knudson-Martin, C., & Huenergardt, D. (2014). Practicing socio-cultural attunement: A study of couple therapists. *Journal of Contemporary Family Therapy, 36*(4), 518–528.

Paré, D. (2014). Social justice and the word: Keeping diversity alive in therapeutic conversations. *Canadian Journal of Counselling and Psychotherapy, 48*(3), 206–217.

St. George, S., & Wulff, D. (2014). Braiding SCIPS into therapy. In K. Tomm, S. St. George, D. Wulff, & T. Strong (Eds.), *Patterns in interpersonal interactions: Inviting relational understanding for therapeutic change* (pp. 124–142). New York, NY: Routledge.

St. George, S., & Wulff, D. (2016). Family therapy = social justice = daily practices = transforming therapy. In S. St. George & D. Wulff (Eds.), *Family therapy as socially transformative practice: Practical strategies* (pp. 1–7). New York, NY: Springer.

Sutherland, O., Turner, J., & Dienhart, A. (2013). Responsive persistence part I: Therapist influence in postmodern practice. *Journal of Marital and Family Therapy, 39*(4), 470–487.

Tamasese, T. K., & Waldegrave, C. (2003). Family therapy and the question of power. In C. Waldegrave, K. Tamasese, F. Tuhaka, & W. Campbell (Eds.), *Just therapy—a journey* (pp. 131–146). Adelaide, South Australia: Dulwich Centre Publications.

Tamasese, T. K., & Waldegrave, C. (2012a). Belonging, sacredness, and liberation: Therapeutic conversations X. Vancouver, BC. May 12.

Tamasese, T. K., & Waldegrave, C. (2012b). Working with families in context of climate change. Pre-conference workshop: Therapeutic conversations X. Vancouver, BC. May 9.

Tamasese, K., Waldegrave, C., Tuhaka, F., & Campbell, W. (2003). Furthering conversations about partnerships of accountability: Talking about issues of leadership, ethics, and care. In C. Waldegrave, K. Tamasese, F. Tuhaka, & W. Campbell (Eds.), *Just therapy—a journey* (pp. 97–120). Adelaide, South Australia: Dulwich Centre Publications.

Waldegrave, C. (2003). "Just therapy" with families and communities. In C. Waldegrave, K. Tamasese, F. Tuhaka, & W. Campbell (Eds.), *Just therapy—a journey* (pp. 63–78). Adelaide, South Australia: Dulwich Centre Publications.

Waldegrave, C. (2009). Cultural, gender, and socioeconomic contexts in therapeutic and social policy work. *Family Process, 48*(1), 85–101.

Williams, K., Galick, A., Knudson-Martin, C., & Huenergardt, D. (2013). Toward mutual support: A task analysis of the relational justice approach to infidelity. *Journal of Marital and Family Therapy. 39*(3), 285–298.

Index